SOCIAL
CONTROL
OF THE
DRINKING
DRIVER

SOCIAL CONTROL
OF THE
DRINKING
DRIVER

Edited by
Michael D. Laurence
John R. Snortum
Franklin E. Zimring

The University of Chicago Press
Chicago and London

DISCARDED

MICHAEL D. LAURENCE is a fellow of the Earl Warren Legal Institute
of the University of California, Berkeley. JOHN R. SNORTUM is the
George C. S. Benson Professor of Public Affairs at Claremont McKenna
College. FRANKLIN E. ZIMRING is professor of law and director of the
Earl Warren Legal Institute of the University of California, Berkeley.

The University of Chicago Press, Chicago 60637
The University of Chicago Press, Ltd., London
© 1988 by The University of Chicago
All rights reserved. Published 1988
Printed in the United States of America

97 96 95 94 93 92 91 90 89 88   54321

An Earl Warren Legal Institute Study

Library of Congress Cataloging-in-Publication Data

Social control of the drinking driver

   (Studies in crime and justice)
   Bibliography: p.
   Includes index.
   1. Drinking and traffic accidents. 2. Drunk
driving. I. Laurence, Michael D. II. Snortum, John R.
III. Zimring, Franklin E. IV. Series.
HE5620.D7S66 1988   363.1'256   87–19111
ISBN:0-226-46953-0 (cloth)
    0-226-46954-9 (paper)

For
Johannes Andenaes
Scholar and Teacher

Contents

Contributors

Johannes Andenaes is professor of law at the University of Oslo. He has written extensively on criminal law, criminology, and constitutional law. Andenaes has also served as the chairman of the Royal Commission on Criminal Procedures and of the Permanent Advisory Council of Criminal Law, and as president of the Norwegian Academy of Science and Letters. In 1979, he received the Sellin-Glueck Award for international contributions to criminology.

Alan Donelson, Ph.D. (Pharmacology, Indiana University), is Senior Research Scientist with the Traffic Injury Research Foundation of Canada (TIRF). Besides conducting studies that better define relationships between alcohol, other drugs, and road accidents, he and his colleagues have worked to develop comprehensive perspectives on this problem area and strategic approaches to deal more effectively with impaired driving. Prior to joining TIRF in 1981, Dr. Donelson worked in the policy analysis division of the University of Michigan Highway Safety Research Institute (now the Transportation Research Institute).

E. Scott Geller is professor of psychology at Virginia Polytechnic Institute and State University. He earned M.A. and Ph.D. degrees in experimental psychology from Southern Illinois University, and is a fellow of the American Psychological Association. In 1982 Geller coauthored *Preserving the Environment: New Strategies for Behavior Change* (Pergamon Press) with Richard A. Winett and Peter B. Everett. He has published extensively in the areas of cognitive psychology, community behavior analysis, and occupational health and safety.

Joseph R. Gusfield is professor of sociology at the University of California, San Diego. He has conducted research and published in the fields of social movements, the sociology of higher education, sociological theory, Indian society, and alcohol studies. Gusfield is the author of *Symbolic Crusade: Status Politics and the American Temperance Movement* (1963) and *The Culture of Public Problems: Drinking-Driving and the Symbolic Order* (1981). Although his interest in alcohol studies has dealt with many aspects of the use and control of alcohol, his major concern is with alcohol as the subject of public policy, law, and political conflict.

Ragnar Hauge is director of research at the National Institute for Alcohol Research, Oslo, Norway, and professor of criminology at the University of Oslo. He received his training in criminology at Cambridge University, and has published a number of books and articles on criminology and alcohol research.

James Jacobs is currently professor of law and director of the Center for Research in Crime and Justice, New York University School of Law. He received his J.D. and Ph.D. in sociology at the University of Chicago. He has authored *Stateville: The Penitentiary in Mass Society* (1977); *New Perspectives on Prisons and Imprisonment* (1983); and *Socio-Legal Foundations of Civil-Military Relations* (1986).

Günter Kroj is head of the evaluation section of the Federal Highway Research Institute, Federal Republic of Germany. His research interests include accident research, driver improvement, and safety education. Kroj has degrees in psychology and natural sciences.

Michael D. Laurence is a fellow at the Earl Warren Legal Institute, University of California, Berkeley. He earned his B.A. in History from Bates College, Lewiston, Maine, and his J.D. from the University of California, Davis. His writings on the criminal justice system include works on drunk driving and capital punishment.

Galen R. Lehman is assistant professor of psychology at Eastern Mennonite College. He earned an M.A. Degree from Hollins College, Roanoke, Virginia. Currently he is completing his dissertation under the supervision of Professor E. Scott Geller for a Ph.D. in applied psychology. His research interests focus on the application of behavior analysis to effecting change in the public domain.

Robert E. Mann received his doctorate in psychology from the University of Waterloo. Since then he has been affiliated with the Addiction Research Foundation, where he is currently a scientist in the Drinking Driving Research Program. In addition to alcohol and traffic safety issues, his research interests have included psychological factors in impairment and the epidemiology and treatment of alcohol and drug problems.

H. Laurence Ross is professor of sociology at the University of New Mexico. His interest in what the law can and cannot do as a tool of social policy has led to numerous empirical investigations in the United Kingdom, France, and Scandinavia as well as the United States, and to his book *Deterring the Drinking Driver: Legal Policy and Social Control.* His overseas appointments have included periods as visiting scholar at Oxford and Geneva Universities, and as Fulbright Lecturer to Belgium and Finland.

John R. Snortum is the George C.S. Benson Professor of Public Affairs at Claremont McKenna College, California. In pursuing interest in comparative criminal justice, he has held faculty and research appointments in Norway, Sweden, and Switzerland. He was coeditor of *Criminal Justice: Allies and Adversaries* (1978). Snortum's recent comparative analysis of alcohol-impaired driving in Norway and the United States (conducted with Ragnar Hauge and Dale Berger) received the Anderson Outstanding Paper Award from the Academy of Criminal Justice Sciences in 1986.

Kathryn Stewart is senior research scientist at the Pacific Institute for Research and Evaluation. Her areas of research include a major evaluation of judicial processing and rehabilitative countermeasures for drinking drivers, and a study of administrative license revocation. Stewart was trained in sociology at the University of Wisconsin, Madison.

Evelyn R. Vingilis is research scientist and psychologist at the Ontario Alcohol and Drug Addiction Research Foundation. On the editorial board of the international journal *Accident Analysis and Prevention,* she was the guest editor of a special issue of this journal entitled "Perspectives on Drinking-Driving Countermeasures." She is also an advisor to interministerial governmental committees on drinking and driving, and the author of numerous articles.

Robert B. Voas is director of alcohol programs at the National Public Service Research Institute in Alexandria, Virginia. His research for federal and state agencies on alcohol countermeasures includes investigations on enforcement technology, sobriety checkpoints, and alcohol sensing. Voas is the former director of the Office of Evaluation for the National Highway Traffic Safety Administration, where he was responsible for the evaluation of demonstration projects as well as being involved in the development of the ASAP program.

Harold L. Votey, Jr. is professor of economics at the University of California, Santa Barbara. He earned his Ph.D. from the University of California, Berkeley, and earlier degrees from the University of Michigan. His research on the economics of crime and justice has been supported by the National Science Foundation, the National Institute of Justice, National Institute of Mental Health, the Ford Foundation, and governmental agencies in Norway and Sweden.

Franklin E. Zimring has been professor of law and director of the Earl Warren Legal Institute at the University of California, Berkeley, since 1985. Prior to that, he was on the faculty of the University of Chicago for eighteen years, most recently as Llewellyn Professor of Jurisprudence and director of the Center for Studies in Criminal Justice. His recent books include *The Changing Legal World of Adolescence* and, with Gordon Hawkins, *Capital Punishment and the American Agenda* and *The Citizen's Guide to Gun Control*. Zimring's special interests include criminal and family law and the empirical study of legal institutions.

Introduction

The problem of drunken driving is a byproduct of both technological progress and economic privilege. The special dangers and large aggregate social costs that result when drinking and driving overlap en masse are twentieth century phenomena. Like gout, drunken driving is a disease of the privileged, expanding in scope with general prosperity, and exacting its greatest toll when the opportunity to drive is democratically distributed throughout a social system. Drunken driving is thus specifically a disorder of the industrialized West. And the greater our success in achieving prosperity, the more attention that needs to be paid to the problem of alcohol and traffic safety.

The history of efforts to cope with the traffic safety costs of alcohol may be short but it is complicated. Understanding the social impact of drinking and driving is a task that implicates all of the social and behavioral sciences, as well as areas ranging from biology to highway engineering. Important insights about the social control of drinking and driving are scattered throughout many academic disciplines, and are found in the experience of many countries. Although these circumstances always risk a Tower of Babel effect, there are positive aspects as well. The parochial boundaries of a traditional social or behavioral science are simply unthinkable. Data on this new topic can provide an important test of theories of social behavior and social control that have evolved from other topical studies.

This volume is an attempt to assemble a nearly comprehensive statement of knowledge about social control of the drinking driver as a problem of public health and public law. Our editorial undertaking was to attempt a conceptual mapping of issues involved in drunken driving as a problem in law and society, and then to locate appropriate scholars in the United States and Europe to fill in the intellectual landscape.

The ultimate success of this effort is a matter for the reader to judge. But the process of assembling this volume was heartening evidence in two respects that the venture was worthwhile. First, some rational subdivision of topics seemed to emerge from our efforts, and is reflected in the sequence of sections and chapters to be presently discussed. Second, enthusiasm for the venture appears widespread: Of the fourteen scholars who were approached for contributions, thirteen joined the venture. The result, divided into five sections and fourteen chapters, is reported in these pages.

The first section of the book is a panoramic overview of research on alcohol and traffic safety by Alan Donelson. This treatment is intended to introduce readers to the major issues on the linkages between alcohol and crashes as well as to some research findings on these issues. It is both a useful summary for those with deep backgrounds on these issues, and an indispensable introduction for those new to the topic.

Part Two of the book relates the experience of a number of Western nations with the problem of alcohol and traffic safety. Johannes Andenaes reports in Chapter Two on the history of the isssue in Scandinavia. He also surveys recent developments in Norway, Sweden, Denmark, and Finland. His essay can be used as an introduction for readers with no prior exposure to the Scandinavian systems of control. The chapter also provides an update on significant recent developments that even specialized scholars will find useful.

H. Laurence Ross examines the origins, content, and apparent effect of deterrence-based policies in Britain, Canada, and Australia in Chapter Three, and in Chapter Four, the comparative perspective is expanded by Gunter Kroj to include the Federal Republic of Germany and the Netherlands.

This list of countries is not a comprehensive sample of nations that have significant experience with drinking drivers. Nine countries on three continents are, however, a substantial sample for comparative study, and an important backdrop for more detailed considerations and developments in the United States.

The task of Part Three is to profile the special characteristics of law, governmental structure, and history as they are important for appreciating the relationship between governmental action and drunken driving in the United States. Joseph Gusfield begins this process in Chapter Five with an essay on the social history of the offense of drunken driving in the United States in recent years.

Michael Laurence continues the parade of American peculiarity in Chapter Six, mapping the major dimensions of federalism as it affects the distribution of power between levels of government in the United States and analyzing constitutional constraints imposed by the Bill of Rights on drunken driving controls at all levels of government.

The fourth part of the book is organized around the various tactics or types of intervention used to combat drunken driving. The chapters in this section are both more general and more specific than earlier contributions to the book. They are more general in the sense that the authors attempt to accumulate evidence across all national boundaries in discussing a particular approach. The chapters are more specific because each type of countermeasure is the focus of sustained individual analysis.

Ragner Hauge discusses governmental efforts to make changes in the availability of alcoholic beverages in Chapter Seven. John Snortum in Chapter Eight surveys the deterrent impact of criminal legal threats directed to driving under the influence of alcohol, and in Chapter Nine, James Jacobs reviews the use of insurance and tort law devices. Robert Mann, Evelyn Vingilis, and Kathryn Stewart examine the impact of programs that attempt to treat the propensities of identified individuals in Chapter Ten. Finally, Harold Votey presents a unified economic perspective in Chapter Eleven that integrates the diverse strategies discussed in the previous chapters under a single rubric, both conceptually and with respect to evaluation.

The fifth section of the book is explicitly future-oriented. In Chapter Twelve, E. Scott Geller and Galen Lehman summarize promising research on the social and psychological contexts of drinking-and-driving behavior, searching for elements of a social psychology of prevention. Robert Voas profiles the innovations in hard technology that are on the horizon in Chapter Thirteen. Finally, in Chapter Fourteen, Franklin Zimring attempts to integrate major themes of earlier chapters into a statement of developing trends in government and society.

What are the uses of this book? We hope it provides an almost comprehensive statement of knowledge about drunken driving and its control in the Western world. We intend the individual chapters to serve as basic references for their specific topics. As a whole, the volume is intended to serve as a detailed introduction to the issues and the literature for scholars and students of public policy. We also hope that our efforts to integrate across disciplinary and political borders will inspire other synthetic efforts.

M.D.L.
J.R.S.
F.E.Z.

March 1987

A Note on Terminology

As will be apparent in this volume, there is little uniformity in the terminology applied to the study of drinking and driving. Some of these differences in usage are national in origin, others reflect methodological and disciplinary differences, and still others reflect changing preferences over time. Because good arguments can be mustered both for and against each of the various terms that identify the "target behavior" in question, we have encouraged authors to use the legal and technical terms that best suit their own purposes.

A few examples may suffice to illustrate why terminology is still in a state of flux: The term *drunken driving* has the historical weight of common usage behind it; however, there is some feeling that the term was more descriptive in the era of classical laws (before reliance upon blood alcohol measurements), when police officers had to document that the driver's behavior was manifestly at the "drunken" extreme. *Drunk driving* is grammatically awkward, but it is a convenient shorthand term for any violation of the so-called drunk-driving laws. Although *drunk driving* is now standard parlance in the popular press, the concept is strained in some research contexts, for example, self-reported violations that are not authenticated by the criminal justice system. *Drinking-driving behavior* is a broadly applicable and innocuous term but it suffers from imprecision and overinclusiveness because it seems to encompass any amount of drinking before driving. The American acronyms *DUI (driving under the influence)* and *DWI (driving while intoxicated)* have a precise legal and technical meaning within a given state in the absence of common federal standards. They may add confusion rather than clarity when used generically. *Alcohol-impaired driving* is a useful term in scientific discussions, especially when it is operationally defined according to a particular blood alcohol level. Nevertheless, it must be acknowledged that there is little consensus in identifying the blood alcohol level at which driving behavior becomes "significantly" impaired. Futhermore, the term is somewhat cumbersome when communicating in public forum where the offense of *drunk driving* has become the conventional focus.

Although the current differences of opinion about general terminology cannot be easily resolved, the situation is quite different in the narrow, technical domain pertaining to *blood alcohol concentration* (called *BAC* in the United States). Despite the apparent international diversity of measures for BAC, all can be "translated" into equivalent scientific scales. Thus, if an American driver is recorded as having .08 percent BAC, this means that the blood sample showed .08 *grams* of alcohol per 100 milliliters of blood. However, the scale in Canada and the United Kingdom is based upon *milligrams* of alcohol in 100 milliliters of blood; therefore, the blood alcohol level comparable to that reported for the American driver would be 80 milligrams per 100 milliliters of blood. In still another variation of decimal displacement, the Scandinavian countries favor a scale based on 100 milligrams per 100 *liters* of blood so that a value of 80 milligrams per 100 liters would be reported as .8 per mille. The BAC limit that defines a drinking-driving violation per se varies across national boundaries, with a relatively strict limit imposed in Norway, Sweden, the Netherlands, and most of Australia (.05 percent BAC); a moderate limit in Canada, the United Kingdom, and the Federal Republic of Germany (.08 percent BAC); and a relatively lenient limit in most of the United States (.10 percent BAC).

Acknowledgments

The material and intellectual assistance necessary to compile this volume was substantial. Our greatest debt is to the authors of the chapters of this book. Their hard work, good humor, flexibility, and sense of the importance of the volume have carried the project forward in near-record time for an international and interdisciplinary project.

The principal financial support for this effort came from the Earl Warren Legal Institute at the Law School of the University of California at Berkeley.

The staff at the Earl Warren Legal Institute was both patient and helpful through the two-year gestation of this book. Cathleen Hill provided administrative support to the enterprise and the editors. Karen Chin word-processed so many different versions of the chapters that she became an involuntary expert on the subject matter. Thanks to all.

In the 1980s, there is no novelty to legal scholars paying sustained attention to the social control of the drinking driver. The contemporary involvement of many of us in these studies stem from the pioneering work of Johannes Andenaes, a debt we acknowledge in the dedication of this volume.

PART

1 Dimensions of the Problem

1   The Alcohol-Crash Problem

Alan C. Donelson

This chapter describes the nature and magnitude of the alcohol-crash problem and summarizes what is known—and not known—about its etiology. Section 1 overviews the state of knowledge, and the topics represent well-traveled ground: the pharmacology of beverage alcohol, the effects of alcohol on driving, alcohol and the risk of crash involvement, and the magnitude of the alcohol-crash problem. Emphasis is placed, however, on identifying important questions that research has not yet answered. Section 2 addresses the issue of perspective—how one conceptualizes the alcohol-crash problem. Finally, section 3 discusses implications of present knowledge for the social control of drinking and driving.

1. The State of Knowledge

The scientific study of alcohol and road accidents began over fifty years ago and continues today. In general, this activity has never evidenced the systematic, methodical inquiry characteristic of other scientific endeavors. One explanation is that research findings more often were used to mobilize public opinion and to justify programs than to understand a suspected though ill-defined alcohol-crash problem.

> This activity provided objective evidence to help gain support in the fight against this basic accident cause. Since drinking of alcoholic beverages does not generally carry a serious social stigma, an unspoken "drinking partnership" was recognized to exist between a large segment of the public and the drinking-driver defendant. This affinity often results in less-than-energetic prosecution of this conduct that is dangerous from the traffic safety standpoint. Thus, *one of the basic reasons for the extensive research efforts has been to attempt to dramatize the enormity of the problem and the seriousness of its effects on a complex and fast-moving society.* (Borkenstein et al. 1963, 144, emphasis added)

3

Nonetheless, early studies confirmed what many already believed as true, namely that alcohol can impair skills related to driving; drivers impaired by alcohol are more likely to have road accidents than their nondrinking counterparts; and increasing amounts of alcohol produce greater impairment and higher risks of crash involvement. Subsequently, refined and more rigorous methods have allowed study of how alcohol affects driving performance, how often alcohol-involved traffic accidents occur, and how little alcohol in the body impairs driving skills. By the end of the 1960s as many countries initiated large-scale countermeasure programs, research had demonstrated a strong association between alcohol use among road users and road accidents, especially fatal accidents. Although the statement that "alcohol causes accidents" remained unproved in the strict scientific sense, the public seemed not to doubt its causal role and supported both the enactment of unprecedented laws and the large expenditure of funds for drinking-driving countermeasures.

Present knowledge about the relationship between alcohol and road accidents can be summarized in four general areas. First, the pharmacology of beverage alcohol principally concerns the biochemical and physiological effects of alcohol in relation to its absorption, distribution, and elimination after ingestion. Second, experimental research has measured the effects of alcohol on driving-related skills and defined alcohol impairment in terms of breath or blood alcohol concentration (BAC). Third, epidemiologic research has estimated the relative risk of crash involvement as a function of BAC. Fourth, based on knowledge from pharmacology, experimentation, and epidemiology, the approximate magnitude of the alcohol-crash problem can be determined.

The Pharmacology of Beverage Alcohol

Pharmacology has two major branches: (1) pharmacokinetics, the absorption, distribution, biotransformation (metabolism), and elimination of drugs; and (2) pharmacodynamics, the effects of drugs and their mechanisms of action. Here, the pharmacokinetics of alcohol and BAC as a measure of the presence and degree of alcohol's effects are considered. For more complete and detailed information, the interested reader should consult one or more of the following references, which also provide entry points to the scientific literature: Dubowski (1963, 1985); Fingl and Woodbury (1975); Forney and Harger (1971); Goldberg (1963); Greenberg (1968); Ritchie (1975); Roach (1982); Wallgren and Barry (1970); and Wayne (1963).

The pharmacokinetics of alcohol is well understood; the thoroughness of research in this area is due in large measure to its importance in the field of alcohol and traffic safety (e.g., Dubowski 1985; Forney and Harger 1971). For example, chemical testing of body fluids and breath for alcohol has played a pivotal role in the enforcement of impaired-driving laws and in the adjudication of impaired-driving offenses. Interpretation of the meaning and significance of chemical test results, which is central to the implementation of law and to research on the alcohol-crash problem, relies heavily on knowledge of the pharmacokinetics of alcohol. In this regard, blood (and breath) alcohol concentration (BAC) quickly became the most critical variable for alcohol and traffic safety (Donelson, Marks, Jones, and Joscelyn 1980, 25–27; Dubowski 1985; Jones and Joscelyn 1978, 2).[1]

In fact, the importance of BAC as a measure of the amount of alcohol present in the body and as a measure of alcohol's effects cannot be overemphasized. At the same time, because myriad factors influence BAC and the intensity of alcohol's effects, relationships among key variables—the dose of alcohol consumed, BAC, and the effects of alcohol on behavior—are anything but simple. The following brief review of the pharmacology of alcohol will illustrate this point.

Alcohol (known chemically as ethyl alcohol) is a small, simple molecule. A liquid at room temperature, alcohol is completely miscible with water. When consumed, beverage alcohol is readily and rapidly absorbed from the stomach and, especially, from the small intestine. Alcohol readily distributes throughout tissues and fluids of the body in a manner similar to that of water. Alcohol is eliminated from the body mostly through metabolism (enzymatic breakdown). A very small percentage of alcohol is excreted unchanged in breath, urine, and sweat. After consumption of alcoholic beverages, the amount of alcohol present in body fluids, organs, and other tissues at any point in time is determined by rates of absorption, distribution, and elimination of alcohol. These rates, in turn, are influenced to a greater or lesser degree by many factors, for example, the amount and concentration of beverage alcohol consumed, the rate of consumption, and the quantity and type of food in the stomach.

Blood and breath alcohol concentrations (BAC) are resultants, or outcomes, of all three processes: absorption, distribution, and elimination. Where one chooses to measure BAC (usually in venous blood or breath)—and when—determine not only what one observes but also the significance of that observation. For example, concentrations of alcohol in urine have virtually no medicolegal meaning for two reasons: (1) laws are written in terms of blood (or breath) alcohol concentration, and (2) BAC cannot be reliably determined from chemical tests that measure the presence and amount of alcohol in urine. Even the relation of breath alcohol concentration to blood alcohol concentration, which depends on a partition factor between blood and breath in the postabsorptive phase, is subject to debate (Dubowski 1985). As Dubowski pointed out, the agreed-upon value for the partition factor (on which breathtesting equipment used by police is calibrated) represents a "population mean." "However, significant variations from this population mean exist during active alcohol absorption and in some individuals even in the postabsorptive phase" (Dubowski 1985, 102). Based on a review of research findings and their implications, Mason and Dubowski (1976) "proposed that the offense of driving under the influence of alcohol be statutorily defined in terms of the concentration of alcohol both in the breath and in the blood, that breath alcohol analysis continue to be employed in traffic law enforcement but that conversion of breath alcohol concentrations to blood alcohol concentrations be abandoned for forensic purposes" (Dubowski 1985, 102).

Whether measured as blood or breath alcohol concentration, the amount of alcohol present in the body determines, in part, the degree of its effects on behavior. The general relationship between BAC and the effects of alcohol (which relates to the *pharmacodynamics* of alcohol) is straightforward: the greater the amount of alcohol present in the body, the greater the effects of alcohol. When the effects of identical doses of alcohol are compared among individuals, however, the variability of effects measured is substantial. When the effects of alcohol are measured in individuals grouped according to BAC, the relationship between BAC and the degree of effects of alcohol appears much more complicated. For example, Harger and Hulpieu (1956) reviewed seven studies that examined the frequency with which subjects were judged to display common signs of drunkenness (that is, slurred speech, difficulty of locomotion) at different BACs. Of 5,850 subjects, 34 percent were judged intoxicated at BACs between 51 and 100 mg%; 64 percent between 101 and 150 mg%; and 86% between 151 and 200 mg%. Forney and Harger (1971) reviewed studies of alcohol effects published prior to 1963. They found that the BAC at which most subjects displayed measurable deficits in performance ranged from a low of 25 mg% to a high of 150 mg%. Personal characteristics of drinkers (for example, tolerance to alcohol), social situations (for example, drinking setting), and many other factors can influence the relationship between BAC and alcohol's effects. This suggests that BAC differences among various groups (and subgroups) of drinking drivers must be sufficiently great to support contentions that the effects of alcohol were also significantly different.

Little is known about exactly how alcohol produces its primary pharmacological effects. The sedative, or depressant, effect of alcohol is generally thought to result from the drug's inhibiting or slowing of brain functions, particularly those responsible for alertness and wakefulness (that is, the brainstem reticular formation). Thus, for many people, alcohol relieves tension or anxiety, and facilitates social interactions (e.g., Wallgren and Barry 1970). The euphoric effects often associated with alcohol consumption appear to depend on the expectations and psychological state of the individual as well as on the dose of alcohol consumed.

Although in general the pharmacologic effects of alcohol are proportional to the concentration of the drug in the body, relationships between dose and response are not necessarily monotonic, for it has been repeatedly shown that small amounts of alcohol can produce a paradoxical improvement in performance (e.g., Perrine 1973). The notion that beverage alcohol consumed in moderate amounts has beneficial effects is understandably controversial (e.g., Baum-Baicker 1985a, b). This is not to say that "two drinks make better drivers." Nonetheless, some people in some circumstances do perform certain tasks more proficiently after consuming small amounts of alcohol. This biphasic action of alcohol—improved performance at low BACs, decreased performance at higher BACs—complicates the relationship between BAC and performance changes.

The Effects of Alcohol on Driving

The primary purpose of experimental research in the field of alcohol and traffic safety has been twofold: (1) to determine how alcohol impairs driving ability, and (2) to define driving impairment in terms of BAC. This line of investigation began early in this century in Sweden, where Widmark first defined the "alcoholic influence syndrome" by combining established methods for testing neurological disorders with those for determining the presence and amount of alcohol in body fluids.

During this same period, in the United States, Heise was examining drivers suspected of operating under the influence of alcohol for the Pennsylvania State Police. At first his examinations were based on physical tests and observations without chemical tests for alcohol. Bitter courtroom experience rapidly taught the need for showing the cause for abnormal behavior. He turned to the work being conducted in Sweden by Widmark. Thus, the Widmark philosophy was brought to the United States.

As a result of this chain of events, the pattern of the approach to the problem was quite firmly established, comprising a battery of psychophysical tests to demonstrate impairment, coupled with a chemical test to show the presence of alcohol as the cause. This form remains substantially the same today. (Borkenstein et al. 1963, 140)

Early research correlating the effects of alcohol with its concentration in blood and urine soon found application. In this regard, the National Safety Council Committee on Tests for Intoxication was a potent force in the area of alcohol and traffic safety, even though "its role has been limited to developing recommendations for . . . legislation, enforcement, education, chemical testing equipment, training of testing personnel, and other aspects of alcohol countermeasure programs" (National Safety Council 1978, 1). Among its more important contributions were standards interpreting the significance of blood alcohol concentrations, thus defining the vague legal phrase "under the influence of alcohol":

less than 0.05% w/v—no influence of alcohol within the meaning of the law;
between 0.05% and 0.15% w/v—alcoholic influence usually present, but courts of law should consider driver behavior and circumstances leading to arrest;
0.15% w/v and greater—definite evidence (prima facie) of being "under the influence."

Although these standards were incorporated by lawmakers into statutes prohibiting driving under the influence of alcohol, they were largely derived from laboratory tests that bore little relation to actual driving.

In the decades following, a remarkable number of studies have been conducted on the effects of alcohol, although their cumulative value in advancing knowledge in alcohol and traffic safety has been less than might be expected (Carpenter 1963; Levine et al. 1973; Perrine 1974). A wide range of behavioral and other effects of alcohol was reported (e.g., Wallgren and Barry 1970), but the comparability of studies was poor and the relevance of their results to the impairment of driving ability remained uncertain. Obvious limitations of many laboratory tests led to an emphasis on techniques and methods with greater face validity, for example, driving simulators and vehicle-based tests conducted on closed driving courses.

In reviewing the experimental literature, Jones and Joscelyn (1978) concluded:

> Simulator studies of behavior thought to be related to driving have shown highly conflicting results, but seem to indicate that one's ability to perform complex tasks is more impaired by alcohol than for simpler tasks. The relationship between simulator tasks and street driving has been seriously questioned in the literature.
>
> Closed course driving experiments indicate that the ability of many drivers to perform parking maneuvers becomes impaired at low BACs (i.e., .04% to .06% w/v). Closed course driving performance at low speeds appears to be degraded for average drinkers at BACs of .08% to .10% w/v, but less so for heavy drinkers. Closed course driving performance at moderate speeds has been shown to be impaired at BACs as low as .05% to .07% w/v.
>
> Thus, there is evidence that some behavior that appears to be related to driving performance is impaired by alcohol. The exact nature and extent of these impairments and their frequency of occurrence among different individuals at given BACs cannot be stated. Lacking explicit relationships between the behavior studied and critical driving tasks, it cannot be said precisely how these impairments affect one's probability to being involved in a crash. What emerges, however, is the behavior that has been studied is consistently and significantly impaired in virtually all individuals as BACs approach .10% w/v. Many persons, particularly lighter drinkers, have shown impairment at much lower BACs. Only a relatively few of the heaviest drinkers appear to suffer little impairment at BACs much greater than .10% w/v. (49)

Experimentation in alcohol and traffic safety, such as that described above, indicated that the presumptive BAC limit for "under the influence" (0.15% w/v in many U.S. jurisdictions) had been set too high. The influence of alcohol on driving skills included amounts of the drug well below those associated with drunkenness or intoxication. Laws were revised based on this knowledge, and lower BAC values were adopted (e.g., .05%, .08%, and .10% w/v).

Still at issue for the social control of drinking and driving is the BAC limit above which driving should be illegal per se. Many jurisdictions have impaired-driving statutes similar to those in Canada:

> 237. Every one commits an offence who operates a motor vehicle or vessel or operates or assists in the operation of an aircraft or

has the care or control of a motor vehicle, vessel or aircraft whether it is in motion or not,

(a) while his ability to operate the vehicle, vessel or aircraft is impaired by alcohol or a drug; or

(b) having consumed alcohol in such a quantity that the concentration thereof in his blood exceeds eighty milligrams of alcohol in one hundred milliliters of blood.

Section 237(a) is an example of a behavior-based impaired-driving statute as the phrases "ability to operate the motor vehicle" and "impaired by alcohol" suggest. To obtain a conviction under this statute requires evidence not only of the consumption of alcohol by the accused but also of behavior or actions indicative of alcohol impairment. Partly because the terms "ability to operate" and "impaired" are vague and have no operational definition, courts have encountered difficulties. Even evidence that defendants had BACs in ranges normally presumed to impair the ability to drive (for example, BACs exceeding .15% w/v) was often insufficient to obtain convictions.

These and other difficulties prompted enactment of per se statutes, such as Section 237(b) above, to complement existing behavior-based laws. These statutes, however, do not refer to behavior related to driving. Per se statutes make it an offense simply to have, under the circumstances described, a BAC exceeding the specified limit. Nevertheless, implicit in per se statutes is the intrinsic link between the specified limit and alcohol impairment of the ability to drive. Without this link, per se statutes would have little meaning and no inherent justification. Proposals to lower present BAC limits must be evaluated in terms of the strength of association between any new limit and behavior-based criteria.

In this context, the word *impair* means to reduce or make worse. This implies a change from some criterion in a negative direction or in a detrimental fashion. Experimental researchers operationalize their definition of impairment by establishing a base-line measure of performance for the drug-free or "sober" condition. They then compare performance of tasks under conditions of alcoholic influence with base-line performance. In this way, impairment of performance due to alcohol can be evaluated on an individual or group basis. Impairment is not an absolute; it is relative to some criterion.

This approach to studying the effects of alcohol—measuring changes in performance due to alcohol relative to standards or norms of performance for identical, but alcohol-free, conditions—works well with discrete, well-defined skills. Laboratory tests are readily available for such skills as reaction time, sensory-perceptual functions, and the like. The ability to drive, however, is not discrete or well-defined. Present laboratory and other techniques do not reproduce the driving task adequately for studying alcohol's effects on driving ability. Existing technology could be, and has been, applied in experimental studies of real-world tasks and the effects of alcohol (for example, flight simulators). Unfortunately, this has not been done for research on the driving task per se.

Researchers have circumvented the issue of reproducing the driving task by developing models of real-world driving and by identifying skills and abilities important to competent, safe performance. They have conceptually disassembled the driving task into component "parts," studied each part under alcohol and nonalcohol conditions, and "reassembled" the results to describe the possible effects of alcohol on real-world driving. The difficulties (and dangers) inherent in this approach have been well documented (Huntley 1973; Moskowitz 1973; Perrine 1973). The question that remains unanswered is whether or not the effects of alcohol on skills and abilities isolated for study are definitive of alcohol's influence on actual driving.

The ability of the researcher to manipulate or control the conditions of an experiment compounds the artificiality of the methods employed. For example, eliminating, or controlling for, other factors that influence the ability to perform tasks increases the precision of measuring alcohol's effects. At the same time, such experimental control widens the gap between the laboratory and the real world. Thus, many of the strengths of experimental research become its weaknesses when we wish to generalize or to apply research findings to actual driving (Chapanis 1967). These considerations are very important because uncritical reading of experimental findings may produce erroneous conclusions.

Another potential pitfall in assessing the import of experimental research is the variability inherent in alcohol's effects. Even in carefully controlled laboratory studies, subjects differ in their responses to alcohol, not only among others in a common group, but also compared to themselves at different times. *Perhaps the most common effect of moderate amounts of alcohol is the resultant increase in performance variability* (e.g., Perrine 1973). Moreover, variability in performance appears greater with higher BACs (Levine et al. 1975). In summarizing the findings of experimental studies, it is common practice to report the *average* decrease (or increase) of performance at an *average* BAC. This practice, however, conceals the variability of the effects of alcohol in groups of subjects. At low to moderate BACs, some individuals may show little or no change in performance skills whereas others will appear much more affected.

With these cautionary notes in mind, the experimental research pertinent to the issue of BAC limits can be summarized as follows. Many different effects of alcohol begin to appear in the range of BACs between 30 and 80 mg%. The magnitude of alcohol effects in this range is generally small. Although many individuals do not perform certain tasks as well as when alcohol-free, many others do not show any decrements in performance. Moreover, many functions, such as perceptual skills, are not substantially altered until higher concentrations of alcohol are reached (Donelson and Beirness 1985; Mitchell 1985). It is fair to conclude, therefore, that present experimental evidence shows that BACs between 50 and 80 mg% can affect performance of certain skills and behaviors related to driving. Most measured effects, given the designs and methods used, are adverse. The lack of valid methods to assess alcohol's effects on the ability to drive—which involves the integration of many different functions and skills—precludes definitive judgments on whether BACs in this range so influence the ability to drive as to constitute "impairment." For example, some vehicle-based studies indicate that people with moderate BACs can drive in a normal, safe, and prudent manner (e.g., Attwood et al. 1980). Variability in responses to alcohol, however, makes it just as wrong to state that *no one* is impaired between 50 and 80 mg% as it is to state that *everyone* is impaired. Perhaps the central question is, What *percentage* of people with BACs between 50 and 80 mg% have their ability to drive impaired by alcohol? Although this question also has no definitive answer (even to estimate ranges of percentages would appear highly speculative), the best available evidence indicates that many persons do not have their ability to drive impaired at BACs between 50 and 80 mg%.

The question above can be rephrased for purposes of policy-making and legislation: Is it acceptable (that is, fair and just) to make it a criminal offense for everyone to drive with a BAC between 50 and 80 mg% when many (and possibly most) people may not have their ability to drive impaired by alcohol in this range of concentration? Some might argue that any effect of alcohol is, by definition, impairing, and (by extrapolation) that any positive BAC would impair a person's ability to drive. Such arguments, if used to support legislation that prohibited all persons from driving with a positive BAC, would probably receive little or no consideration. This line of reasoning, however, differs only in degree when BAC limits lower than 80 mg% or 100 mg% are proposed. We can assume that a higher percentage of people have their ability to drive impaired at BACs between 50 and 80 mg% than between 0 and 49 mg%. Nevertheless, given consequences of convictions under per se laws—a criminal record, temporary loss of driving privileges, fines, increased insurance rates, and less tangible social and personal losses—more definitive evidence of impaired driving associated with BACs lower than current BAC limits in North America would seem required in a court of law.

Unfortunately, emphasis on establishing and justifying statutory BAC limits has detracted from the study of variability in human response to alcohol consumption. In addition, the emphasis on driving skills to the exclusion of alcohol's effects on attitudes toward safe driving and risk-taking leaves large gaps in present knowledge. Yet, paradoxically, this is an area well suited to experimental inquiry. For example, few investigators have selected subjects representative of individuals who drive while impaired. Experimental studies using the best available methods should be conducted with subjects drawn from the population of persons convicted of impaired-driving offenses. Such research would provide important insights not possible at present.

Similarly, experimental research might investigate the behavioral effects of alcohol on subjects drawn from "high risk" groups of drinking drivers, particularly young drivers, infrequent drinkers, "alcoholic" drivers, and older persons lacking in driving experience (e.g., Allsop 1966; Donelson, Beirness, and Mayhew 1984; Donovan et al. 1983). Little experimental research has been conducted upon the effects of alcohol on skills required for the safe operation of special classes of vehicles (for example, tractor trailers, motorcycles, snowmobiles, etc.). Even gender differences are not documented adequately in the literature, despite the dramatic variances in the collision experiences of men and women drivers (Warren and Simpson 1982). As well, few experimental studies have attempted to document variability in alcohol-related responses among "risk-taking" and "risk-aversive" subpopulations, although the former seem much more characteristic of collision-involved drivers than do the latter.

In sum, it would appear that (in the absence of methods better approximating the driving task) further experimental research justifying present statutory BAC limits is likely to contribute little. By contrast, individual variations in response to alcohol consumption remain a fertile area of inquiry. Further experimentation must focus much more explicitly on specific characteristics of high-risk groups as identified in the epidemiologic literature. Such research is a crucial adjunct to better understanding of the alcohol-crash problem.

Alcohol and the Risk of Crash Involvement

The term *risk* means the likelihood, or probability, of an event or condition. The risk of road accidents can be estimated, but only very indirectly. A common estimate of risk is the number of fatal road accidents per one hundred million vehicle miles traveled. The number of fatal road accidents is reliably recorded. The number of miles traveled by vehicles, however, is calculated based on fuel-sales data and estimates of the average number of miles traveled per gallon of fuel used by motor vehicles. This gross estimate of "accident risk" serves as an indicator of overall road safety, but does little to define the risk of accident involvement due to such specific factors as alcohol-impaired driving. In fact, given constraints on the collection of needed data, directly measuring the risk of road accidents—much less the risk associated with alcohol-impaired driving—seems remote indeed. Nevertheless, methods of epidemiology offer a way to estimate the extent to which drinking drivers have an increased risk of accident involvement compared to that of non-drinking drivers.

To demonstrate that alcohol in and of itself increases accident risk, researchers have employed epidemiologic methods first used in the study and control of infectious disease. In particular, case-control studies have compared accident- and nonaccident-involved drivers and pedestrians for their use of alcohol, controlling for as many other relevant factors as deemed needful or feasible (for example, time of day, day of week, and place of prior accident; age and sex of subject; etc.). This kind of comparison is critical. Although alcohol may be strongly associated with certain types of accidents, no statement about alcohol's influence on the risk of crash-involvement can be made without comparing accidents with at-risk populations. Among the more rigorous of formulations, the results of these surveys have been expressed as the *relative probability* of accident involvement as a function of BAC (Hurst 1970, 1974; Donelson et al. 1980; Donelson and Beirness 1985, 16–22, 44–51).

A consistent finding from epidemiologic research is that, as drivers' BAC exceeds .08 to .10% w/v, the risk of being involved in a traffic accident increases relative to the (unknown) risk associated with the zero-BAC level. As reviewed by Hurst (1974), this general relationship has limitations with regard to inferences about the influence of alcohol on the ability to drive, even when combined with experimental data:

> We have on the one hand laboratory data which may be partially irrelevant and on the other hand field data which do not reveal individual difference distributions except in the gross sense of differentiating demographical sub-groups. As a last resort, we can "combine" the field and laboratory results and draw some tentative inferences. Since the laboratory studies usually show continuous or quasi-normal distributions of individual impairment levels, we may infer that a substantial rise in crash incidence at a given BAC, from field data, is the result of a fairly large number of individual impairments, with everyone else being unaffected. This introduces some iffy propositions, however, and seems inadequate to answer the question of just what percent of a population drives less safely at a given BAC. It is even further from determining the BAC at which a particular individual may rationally be presumed to drive less safely, or presumed not to drive less safely. I would question the basis of laws that set levels for "presumed to be impaired" or "presumed not impaired." (131)

Identifiable subgroups within the population of drinking drivers may have differing relative probabilities of crash-involvement at given BACs. For example, the average driver who reports drinking daily has about the same relative probability of crash involvement at .09% w/v as the average driver who does not drink at all (Hurst 1974).

In addition to the presence of alcohol and the frequency and quantity of its use, accident- and nonaccident-involved drivers have been compared with respect to such other variables as age, sex, estimated annual mileage driven, education, race or nationality, marital status, and occupation. The large-scale controlled study conducted by Borkenstein et al. (1964) permitted an assessment of the increased (or decreased) accident risk associated with these factors. Controlling for these factors, alcohol use resulting in *higher* BACs emerged as the dominant, explanatory variable for increased accident risk.

> Factors other than alcohol are associated with individual accident experience. In general, the classes with the worst accident expe-

rience were those that we anticipated. The frequency with which the young, the very old, the inexperienced, and the uneducated were involved in accidents was out of proportion to their exposure to traffic. At the same time, the identifiers of the safest groups seemed entirely logical. The most highly educated, those with the best employment and the middle-aged have the best records of low accident involvement.

Since many other factors other than alcohol are involved in accident experience, further control was necessary. Tests of the data again showed that within all of the sub-classes of the major factors, the accident rate mounted as the blood alcohol level rose. Then, just as in the preceding analyses, we found that above 0.08 percent blood alcohol level, factors other than alcohol became less and less significant and eventually seemed to disappear. In every case, the higher alcohol levels were associated with more frequent accident experience, and in general, accident involvement increased rapidly as the alcohol levels exceeded 0.05 percent. This association was so strong that other explanations of the excessive accident experience of drivers in the highest alcohol ranges were substantially ruled out. (Borkenstein et al. 1964, 6–7)

The final sentence in the above quote may leave the impression that no other factors could explain the increased risk of accident involvement among high-BAC drivers. Clearly, high BACs contribute to increased risk. Nonetheless, *personal characteristics* and *social circumstances* of alcohol-impaired drivers may also contribute to (and thus partly explain) their more likely involvement in road accidents (Donelson, Beirness, and Mayhew 1984; Donovan et al. 1983). For this and other reasons, we have to interpret values of relative risk associated with BAC with caution.

For example, a statement to the effect that "a BAC of .08% w/v doubles or quadruples the risk of an accident" is not only simplistic but also misleading. Relative risk estimates are simply that: estimates, subject to some degree of uncertainty. This uncertainty may have much more to do with the variability of the phenomenon measured than with mistakes or errors made when measuring.

In epidemiologic research, the calculation of *confidence intervals* indicates the precision of relative risk estimates (Armitage 1971; Gart 1962). The 95 percent confidence interval—a common standard in scientific studies—predicts that, in repeated surveys of the same sample size, the value of the relative risk estimate will fall within the specified range 95 out of 100 times. This confidence interval is, essentially, a "test of significance" of the relative risk estimate.

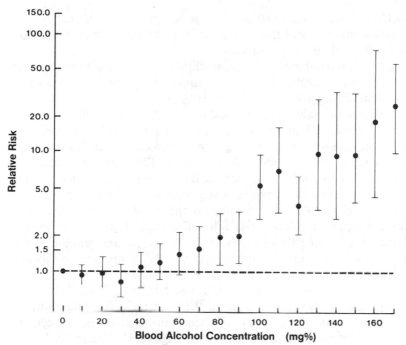

Fig. 1.1. Blood alcohol concentration and relative risk of accident involvement:
The Grand Rapids Study (Borkenstein et al. 1964).

Values outside the confidence interval would be considered highly
unlikely, given the results of the scientific study.

Figure 1.1 provides a case in point. Here, 95 percent confidence
intervals for relative risk associated with BAC ranges between 10
and 170+ mg% have been calculated for data from the Grand Rapids
study (Borkenstein et al. 1964). The value of 1.0 for relative risk
represents the (uncalculated) risk of accident involvement for the
average nondrinking driver. For ease of comparison, a dashed line
has been drawn parallel to the line for BAC. Without confidence
limits (shown by vertical lines through each point on the graph), we
might conclude that drivers with BACs of 30 mg% or lower have a
decreased risk of accident involvement relative to the nondrinking
driver. Similarly we might decide that drivers with BACs greater
than 40 mg% have a higher risk of accident involvement. The confidence limits for all points up to 80 mg%, however, indicate that no
estimate differs significantly from the risk of accident involvement
associated with the average nondrinking driver. Given this information, one could not conclude with confidence that drivers with

BACs between 50 and 80 mg% have a significantly higher risk of accident involvement than the average nondrinking driver (cf. Borkenstein et al. 1964, 117–124).

BAC data combined in larger or different intervals, however, can yield different results. This is a common procedure employed when the number of cases for smaller BAC intervals is inadequate for more detailed analyses, or when data are analysed for different purposes. Figure 1.2 presents the same data graphed in Figure 1.1; however, the data have been grouped to form larger BAC ranges: 10–49 mg%, 50–79 mg%, 80–119 mg%, 120–149 mg%, 150–179 mg%, and 180 + mg%. A confidence interval is given for each relative risk estimate and the range of BACs included in the estimate is also shown. This establishes an area on the graph in which the most likely estimate of relative risk falls. The shaded portions represent these areas. Using these *areas of estimation,* maximum and minimum risk curves can be approximated. By comparing confidence intervals for the relative risk estimates for 50 through 70 mg% in Figure 1.1 with that for the BAC range 50–79 mg% in Figure 1.2, we find an apparent contradiction. Whereas the three data points in Figure 1.1 are not statistically significant, the relative risk of accident involvement associated with the BAC range of 50–79 mg% in Figure 1.2 *is* significantly different from that of the average nondrinking driver! How can smaller intervals of BAC, each of which does *not* differ significantly from 1.0, when combined, now produce a statistically significant value? The answer lies in the method of calculating confidence intervals for relative risk estimates. Basically, increasing group size (that is, the number of individual cases included in a BAC range) tends to shrink the confidence interval. In addition, all values in the intervals combined were closely related and greater than 1.0. As a result, the average value for the larger BAC range is also greater than 1.0 and becomes statistically significant.

This "mathematical explanation" for the apparent contradiction described above does little to resolve the issue of whether or not BACs between 50 and 80 mg% increase the risk of accident involvement compared to the average nondrinking driver. Here we encounter—in a single study—a fundamental problem: how to apply findings for groups of persons to individuals, based on a single characteristic like BAC. For example, if an individual has a BAC of 60 mg%, then do we consider that person a member of the smaller 60 mg% group or a member of the larger 50–80 mg% group? The former group does not have a relative risk that differs significantly from the average nondrinking driver while the latter group does.

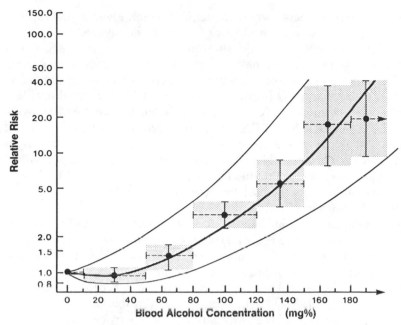

Fig. 1.2. Relative risk of crash involvement by blood alcohol concentration (Bor-
      kenstein et al. 1964).

This problem is one of a cluster of problems that stem from basic differences in the disciplines of science and law. These differences warrant separate study for their general policy implications concerning the role of science in law. For present, more restricted purposes, a brief discussion may prove useful in defining the issue.

Scientific research uses groups of "cases" to discover general principles or rules of behavior—which may or may not apply to some individuals, even those in the groups studied. Research findings are probabilistic, indicating the likelihood of their being correct. Thus, there always exists the possibility of exceptions to the rule. The rules of law, especially as applied to adjudicating the guilt or innocence of individuals charged with committing an offense, operate on an individual, case-specific basis. Judges, for example, do not review a set of similar cases as the sole basis for deciding the outcome of a proceeding. They weigh the evidence presented for that case and decide accordingly. This difference can be summarized briefly as follows: A scientific expert might indicate, based on relevant studies, the likelihood that an individual belonging to a group with a certain BAC had an increased risk of accident involvement.

A judge has to decide whether that individual, given actual facts in evidence, had an increased risk of accident involvement.

Unfortunately, this basic difference between science and law is blurred by statutes that make driving with a BAC exceeding certain limits an offense per se. Although implicitly based on scientific research showing *likely* impairment and *probably* increased accident risk, such statutes only require evidence from chemical tests showing that the accused had a BAC over the legal limit—whether or not that individual was actually impaired or had a demonstrably increased risk of an accident. In other words, even if that individual were an *exception* to the rule that persons above the legal BAC limit are impaired, nonetheless, that person would be convicted of an "impaired-driving" offense.

Depending on the jurisdiction, present statutory limits of 50, 80, and 100 mg% have received general (but not complete) acceptance as fairly defining the offense of alcohol-impaired driving. Those persons who drive with BACs over those limits are considered impaired to an unacceptable degree and are assumed to have an unacceptably high risk of accident involvement. The fact is, however, that an overwhelming majority of driving trips by persons with BACs twice legal limits are completed without accident or arrest. Reference to the distinction between "relative risk" and "absolute risk" may help clarify this point. Statements that drivers with illegal BACs have an increased risk of accident compared to the average nondrinking driver refer to relative risk. The actual probability (or absolute risk) of a serious traffic crash, even with high BACs, is extremely low. Thus, "increased risk" does not necessarily mean "very likely," especially for drivers with BACs between 50 and 80 mg%.

The real issue is why *some* of the many drivers with high BACs cause traffic crashes. How do accident-involved drivers with high BACs differ from impaired drivers who do not have accidents? Limited research relevant to this question suggests that such personal attributes as hostility, alienation, impulsiveness, inability to cope with stress, and rebelliousness are more frequently found in groups of high-risk drinking drivers (Donelson, Beirness, and Mayhew 1984; Donovan et al. 1983). Unfortunately, not unlike experimental research described earlier, epidemiologic inquiry has focused on demonstrating that a problem exists and on establishing a general relationship between BAC and relative risk. This focus, dictated historically by interest in setting BAC limits for drivers, has tended to detract from the study of risk variability. Aggregation of data to study the relationship between alcohol and accident risk tends to oversimplify an extremely complex phenomenon. It seems very likely that crash risk varies dramatically, not only as a function of BAC, but also as a function of myriad other factors. Fatal crash risk (as a function of BAC) varies across the spectrum of young, middle-aged, and aging drivers; infrequent drinkers and "alcoholic" drivers; drivers of different types and classes of vehicles; and inexperienced and experienced drivers, to name but a few. Considerably greater emphasis now must be placed on documentation of *variability* rather than uniformity in alcohol-related effects, so that the specificity and efficacy of social control strategies can be increased.

The Magnitude of the Alcohol-Crash Problem

Many people, especially journalists on their first search for statistics on alcohol and road accidents, express great surprise when they learn that certain key questions cannot be answered reliably with present knowledge:

> How many road accidents are due, at least in part, to alcohol impairment?
> How many victims are killed and injured by alcohol-impaired drivers each year?
> How many road accidents occur in which the person responsible was alcohol-impaired *and* had one or more previous convictions for alcohol-impaired driving offenses?

The answers to these and other questions are not forthcoming for a variety of reasons. One reason is that available data are scattered among many sources—coroners, hospitals, police, courts, and traffic-accident and driver-licensing data systems. The special studies required to gather relevant data from each source are rarely funded and are certainly not done routinely on a state or national basis.

In many cases, needed data simply are unavailable. For example, police and medical personnel do not obtain objective data on the presence and amount of alcohol in the vast majority of accident-involved road users. Subjective information included in police accident reports has proved unreliable (e.g., Waller 1971). Even when objective data from chemical tests are available, the degree to which the effects of alcohol influenced behavior contributing to the occurrence of a given accident remains problematic. For example, inattention, careless or reckless driving, poor judgment, and failure to respond quickly enough in traffic situations often occur in the absence of alcohol. Other physiological and medical conditions (for example, fatigue, mental and physical disease) are not or cannot be detected; these factors may also contribute to some proportion of traffic accidents in which alcohol is either present or absent. In addition, inferences about impairment based solely on BAC data (legal definitions aside) cannot be made with certainty at concentrations below those associated with frank intoxication and in the absence of detailed accident descriptions. Some uncertainty persists even in clinical accident investigations.

To estimate, at a minimum, the magnitude of the alcohol-crash problem we must ask a less precise question: "How many road accidents involve alcohol-impaired road users?" We define "alcohol-impaired" as a BAC equal to or exceeding some value, usually the statutory BAC limit (for example, .08 or .10% w/v). We presume, based on this defintion, that persons above the legal limit were alcohol-impaired, and those below the limit were not. This approach, although subject to error, is based on experimental and epidemiologic data indicating that certain blood alcohol concentrations are associated with decreased performance of skills related to driving and an increased risk of accident involvement. Practical limits on available data necessitate these assumptions. Some proportion of road users with BACs above the "minimum" BAC for alcohol impairment will not have "caused" the accident and may not have been "impaired"; however, some proportion of road users with BACs *below* that threshold concentration will have "caused" the accident and may have been "impaired" as well. The presumption is arbitrary but not capricious—and essential to further analysis.

Among the most serious of traffic crashes are those resulting in death. Investigations of accidental death, especially those due to motor vehicle accidents, often include routine tests for the presence and amount of alcohol in fatally injured drivers and pedestrians. Although fatal accidents comprise only about 1 percent of all traffic accidents, more information about alcohol involvement is available for this category of accidents than for any other. In fact, perceptions about the magnitude of the alcohol-crash problem seem based almost exclusively on fatality data.

Early official statistics underreported alcohol involvement in fatal accidents, varied greatly from jurisdiction to jurisdiction, and created an impression that alcohol was not a significant risk factor (Schmidt and Smart 1963). Special studied (uncontrolled and controlled) conducted over a period of thirty years reversed this perception. At present, for example, a common statement in the literature is that alcohol-impaired drivers cause 50 percent of all fatal accidents. This, however, seems demonstrably untrue (Zylman 1974a).

Jones and Joscelyn (1978) summarized findings from epidemiologic studies of fatally injured drivers in the United States. In those studies, selected for adequate design, execution, and number of subjects, 40 to 55 percent of fatally injured drivers had BACs exceeding the legal limit (.10% w/v) in most states. In European countries reporting comparable data, the proportion of drivers exceeding .10% w/v may be somewhat less than this range (Organisation for Economic Cooperation and Development 1978).

In Canada, the Traffic Injury Research Foundation of Canada (TIRF) is the principle source of statistics on alcohol use by persons fatally injured in road accidents. In projects sponsored by several governmental and private agencies, the foundation has collated data from police accident reports and coroners' records for seven of the ten Canadian provinces since 1974. The data base on traffic fatalities, established and maintained at TIRF (see Simpson, Page-Valin, and Warren 1979), provided the basis for a recent report entitled "Alcohol and Fatal Road Accidents in Canada: A Statistical Look at Its Magnitude and Persistence" (Beirness et al. 1985). This report presented detailed data on the use of alcohol by persons fatally injured in road accidents, focusing on alcohol-impaired drivers. Although the number of drivers has increased and decreased over the years, the percentage of tested drivers with a BAC exceeding the present statutory limit (.08% w/v) has remained remarkably constant: between 45 and 51 percent!

Although personal injury accidents (those involving no fatalities) occur much more frequently than fatal accidents, only fragmentary data exist in North America on the involvement of alcohol in these incidents. A study by Holcomb (1938) found that 25 percent of injured drivers, compared to 2 percent of at-risk drivers, had BACs exceeding today's legal standards for alcohol impairment. Since that study, only a handful of special research studies have produced data on alcohol and injury accidents. Problems related to legal and practical constraints (for example, the requirement for informed consent, the ability and willingness of hospital emergency departments to cooperate) account for the paucity of present information (Donelson, McNair, Ruschmann, and Joscelyn 1980). What data exist indicate that the prevalence of alcohol use among all injured drivers is less than that among fatally injured drivers, and that the prevalence of alcohol use among injured drivers increases with increasing injury severity.

For example, Jones and Joscelyn (1978) reviewed North American studies of alcohol involvement in nonfatal injury crashes. Allowing for differences in key variables (for example, time of day, geographical area, etc.), they estimated that between 9 percent and 13 percent of drivers injured in traffic accidents had BACs exceeding 0.10% w/v Farris et al. (1977) combined Huntsville, Alabama, and San Diego, California, data on injured drivers and reported that 12 percent had BACs of .10% w/v or greater. McLean and Robinson (1979), reporting results of the Adelaide In-Depth Accident Study, found 14 percent of injured automobile drivers had BACs greater than .08% w/v.

Other studies suggest somewhat higher rates of alcohol involvement in injury-producing collisions. One study conducted in Australia found that 20% of injured drivers had BACs greater than .05% w/v (Gay et al. 1978, cited in Rockerbie 1979, 1). Terhune and Fell (1981) reported that 25% of drivers participating in a New York study had been drinking, and that 20% had BACs of .10% w/v or greater. They noted that this finding is a conservative estimate for several reasons, not least of which is the fact that 311 persons refused to cooperate in the study (about 30% of the total number of eligible cases).

Two recent studies of alcohol use among persons injured in traffic accidents have been conducted in Canada. Rockerbie (1979) and Parkin et al. (1980) reported a study on 728 traffic accident victims admitted to the emergency ward of a British Columbia hospital. Of the 422 drivers included in the study, 26 percent had BACs in excess of .08% w/v. Warren et al. (1982) reported a year-long study conducted at four major hospitals in the Province of New Brunswick. Findings indicated that, among drivers: at least 28 percent had been drinking (greater than or equal to .02% w/v); at least 21 percent had BACs in excess of the statutory limit (greater than or equal to .08% w/v); and at least 10 percent had BACs in excess of .15% w/v. Using a method to infer BACs of nonrespondents, Warren estimated that at least 34 percent of the injured drivers reporting to emergency wards had been drinking, 27 percent having BACs in excess of the statutory limit. In addition, percentages of those evidencing use of alcohol increased with injury severity. The results of these Canadian studies provide additional evidence that alcohol use among injured drivers, especially among those who are seriously injured, may generally exceed earlier estimates of 9 to 13 percent (Jones and Joscelyn 1978).

The most common type of traffic accident involves "only" property damage. The relationship between alcohol use by drivers and property damage accidents has received little attention from researchers. In one of the few research studies to investigate alcohol involvement in crashes with no indication of personal injury, Borkenstein et al. (1964) found that 5 percent of 4,570 drivers had BACs of .10% w/v or greater. One might assume that routine investigations of property damage accidents by police would provide extensive data on alcohol involvement. However, for numerous reasons summarized by Zelhart and Schurr (1977), reliable estimates of the extent of drinking among these accident-involved drivers are not possible based on police accident reports or adjudication statistics.

The findings above provide a starting point for estimating the magnitude of the alcohol-crash problem, that is, the percentage of road accidents of different severity attributable, at least in part, to the impairment of road users by alcohol.

Because of constraints on the depth and quality of information about alcohol and road accidents, one convenient approach to estimating the magnitude of the problem is to consider "alcohol-involved" road accidents as "alcohol-caused" road accidents. In other words, if alcohol is found present in one or more persons involved in a road accident, then we assume that the alcohol present had an effect on behavior but for which the road accident would not have occurred. Obviously, very low amounts of alcohol, if present, make this assumption tenuous. As discussed above, we usually select a BAC (for example, the statutory BAC limit) beyond which we can assume with greater certainty not only the presence of alcohol but also the adverse effects of alcohol on the ability to drive. This approach to estimating the magnitude of the alcohol-crash problem results in the following figures: 50 percent of fatal road accidents, 25 to 30 percent of injury road accidents, and 5 to 10 percent of property-damage-only road accidents involve alcohol use. These rates are often used in conjunction with statistics on the number of road accidents occurring in different jurisdictions at different times, even though objective data on alcohol use by persons involved in those road accidents are not obtained or available (e.g., Organisation for Economic Cooperation and Development 1978; Comptroller General of the United States 1979; U.S. Department of Transportation 1968; Jones and Joscelyn 1978).

In their analysis of the alcohol-crash problem in the United States, Jones and Joscelyn (1978) cautioned potential users of these kinds of estimates:

The above figures, while indicative of a large-scale national problem, do not, of course, prove that alcohol *caused* the crashes in which drinking was involved. Traffic accidents are probabilistic, with many factors entering into the probability equation. The most that can be said on the basis of epidemiologic evidence is that, on the average, alcohol, present beyond a certain amount, is associated with increased crash risk. In-depth analyses of the conditions surrounding the crashes would have to be made to support stronger statements about causation. While such analyses have been made of the roles of many other factors, the role of alcohol has not been subject to the same close scrutiny. Only rough assessments have been made of alcohol as a causal factor in crashes. (33–34)

Other authors have taken stronger exception to estimates of "alcohol-involved" road accidents. Of particular note, Zylman (1974a) published a detailed analysis that stands today, in this author's opinion, as a definitive study of issues surrounding statements of "alcohol involvement" in *fatal* road accidents. He developed his estimates "based largely on the most reliable research available, and partially on empirically based guesses" (200). He also carefully disaggregated highway deaths into numerous subcategories of victims and circumstances to assess the portion of each that may have "involved alcohol" in some causal way. Zylman concluded that, based on his analysis, "the actual frequency of alcohol-involvement in fatal crashes is in the range of 25–34 percent" (202). Despite the report by Zylman, the tendency to overestimate and "overdramatize" the magnitude of the alcohol-crash problem with uncritical use of road accident statistics has continued (Gusfield 1981a; Reed 1981). One concern of experts in the field is that "overemphasis on alcohol" detracts from efforts to increase knowledge of the complexity of the problem beyond the citing of large numbers as a preface to informational campaigns (Zylman 1974b).

As the issue of "drunk driving" once again began to command attention in North America, another attempt to develop more precise estimates of the magnitude of the problem was published. Reed (1981), following the work of Hurst (1970), reanalyzed data from controlled studies to estimate the number of road accidents that would *not* have occurred had all drivers *not* consumed alcoholic beverages—in other words, the number of accidents prevented by a "perfect" drinking-driving countermeasure. Based on his reanalyses of fatal crash data from Vermont (Perrine et al. 1971), injury crash data from Huntsville, Alabama (Farris et al. 1976), and property damage crash data from Grand Rapids, Michigan (Borkenstein et al. 1964), Reed estimated expected reductions in road accidents if all drivers had a zero, or negative, BAC: 23.7 percent of fatal road accidents, between 8.2 and 15.8 percent of injury accidents, and 5.7 percent of property-damage-only accidents. These figures are about half those based on estimates of "alcohol-involved" road accidents. Because Reed assumed for the purposes of his analysis a "perfect countermeasure," his estimates represent the *maximal* gains possible by focusing solely on alcohol use by road users and by *completely* separating driving from drinking.

Discussions of the magnitude of the alcohol-crash problem often seem unduly academic and undoubtedly leave those concerned with "doing something about the problem" with a dispirited view of ivory-tower types who love playing with numbers, not working toward the goal of reducing the problem. Issues related to the magnitude of the problem run deeper than they might first appear. Let us first agree that the problem is big, whether 24 percent or 50 percent of fatal road accidents are "caused" by alcohol. Next, let us accept that "something must be done" to reduce the problem. Finally, we are left with the question, "Have we made any difference?"

In the absence of precise measures of the magnitude of the problem over time, the effectiveness of our overall response, and the effectiveness of specific programs, cannot be known. The complexity and diffuseness of the problem allow a great diversity of independent action programs. Without adequate knowledge of how and to what degree the extent and characteristics of the problem change over time, we can never know how, or which, programs proved effective. If we acknowledge the need for such information, then we also must accept long-standing recommendations from researchers concerning the development and application of methods to monitor and to define more accurately the magnitude and characteristics of the alcohol-crash problem. Viewed in this way, research supports action programs and assists in their refinement. To ignore this issue is to bestow on the next decade's reviewers the unenviable task of reciting once again the litany of informational gaps that hinder progress in this field.

2. The Issue of Perspective

One inherent, frequently covert issue that haunts discussions of the alcohol-crash problem is that of perspective: how one views the problem, how one defines the problem, and how different views and definitions contrast, conflict, or complement each other. The nature of the problem itself gives rise to this issue. The alcohol-crash problem is a behavioral and social phenomenon with legal, moral, political, economic, philosophic, and emotional implications. Considering the number and diversity of individuals, groups, organizations, and institutions that have or claim part or whole ownership of the problem, a single, consensual perspective would be astonishing. Unfortunately, the panoply of perspectives that do exist often transforms the "war against drunk drivers" into a battle of contending theories, none of which has ever gained sufficient support to acquire sole status as paradigm or policy (Warren and Donelson 1982).

If the issue of perspective were only a matter of academic or semantic interest, its relevance might well be questioned. Its importance, however, relates directly to the ineffectiveness of social control policies, evidenced by the persistence of the alcohol-crash problem itself. As Bacon (1973) argued:

> The failure to achieve successful control does not primarily stem from lack of energy, know-how, money, or even from public disinterest, . . . it arises basically from conflicting and often ill-defined notions of what the problem is with the consequent adoption by different groups of quite different goals. In turn, these varying notions of the nature of the problem together with their contrasting goals reinforce the adoption of quite different methods for attempted control. These basic disagreements practically deny the possibility of objective evaluation of results, create antagonisms among those attempting programs, and minimize public support. (311)

The confluence of perspectives thus manifests as the fragmentation of effort and the lack of coordinated activity endemic to a demonstrably impotent societal response.

Perspective at Issue

One can appreciate the still frequent use of an otherwise hackneyed metaphor—the blind-men-and-the-elephant story—when one considers its sadly accurate portrayal of group problem-solving behavior. For example, the struggle to define "the problem" at a recent workshop evidenced that each expert, if not blind, at lease had blind spots. One outcome of the meeting was merely a restatement of the moral of the story: "The answers [to the question "What is the problem?''] describe points of view—some narrow, some broad—and determine how and where emphasis is placed in dealing with the problem of alcohol and road accidents'' (Donelson 1983, 12). Although the group as a whole recommended a long-term, systematic, comprehensive, coordinated, strategic approach to the problem, it became clear that barriers to the development of a strategic plan and its implementation include continuing disagreements over means (methods, programs) and ends (aims, objectives), the chronic symptoms of conflicting perspectives.

The critical questions now are whether debate among the (partially) blind will (or can) lead to dialogue, and whether contention among advocates of different perspectives will lead to cooperation. The solution appears simple but not easy: accepting the fact that all of us touch part of, but do not see, the whole problem. That the alcohol-crash problem *is* remarkably complex—an idea, perhaps, whose time has finally come—is no excuse for retreating to past oversimplification. Developing, discussing, and refining a mutually satisfactory framework of thought to encompass major viewpoints appears the only recourse at present. In this context, two recent developments point to the urgency of the task.

First, a tidal influx of people new to the field of alcohol and highway safety has occurred, including whole agencies and organizations with little appreciation of its history. Many appear engaged in "reinventing the wheel," a syndrome characteristic of past efforts to deal with the alcohol-crash problem. Consistent with Bacon's (1973) Stage I of social problems, definitions of the nature, extent, and causes of the problem phenomenon are, once again, sweeping and ill-defined.

As in the past, "the problem" is popularly viewed as the overlap between two otherwise legal and socially acceptable behaviors. The consumption of alcoholic beverages in combination with the driving of motor vehicles gives rise to drinking-and-driving behavior. The adverse outcomes of this behavior—alcohol-impaired driving and alcohol-related traffic crashes—result in human, economic, and other losses and costs to people and society, presumably our ultimate concern. This conceptualization of the problem inspires the obvious solution: separate drinking from driving. The past fifty years, reflected in the recurrent message "don't drink and drive," have been spent for the most part in searching for *the* solution, the "magic bullet" to end the problem once and for all. There is now growing acceptance that past ways of thinking about the problem have been too simple, even simplistic. Certainly, almost all frontal assaults aimed at separating drinking from driving have failed to reduce alcohol-crash losses measurably, if at all.

When we recognize that *alcohol and highway safety* involves considerations ranging from the molecular to the societal, even to the international, then we can also appreciate that such phrases as "alcohol and road accidents," "drinking and driving," and "drunk driving" conceal more than they reveal about the complexity of problems in this area of social and political concern. Even to suggest that these problems stem from the overlap of two ubiquitous behaviors—the consumption of alcoholic beverages and the use of motor vehicles—tends to oversimplify. For example, both "behaviors" include a wide range of personal and social *patterns* of use, some problematic, others not. The manufacture, distribution, and sale of motor vehicles and alcoholic beverages represent billion-dollar enterprises and key strands in the fabric of society. Laws and regulations pertaining to each have a complexity all their own, stemming from social control policies that attempt to reconcile conflicting aims of economy, justice, health, and safety. Beyond the use of motor vehicles and alcohol, beyond individual behavior, the structures of society and current social practice contribute to the alcohol-crash problem and alcohol-impaired driving. Separating drinking from driving, or vice versa, admits to no one simple solution, even in the abstract.

The second development underscoring the importance of a broad, unifying perspective relates to the alcohol-crash problem as a high-profile social and political issue, an issue that currently serves as a rallying point for agencies and organizations generally concerned with "alcohol problems" or "traffic safety." To appreciate this trend, we have to acknowledge that health and safety problems associated with alcohol and with traffic crashes are not yet, in and of themselves, critical issues. At present, *the* issue is "drunk driving." Thus, alcohol-specific control policies and crash-loss reduction measures are frequently advocated in the name of dealing with the alcohol-crash problem (e.g., Presidential Commission on Drunk Driving 1983; Task Force on Drinking and Driving 1983; Douglass 1980). This development may have strong implications for the integrity of efforts to reduce alcohol-crash losses. The focus of the grassroots movement has inevitably expanded to include other alcohol problems and traffic-crash problems as well. One question is whether or not measures with more general thrust will diffuse energies, create dissension within the swelling ranks, and, perhaps, even miss the original target. Another question is to what extent the broader public health perspective, a welcome contribution in itself (e.g., Room 1984; Mäkelä et al. 1981), will carry with it a return to a temperance view of alcohol as *the* cause of this social problem (Levine 1984).

In this context, the recurrent notion that "alcohol causes traffic crashes" may seriously undermine efforts to broaden the scope of inquiry into the etiology of the alcohol-crash problem. Richard Zylman—whom Douglass (1982) perceptively described as "a voice crying out in the wilderness"—identified as one of the barriers to change in dealing effectively with the alcohol-crash problem "the power of single-cause and simple interpretations of complex problems, which have dominated American thinking about alcohol" (1968, 23). Based on his conceptualization of the problem as a multivariate phenomenon, Zylman (1974a) also challenged popular statistics on the magnitude of the alcohol–fatal crash problem (cf. Reed 1981). His rational, scientific approach, not to mention his conclusions, fell on mostly deaf ears. Gusfield (1981a) and Bacon (1984) provide cogent, sociological reasons that indirectly explain why Zylman has had so little apparent influence on subsequent developments in the field.

As quoted earlier, Borkenstein et al. (1963) once wrote that "one of the basic reasons for the extensive research efforts has been to attempt to dramatize the enormity of the problem and the seriousness of its effects on a complex and fast-moving society" (144). In practice, research *has* served to provide "facts" in support of a priori assertions and positions. The frequent failure of this tactic in the past has not deterred the resurgent movement "against drunk drivers," a loose but powerful coalition that still employs simple definitions of the alcohol-crash problem. This merely underscores the critical need to resolve the issue of perspective and to support efforts to communicate a more comprehensive way of thinking about the alcohol-crash problem.

Complexity of the Alcohol-Crash Problem

The need for a broader, more comprehensive perspective of the alcohol-crash problem, therefore, is also indicated by the complexity of phenomena associated with the alcohol-crash problem. Even such truisms as "alcohol impairs the ability to drive" and "alcohol increases the risk of traffic crashes" become sharply qualified as research findings receive critical review (Donelson 1985a; Donelson and Beirness 1985). Perhaps the most disturbing oversimplification concerns "drinking drivers," often vilified and lumped together as social reprobates. Thus, underlying issues relate to two key problems, both crucial for assessing the potential value of social control strategies: (1) how we view and conceive of the drinking driver; and (2) the limited state of knowledge beyond basic, descriptive data (for example, age, sex, and BAC). In the longer term, these issues may have more import for formulating policy and designing programs than present information from past scientific studies.

When we look beyond alcohol per se as a "cause" of road accidents to the people who consume alcoholic beverages and drive, we usually begin by categorizing drinking drivers. The general population of interest includes all drivers who consume alcoholic beverages at least occasionally (or, conversely, all people who drink and sometimes operate motor vehicles). In the general population of interest, we can define several target groups for study or action: *drinking drivers* (those who drive with positive BACs); *alcohol-impaired drivers* (those who drive with BACs in excess of the statutory limit or who become impaired at lower BACs); and *accident-involved drinking drivers*. Unfortunately, this approach to defining target groups has certain drawbacks that limit its usefulness.

First, the various labels (for example, "drinking drivers") do not describe durable attributes or characteristics of people or groups of people. Like alcohol impairment, a temporary condition or state, the act of driving after drinking usually lasts only a fraction of the time a person spends in a given period. Exceptions undoubtedly exist, for instance, an alcoholic taxi driver. For the majority of people, however, we can safely assume that each becomes a "drinking driver" for a relatively short time, and then exits that population— safely, under arrest, or accident-involved, in decreasing order of probability.

Second, the labels lend themselves to stereotyping. The so-called "killer drunk" as well as the "drunk driver" become mythologized, obscuring a more complicated reality, which features diverse patterns and outcomes of drinking-driving behavior as well as diverse types of people who engage in that behavior. They tend to connote moral reprehensibleness, social pathology, alcohol dependency, and general irresponsibility. Otherwise upstanding people (understandably) do not relate to such images in a personal way, especially when associated with impersonal informational campaigns on drinking and driving. Stereotyping may encourage public indignation but not necessarily the average individual's accepting responsibility for solution of the problem.

Third, labeling populations of interest (pejoratively or not) provides only a vague set of nonoperational categories for identifying high-risk subsets of drinking drivers for preventive measures designed to reduce the alcohol-crash problem. Furthermore, the categories are not mutually exclusive over time. Variables such as age, sex, and BAC assist in stratifying populations within categories. Social and psychological data, especially those that measure personal and behavioral attributes of persons who drink and drive, provide information of greatest value. Labeling as a basis for target group identification merely encourages the notion that present knowledge is adequate for new initiatives in the absence of more informative data.

Cross-sectional descriptions of populations of interest cannot capture the dynamic nature of drinking-driving phenomena. Yet past research, with a few exceptional studies, has scarcely gone beyond looking at unrepresentative samples of different populations of interest. Information from past studies allows a general description of people found in those populations at specific times and circumstances. The data do not describe how people enter and exit different populations (or, more accurately, *risk states*), how often, why, and with what likelihood of particular outcomes. Moreover, the identification of high-risk target groups for preventive measures—as opposed to punitive action—remains far from complete.

Past beliefs about drinking drivers have reflected, for the most part, prevailing notions about people who drive and people who drink. The "drunk driver" became the target of legal measures aimed at reducing a perceived but ill-defined alcohol-crash problem. This stereotype mirrored the picture of all those who succumbed to "demon rum," the difference being only that these people happened to own and operate "motorized wagons." As the medical community came to accept certain patterns of alcohol consumption as addiction (similar to the chronic, compulsive use of opium-derived drugs), the "disease model" of alcohol-related problems gained ground (Jellinek 1960). By the late 1960s, experts in the area of drinking and driving had conceived of the *health-legal approach* (Jones and Joscelyn 1978). The criminal justice system would act as a "case-finding mechanism"; the health care system would function in its traditional role, providing treatment and rehabilitation for those dependent on alcohol. This approach paralleled the trend in Western society to view drunkenness per se as unsafe or unhealthy as opposed to immoral or illegal. The degree to which the medical paradigm had a lasting impact on the public or the judiciary seems debatable. For example, in recent years citizen activist groups have insisted that drunk drivers be considered and treated as criminals, whether or not offenders evidence problem drinking or alcoholism.

The predominance of scientific and legal definitions of drunk driving extends past medical considerations to more practical ones. Some evidence indicates that most people cannot calculate (nor even can conceive of calculating) their BAC after drinking (Beirness and Donelson 1985). This is analogous to enforcing posted speed limits, knowing drivers have no speedometers in their vehicles. Not well appreciated, therefore, is that many people may be unable to comply with a law cast in terms they do not understand and for which they have no reference to objective measures, even if they do exercise some control over their use of alcohol.

This illustrates another prevalent idea about the "problem drinking-driver": that people who drive with BACs above statutory limits are simply unaware, ill-informed, or uneducated. Notions that "people should know better" and that "people are basically irresponsible" have led in recent years to a reemphasis of the "stick approach": law-based, punitive measures and consistent calls for "harsher laws and stiffer penalties" by citizens' groups. Almost forgotten now (or at least neglected) are findings from past studies showing that many persons convicted of alcohol-impaired driving offenses are "alcoholics" (Vingilis 1983a). Not taken into account are prevailing (and paradoxical) attitudes among the drinking-driver population, which lead to acceptance of this behavior as essentially noncriminal, if not normative. Moreover, depictions of drinking drivers in general as ignorant, irrational, and irresponsible are not consistent with the subjective judgments and experiences of those who drive after drinking. As discussed in detail elsewhere (Warren 1982), the fact that the vast majority of "drunk-driving" trips results in no damage or arrest tends to reinforce and even justify the behavior as rational and "safe" in the minds of those who engage in it. Small wonder many pay lip service to the admonition "don't drink and drive"— and do otherwise. This gap between social goals and personal perceptions greatly complicates efforts to decrease the acceptability of drinking and driving. It also greatly separates popular views of stereotypical drinking drivers from the real world of people and their actual behavior, further hindering progress of those efforts.

3. Present Knowledge: Implications for Social Control

Medicine distinguishes palliative treatment from curing a disease. In law, a rough analogy might be the difference between retribution and rehabilitation. For those concerned with the alcohol-crash problem, there is control and, ultimately, elimination. Historically, however, even attempts to control the alcohol-crash problem have engendered frustration. This is not to say that past experience is bereft of success stories or progress, only that recorded gains do not appear commensurate with the level of on-going efforts or the magnitude of resources invested each year.

With hindsight sharpened by a century of control strategies and intervention tactics (e.g., Borkenstein 1985), lessons have been learned. No one law or program, in and of itself, guarantees substantial, sustained reductions in the problem as a whole (e.g., Ross 1984a). Deterrent-based approaches, however necessary, are insufficient; rather, at a minimum, *systems* approaches seem required to integrate and coordinate legal, health, public informational, educational, and technological measures (Jones and Joscelyn 1978). As a response to periodic public outcry and demands for action, the traditional triad of tougher laws, stricter enforcement, and harsher penalties has limits imposed not only by the criminal justice system itself but also by society at large (e.g., Gusfield 1981a). Ironically, one fruit of the labors of activist groups—which initiated the most recent battle in the "war against drunk drivers" in North America (Gusfield 1981b; Haskins and Haskins 1985; Lightner 1981)—has been formal recognition of the need for long-term, *comprehensive* approaches to the alcohol-crash problem (Presidential Commission on Drunk Driving 1983; cf. Donelson 1983).

Because the alcohol-crash problem has persisted, resistant to traditional approaches based on deterrence, the concept of "control" has expanded. Not surprisingly, measures to control the use, distribution, sales, and marketing of alcoholic beverages have been advocated as ways to reduce alcohol consumption and, by extension, such problems as impaired driving and alcohol-related traffic crashes (e.g., Moore and Gerstein, 1981, 61–78; Simpson et al. 1985). Informal social controls have received greater emphasis, from practicing and encouraging moderation in drinking to ensuring that guests or employees do not drive after drinking too much (e.g., Chafetz 1983).

In Canada, the Traffic Injury Research Foundation (TIRF) has fostered the notion of "community-based initiatives" in alcohol and traffic safety, influenced greatly by advances in the area of disease prevention and health promotion (Donelson, Mayhew, and Simpson 1985). This "bottom-up" approach, in which individuals would act as agents for change in relationships, families and groups, organizations, and communities, would complement "top-down" control measures designed to do something *to* or *for* people (Traffic Injury Research Foundation 1984; Simpson 1986). The phrase "humane intervention" was used to distinguish this approach from the usual meaning or connotation of control (or external intervention); participation in the prevention of impaired driving was described as "an expression of people's willingness and ability to take personal and individual responsibility for the problem" (Donelson 1985b).

Acknowledgment of the importance of community involvement and individual participation—a refreshingly new and positive development—no doubt reflects the influence of the grass-roots movement in North America (Donelson 1985a, 216–220). But it also points to a profound though subtle shift in perspective that coincided with the emergence of citizen activist groups. Before 1980, some social and cultural "factors" were recognized as contributing to the alcohol-crash problem, for example, the availability of beverage alcohol, the necessity of private transportation, the "inevitable" overlap of drinking and driving behaviors, the social acceptability and public tolerance of alcohol-impaired driving ("There by for the grace of God go I"). These conditions and forces were to be neutralized and overcome by countermeasures ranging from legal threats to persuasion to treatment for problem drinking. Currently, however, we encounter as explicit aims of policies and programs such phrases as "changing attitudes and social norms," "making drunk driving socially unacceptable," and "creating a society in which impaired driving is not only unacceptable but also unnecessary" (e.g., Presidential Commission on Drunk Driving 1983; Donelson 1985a; Chafetz 1983). What we find is a more explicit recognition that the alcohol-crash problem occurs in a "sociocultural environment" (Donelson 1985c), and that drinking and driving as behaviors have social and cultural contexts (Gusfield 1985). Indeed, a more active, focused search has begun for social and cultural *determinants* of the alcohol-crash problem, the findings of which should eventually guide efforts to alter the sociocultural environment to prevent impaired driving. Remarkably, MADD, RID, SADD, and many other grass-roots groups themselves *became* social determinants, suggesting the possibility that, in the end, people make the difference, not laws, regulations, and other countermeasures per se.

To appreciate this shift in perspective, we have only to recall that, in the past, the field of alcohol and traffic safety generally ignored the sociocultural context in which the alcohol-crash problem occurred. Discussions of social and cultural factors are (in retrospect) conspicuously absent from major reviews of the state of knowledge (e.g., Jones and Joscelyn 1978; Perrine 1974). Rare exceptions were often provided by sociologists who entered the field through the gateway of alcohol studies (Bacon 1973; Cisin 1963; Cosper and Mozersky 1968; Gusfield 1981a), an area increasingly sensitive to the *etiologic* significance of social and cultural factors (e.g., White 1982; Room 1982). In contrast, the field of highway safety has evidenced few serious investigations into the sociocultural environment and its relation to traffic crashes and deviant driving. For example, Klein and Waller (1970) found few " 'hard', empirical data" to support their attempt "to delineate . . . some of the broader social forces that may foster deviant driving behaviour" (205). That such forces can affect trends in motor vehicle accidents was observed after the 1974 "oil panic" (Haight 1983) and recent economic recessions (Hedlund 1985). Of interest, although the *number* of driver fatalities fluctuated, the *proportion* of drivers with illegal blood alcohol concentrations (BACs) remained relatively constant, at least in Canada (Beirness et al. 1985). The inability to explain these phenomena reflects an abysmally poor knowledge base and the near total lack of sociological research in highway safety.

As reviewed in this paper, the preponderence of research in the field of alcohol and traffic safety has primarily and narrowly focused on alcohol per se—the relationship between beverage alcohol consumption and BAC; the effects of alcohol on driving; alcohol as a contributing factor to traffic crashes. Secondarily, some studies have described the attributes and characteristics of drinking drivers. Rarely, however, have investigators looked beyond alcohol and the people who drink and drive to the social and cultural environment in which the alcohol-crash problem occurs.

Much of the current interest in the control of drinking and driving relates to social and cultural domains. For example, the final report of the Presidential Commission on Drunk Driving (1983), which promulgated a remarkable call for a decade-long, nationwide response to the alcohol-crash problem, recommended as the first two of six key elements of any program the following:

First, drunk driving must be recognized as socially unacceptable. We must focus on bringing about changes in society's attitude of toleration toward drunkenness and drunk driving. The public must realize that the grave consequences of driving under the influence require each of us to take the personal responsibility for *prevention* in our own social circles.

Second, since attitudes about drinking and driving are largely shaped within the community, and because the primary administrative responsibility for our efforts to combat drunk driving rests with the groups and governments at that level, efforts must have a *community focus*. (5)

The nature and prominence of these programmatic elements are unprecedented, given the history of alcohol and highway safety. The Commission's report also contained recommendations for a broad array of measures concerned with alcohol consumption, traffic safety, and "drunk driving." Yet no obvious mention was made of any need to advance the present state of knowledge in any area of recommended action. In fact, as Ross (1985b) commented, the report as a whole was not based on an analysis of the problem and its etiology.

Decades ago, efforts to control the alcohol-crash problem proceeded in earnest based on assumptions that in retrospect seem simplistic. Emerging, broader perspectives, along with knowledge gained from experience and research, indicate the value of revising the etiology of the alcohol-crash problem to include social and cultural factors (Donelson 1985c). At the very least, factual information about prevailing conditions and forces, whether aligned with or opposed to the social control of drinking and driving, would be operationally useful in planning intervention strategies. Two related subject areas—alcohol control policy and deterrence of impaired driving—have benefitted from a broader conceptual framework (Mäkelä et al. 1981; Room 1984; Snortum 1984b).

Basic questions that flow from both bodies of knowledge have to do with *why* various control policies and intervention tactics did or did not have an impact. Answers to these questions would increase our understanding of *how* the sociocultural environment, in which we must deal with different social problems, facilitates or impedes our programmatic efforts. It seems logically compelling that rational, systematic, comprehensive, strategic approaches to the alcohol-crash problem require, as a basis for effective action, better knowledge of the social and cultural factors we face in our mission to reduce alcohol-crash losses. If history best predicts the future, then the relative ineffectiveness of past efforts to deal with this problem indicates that continued ignorance will engender further frustration.

Systematic, coordinated, societywide efforts to control the alcohol-crash problem may well be considered by many as far-fetched or naively idealistic. As Gusfield (1981a) wrote:

> There has long existed an orientation that has explained alcohol problems as aspects of larger institutional and historical elements. . . . An emphasis on the general cultural and social conditions should not be dismissed but, by themselves, are too global for preventive strategies. Measures to deal with such deeply-seated institutional elements are beyond the ken of the fundamentally reformist orientation which dominates alcohol policies. Often they rest on nothing more than a series of assertions about the relation between background conditions and alcohol use. (417)

He went on to add, however:

> This discussion of the sociocultural context . . . suggests an important dimension in preventive measures and programs. Research and policy contribute significantly to the sociocultural climate because they affect the conception of the object—alcohol—and of the alcohol problem. They aid in maintaining or developing new governing images. In turn, they are themselves a part of changing conceptions which bear on the images of alcohol problems and their resolution. They influence the development of the very sociocultural environments from which they are drawn. (418)

A more completely developed concept of social control, if based on a broader perspective of the alcohol-crash problem and designed to address social and cultural factors, might also assist in creating "new governing images." Admittedly, from a social scientific perspective, this approach has little to offer yet due to its weak theoretical support. In general, those concerned with social and cultural factors face an incredible task of conceptually and empirically tying those gossamerlike strands to existing schema better grounded in "hard data." Before moving forward to pursue single-factor analyses of specific factors, however, we might first take note of some basic, summary questions pertaining to the above.

> How, and to what degree, do social and cultural factors influence the magnitude, characteristics, and persistence of the alcohol-crash problem?
>
> To what extent can we expect substantial reductions in losses due to alcohol-related road accidents in the absence of sustained shifts in social norms related to drinking and driving?

Can we develop integrated sociological models that relate functionally with other frameworks of thought (social psychological, behavioral, pharmacologic) and that assist in rationalizing a diffuse, complex set of factors already identified?

Does there exist an embryonic *technology of social change?* Can we develop one to address the alcohol-crash problem based in part, perhaps, on theory and practice applied to deal with other social problems (e.g., littering, tobacco smoking, heart disease, infectious disease)?

To what extent can research in this area of alcohol and highway safety contribute to changes in the sociocultural environment that would promote and effect substantial reductions in the magnitude of the alcohol-crash problem?

These and other questions will serve to uncover our presuppositions concerning the problem we seek to address and to challenge our present frameworks of thought. If we are ever to develop strategies (as opposed to tactics) in "the war against drunk drivers," then we have to assess the nature, scope, and possible duration of our undertaking. We also have to consider the distinct possibility that sociocultural change along several (as yet undefined) dimensions will dictate the success of our overall campaign. Research focused on social and cultural factors and expressed in the forms of idea generation, problem reconceptualization, problem definition, program development, and program evaluation can play an important role in this process.

PART

2   Social Control in Other Countries

2 The Scandinavian Experience

Johannes Andenaes

In the field of drinking and driving the "Scandinavian model" has become a familiar concept.[1] The model could be characterized by three features: (1) per se legislation, that is, statutes that make driving with a blood alcohol content (BAC) exceeding a certain limit an offense in itself, without requiring additional evidence of drunkenness or impairment of driving capability; (2) strict enforcement of the legislation with extensive use of breath and blood tests of drivers suspected of drinking and driving, and in recent years also by random roadside checks; and (3) stiff sanctions with a considerable use of imprisonment and temporary or permanent loss of driver's license.

For many, the Scandinavian model exemplifies the way to fight the all-too-many motor accidents caused by drunk drivers. Thus the movement in the United States in recent years for stiffer legislation against drunken driving often has referred to the Scandinavian example. Others consider the Scandinavian laws in this field excessively repressive, and critics have cast doubt on their supposed effectiveness in preventing alcohol-related accidents. The classic critic is Professor H. Laurence Ross who in one of his first writings on the subject used the expression "the Scandinavian myth" to characterize the unquestioning belief in the effectiveness of the Scandinavian drinking-and-driving laws.[2] The expression may easily be misinterpreted. Ross did not assert that the efficacy of the Scandinavian system was disproved. His claim was that there was no convincing evidence of the effects, and the myth was that such evidence existed. After examining accident statistics he found no effects from the introduction of the per se legislation in Norway and Sweden, and he concluded that other types of evidence were weak and unconvincing. In a later paper he castigated "the sacredness and smugness with which some Scandinavian sources treat the existing law."[3]

The provocative statements of Ross may have worked as a stimulus to self-scrutiny. There are still many blank spots on the map, but research within the past decade has greatly increased our knowledge about basic facts, such as the actual frequency of drinking and driving, the distribution for different levels of BAC, the increased accident risk at higher BACs, and the role of alcohol in different types of traffic accidents. American social scientists such as Professors John Snortum and Harold Votey have made valuable contributions to the discussion.

Geographically, Scandinavia comprises Denmark, Norway, and Sweden. Culturally, Finland and Iceland should be included, and in this paper Scandinavia is taken in this broad meaning. In the field of drinking and driving, Finnish experiences in later years are especially interesting, and less known internationally than those of Norway and Sweden. Iceland's experience has produced little material, and to simplify the exposition this small and sparsely populated country is not included in the discussion.

Although Scandinavia may appear to the outsider as a rather uniform corner of the world, on closer observation the individual countries show substantial differences. This also holds true for the field of drinking and driving. For example, public attitudes toward alcohol, and also to the combination of alcohol consumption and driving, are more liberal in Denmark than in Finland, Norway, and Sweden, and this is reflected in legislation as well as in law enforcement. Moreover, considerable changes have taken place over time.

This essay discusses the evolution of Scandinavian policy toward drinking and driving under six headings. I deal first with the development of Scandinavian legislation and the enforcement of the law on the highways, followed by patterns of sentencing and the effects of this regime on driving behavior and on traffic accidents. A concluding section of the essay discusses recent proposals for change in Sweden and Norway.

Legislation

The development of drinking-and-driving laws has differed from one country to another. The statutes from the first decades of this century made it an offense to drive while being intoxicated (or drunk). Later, the law was expanded to driving under the influence of alcohol, a much broader concept. For example, a Norwegian study conducted in 1932 found that of 373 drivers who were medically examined, 212 were characterized as being under the influence, but only 45 as intoxicated.[4] In the early 1930s, blood-alcohol analysis began to be used in Scandinavia as part of the medical examination of the accused, first on a voluntary basis, later based on statutory authority. The chemical analysis results, however, were not binding on the examining doctor or the court.

Norway was the first country to make it a criminal offense per se to drive with a BAC exceeding a certain limit. This was done by an act of 1936, which added to the existing prohibition against driving under the influence of alcohol a provision that defined "under the influence" as a blood alcohol concentration of more than 0.5 per mille (0.05 percent).[5] This limit has remained in force ever since. It is therefore somewhat misleading to speak about "drunken driving" legislation, and to describe the offenders as "drunk drivers." The law goes far beyond what these words mean in ordinary usage. It is preferable to speak about drinking-and-driving legislation.

The first country to follow the Norwegian example was Sweden, which in 1941 introduced a limit of 0.8 per mille. In 1957 the limit was lowered to 0.5 per mille as in Norway.[6] It was not until 1976 that Denmark and Finland introduced per se laws.[7] Denmark fixed the limit at 0.8 per mille, the same as in England, whereas Finland chose 0.5 as in Norway and Sweden. It should be mentioned that both in Denmark and Finland the blood alcohol concentration had played an important role in the courts even before a legal limit was established. In most cases the courts would declare the driver to be under the influence if the analysis showed a BAC of more than 1 per mille.

It is remarkable that the system of per se legislation, which has been emulated by most of the industrial world, was invented in a small country in a corner of Europe, where motor traffic was still in its infancy. In 1936 Norway had about eighty-thousand motorcars and a population of 2.9 million—one car per thirty-six persons. The new act met with little opposition. Medical authorities stated as an established fact that driving ability usually was impaired when a driver had a BAC above 0.5 per mille. Legal practitioners were pleased with the simplification of trials that would be a consequence of the new rule. In addition, the temperance movement, which has played a strong role in Norwegian politics, welcomed the law as a victory in the fight against alcohol.

The new legislation was well suited to act as a symbol of the dangers of drinking. However, in striking contrast to what occurred in England when its per se law was introduced in 1967, little publicity surrounded the enactment of the 1936 act and its implementation.

During the discussion of the bill in the Storting (Parliament), the spokesman for the Parliamentary committee in question expressed surprise over the fact that there had not been more discussion of the matter in the press, as a step was being taken that had no precedent in the legislation of any country. And a perusal of the country's two leading motoring journals of that time yields the surprising fact that neither the act nor the practice to which it gave rise are mentioned at all in 1936 or 1937.

When Sweden introduced a fixed BAC limit in 1941, a distinction was made between exceeding the limit (called driving when not sober) and driving in a state of intoxication (drunken driving). Drivers would be convicted of the latter offense if they were so much under the influence that it could be assumed that they could not drive the vehicle in a satisfactory manner. Drivers with a BAC of 1.5 per mille or more are considered to have been so much under the influence as to fall within the above provision. Normally the less serious offense (driving when not sober) will lead to a fine, the more serious offense (drunken driving) to a prison sentence. Denmark and Finland have a similar distinction between two degrees of the offense, whereas in Norway all driving with a BAC above 0.5 falls under the same provision regardless of the degree of intoxication. (In popular usage all these drivers are called "per mille drivers.") This difference is very important when it comes to sentencing. In Norway even the smallest transgression of the legal limit will normally lead to an unsuspended prison sentence. Further details of sentencing will be given below.

Legislation was later enacted to close some loopholes in the law. When first introduced, the per se laws provided that the BAC at the time of driving was conclusive proof of guilt. In a number of cases in which the analysis showed a BAC of more than 0.5 per mille the driver was acquitted because he claimed that he had consumed alcohol immediately before driving so that the alcohol had not been absorbed into the blood at the time of driving. To prevent acquittals on this basis, the Norwegian law was amended in 1959 so as to apply not only to driving with a BAC above 0.5 per mille, but also to driving after having consumed so much alcohol that it would later result in a BAC above the legal limit.[8] Thus, if the blood test showed that the per mille limit had been exceeded, criminal liability was incurred without any need to establish by means of a retrospective calculation that the per mille limit had also been reached during the course of the driving. Other countries also have made similar amendments.

The greatest zeal to prevent unjustified acquittals has been shown by the Norwegian legislators. It sometimes happens that a driver suspected of drunken driving, for example in connection with a traffic accident, has left the scene and temporarily has succeeded in evading the police. A blood test taken later shows a BAC above the legal limit, but the driver explains that this is due to alcohol consumption after driving. He was so shocked by the accident that he drank to calm himself down. In order to prevent this excuse, the act was amended in 1959 so that the consumption of alcohol during the six hours immediately after driving was equated with driving under the influence if the driver knew or should have known that the said driving might be the subject of police investigation.[9] This example has not been followed by the other Scandinavian countries. The Norwegian law also has a stringent provision against car owners who let others drive their cars without ensuring that the drivers are sober.

Breath tests are used as a screening device, but breath alcohol content is not a legal alternative to blood alcohol content, as it is in England and some other countries. The question of basing conviction directly on breath alcohol content has been discussed in public reports in Sweden (1985) and Norway (1986), but because of the greater unreliability of breath tests as compared with blood tests, the conclusion in both countries so far has been negative. Blood tests may also be the preferred method because, due to the long experience with such tests in the Scandinavian countries, the taking of a blood test is not considered to be such an intrusive procedure as in many other countries.

Enforcement

When the British Road Safety Act of 1967 introduced a fixed limit of 0.8 per mille, it resulted in a considerable reduction in alcohol-related accidents, but most of this effect seemed to have dissipated by the end of 1970. Professor H. Laurence Ross, in his thorough study of the British act, explains this primarily by the weak enforcement of the law.[10] The great publicity accompanying the new law had given the public unrealistic ideas about the risk of detection and conviction, but in fact little was done to enforce the law. The police did not consider enforcement of the new provisions an important task, and the public learned that they had overestimated the risk.

In the Scandinavian countries, enforcement of the drinking-and-driving laws are taken seriously—though perhaps somewhat less seriously in Denmark than in the other countries. The police consider control of drinking and driving an important task, and detected offenders are promptly prosecuted. If there is reasonable cause to suspect a violation, the police are authorized to order a blood test. The normal procedure will be first to take a breath test, and if this confirms that the suspicion is well founded, a blood test is administered. In recent years, the police have been authorized to make random breath tests in connection with traffic control (roadblocks), and if the driver has been involved in an accident or committed a violation of traffic rules, a breath test can be taken routinely without specific reason for suspicion. The purpose of these provisions is, of course, to increase the risk of detection, and thereby enhance the deterrent effect of the law. Legislation authorizing random tests was first introduced in Sweden in 1976, and the example has been followed by other Scandinavian countries. In Sweden, and even more so in Finland, such random controls have been used as an important part of the traffic safety work of the police. Such controls also provide information needed for assessing the incidence of drinking and driving in normal traffic and the distribution on different levels of BAC. Thus, in 1981–82 in Norway a research program with this purpose, including 72,000 breath tests, was carried out in cooperation between the police and the Institute of Transport Economics.

Sentencing

As mentioned, the pattern of sentencing for drinking and driving varies considerably among the Scandinavian countries. Norwegian sentencing practice is by far the most severe. Whereas Norwegian laws normally give the courts wide discretion in sentencing, and a suspended sentence is the normal sanction for a first offender if the crime is not very serious, the Road Traffic Act specifies imprisonment for driving with a BAC of more than 0.5 per mille, unless there are special mitigating circumstances. The present act was passed in 1965, but the provision in question dates back to 1926. It originally referred to intoxicated drivers. In 1935 it was extended to driving under the influence of alcohol, which as we have seen is a considerably wider concept. And when the fixed BAC limit of 0.5 per mille was introduced in 1936, and defined as equivalent to influence, the presumption of imprisonment acquired a vastly extended field of application. The act does not state that the sentence shall be mandatory, but this has become the settled practice of the courts under the leadership of the Supreme Court. Only rarely is the sentence suspended, and then almost invariably combined with a heavy fine.

This penalty is given to about 15 percent of the convicted drivers. Fines alone are used in a handful of cases only. The term of imprisonment for a first offender is usually between twenty-one and thirty-six days, with twenty-one days as the standard minimum term for imprisonment.

In cases of recidivism, the sentence can be much higher. Some of the convicted drunken drivers have a very long record. In one case tried in 1979, the defendant had nine previous convictions for the same offense, and was now prosecuted for four cases of driving with very high levels of BAC (2.84, 2.45, 3.24, and 2.93, respectively).[11] The district court sentenced him to one year of imprisonment, but on appeal the sentence was reduced to nine months, taking into consideration that he was about to serve two previous sentences that together totaled one year of imprisonment.

Other Scandinavian countries exhibit less draconian patterns of sentencing, and the difference has been widening. In Sweden the normal penalty for "driving when not sober" (with a BAC between 0.5 and 1.5) is a heavy fine, and for drunken driving (with a BAC of 1.5 or more) a month of imprisonment. In cases of recidivism, the sentence sometimes is increased to two months. In Denmark the pattern is similar, but with somewhat shorter sentences. Through an amendment in 1981, the limit for which fines are the normal punishment was raised from 1.5 to 2 per mille BAC.[12] It should be added that this change was motivated more by the desire to save prison space and thus reduce the number of convicts waiting to serve their sentences than by considerations of what, in itself, was the most desirable course of action.

The greatest change in recent years has taken place in Finland. Traditionally the sentences for drunken driving in Finland have been very severe, often unsuspended prison terms of three to six months. Legislation enacted in 1976 brought a fundamental change.[13] For driving with a BAC up to 1.5 per mille the sentence now will be a fine; this even applies to the bulk of recidivists. For aggravated drunken driving, that is if the BAC is at least 1.5 per mille or the driving has been dangerous, the normal penalty for a first offender will be a suspended prison sentence of one to three months plus a fine. Of the total number of offenders convicted in 1980 of having driven with more than the legal limit of 0.5 per mille, only 12 percent received an unsuspended prison sentence.

It would be somewhat misleading to discuss sentencing without mentioning the revocation of the driving license, which is a normal consequence of a conviction of drinking and driving. The revocation is considered a withdrawal of a privilege rather than the imposition of a penalty, but for the convicted drivers this legal distinction hardly seems important. For many of them, the revocation of the driving license is what hurts most. Again Norway has the harshest system. A first offender will lose the license for at least one and normally two years. In cases of recidivism the loss will be permanent, but with a possibility for the Ministry of Justice to grant a mitigation. Other countries employ revocation of the driving license as an important part of the sanctions system, but the periods are shorter. In Denmark the revocation is suspended if the BAC does not surpass 1.2 per mille. It could be added that whereas the revocation of the driving license in Norway is made by the police, in Denmark and Finland it is a matter for the ordinary court, and in Sweden for an administrative tribunal.

It could be stated as a political fact that the temperance movement has been a strong and vigilant pressure group, at least in Norway and Sweden. Although the temperance movement has suffered great losses in membership and influence during the past fifty years, it still has considerable political power, especially in questions where it does not collide with other pressure groups. Few politicians feel inclined to speak up for the drinking driver. A glaring example was the discussion in the Norwegian Storting in 1985 on a bill lowering the general minimum term of imprisonment from twenty-one to fourteen days. The bill was enacted, but an exception was made for drinking and driving. For crimes like robbery, drug pushing, or negligent homicide the legal minimum term is now fourteen days, but for the misdemeanor of drinking and driving it remains twenty-one days.[14]

The Effects of the Legislation: Driver Behavior

One effect of the Scandinavian system is indisputable: it has created a considerable strain on the prison system. This is especially true in Norway. The number of convicted drivers has increased approximately in the same proportion as the number of motorcars, although there has been a small decline since 1977. Of all persons given unsuspended prison sentences in Norway, about one-half are motorists convicted of drinking and driving. Since the prison terms for this offense are quite short, the offenders do not constitute a corresponding part of the prison population, but they do constitute approximately 20 percent of the prison population. In other Scandinavian countries, the corresponding figure is between 10 and 15 percent. To avoid misunderstanding it should be noted that the Scandinavian countries do not distinguish between prison and jails.

What then about the effect of the law upon the behavior of the drivers and on the volume of alcohol-related traffic accidents?[15] These are two questions that should be dealt with separately.

First, driver behavior. On impressionistic evidence, it has been generally accepted in the past that drinking and driving is rare in the Scandinavian countries, and that this to a great extent is due to strict legislation and effective law enforcement. In a paper many years ago, I summed up the situation in this way:

> A person moving between Norway and the United States can hardly avoid noticing the radical difference in the attitudes toward automobile driving and alcohol. There is no reason to doubt that the difference in legal provision plays a substantial role in this difference in attitudes. The awareness of hazards of imprisonment for intoxicated driving is in our country a living reality to every driver, and for most people the risk seems too great. When a man goes to a party where alcoholic drinks are likely to be served, and if he is not fortunate enough to have a wife who drives but does not drink, he will leave his car at home or he will limit his consumption to a minimum. It is also my feeling—although I am here on uncertain grounds—that the legislation has been instrumental in forming or sustaining the widespread conviction that it is wrong, or irresponsible, to place oneself behind the wheel when intoxicated.[16]

One objection to this impressionistic sketch is that it describes only the situation as it presents itself to middle class or upper-middle class groups. However, later research has on the whole confirmed the picture. Roadside surveys from recent years have shown that the frequency of drinking and driving in Scandinavian countries is, in fact, much lower than in most other industrialized countries. In the United States, Canada, and the Netherlands, roadside surveys at night have found as many as 10 to 15 percent of drivers with a BAC above 0.5 per mille. In Norway and Sweden findings in similar surveys have been from 1 to 2 percent.[17] And large-scale roadside surveys, distributed to obtain a representative sample of all motor traffic, have shown extremely low figures of drivers under the influence of alcohol. Thus, the Norwegian research mentioned earlier, with 72,000 breath tests, found only between two and three out of one thousand drivers with a BAC above the legal limit of 0.5 per mille.[18] Swedish large-scale surveys show similar or even lower results. Recent findings from Finland give figures of the same order of magnitude. Although such surveys are not undertaken in Denmark, my guess is that there would be found a higher proportion of drinking drivers in that country. A recent study by Snortum, Hauge, and Berger offers "resounding confirmation" of the radical differences in Norwegian and American attitudes toward drinking and driving, and even confirms the description of specific tactics, including alternative drivers, limited consumption by drivers, and the use of public transportation.[19]

The Norwegian roadside survey also shows the distribution on different BAC levels. About one-half of the violators had between 0.5 and 1.0 per mille, about 30 percent between 1.0 and 1.5 per mille, and about 20 percent above 1.5 per mille. Thus, the moderate degrees of intoxication are dominating. This distribution is very different from the distribution among convicted drivers. Of this group only 10 to 15 percent have less than 1.0 per mille BAC, and about one-half have more than 1.5 per mille. This means that the risk of detection is much smaller for drivers with a low BAC than for those with a high BAC. Of drinking drivers involved in fatal accidents 80 percent were above the 1.5 limit.[20] Thus, in Norway, and probably also in the other Scandinavian countries, the small group of excessively drunk drivers represents the great majority of serious alcohol accidents.

A somewhat unexpected finding in the Norwegian survey was that the frequency of drinking and driving was lower among young drivers than among middle-aged and elderly drivers. For drivers under twenty-five years, 0.21 percent had BACs above the legal limit whereas the corresponding figure for drivers between forty and sixty was 0.33, and for drivers above sixty years, 0.37.[21] Young motorists, however, represent a much larger proportion of convicted drivers and an even greater proportion of drivers involved in serious accidents.

Although the relative frequency of drinking and driving is very low, the total amount of such driving adds up to impressive numbers. On the basis of the Norwegian roadside study, the total number of drivers with a BAC above 0.5 per mille was estimated to be about eleven thousand per day, or four million per year. The number of convictions amounts to about seven thousand per year.[22] Consequently, the risk of detection is very small, on the average less than two in one thousand. The risk increases with increasing BAC. For BAC levels below 1.5 per mille the risk is estimated to be one in one thousand; for BAC levels above 1.5 per mille, four in one thousand. Obviously this low risk of detection weakens the deterrent effect of the threat of punishment, although most drivers probably overestimate the risk.

It is, of course, impossible to know for certain how much the laws and law enforcement have contributed to the low figures of drinking and driving. Several other explanations may be offered, for example, the general attitude to alcohol in society, the availability of public means of transportation, the pattern of drinking in homes versus bars. Such factors may be important, but none undermines the plausibility of seeing the strict law and effective enforcement as a major factor in the achievement of compliance. In my view, few fields of criminal law give a clearer picture of the three different elements in the creation of conformity by means of law: fear of punishment (deterrence), moral impact, and habit formation.

In this field impressionistic evidence should not be dismissed as unscientific, and the best informants are the drivers of the countries in question. As a member of this group, I offer myself as a witness. Other sources give indirect confirmation of the reliability of the spontaneous impressions. A Norwegian public opinion poll in 1976 contains information about the public's knowledge of and attitudes toward drinking-and-driving legislation.[23] The standard of knowledge was very high, and higher for holders of driving licenses than for the rest of the population. This is natural enough, since the question is of less importance for nondrivers than for drivers. Ninety percent of licensed drivers knew that the legal limit was 0.5 per mille. They were also well informed about how much consumption of alcohol was required to reach this level, even though there was a tendency to underestimate how much they could drink. Ninety percent of the drivers knew that the normal penalty for a first offense was a term of imprisonment of between twenty-one and thirty days' duration. Eighty percent were aware that the driver's license was always revoked, and the great majority of these drivers realized that the period of revocation was one to two years. This impressive level of knowledge is a strong indication that the sanctions for drinking and driving are a matter of great importance to drivers. In the United States it would for many reasons be impossible to reach a comparable level of knowledge.

A similar poll in Denmark in 1977, shortly after the introduction of per se legislation in 1976, gave quite different results.[24] Knowledge among drivers of both the legal BAC limit and the likely sanction was weak. The high level of knowledge in Norway is due to a law and practice that have remained virtually unchanged for half a century, and in addition are so uncomplicated that the principles are easy to understand and to learn.

It is sometimes said that the risk of detection of drinking and driving is so low that deterrence cannot possibly work. This is a speculation that does not hold up in real life. When the sanction is so severe as in Norway, and the gain by violating the law is so limited, the awareness of even a small risk may be a reasonably effective deterrent. Moreover, most drivers probably overestimate the risk or they have just a vague idea of it. It should also be recognized that the choice of violation or compliance is not a once-in-a-lifetime decision. For a social drinker this situation of choice arises in connection with every party away from home. If a driver regularly violates the law, the risk of being arrested sooner or later will reach a quite different magnitude than the risk connected with a single trip. Probably very few of the drivers convicted of drinking and driving are one-time offenders.

The question of moral effects is more complex. The law can exert influence as an authoritative statement that a certain conduct is bad and should be avoided by a responsible citizen. Or it may work as a moral eye-opener bringing the citizens to reflect on the socially harmful character of the act. Moral condemnation of a certain type of conduct, however, has many other sources than the law.[25] It is no doubt true that the general public in the Scandinavian countries looks upon drinking and driving as a more serious offense than has traditionally been the case in the United States. It may be argued that the strict legislation and practice are results of the moral condemnation, and not the other way around. Probably an interaction takes place. In the Scandinavian countries strict legislation and uniform enforcement have lasted for decades. Police controls and court cases involving drinking and driving are regularly reported in the press, at least in Norway. The legal condemnation of drinking and driving has given ammunition to the continuous traffic safety propaganda from public authorities and private organizations, elaborating on the hazards involved, the irresponsibility of drinking drivers, and the strict sanctions. The slogan "alcohol and driving do not belong together" has become generally accepted.

A Norwegian opinion poll in 1976 included questions about attitudes toward the drinking and driving legislation. The great majority of drivers believed that driving ability is reduced at a BAC of 0.5

per mille and that this is a proper legal limit, but twenty-five percent thought that the limit should be lower. Only a few percent thought that it should be higher. The strong acceptance of this precise legal limit indicates that the legislation has succeeded in impressing its values on the citizens. As Ragnar Hauge puts it in his commentary to the poll:

> The result of a biochemical analysis has not only been established by legislation as the criterion of criminality, but it has also been adopted by popular opinion as the criterion that decides the essential morality of the act.[26]

From other Norwegian polls we know that the overwhelming majority favors random roadside breath tests by the police. Only toward the penalties imposed have the polls revealed a critical attitude. The results are somewhat at variance, depending on the formulation of the questions, but it seems that a slim majority is in favor of fines instead of imprisonment for the lower BAC degrees.

Most drivers acquire habits with regard to drinking and driving, relieving them from weighing advantages and disadvantages in the individual case. A few may habitually disregard the rules. Many have accepted the principle not to drink at all when they are going to drive. In a comparative study by Snortum, Hauge, and Berger of Norway and the United States, 88 percent of the Norwegian sample (and 55 percent of the American sample) said "I never drink before driving."[27] (The Norwegian abstention figure is higher than I would have expected. It is not taken as a matter of course that a guest who has driven to the event will refuse an offer of drinks, but if the refusal to drink is because of driving, this is seen as natural and legitimate behavior.)

The effects of the Finnish reform of drinking-and-driving legislation in 1976 have great relevance in discussing deterrence. Drunken driving has traditionally been considered a serious problem in Finland. Conviction rates have been high, and before the reform the penalties were very severe, normally three to six months' imprisonment. Demands for still harsher penalties were politically popular. In the Ministry of Justice and among criminologists and alcohol researchers the view was different, and by some kind of miracle their view was made the basis of the new law of December 1976, in force since April 1, 1977. The leading idea in the new legislation was to stake more on the risk of detection, and less on the severity of punishment. The changes can be summarized in three points: (1)

The law introduced a fixed BAC limit of 0.5 per mille as in Norway and Sweden. Previously there had been no fixed limit, but the court practice was to consider influence of alcohol proved around 1.0 per mille. (2) The severity of punishment was radically reduced. Fines and suspended sentences became normal penalties. Also, the length of revocation of the driver's license was shortened, and graduated according to the seriousness of the offense. (3) Random breath tests were introduced, and the number of such tests has been drastically increased. The police made about 10,000 tests in 1977, gradually increasing to 390,000 in 1981 and 725,000 in 1984.

A working group appointed by the Ministry of Justice with the mandate to evaluate the effects of the changes published a comprehensive report in May 1985.[28] The number of convictions increased by 10 percent in the years after the new law, but the report found that in the same time the risk of detection had doubled. This means that the real incidence of drinking and driving has been reduced to about half. The reduction is confirmed by roadside surveys from the most populous province, Nylands län, where such surveys have been made regularly since 1979. The percentage of drivers with a BAC over the legal limit showed this development from 1979 to 1985: 0.46, 0.39, 0.36, 0.34, 0.24, 0.20, 0.20. (The effect on traffic accidents will be discussed below.) The Ministry of Justice said in the press release of the report: "Finland today belongs beside Sweden and Norway as the countries which have the most sober traffic in the industrialized world." In order to further reduce drinking and driving the working group recommended continued increase of surveillance. It seems likely that the perception of risk among drivers as a result of the frequent tests has increased even more than the objective risk of detection.

On common-sense grounds it must be assumed that an increased risk of detection primarily affects the deterrent rather than the moral effects of the law. The Finnish experience leaves us with two tentative conclusions: (1) drinking and driving can be substantially deterred through traffic control; and (2) the amount of control is of greater importance than the severity of sanction. To the latter point it should be noted that the sanction in this case—a stiff fine and a temporary loss of driving license—still has quite serious consequences for the offender.

It deserves to be emphasized that the new Finnish policy is not an enforcement crackdown, but rather represents a sustained and gradually increased control effort. Experience shows that well-publicized crackdowns may have a momentary effect, but the effect tends to be limited to the duration of the campaign. This finding is interesting as far as it goes, but has no bearing with regard to a permanent change to a higher level of control.

The Effects of the Legislation: Traffic Accidents

The aim of the criminalization of driving and drinking is to reduce traffic accidents. The ultimate test of the success of the system is how many accidents it prevents, not how much the volume of driving and drinking is reduced. Whereas Scandinavian law seems to have been successful in minimizing drinking and driving generally, the evidence for a strong effect on accidents is less impressive. Professor Ross in his paper on the "Scandinavian Myth" applied interrupted time-series analysis to the introduction of the per se legislation in Norway in 1936 and Sweden in 1941 without finding any decrease in fatal accidents that could serve as evidence of an effect of the new legislation.[29] However, in later writings he recognized that the laws were introduced at a time when other historical events may have been strongly influencing accident rates, and the measures of the effect variables were relatively insensitive.[30] Thus, it would have been surprising to find clear statistical evidence of a deterrent effect even if such effects were in fact achieved.

The greatest change in the law of the Scandinavian countries in recent years has been the Finnish reform of 1977. As previously mentioned, the Finnish working group estimates that the frequency of drinking and driving has been reduced to about half. The report also gives official statistics for persons killed or injured in accidents involving a drinking driver. In absolute numbers there has been almost a 50 percent decrease since 1977. In the same period, however, the official total number of people killed or injured was also reduced, partly due to changes in the statistics, so the proportionate decrease of alcohol-involved accidents was much smaller. In the years 1974–76 alcohol-involved accidents were on the average responsible for 12.1 percent of all persons killed or injured in traffic accidents. The share gradually diminished, and in 1982–84 was, on the average, 9.3 percent, approximately one-quarter less than before the reform. The pattern for fatalities alone is similar, but since the figures are much smaller the curve is less regular. In 1974–76 persons killed in alcohol-involved accidents represented 14.7 percent of all deceased traffic victims. In 1982–84 the corresponding figure was

12.3 percent.[31] The effect seems clear, but is not of the same size as the effect on the incidence of drinking and driving.

Another approach is to compare the frequency of alcohol-related accidents in different countries. One weakness in this method is that if we find lower figures in one country than in another it is hard to know whether this is due to differences in legislation and enforcement. Another great difficulty lies in identifying comparable figures. Police statistics give a poor basis for comparison, and even research reports based on other sources are often difficult to compare. One of the most objective measures is the percentage of intoxicated drivers among drivers killed in motor accidents. The most comprehensive Scandinavian study of this type included all fatal accidents in Norway during one year (1976–77).[32] The police had instructions to take blood tests of all drivers killed in this period; in fact, blood tests were taken in 80 percent of the cases. Thirty-two percent of the tested drivers and 26 percent of all the deceased drivers had a BAC above 0.5 per mille. The authors concluded that the real share must lie somewhere between these two figures. Other studies in Norway and Sweden have given similar results, some higher, some lower.[33] The discrepancies may be due to chance variations, regional differences, changes over time, or biased samples. In Denmark the proportion of drunk drivers seems to be higher.

The figures for Norway and Sweden are moderate in an international perspective, and certainly lower than in the United States, but they do not stand out as something exceptional. They seem, to mention just one example for comparison, to be about on the same level as figures from the United Kingdom before the introduction of the British per se law in 1967. To avoid misunderstanding it should be added that the toll which drunken drivers take among other accident victims is much lower. Thus, the Norwegian study just cited found that in accidents in which the driver survived but other persons were killed, a drinking driver was involved in only 5 to 8 percent of the cases. Of all fatal accidents the authors estimated that a drinking driver was involved in 12 to 16 percent. Drinking and driving is much more dangerous for the driver than for other users of the road. The typical serious alcohol accident is a single vehicle accident at night.

By comparing the incidence of drinking and driving in ordinary traffic and in traffic accidents, it is possible to give estimates of the risk on different BAC levels. For Swedish traffic accidents with personal injuries the following risk figures have been found (decimals omitted): 6 for BAC between 0.5 and 0.8, 15 for BAC between 0.8

and 1.5, and 54 for BAC above 1.5.[34] The risk figures are especially
high with regard to fatal accidents in which the driver is killed. For
such accidents in Norway the risk figures according to Alf Glad were
as follows: 13 for BAC between 0.5 and 1.0, 100 for BAC between
1.0 and 1.5, and 550 for BAC above 1.5.[35]

The increase in risk was much greater for young than for middle-
aged and elderly drivers. The apparent exactitude of such compu-
tations is, of course, an illusion because of the uncertainty of the
basic figures. Moreover, it could not be taken for granted that the
total increase in risk is due to alcohol consumption. Drunk drivers
involved in accidents are not a representative sample of all drivers.
It seems likely that this group of drivers is a negative selection, and
would have had higher accident risk than the normal driver even
without the actual alcohol consumption. Nonetheless, the figures
illustrate the enormous increase of risk for drivers with high BAC.

Without going into further detail, it could be safely stated that
the Scandinavian countries have not been as effective in combating
alcohol accidents as in combating driving after alcohol consumption.
How could this apparent contradiction be explained? A definite answer cannot be given. The chain between prevention of behavior
and prevention of accidents should be more in focus than has been
the case. However, a reasonable hypothesis seems to be this: The
law has been successful with regard to the ordinary social drinker.
Most of these are people who, even without the strict alcohol policy,
would have shown some feeling of responsibility while driving after
moderate alcohol consumption, in spite of being under the influence
to some extent. Motorists driving with very high BAC levels, and
therefore representing a high risk, more often than not are persons
with serious alcohol problems, often aggravated by other social
shortcomings. These people are poor targets for the deterrent and
moral effects of the law. The Norwegian recidivist case cited above
gives an impressive illustration. In short, it is reasonable to believe
that the law's motivating effect is strongest among those who would
have represented only a moderate traffic risk even if they had consumed alcohol in excess of the legal limit.

Another important aspect of criminal policy deserves to be mentioned. Up to now criticism of the Norwegian practice of imposing
prison sentences for even very small violations of the legal limit has
been met with the argument that any mitigation would reduce the
deterrent and moral effects of the law, and that no such experiments
should be tried when life and health are at stake. However, available

data from recent research tend to show that there is no more drinking and driving, and no more alcohol-related accidents, in Sweden than in its neighboring country Norway, despite a very different pattern of sentencing. If there is a difference it seems to be in favor of Sweden. This gives reason to believe that the effect of the prison sentence for low degrees of BAC has been strongly overstated in Norwegian discussions. The results of the Finnish reform of 1977 point most clearly in the same direction. This reform brought a drastic reduction of prison sentences, and at the same time introduced the per se system and authorized random checks. The reform emphasized increased risk of detection instead of severity of sanction. For the years following the reform, the effect upon drinking and driving and on alcohol-related accidents seems to have been very favorable. The weak point in the deterrence mechanism in this field is not the severity of the sanction, but the low risk of detection.

Recent Proposals for Change

How to deal with drinking and driving is a recurrent subject of public discussion in the Scandinavian countries, but on the whole proposals for change have met fierce resistance. The most conspicuous exception is the Finnish reform of 1977. For the time being, Sweden and Norway are the countries in which the question of change in drinking-and-driving legislation is on the political agenda.

In Sweden a government bill of 1984 proposed to reduce the use of imprisonment for drunken driving, and to lower the legal limit from 0.5 to 0.4 per mille BAC. The lowering of the legal limit was officially motivated by considerations of traffic safety, but was in fact politically formulated to make the bill more acceptable to the temperance movement. The tactic, however, was unsuccessful. The proposal to reduce the use of prison sentences met such strong political opposition that the bill was withdrawn. In 1986 a new Law Committee report on criminal sanctions in general nevertheless proposed a greater use of heavy fines, and consequently a reduced use of imprisonment for drunk driving.[36]

In Norway a report of a Law Committee in November 1986 dealt at length with the question of sanction of drinking and driving.[37] The mandate for the committee expressly stated that the report should be based on new research results, for example, on the incidence of drinking and driving, the effect of low BAC, and new estimates of accidents and risks. In its report, the committee proposed to mitigate the penalties for low and moderate BAC, with a heavy fine as the ordinary penalty for a BAC up to 1.0 per mille, and suspended prison plus a fine for the interval between 1.0 and 1.5 per mille. The report recommends to shorten the periods of revocation of the driving license, to fix the period in proportion to the seriousness of the offense, and to transfer the question of revocation from the police to the court. The report makes extensive use of the experience from Finland, and recommends a substantial increase in the use of breath tests in traffic control. It is stated as a reasonable goal that all drivers be alcohol tested on the average once in two years, preferably in connection with control of the license and the car. This would mean an increase from about 200,000 to one million breath tests a year, and establish a higher control level than Sweden and Finland currently have. The committee is confident that the increase in alcohol control will lead to a reduction in drinking and driving, and expects also a decrease in alcohol accidents, but makes it clear that the effect on accidents cannot be expected to be of the same magnitude as the effect on the amount of drinking and driving. If implemented, the proposals would reduce the number of prison sentences to about half, and bring Norwegian law closer to the other Scandinavian countries, but Norway would still have the strictest law. The proposed changes may seem modest seen from the outside, but time will show whether they are acceptable to the government and Storting. As chairman of the committee, I do not feel optimistic.

Summary and Discussion

A characteristic feature in the Scandinavian system of combating alcohol-related accidents is the per se legislation, which makes driving with a BAC above a certain limit an offense in itself, without the necessity of proving that the driver was drunk or unfit to drive. This system was first introduced in Norway in 1936, and has been accepted by most countries in the industrialized world.

The objection to per se legislation has often been that people react differently on alcohol, and that a BAC that makes one driver unfit to drive does not have the same effect on others. A similar argument could be made against speed limits: one driver may be able to drive safely with a speed that would make another a danger on the road. The objection is not convincing. The point is that alcohol consumption above a certain level for most people reduces their ability to drive safely; that this effect increases very strongly with increased BAC; and that BAC levels therefore give an objective indication of reduced fitness for driving, whereas clinical examinations or other evidence of the influence of the alcohol consumption is of a very subjective nature. It is next to unthinkable that any of the Scandinavian countries should abolish the per se system or raise the permissible levels of BAC.

The per se system, combined with effective enforcement and severe sanctions, seems to have worked well to reduce the frequency of drinking and driving, but it should be acknowledged that the effect on alcohol-related accidents is not of the same magnitude as the effect on driver behavior. The main reason for this may be that a great part of the alcohol accidents are caused by drivers with serious alcohol problems, who do not react to the threat of punishment in the same way as the average driver.

The gains in traffic safety are achieved with a considerable cost, for society as well as for the individuals concerned. This is especially so in Norway, where the normal penalty is imprisonment even for slight violations of the legal limit. Comparisons between Norway and Sweden, and experiences of a law reform in Finland in 1977, indicate strongly that this extraordinary severity does not have any appreciable payoff in traffic safety. Norway, which was the pioneer in the field, has up to now clung stubbornly to a system of sanctions created in the 1930s, with little willingness to make use of new insights and experiences from other countries. Thus, the example of Norway illustrates one pitfall in the per se system: It may lead to an overemphasis on the violation of the legal limit of BAC as such without taking sufficient account of the enormous differences in risk which the various levels of intoxication represent. This has led to excessive severity in dealing with minor violations. The other Scandinavian countries have been better equipped to avoid this danger by establishing two limits of BAC, and reserving imprisonment for the aggravated or repeated offense of drinking and driving. Moreover, the development in these countries has been moving toward less use of imprisonment. Instead of relying on the severity of the sanction, more emphasis is laid on increasing the risk of detection by random checks. It is to be hoped that Norway will enter the same course.

However, it should be realized that the criminal law approach to the problem of drinking as a factor in traffic accidents has its limitations. We know these limitations from other fields. We can never have realistic hopes of being able to eradicate crime. At best we can keep it at a tolerable level, and investment in increased severity tends to yield diminishing returns. The situation with regard to drunken driving is basically the same, but has its specific features. To put it in somewhat provocative terms: The moderate cases of drinking and driving can be quite effectively combated by threat of punishment and strict enforcement, but this does not mean much for the number of accidents. The dangerous cases of drunken driving are hard to combat, since the greater part of such drivers are persons with heavy alcohol problems whose behavior is difficult to influence by the threat of punishment. As long as we have our present drinking customs with their production of problem drinkers—and I see no prospect of a change in this situation in the future—we shall have to live with drunken driving as an important cause of traffic accidents.

If we succeed in reducing the total amount of accidents by providing better roads, safer cars, more effective traffic regulation, and other measures, this will, however, also reduce the amount of alcohol-related accidents. The introduction of compulsory seat-belt usage has probably saved more lives than many prison sentences have. Ross and others have discussed the merits and weaknesses of deterrence policy vis-à-vis other means of improving safety.[38]

In the 1970s and the beginning of the 1980s, the number of traffic fatalities and serious injuries in Norway and the other Scandinavian countries decreased year by year in spite of the steady growth of traffic. It became safer on the road, and this, of course, also benefited the drinking driver. An improvement of this magnitude would not have been attainable by legal threats and law enforcement toward the drivers. Fatalities on the road in proportion to the number of cars are about the same level as in the United States—somewhat higher in Denmark and Finland, somewhat lower in Norway and Sweden (1984).

It seems as if this improvement in safety has now come to a halt. Probably the technical methods to prevent accidents have met the law of diminishing returns, just like the method of influencing driver behavior by threat of punishment. When the easy gains in traffic safety have been made, a further reduction of accidents demands greater effort. Rational deterrence policy and technical improvement represent different approaches to the same problem. Neither approach can be discarded. The effect of changes should be closely monitored by research on costs and benefits that may assist us in making better policy decisions.

3 Deterrence-based Policies in Britain, Canada, and Australia

H. Laurence Ross

Traffic safety interventions have traditionally been divided into those that focus on the vehicle, the highway, or the driver. A related distinction is between policies stressing occupant protection, traffic engineering, or human factors. In the United States, following passage of the Highway Safety Act of 1966, traffic safety policy became committed to the occupant protection approach, which was embodied in the Federal Motor Vehicle Safety Standards issued by the National Highway Traffic Safety Administration. This commitment remained at the heart of American policy for more than a decade, although it met determined opposition from the automobile industry, which had to add the price of the expenses imposed by the policy to its products. A shift in emphasis to human factors occurred following the inception of the more conservative, pro-industry, law-and-order Reagan administration in 1981.

In contrast, governments in the United Kingdom, Canada, and Australia have entertained the human factors approach over a longer time period (Irwin 1985). Deterrence-based policies have been central to this approach. Therefore, these countries have a longer history of drunk-driving interventions than we do in America, and their experiences can perhaps provide some lessons concerning the potential accomplishments and limitations of deterrence-based policies. In reviewing these experiences I hope to suggest their implications for wise decisions relative to traffic safety in other countries, including our own.

Perhaps the main lessons of these experiences are, first, that measures designed to increase the objective certainty of apprehension and punishment for drunk driving can, with adequate publicity, attain at least short-term increments of deterrence. This is true despite the fact that a large proportion of drunk driving is done by problem drinkers and alcoholics, who may be disproportionately difficult to deter from drinking. Second, this accomplishment has been achieved

64

with relatively modest sanctions. Severe punishment, on the order of heavy fines, vehicle confiscation, and incarceration, does not seem necessary to achieve deterrence. Third, increments of deterrence that have continued over a considerable time period have been achieved by investing massive resources for apprehending drunk drivers; it seems to be within the limits of practicality in at least some countries to raise the objective chances of apprehension for drunk driving to the point where they are not regarded as negligible.

The United Kingdom

If there is an external gadfly to the government in the case of traffic safety policy in the United Kingdom it is the prestigious British Medical Association (BMA), which has historically viewed injuries suffered in traffic accidents as a medical problem and urged the application of political as well as other countermeasures. The BMA was, of course, in the best position to understand the technological advances in the ability to measure alcohol consumption of individuals that had permitted Norway and Sweden to enact an innovative drunk-driving law prior to World War II. This new type of law defined the prohibited offense in terms of exceeding a specified blood alcohol concentration and it utilized newly available technology to obtain evidence of the violation. Although, initially, sufficient precision for evidentiary purposes in court required the taking of a blood sample, rough estimates of blood alcohol suitable for screening purposes could be obtained through small portable instruments that tested breath samples.

The Road Safety Act of 1962 acknowledged this technology by permitting the use of blood alcohol evidence in drunk-driving cases, but that law did not provide for mandatory testing. In fact, it permitted comparison of blood alcohol test results with the outcomes of prosecutions, leading to the conclusion that many seriously impaired drivers charged under the classical law were escaping conviction and punishment.

The proposal for a new, Scandinavian-type law in Britain rested on evidence (Garwood and Johnson 1968) from both laboratory and field studies demonstrating the impairing effect of blood alcohol concentrations over 0.08 percent. (Evidence of significant impairment at much lower levels, potentially justifying limits of 0.5 percent or even less, did not appear until the 1980s.) The proposed law authorized police officers to test any driver for evidence of alcohol consumption. However, this broad "random" permission proved controversial, and during the Parliamentary process it was replaced by provisions that allowed police to demand a test from a driver who was involved in an accident or a traffic-law violation, but not otherwise without reasonable cause to suspect that the driver had been drinking. Attempts to meet civil liberties objections also resulted in the law's specifying a complex procedure to be followed in requesting and performing the necessary chemical tests.

The Road Safety Act of 1967 represented a revolutionary change in British law. Even without the random testing provision, it was highly controversial and thus highly newsworthy for a long time prior to its imposition in October of that year. Moreover, its complexity provided the opportunity for numerous legal challenges that kept it in the media for a long time thereafter. The law appears to have been among the best-known statutes in British history, and its promise of apprehension and punishment of drunk drivers was prominently advertised far beyond the government's official publicity campaign.

The Road Safety Act appears in some ways to have been the most successful deterrence-based measure ever launched against drunk driving. The extent of casualty saving was so great that the law was immediately declared a success by the government and by the media, and this apparent success was confirmed in numerous subsequent scientific evaluations (Beaumont and Newby 1972; Ross 1973). My own interrupted time-series analysis found serious injuries and fatalities during weekend drinking hours to have been reduced by 66 percent at the inception of the law. Various supplementary analyses suggested that the effect was due to motorists separating their driving from their drinking, rather than merely drinking less or driving fewer miles.

These attainments, however, proved to be only temporary. The time-series curve of casualties, reproduced in Figure 3.1, showed a change in slope compensating for the change in level at the inception of the Road Safety Act. Extrapolating the series led to the conclusion that matters were tending to return to the status quo ante within a very short time. Further evidence came from the fact that the proportion of fatalities involving illegal blood alcohol concentrations returned to and then surpassed pre-1967 levels within a few years. Even during the first year, successive polls by the Automobile Association showed reductions in the numbers of drivers acknowledging changes in their behavior.

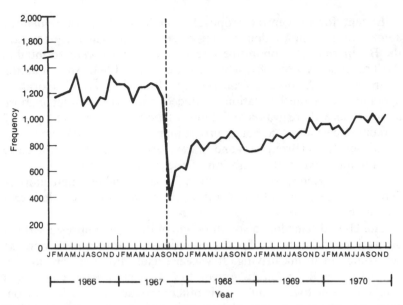

Fig 3 1   Fatalities and serious injuries in the United Kingdom. Combined for Friday, 10 P.M.–midnight; Saturday, midnight–4 A.M.; Saturday, 10 P.M.–midnight; Sunday, midnight–4 A.M.; corrected for weekend days per month and with seasonal variations removed (Ross 1973:33).

The government conceded its concern by appointing a departmental committee in July 1974 "to review the operation of the law relating to drinking and driving and to make recommendations." The Blennerhassett Committee issued its report in early 1976 (Department of the Environment 1976).

The Blennerhassett Committee recommended eliminating the limitations on the power of police to stop and test drivers. "We regard this as an essential and integral part of our proposals" (p. 4). Furthermore, the committee proposed that "proof of an offense should not be unreasonably dependent on compliance with procedural requirements" (p. 6), and urged the use of evidentiary breath tests rather than blood tests, the relevant technology having greatly improved since the 1960s. In most other ways the committee recommended preserving the legal status quo, for instance, in the level of permitted blood alcohol concentration and the duration of the mandatory disqualification or license suspension, despite pressures for change. The committee also recommended special procedures for treating "high-risk" offenders, and continued publicity and education regarding drunk driving.

Except for its central proposal, which would have reinstated something like the random testing originally envisaged for the law, the Blennerhassett Committee's recommendations were adopted in the Transport Act of 1981, which took effect in 1983. An evaluation by the staff of the official Transport and Road Research Laboratory concluded that the legislation produced a deterrent effect in rural areas, where there was a reduction of between 5 percent and 12 percent in casualties, although no comparable results were achieved in built-up areas (Broughton and Stark 1986). It is probably too early to estimate reliably the duration of the apparent effect. However, this new experience seems to confirm the ability of laws that simplify detection and prosecution of offenders to obtain some deterrent increment.

The United Kingdom also offers one of the most impressive demonstrations of the ability of police enforcement campaigns to increase deterrence of drunk driving. It was precisely the apparent loss of effect for the Road Safety Act of 1967 that stimulated Cheshire's chief constable to demand that his officers request a breath test from motorists whenever permissible under the terms of the act. An initial week's experience with no publicity produced no deterrent effect, but suggested that police discretion in ordinary times resulted in a failure to test fully half of all drunk drivers who had been interrogated by police on the occasion of an accident or violation. A deterrent effect became evident in the subsequent month when the press "discovered" and negatively commented on the "blitz" (Ross 1977).

The ability of publicized enforcement to produce deterrent results is also demonstrated by the "Christmas Crusade" of December 1983. Not a planned intervention, the crusade was a fortuitous conjunction of several factors likely to affect the perception of punishment for drunk driving. First, a budget reduction at the national level forced narrowing of the usual Christmas safety campaign to deterrence-related themes alone. Second, an unusually vigorous crackdown in one police jurisdiction gained national attention. Third, a coincidental wave of drunk-driving convictions occurred, following appellate resolution of a case that had held up numerous prosecutions. Fourth, the unprecedented use by one jurisdiction of short periods of detention in police cells received extensive publicity. Fifth, a few especially poignant and unusual drunk-driving incidents occurred and were highly publicized in the media. Interrupted time-series analysis found a significant 23 percent reduction in total crash-related fatalities nationally during the month of the crusade. It seems reasonable to attribute this to the conjunction of measures mentioned (Ross 1986).

In brief, British experience furnishes multiple examples of the ability of well-publicized deterrence-based measures to obtain intended results. This is true for the adoption of Scandinavian-type per se laws and also for apparently intense enforcement efforts based on existing law, and it obtains even though the penalty of a year's license suspension in a country with superb public transportation does not appear to be especially severe in the context of contemporary American developments. The principal shortcoming of the deterrence-based measures in Britain has been their short duration, whether by necessity as in the case of a time-limited campaign, or unintentionally as with the decay of effects that theoretically ought to be permanent, such as the laws permitting more efficient apprehension and punishment of drunk drivers. A reasonable interpretation of the decay phenomenon is that deterrent accomplishments hinge on exceeding a certain threshold of likelihood of punishment for violations. Beneath this level, a threat of increased punishment is ineffective because the threat is sooner or later perceived as negligible. The question can be raised whether such a threshold can be passed within the limits of political possibility. This question may have to be answered differently from jurisdiction to jurisdiction depending on the ranking of drunk driving among priorities on the political agenda.

Canada

Because it is a federal state, drunk-driving interventions in Canada occur under different auspices. The basic Canadian criminal law is federal, but the level of enforcement is a matter for the provinces. On the federal level, Canada offers another look at the adoption of a Scandinavian-type law, while several provinces offer enlightening examples of enforcement campaigns or "blitzes." The findings in Canada can be compared with and related to those in Britain, where apparently successful experiences stimulated the Canadian copies.

The Criminal Law Amendment Act of 1969 was directly inspired by the British Road Safety Act two years earlier. Word of the impressive initial results of the latter was current in English-speaking circles, whereas its limitations were not yet generally evident. The Canadian law, like the British, prohibited driving with more than .08 percent blood alcohol content. The police were authorized to demand a breath test from someone who they had "reasonable and probable" cause to believe was violating the law. Unlike the British police, they were not empowered to demand tests in the absence of such suspicion for those involved in accidents or violations. Moreover, the legislation did not mandate license suspension but utilized fines as the main punishment. In terms of both certainty and severity of punishment the Canadian law appears weaker and less innovative than the British prototype.

There was a publicity campaign at the inception of the Canadian law. However, the law seems to have been less newsworthy, because less revolutionary in its context, than was the British Road Safety Act. Although surveys found increases in knowledge about the law from before its inception to ten weeks later, there had been no changes in attitudes toward drunk driving or in declared behavior.

The chief evaluation of the Canadian Criminal Law Amendment (Carr et al. 1975) found evidence of a reduction in nighttime and weekend casualties, but it was much smaller than had been achieved in Britain, and it appeared to be very brief in duration. A second, apparently more sophisticated, evaluation (Chambers et al. 1976) confirmed the law's deterrent effect but likewise found it to be of short duration.

The relatively less impressive consequences of the Canadian law as compared with the British very likely are a consequence of the lesser credibility of the threatened punishment. Canadian police had to develop suspicion of alcohol influence on the basis of behavioral cues before they could turn to the scientific handmaiden, the breath test, and the mere fact of an accident or violation did not warrant this suspicion. Moreover, the police were not provided with convenient, portable, breath-screening devices, rendering the procedure more cumbersome and less likely to be utilized than the British. As noted above, the law was less newsworthy, and the official publicity did not encourage fear of apprehension. That some deterrent results were nonetheless achieved seems quite fortunate under the circumstances.

Although experience with the Canadian federal law illustrates the limitations of the deterrence-based drunk-driving policy, much experience in the provinces probes the potential of enforcement. A copious outpouring of studies comes from British Columbia under the aegis of Project Counterattack, lodged in the Ministry of the Attorney General. The typical intervention is a well-publicized "blitz." Although the evaluations are all in-house and suffer from overdependence on the single criterion of police-reported alcohol-related accidents, the amalgamation of comparable experiences is noteworthy. For example, when publicity peaked at a time different from the blitz, it was the publicity barrage rather than the police activity that seemed to produce the greatest reduction in drunk driving (Mercer 1984a). Indeed, police enforcement of the law produced no results at all when the news was blacked out by a newspaper strike and the only way for the public to know about the blitz was through experience or word-of-mouth (Mercer 1984b). At least at the levels of police activity prevailing at the time and the place, personal experience and communication were not sufficient to translate enforcement into deterrence.

The Province of Alberta, in its Check-Stop program, also housed in the office of its Attorney General, likewise found deterrent results for publicized enforcement. A year-to-year comparison found a 10 percent increase in fatal accidents and a 16 percent decrease in alcohol involvement reported among fatalities (Alberta Solicitor General 1974). However, the method used in this evaluation is weak and only limited confidence in the conclusions is warranted.

Similar activity was undertaken in Ontario, where it was evaluated by the staff of the Addiction Research Foundation. A check-stop-type program in a small part of metropolitan Toronto (Reduced Impaired Driving in Etobicoke, or RIDE) was accompanied by flyers distributed to all postal customers, and obtained a good deal of media coverage. The somewhat inconclusive results of the broader effort (Vingilis and Salutin 1980) were favorably interpreted and the program was expanded to the entire metropolitan area (Reduce Impaired Driving Everywhere). The evaluation (Vingilis et al. 1981) did not find evidence of a deterrent impact. Although a variety of methodological problems could be cited to explain the results, the experience may be taken as evidence that a successful blitz requires quantum increases in both enforcement and publicity.

On the whole, the experience of Canada in utilizing deterrence-based measures to counter drunk driving has been less successful than that of Britain. Perhaps both the form of the interventions and the nature of the drunk-driving problem in Canada may help to explain this fact. The Criminal Law Amendment Act lacked color and teeth, yielding the impression that things had changed very little with regard to the chances of a drunk driver's being punished. Likewise, blitzes when routinized in an area may eventually be perceived as not newsworthy, like the fabled cry of "wolf!" More than in the

United Kingdom, Canadian policy has been veering to the view that drunk driving is an aspect of the broader problem of alcohol use, which must be attacked by such means as restrictions on sales and tax-induced price increases. Evaluation of policies based on this understanding has yielded some interesting and surprising results (Liban et al. 1985), but these are beyond the scope of the present essay.

Australia

Although it is a federal country like Canada, Australia's drunk-driving law is entirely a matter for the state governments. And unlike the case in the United States, there is no strong leadership from the federal government for state action in the drunk-driving area. In practice the laws and enforcement practices of the various states have been divergent, making Australia one of the more interesting places in the world in which to compare the effects of legal policies.

The State of Victoria pioneered adoption of a Scandinavian-type law in Australia, setting a tolerance limit of .05 percent, in 1966. Adoption of similar laws in other states was encouraged by the initial successes of the British Road Safety Act of 1967. The British specification for the permitted blood alcohol concentration of .08 percent was initially followed, but many states subsequently changed to .05 percent, joining the Scandinavians (but not Canada or the United States) in prohibiting driving after relatively moderate or "social" drinking. Surprisingly, there have been few notable evaluations of the effects of adopting these laws, or of changing the permissible blood alcohol concentration. According to Ian Johnston (1982, 5), the consensus among Australian scholars is "that there is no acceptable evidence of the effectiveness of per se legislation in Australia."

However, the laws of many Australian states accomplish what the British Road Safety Act and the Canadian law dared not do— they authorize random testing by police. This authorization permits the testing of all drivers passing through safety-check roadblocks. Such freedom for police in enforcing drunk-driving laws was not even permitted in Scandinavia until the late 1970s. It offers an important opportunity to raise the perceived risk of punishment for drunk drivers. Not only can numerous tests efficiently be given in this fashion (though with a low yield of drunk drivers), but the practice subverts a possible psychological mechanism for underestimating the risk of apprehension: the belief that an impaired person can drive in a manner that does not excite the attention of the police.

Indeed, it is very likely that the formal law is less important for deterrence than the actual and declared practice of the police. Ross Homel (1986) notes that the practice of police in Western Australia of setting up roadblocks for the ostensible purpose of checking equipment and licenses closely approximates random breath testing, although the law does not provide for the latter. In South Australia, according to Homel, the provision of random breath-testing authority is so seldom used that the law is a dead letter. In Victoria, roadblocks are confined almost entirely to blitzes of specific and short duration. Only in New South Wales and Tasmania is there "RBT, boots and all," that is, programs of intensive and continuous enforcement with publicity.

Australia has a vigorous traffic safety research community, and there are several important and illuminating studies of the effect of random breath-testing laws in the various states. This even includes South Australia, which Homel characterizes as possessing "Clayton's RBT," referring to the advertisements for an alcohol-free beverage that allows one to have a "drink" when one is not drinking. Despite what Homel claims is minimal enforcement, McLean et al. (1984), using breath alcohol surveys of drivers, found a decline of 14 percent in those who had been drinking after seven months of the South Australian law. After a year, there was still a notable effect, a 10 percent reduction. There was also a reduction, albeit confined to the city and short-lived, in the numbers of late-night fatalities.

Studies of the Victorian blitzes (e.g., Cameron et al. 1980) report positive deterrent results, but lacunae and unexplainable aberrations in statistics for Victoria militate against strong reliance on these studies (see Johnston 1982). Positive claims are also made for enforcement practices in Western Australia, where a year-to-year comparison found nighttime casualty declines of 28 percent in Perth and 37 percent in the country (Maisey and Saunders 1981), but again methodological reservations apply.

The strongest and most exciting findings concerning the deterrent effects of random breath testing in roadblocks come from New South Wales, where enforcement has been vigorous and evaluation detailed and competent. The New South Wales law was proposed by a governmental commission with the acronym of STAYSAFE in 1982, when relevant experience in Victoria and South Australia was available for study and guidance. It was implemented on a three-year trial basis on December 17 of that year, and subsequently made permanent.

Vigorous enforcement accompanied random breath testing in New South Wales from the beginning. During the first year, police administered nearly a million breath tests in a driving population of three million. This might be compared to approximately 100,000 administered in the jurisdiction during the prior year. (Tasmanian enforcement was more vigorous yet; in 1985, 200,000 tests were made in a driving population of less than 270,000 [Sutton 1986].) Furthermore, police activity was supported with the investment of millions of dollars in advertising, along with free coverage generated by intense media interest.

Evaluation of the New South Wales experience includes interrupted time-series analysis of fatalities and numerous surveys of information, opinion, and behavior. The general evaluation by Cashmore (1985) leans strongly on the statistical work of Arthurson (1985) and the survey data provided by Homel (1986), Carseldine (1985), and others. Perhaps the central item of evidence is the time-series curve of fatal crashes, shown in figure 3.2 (taken from Arthurson 1985, 9). As in Britain in 1967, the change in the level of the curve at the inception of the New South Wales law is clearly visible and significant. Moreover, in contrast to the British case, the post-intervention curve seems to be nearly stationary, with relatively little suggestion of a return to the status quo ante in the future. Additional facts indicating deterrence of drunk driving include a decline in the proportion of crashes occurring late at night and on weekends, a decrease in the proportion of male drivers and of young drivers, a decrease in deceased drivers with any alcohol in their blood, and a decrease in those with illegal levels of blood alcohol (p. 10).

That these results are properly interpreted by deterrence theory is supported by evidence from survey data (Homel 1986). A very high proportion of motorists were aware of the law and police practices. More than one driver in ten had been tested within the first three months of the law. The number of friends that had been tested correlated with the driver's estimates of the risk of apprehension and punishment, and this risk in turn related to claimed changes in behavior that reduced the amount of drinking and driving. In sum, there is good reason to agree with the director of the New South Wales Bureau of Crime Statistics and Research that "random breath testing, as implemented in New South Wales, has had a significant

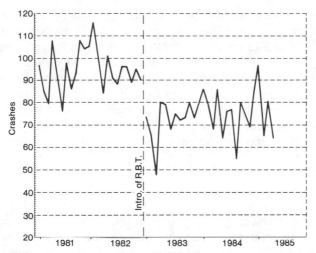

Fig. 3.2. Monthly count of fatal crashes in New South Wales, January 1981–
March 1985.

impact on the road toll, on the number of persons appearing before
courts on drunk-driving charges, and on community attitudes and
drunk-driving behavior'' (A. J. Sutton in Cashmore 1985, ix).

The experience with random breath testing and roadblocks in New
South Wales suggests that drunk-driving law enforcement that man-
ages to breath-test a third of the driving population every year may
exceed the threshold for long-term deterrent effectiveness. Moreover, the intervention appears clearly to be cost-effective. Arthurson
(1985), for instance, estimates the benefits to the community con-
servatively as $130 million with a direct cost to the government of
less than $6 million for the first two years. Although other costs
must be considered, such as lost jobs in the alcohol industry, the
economic balance is still likely to be most favorable.

However, some reservations must be expressed about using the
New South Wales model as a pattern for policy in other places,
especially the United States. Not included in the economic cost-
and-benefit calculation is the fact that this form and degree of policing
would very likely conflict with American conceptions of civil liberties. In a sense, the roadblock constitutes a mass stop and frisk,
which may only marginally be distinguished from, say, stopping all
passing pedestrians to be sniffed by dogs for the possession of drugs
or patted down to see whether they are carrying weapons. Inasmuch
as drunk driving can be held causally responsible for only about a

quarter of traffic fatalities and a much smaller proportion of less serious accidents, and inasmuch as cost-effective countermeasures like airbags and automatic seatbelts are available for reducing traffic deaths and injuries regardless of their cause, why should this sacrifice of liberties be necessary? The Australian experience seems to demonstrate the rationality and benefits of these intrusive laws—they are not merely arbitrary and capricious—but it does not demonstrate their necessity nor their special virtue in reducing traffic deaths and injury, in comparison with alternatives lying beyond deterrence.

Conclusion

The focus of traffic safety policy in these three English-speaking countries on deterrence-based countermeasures may well be in part a matter of following a well-known and apparently successful example. The Canadian law is clearly patterned on the British Road Safety Act of 1967, and its timing further testifies to a filial relationship. Officials in New Zealand have told me that their blitzes were consciously patterned on the experience of the Cheshire Constabulary as I reported it (Ross 1977), and I would speculate that the various Australian enforcement campaigns, including the New South Wales example, also belong in the family.

Beyond this lies the nonadversary and consultative nature of policymaking in parliamentary democracies. The initial stance of the American agency, adversary to the automobile industry, would have been unlikely in the countries reviewed here. A concentration on human factors, especially where the problems are defined as pertaining to a deviant minority rather than to the general driving public, is far more likely to be acceptable to that industry, thus inviting political attention to drunk driving and to deterrence-based policies to counteract it. To the extent that the alcoholic beverage industry would be included in the network of consultation, deterrence-based policies would be preferable to institutional countermeasures exemplified by increasing taxes and restricting advertising of the products. Furthermore, as compared with both occupant protection and social-change alternatives, deterrent countermeasures appear cheap and easy to administer.

Here in America we experience deterrence-based policies as central to the program of citizen-activist groups, motivated by grief and demanding that drunk-driving be regarded as a deliberate crime and be punished in a manner appropriate to that viewpoint. Certainly, the grief of the victims and their demand for justice have been an important political force in helping to redirect American policy from occupant protection to deterrence, but experience in the countries reviewed here suggests that this is not a necessary condition for a deterrence-oriented traffic safety policy. Deterrence thinking comes easily to people like legislators, prosecutors, police, and other affiliates of the legal community. "If all you have is a hammer, then everything looks like a nail." Whether as constituting the membership of a presidential or governor's task force on drunk driving or in their roles as behind-the-scenes administrative policymakers, such individuals can generally be depended on to take existing institutions as given and to prefer policies that avoid the need for antagonizing vested interests and overcoming the inertia of social systems.

The experience of these countries with deterrence-based countermeasures supplies further evidence for the proposition that publicized programs designed to increase the likelihood of apprehension and punishment can reduce drunk driving. When the interventions are whole-hearted and well-publicized, one sees the familiar prompt and important reduction in time series of measures of drunk driving like weekend night casualties. The Australian experiment with "random" breath testing on a hitherto unprecedented scale offers the possibility that a program which will test a third of the drivers every year may achieve permanent reductions in the amount of drunk driving and thus in the number of deaths and injuries on the roads. It should be stressed that this accomplishment, like most of those reviewed here, was attained without the need for heavy fines, permanent license revocation, or incarceration. The need for increments of severity has not been demonstrated in drunk-driving policy experience.

However, these experiences should not be viewed as vouching for the wisdom of the deterrent approach in traffic safety. None of the evaluations reviewed, in my opinion, takes sufficient account of the intrusiveness of the enforcement efforts in calculating the balance between costs and benefits, and I suspect that the clearly favorable balance claimed in Australia might not be so evident in the United States, for example.

Moreover, the wisdom of a deterrence-based policy, even if cost effective, must take alternative policies into account. If the problem is conceived as traffic-related deaths and injuries, drunk-driving interventions are fundamentally limited in their effectiveness by the fact that only a minority of the deaths and injuries can be meaningfully attributed to alcohol as a cause. The National Academy of Science's estimate is that about one-fourth of deaths and considerably less of injuries and property damage can be attributed to alcohol (Reed 1981). In contrast, countermeasures focusing on occupant protection can conceivably be effective in the three-fourths of fatal accidents where alcohol was not a cause, along with those caused by alcohol. One way of looking at the options is to recognize that if drunk driving could somehow be eliminated, while changing nothing else, the death rate on the roads might be reduced by about a quarter; but if all cars had operational airbags, the rate might be reduced by about half. If it is easier to install airbags than to eliminate drunk driving, a policy centering on the former should be preferred to one centering on the latter.

I am arguing here only about the center of a policy, not about its outside limits. If deterrent measures directed at drunk driving can save lives, at a cost that is less than the benefits when all legitimate considerations are properly included, then that policy should be included as an integral part of our total approach to the traffic safety problem. The experiences of Great Britain, Canada, and Australia suggest that these conditions may be met, and that an occupant-protection-centered policy should be complemented by vigorous and publicized enforcement of laws against drunk driving. After all, many of us have only hammers! However, that enforcement should be moderated by scrupulous respect for the civil liberties of the population, whether in or outside of vehicles, and it should be in service of fair penalties appropriate to the actual danger of drunk driving rather than draconian ones tied to the rage of the times.

4 Drinking-and-Driving Laws in the Federal Republic of Germany and the Netherlands

Gunter Kroj

This chapter attempts to provide some insight into the drinking-and-driving problem and government responses in the Federal Republic of Germany and the Netherlands. After briefly describing drinking-and-driving behavior in these two countries, the chapter shifts its attention to the legislative and enforcement strategies designed to reduce drunken driving. Section 3 briefly assesses the effectiveness of current anti-drunken-driving strategies. Finally, this chapter focuses on the German Driver Improvement Program, which combines education and skills training with the penal sanction in an effort to prevent drunken driving recidivism.

1. Drinking-and-Driving Behavior in the Federal Republic of Germany and the Netherlands

The discussion of drinking-and-driving behavior in these two countries begins with patterns of alcohol consumption. In 1983 alcohol consumption amounted to fifteen liters per person (over age fourteen) in the Federal Republic of Germany and nine liters per person in the Netherlands. Approximately 10 to 15 percent of the German population over age fifteen abstain from intoxicating beverages. A representative study of the population age fourteen to nineteen years in 1978 revealed that 78 percent of this age group consume intoxicating beverages. And in the age group from twenty to twenty-nine years the percentage is as high as 94 (Infratest Gesundheitsforschung 1979).

In recent years, significant progress has been made in reducing the total number of fatal accidents in the Federal Republic of Germany and the Netherlands. From 1980 through 1984, the total number of fatal accidents in the Netherlands decreased from 1,837 to 1,477, a 20 percent reduction; and in the Federal Republic of Germany fatal accidents fell from 11,911 to 9,304, a 22 percent reduction

79

Table 4.1. Alcohol- and Nonalcohol-related Accidents (Percentages Rounded)

		Fatal accidents				
		Nonalcohol		Alcohol		Total
	Year	abs.	%	abs.	%	abs.
The Netherlands	1980	1,567	85	270	15	1,837
	1981	1,403	85	247	15	1,650
	1982	1,333	85	236	15	1,569
	1983	1,387	86	233	14	1,620
	1984	1,263	86	214	14	1,477
The Federal	1980	9,105	76	2,806	24	11,911
Republic	1981	8,128	76	2,504	24	10,632
of Germany	1982	8,116	77	2,465	23	10,581
	1983	8,221	77	2,419	23	10,640
	1984	7,201	77	2,103	23	9,304

Source: Federal Bureau of Statistics (1981, 1982, 1983, 1984, 1985).

(table 4.1). These reductions occurred in almost equal proportions in accidents with and without alcohol involvement. In 1980, 14.7 percent of the accidents in the Netherlands were alcohol related, and in 1984, the rate was 14.5 percent. Similarly, the corresponding figures in the Federal Republic of Germany were 23.6 percent and 22.6 percent. Thus, despite important reductions in the absolute numbers of alcohol-related accidents the proportion of alcohol-related accidents has remained about the same.

Demographic surveys of those violating the legal blood alcohol concentration (BAC) limit reveal a relatively young population. In all, 40 percent of drunken drivers involved in accidents in the Federal Republic of Germany in 1983 were between eighteen and twenty-four years old, and another 25 percent belonged to the age group from twenty-five to thirty-four years. Table 4.2 describes how many German drivers of a given age group were involved in alcohol-related accidents resulting in fatalities or injuries or in property damage of DM 1,000 and more (Schwerdtfeger and Küffner 1981). In general, the accident involvement rates of car drivers (including passengers and without distinction by cause of accident) show a much higher accident risk for younger drivers.

In particular, the eighteen to twenty-one age group of car drivers involves the highest risk—with about forty-nine drunken drivers involved in accidents per one million hours of road use. With increasing age, the accident involvement rate declines sharply, reaching a minimum of three for the sixty-five and over age group.

Table 4.2. Time Rate of Accident Involvement of Drunken Drivers According to Age in the Federal Republic of Germany

Age	Sex	Mean frequency of daily car trips (in 1976)	Mean length of one car trip (min)(in 1976)	Inhabitants (12/31/75) (in 1,000)	Sum total of drunken drivers involved in accidents in 1979	Time rate of alcohol-related accident involvement (per million hours of road use)
18– <21	M	0.89	20.6	1,330.3	11,869	49.3
	F	0.56	21.2	1,270.1		
21– <25	M	1.94	23.5	1,694.5	13,672	21.3
	F	0.89	18.9	1,675.1		
25– <35	M	2.27	23.4	4,274.1	19,497	10.7
	F	0.90	20.1	3,983.7		
35– <45	M	2.17	23.0	4,666.2	15,349	8.6
	F	0.69	19.5	4,331.8		
45– <55	M	1.87	22.5	3,497.7	6,627	5.9
	F	0.44	21.1	4,076.2		
55– <65	M	1.34	23.5	2,412.5	2,504	4.4
	F	0.22	23.0	3,527.0		
65 and older	M	0.46	23.5	3,358.7	782	2.9
	F	0.07	21.5	5,646.1		

Sources: Bomsdorf, Schmidt, and Schwabl (1981); Schwerdtfeger and Küffner (1981).

Accurate estimates of the amount of undetected drinking-and-driving violations in the Federal Republic of Germany are not readily available. German law prohibits law enforcement officials from conducting routine breath tests not based on reasonable suspicion and thus precludes random roadside surveys of breath alcohol levels. Thus, personal interviews have been used to gather self-reported violations as an indirect means for assessing drinking and driving in the general population (Kretschmer-Bäumel and Karstedt-Henke 1986; Kretschmer and Riediger 1979).

In a representative sample of German drivers, one-fourth reported driving to a place where they had consumed alcohol (Kretschmer-Bäumel and Karstedt-Henke 1986). Within this group, 84 percent of the persons reported observing the law in this situation, while 16 percent drove with a BAC of 80 mg/100 ml or more. The survey found that the decision to violate the law depended on the general attitude toward the legal BAC limit of 80 mg/100 ml; estimation of the danger associated with drunken driving; general attitudes on heavy drinking; and gender (females drive less often under the influence of alcohol). The probability of drinking-and-driving offenses is highest for drivers who: (1) accept the legal BAC limit of 80 mg/100 ml, but reject any more stringent limit; (2) tend to display a tolerant attitude toward excessive alcohol consumption; and (3) attribute a lower risk for drunken driving than others do.

Most German drivers accept the legal BAC limit of 80 mg/100 ml. One in three drivers even advocates lowering the legal BAC limit. Half of the drivers want the police to check as many drivers as possible so that drunken drivers are removed from the traffic scene; however, 44 percent of the driving population advocate police intervention only if suspicion of drunken driving is justifiable (Kretschmer-Bäumel and Karstedt-Henke 1986). Interview studies and studies on drinking patterns reveal that the majority of drivers generally comply with the law. The estimates are based on the assumption that between 2 percent and 5 percent of the driver population occasionally or frequently use their cars with BACs at or exceeding the legal limit of 80 mg/100 ml (Kerner 1985). However, hardly more than 2 percent of all drinking-and-driving offenses result in apprehension (Kerner 1985).

The high blood alcohol concentrations measured on drinking-and-driving offenders in the Federal Republic of Germany leads to the conclusion that many of these offenders probably require alcohol abuse treatment. Bavarian BAC figures revealed that, in 1983, 30 percent of the offenders involved in accidents had BACs between 150 mg/100 ml and 200 mg/100 ml, 29 percent between 200 mg/100 ml and 300 mg/100 ml, and 2 percent in excess of 300 mg/100 ml (Stephan 1986; Bierau 1985).

In the Netherlands, the Institute for Road Safety Research (SWOV) has conducted extensive and expensive surveys of the alcohol consumption of drivers. In the surveys conducted from 1970 to 1977, 10 to 20 percent of the drivers refused to cooperate (Stichting Wetenschappelijk Onderzoek Verkeersveiligheid 1978, 1984; Mulder and Vis 1983; Noordzij 1984). In 1981, therefore, a new survey concept was tested, and a comprehensive study on the alcohol consumption of drivers was undertaken in 1983, as part of the normal police control activities (Stichting Wetenschappelijk Onderzoek Verkeersveiligheid 1984).

Table 4.3 illustrates the percentage of drivers surveyed by BAC level. The remarkable decline in drunken drivers after passage of the amendments to the drunken driving law in November 1984 is noteworthy. The longer-term effect of the law, however, is much lower than the short-term effect observed in 1974 directly after the "drinking-and-driving law" had been introduced. Apart from the effects of the law itself, this positive short-term effect is also believed to have been caused by more intensive police controls, safety campaigns, and general publicity in this initial period (Stichting Wetenschappelijk Onderzoek Verkeersveiligheid 1984).

Both the alcohol consumption of the Dutch population at large (per capita consumption in 1975, 8 liters; in 1983, 8.9 liters) and that

Table 4.3. Percentage of Intoxicated Drivers in the Netherlands, 1970–1983

| Year | Drivers with BACs of | | |
	20 mg/100 ml	50 mg/100 ml	100 mg/100 ml
1970	24	13	5
1971	31	18	8
1973	32	16	5
1974[a]	20	12	3
1974[b]	5	2	0
1975	23	11	4
1977	25	12	4
1981	25	12	5
1983	24	12	3

[a]Before November 1, 1974.
[b]After November 1, 1974.
Source: Stitching Wetenschappelijk Onderzoek Verkeersveiligheid (1984).

of drivers remained largely unchanged between 1975 and 1983. However, since 1975 consistently lower levels of alcohol consumption have been measured in roadside surveys than before the law amendment in 1974. Despite these findings, the level of drinking and driving by Dutch drivers cannot be considered as acceptable (Stichting Wetenschappelijk Onderzoek Verkeersveiligheid 1984). About fifty thousand alcohol-related accidents are brought to court per year and approximately one out of ten accidents with personal injuries involves alcohol (Stichting Wetenschappelijk Onderzoek Verkeersveiligheid 1984).

2. Drinking-and-Driving Laws in the Federal Republic of Germany and the Netherlands

Drinking-and-Driving Statutory Provisions

Drinking-and-driving offenses incur the following legal consequences in the Federal Republic of Germany:

- A BAC of 30 mg/100 ml or more can bring imprisonment for up to one year or a fine, license revocation and entries in the Central Register of Traffic Offenders *if* police detect signs of unsafe driving, such as weaving. *If* an accident places other persons or property at risk, the penalty is considerably higher: imprisonment for up to five years and license revocation for up to five years.
- A BAC of 80 mg/100 ml constitutes an *administrative* offense even if there is no evidence of faulty driving. This may be followed by license suspension for up to three months, a fine of up to DM 3,000 and entries in the Central Register of Traffic Offenders. If the offense involves an accident, the consequences will be as severe as at a BAC of 30 mg/100 ml.
- BACs of 130 mg/100 ml or more invariably constitute a *criminal* offense, independent of accident occurence. At such BACs, a license is always revoked, the offender imprisoned or fined, and points against him are entered in the Central Register of Traffic Offenders.

Because these blood alcohol limits are so complicated, it is often erroneously believed that one may drive with up to a BAC of 80 mg/100 ml, overlooking the fact that driving is impaired at lower BAC values. The type of penalty and its severity depend on the circumstances in each case. Although binding statements about the likely penalty for a drinking-and-driving offense are not possible, a certain uniformity has developed in the practice of penalty assessment. First-time offenders without any consequential offenses may generally expect a fine amounting to at least a month's salary or even imprisonment if hazards to others are involved. Suspension of a sentence or probation in cases involving severely or fatally injured accident victims are rare and will occur only if considerable contributory negligence on the part of these victims has been demonstrated.

Although license revocation is legally defined as a means for rehabilitation and crime prevention rather than as a form of punishment, license revocation often affects drivers more severely than the sentence itself. Licenses may be revoked for time periods between six months and five years, and, in rare circumstances, for a lifetime. Once the license has been canceled, the driver must apply for a new license after the revocation period. Thus, traffic authorities may require the applicant to retake the driving test or make license renewal contingent on the results of a medical and psychological examination.

Drinking-and-driving offenses account for more than 90 percent of all license revocations. The number of license revocations increased by 18 percent between 1970 and 1980, as shown in table 4.4. Between 1980 and 1985 these figures decreased by 14 percent. In addition to the revocations, about forty thousand of the total thirty million driving licenses in Germany are suspended each year by the courts and the administrative authorities.

A special feature of German law is that the administrative authorities may renew a license only if the reasons for the revocation no longer exist. A medical and psychological report is required under the German Highway Code (§15c, para 3, StVZO) for drivers with one or more previous offenses. About ninety thousand medical and psychological examinations under this provision take place in the Federal Republic of Germany each year, and 50 percent of these involve drinking-and-driving offenders. In 1984, 58 percent of these examinations reported favorably on the driver's competence, and the driving license was renewed or not withdrawn.

After the legal BAC limit of 80 mg/100 ml was introduced in the Federal Republic of Germany in 1973 as constituting an offense incurring a fine, the number of alcohol-related accidents recorded by the police declined by 14 percent (Janiszewsik 1974). The Federal Bureau estimates that about six hundred to seven hundred people were thus saved from death in 1973 (Federal Bureau of Statistics

Table 4.4. Revocation of Driving Licenses of Classes 1 to 5 from 1970 to 1985, Federal Republic of Germany

| Year | License revocation due to an offense in connection with | | |
	Total	Drinking and driving	Traffic accident
1970	129,739	120,140	71,318
1971	130,713	120,795	69,723
1972	142,395	132,634	74,135
1973	142,744	132,841	71,452
1974	137,251	126,395	60,952
1975	147,765	132,584	63,945
1976	149,747	132,600	64,030
1977	158,542	140,140	66,720
1978	162,634	143,905	70,619
1979	157,671	139,436	69,435
1980	159,854	142,038	71,957
1981	157,607	139,617	72,040
1982	153,139	135,069	68,162
1983	155,551	137,220	68,886
1984	147,058	129,856	63,935
1985	138,473	121,781	61,434

Source: Statistische Mitteilungen des Kraftfahrt-Bundesamtes (1986).

1973). A particularly striking fact is the reduction in the number of licenses revoked in 1974 for offenses associated with accidents, which also in the years 1975 to 1979 remained considerably below the revocation figures of 1972, despite a heavy increase in vehicle-kilometers (cf. table 4.4).

Since 1974, the Netherlands has prohibited driving a vehicle when a driver's BAC is in excess of 50 mg/100 ml. If the police suspect a person, the 50 mg/100 ml screening test is obligatory; refusal of such a test constitutes an offense. A positive 50 mg/100 ml test result is followed by an 80 mg/100 ml screening test, usually at a police station. Even if the result is negative (that is, in excess of 50 mg/100 ml but less than 80 mg/100 ml), the driver is not permitted to drive for a period of eight hours.

If the 80 mg/100 ml screening test results are positive, a blood sample will be requested which is taken by a physician. An offender has the right to insist on the sample being taken within an hour of the first contact with the police. If the blood test is refused it will be officially ordered. Refusal of the order constitutes an offense. A positive 80 mg/100 ml screening test result also incurs the prohibition to drive for a period of eight to twelve hours. Upon conviction, the court may impose fines up to Hfl 10,000, imprisonment up to three months, and license revocation for up to five years.

According to the directives for the public prosecutor, the severity of a sentence is dependent on the BAC level. Recidivism is taken into consideration irrespective of whether an accident occurred. Judges are free, within the limits of the law, to sentence as they see fit. However, in practice they generally follow the directives and impose a combination of the punishments. Recently the public prosecutor was given the authority to impose fines ranging from Hfl 250 to Hfl 750 directly without court intervention. However, this procedure is contingent on BACs below 130 mg/100 ml and the absence of further aggravating circumstances.

In the near future, the law will be amended once more. The blood test will be replaced by an obligatory evidential breath test. The legal limit will be 22 ug/100 ml (which is equivalent to 50 mg/100 ml, based on the ratio of 1:2,300 between breath and blood alcohol concentration). If a suspect is not able to complete the breath test, a blood test will be performed.

Police Control

Studies on police control activities in the Federal Republic of Germany have shown that the frequency of such controls varies considerably within short time periods (Beneke 1982). Furthermore, these variations can influence the kinds of drinking-driving offenders that are brought into driver improvement programs. Drawing on data for fifty thousand drinking-and-driving offenders on file in the Central Register of Traffic Offenders, it was noted that a higher proportion of offenders in southern Germany than in the north came to police attention only because of their involvement in an accident (Stephan 1985). Likewise, offenses with accident involvement have been more frequently recorded in larger cities and in rural areas compared with medium-size and small cities. By inference, the data suggest that less intensive police controls allow the gradual buildup of a higher proportion of highly intoxicated drivers who present a greater accident risk.

These findings are consistent with the interpretation that intensive police controls serve to prevent drinking-and-driving offenses. Furthermore, in areas with relatively high control intensity, a lower per capita accident rate has been found without, at the same time, leading to an increased rate of arrests for drinking-and-driving violations in the general flow of traffic. Based upon these findings, it has been proposed to increase the intensity of police control activities as a means to improve compliance and, simultaneously, to reduce alcohol-related accidents (Stephan 1985).

Without sizable increases in police manpower it will be difficult to significantly raise the risk of being stopped in traffic in the Netherlands. Within the framework of a demonstration project, "Special Police Controls," SWOV is now studying possibilities for targeting police surveillance more directly toward the most probable times and locations of drinking-and-driving behavior to achieve more effective results.

Drinking-and-Driving Safety Campaigns

In 1974 and 1975, the German Federal Ministry of Transport conducted a comprehensive safety campaign on alcohol and driving. Subsequent studies revealed that a great number of organizations have engaged in activities in this area (Spoerer 1979); however, the contents, target groups, and range of safety efforts have varied greatly. Safety campaigns were conducted primarily on a regional basis without any apparent coordination between the sponsors or organizers involved. The inefficiencies resulting from these disconnected campaigns toward the same target groups have probably reduced the overall effectiveness of these efforts from the outset (Spoerer 1979).

Based on the results of these studies, the Federal Ministry of Transport together with the German Traffic Safety Council and the Anti-Drinking and Driving Association started work on an integrated approach to planning in 1983. Uniform campaign contents, definitions of target groups, and implementation strategies were thus established. Beginning in 1985, a new action concept, known by the slogan "Sober drivers get there safely," was implemented nationwide by the German Traffic Safety Council (Deutscher Verkehrssicherheitsrat 1985). The most important objectives of the associated campaigns are to increase public awareness of laws and sanctions and to increase informal social pressures upon drivers in drinking situations.

Drinking-and-driving countermeasures recently introduced in the Netherlands include: information campaigns by the Dutch Association for Safe Traffic; information and education projects undertaken in prisons for persons convicted for drinking-and-driving offenses; and information and education projects as an "alternative to punishment" (instead of fines or imprisonment).

3. Assessing the Effectiveness of Current Anti-Drunken-Driving Strategies in the Federal Republic of Germany and the Netherlands

A long-term evaluation of driver improvement programs in the Federal Republic of Germany examined the behavior of convicted drivers in the first five years after their driving license was reissued or renewed (Stephan 1984). The analysis was based on a sample of 1,096 drivers convicted in 1973 for a drinking-and-driving offense and who received entries against them in the Central Registry of Traffic Offenders. In the Netherlands, data on the subsequent behavior of convicted drivers were available covering the time period 1956 to 1966 (Buikhuisen and von Wering 1983). For first-time drinking-and-driving offenders, the German relapse rate after sixty months (35 percent) was found to be considerably higher than in the Netherlands (25 percent). On the other hand, for offenders with more than one conviction, the recidivism rate in the Federal Republic of Germany was much lower than in the Netherlands (table 4.5).

Further differences between countries are revealed in table 4.6, which contrasts the arrest histories within initial samples studied in Germany and the Netherlands. The relative percentage of first-time offenders is higher by one-third in the Dutch than in the German sample, whereas the relative percentage of offenders with one or two or more previous convictions is more than twice as high in the German samples. Both countries' figures thus reveal statistically significant differences particularly for first-time offenders and those with one previous drinking-and-driving conviction.

It has to be assumed that the relapse rates described above are basically the result of two interacting factors: the deviant behavior of drivers and police manpower requirements to deal with it. Because of wide regional differences in the intensity of police controls within a country, regional estimates of relapse rates might be more meaningful than nationwide rates. As previously noted, the analysis of fifty thousand offenses between 1982 and 1983 indicated regional differences in enforcement in the Federal Republic of Germany (Stephan 1985).

There is a striking difference between the Dutch (Buikhuisen and von Wering 1983) and German data (Stephan 1984) with respect to the high relapse rate in Germany of first-time offenders and the low relapse rate in Germany for offenders with one previous drinking-and-driving conviction. With respect to the first difference, the unexpectedly high proportion of relapse among German first offenders

Table 4.5. Relapse Rates in the Federal Republic of Germany and in the Netherlands

Relapse period	Relapse rate for first-time drinking-and-driving offenders		Relapse rate for drivers with one previous drinking-and-driving conviction		Relapse rate for drivers with two or more previous drinking-and-driving convictions	
	FRG	NL	FRG	NL	FRG	NL
0 months[a]	3.7%	1.8%	2.9%	2.9%	7.5%	3.5%
up to 12 months	8.1	7.2	7.2	12.0	12.9	14.4
up to 24 months	16.6	12.9	11.7	21.7	22.6	15.9
up to 36 months	24.9	16.9	16.7	28.2	26.9	33.8
up to 48 months	30.3	20.9	20.4	34.8	30.1	41.8
up to 60 months	34.5	24.5	23.4	40.8	31.2	48.9
Recidivists (N)	669	1,376	334	218	93	60
Confidence interval 1%	+/−4.7%	+/−2.9%	+/−5.9%	+/−8.5%	+/−12.3%	+/−16.6%

[a]A number of recidivists had relapses before their licenses were reissued.

Table 4.6. Arrest History of Offenders in the Federal Republic of Germany and the Netherlands (Percentages Rounded)

Offender groups	Federal Republic of Germany ($N=1{,}096$)	Netherlands ($N=1{,}654$)
First-time drinking-and-driving offenders	61%	83%
Drivers with one previous drinking-and-driving conviction	31	13
Drivers with two or more previous drinking-and-driving convictions	9	4

Source: Stephan (1984).

(35 percent) may be due either to more intensive police controls in detecting recidivists or to the existence of a much more serious drinking-and-driving problem in Germany than was the case in the Netherlands twenty years ago. According to the available evidence (Stephan 1984), it appears that some combination of these two factors may be operating.

The second difference—the very low relapse rate in the group of offenders with one previous drinking-and-driving conviction in the Federal Republic of Germany compared to that in the Netherlands— may be explained by the difficulties encountered by repeat offenders in reobtaining their license under German law compared with first-time offenders. As was explained in section 2, offenders with one previous drinking-and-driving offense are confronted with the fact that license renewal cannot be taken for granted at the end of the revocation period. The authorities generally advise offenders that their drinking-and-driving behavior has given cause to doubt their competence as drivers and that a positive medical and psychological report is required to remove this doubt. The effects on offenders of the uncertainty, the added obstacle of the medical and psychological examination, and the exclusion of high-risk offenders may have contributed to reduced recidivism rates among offenders with one previous drinking-and-driving conviction (Stephan 1984). Such effects on law obedience, however, can only be expected from drivers who still have control of their drinking and can enjoy both drinking and driving separately. In groups of drivers with several previous drinking-and-driving offenses, there are probably many drivers with serious alcohol problems, as is indicated in table 4.7.

Although the extremely small sample sizes in table 4.7 preclude direct interpretation of specific findings, it is safe to generalize that

Table 4.7. Percentages of Offenders with Relapses (Percentages Rounded)

Offender groups	Relapses before the end of the revocation period (N)	Total relapses (N)	%
First-time drinking-and-driving offenders	25	231	11
Drivers with one previous drinking-and-driving conviction	10	79	13
Drivers with two previous drinking-and-driving convictions	3	13	23
Drivers with three previous drinking-and-driving convictions	4	10	40
Drivers with between four and seven previous drinking-and-driving convictions	3	6	50

Source: Stephan (1984).

the relative percentage of relapses during the period of revocation increases with the number of convictions. A breakdown of the relapse rates by age groups and types of offenders shows a great difference between age groups (table 4.8).

4. Driver Improvement Programs in the Federal Republic of Germany

Driver Improvement Programs

In the 1960s and the beginning of the 1970s, the Federal Republic of Germany made intensive efforts to reduce road safety risks through a series of programs for improving the knowledge, attitudes, and behaviors of road users. A survey of the spectrum of measures is given in figure 4.1.

In 1978, the Driver Improvement Program was established at the Federal Highway Research Institute to compile a summary survey of the programs in figure 1 and undertake evaluation studies to determine the success of these programs (Hebenstreit et al. 1978, 1979, 1980, 1981, 1982).

The legal provisions applying to "drinking-and-driving" offenders must be understood to comprehend the German model of interven-

Table 4.8. Relapse Rate by Age Group and Type of Offender

Age group	First-time drinking-and-driving offender		Offender with one previous drinking-and-driving conviction		Offender with two or more previous drinking-and-driving convictions	
	Offenders	Relapse rate	Offenders	Relapse rate	Offenders	Relapse rate
15–20	53	49.1	7	57.1	—	—
21–25	152	42.8	51	23.5	6	50.0
26–30	112	30.4	74	27.0	9	11.1
31–35	127	33.9	74	28.4	30	43.3
36–40	92	31.5	66	22.7	15	33.3
41–45	45	26.7	24	8.3	18	22.2
46–50	34	32.3	16	—	5	20.0
51–55	29	34.5	9	22.2	2	0.0
56 and over	23	4.4	13	15.4	8	25.0

Note: Observation period of 60 months.

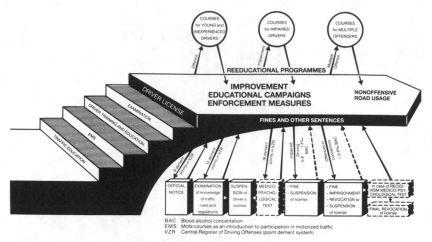

Fig. 4.1. Measures to influence road users in the Federal Republic of Germany.

tions. Program participants' motivations are revealed by examining the procedures outlined in figure 4.2 (Stichting Wetenschappelijk Onderzoek Verkeersveiligheid 1978). The starting point is a *drinking-and-driving offense:* somebody has been caught by the police because of driving under the influence of alcohol.

The first question is whether the offense is serious enough to warrant sentencing the person on the basis of the *penal code.* The most frequent reason for this is a BAC of 130 mg/100 ml or more. If this is the case, the judge will impose license revocation and fix a period of revocation. This period may have a length of about half a year for first-time offenders or two years or more for drivers with two or more previous offenses (in most cases).

The next question is whether we are dealing with a *first-time offender* or a driver with several previous offenses. If he is a first-time offender he has the opportunity to participate in a Driver Improvement Program for first-time drinking-and-driving offenders. If he refuses to cooperate, he must wait for the period of revocation to expire.

If he participates in the program, the court has discretion to accept participation as evidence of improved attitudes and behaviors concerning drinking and driving. If the judge accepts the evidence, the period of revocation will be shortened; if not, the offender will have to wait for the end of the full period. Although the judge's discretion regarding the assessment of the driver improvement program's effect

asp = alcohol safety programme

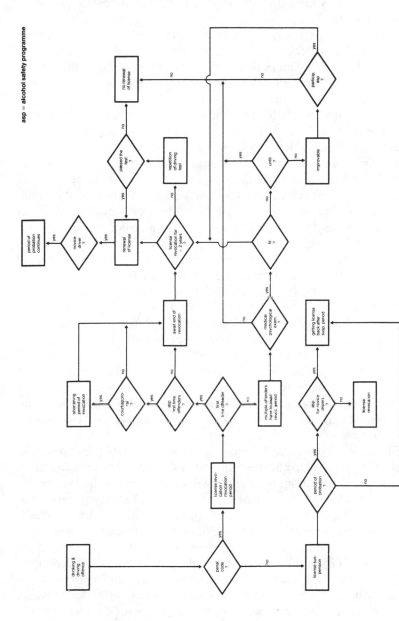

Fig. 4.2. Legal basis of improvement courses for DWI offenders in the Federal Republic of Germany.

on a driver is substantial, most judges find such participation as evidence of reform.

If the revocation period has been completed, but was less than two years, the offender can have his license renewed. In case of license revocation of more than two years he has to repeat the driving test. If the candidate passes the test for license renewal he is given a new license; if not, the license is refused.

The only question after receiving the new license is whether he is a novice driver. In that case the period of probation continues because the intervening time does not count.

Multiple offenders in all cases must await expiration of the whole period of revocation. In addition, they must submit to medical and psychological examinations. Two possibilities emerge if the result of the examinations is negative: either the report considers a driver as fully incompetent—in which case there is no longer any chance of license renewal—or the report confirms the doubts about the driver's present incompetence but believes that it could be corrected by participation in an improvement program. If he refuses to participate, he forfeits his chance of license renewal. If he takes part in a driver improvement program, the subsequent steps again are subject to the conditions mentioned before. Because the revocation period for a repeat offender generally exceeds two years, he will, in most cases, be required to retake the test.

This leaves the last part of the flow chart, which applies to the driver not sentenced on the basis of the penal code. This is generally a driver who violated the legal BAC limit of 80 mg/100 ml. The consequence in this case is license suspension for one (minimum) to three (maximum) months.

The steps taken after the suspension period ends depend on the kind of driver under consideration. If he is not a novice driver in his period of probation, his license will be returned. If he is a novice driver, he will have to participate in an alcohol safety program for young novices. If he refuses to do so, his license will be revoked.

The program described here is not construed as an *alternative* to license revocation or license suspension but rather a means of integrating driver improvement programs into the existing administrative, legal, and social environments. A recent report on the evaluation of improvement programs for repeat offenders reveals the advantages and drawbacks of this integration (Winkler 1985):

• "Traffic authorities generally prefer rehabilitative programs over punitive measures. Therefore, driver improvement programs enjoy a broad measure of official support.

• The authorities themselves are interested in the results of evaluation studies. However, to take part in such studies, statutory provisions are required to assure data protection.
• Even though participation in a driver improvement program often can be a deeply upsetting experience, it may still fail to produce any basic changes in behavior. Driver improvement measures should therefore be reinforced by auxiliary policies requiring periodic reexamination and participation in meetings organized for former program participants in order to attain a lasting effect.
• If the therapeutic aims of driver improvement programs are in conflict with social norms and values (for example, alcohol consumption, speeding, and self-assertion) the measures will have little chance of success. Influencing these social norms and values is an intrinsic part of the whole driver improvement concept, probably as important as influencing individual drivers."

Effectiveness of Driver Improvement Programs and Results of Accompanying Evaluation Studies

Preliminary results and conclusions of evaluation studies now in progress in the Federal Republic of Germany are presented here according to designated target groups.

PROGRAMS FOR YOUNG DRIVERS WITH PREVIOUS MOTORING OFFENSES

The results of the model tests on programs for young novice drivers are incorporated into the 1984 Road Safety Program of the Federal Ministry of Transport with the aim of improving the system of driver education and examination (Bundesminister für Verkehr 1984). Based on these results, a working party of the German Traffic Safety Council developed an improvement program for young drivers with previous motoring offenses. The program will be implemented as part of the provisions for the probationary driving license regulation for novice drivers, officially introduced on November 1, 1986 (Deutscher Verkehrssicherheitsrat 1986). Under this law, drivers must demonstrate their driving competence by not causing an accident or violating traffic regulations for a two-year probation period after their license is issued. An emphasis upon prevention is thus an essential feature of the probationary driving license system.

A novice driver committing traffic offenses in the first two years after having obtained his license is suspected of shortcomings in his competence as a driver and/or having a dangerous degree of risk acceptance. The improvement program aims at gradually reducing individual shortcomings and thus also the high number of accidents caused by this target group. Program participants discuss their experiences and identify ways to reduce their accident risk. The importance of active participation in group discussions is explained by the fact that new insights and knowledge are generally more thoroughly and lastingly acquired if they are processed on an emotional as well as intellectual level. Although these programs are intended for traffic violators rather than for drinking-and-driving offenders, they do attempt to alert novice drivers to common errors of judgment in the use of alcohol in driving situations (Deutscher Verkehrssicherheitsrat 1986).

Driver improvement groups typically include from six to twelve participants. Program leaders are qualified driving instructors and they are further prepared for the task in a one-week introductory training session. The driver improvement program includes four discussion sessions and a driving exercise, which provides an opportunity to observe the driving behavior of participants.

Novice drivers committing drinking-and-driving offenses in the period of probation represent a special target group. A special alcohol safety program has been designed to help participants understand their alcohol problems and to avoid future drinking-and-driving offenses. These programs employ trained psychologists who are familiar with the drinking-and-driving program and experience in group work. The preliminary tests of the model are quite promising (Stephan 1984, 1985, 1986; Justizminister Baden-Württemberg 1981; Bussman and Gebhardt 1984).

DRIVER IMPROVEMENT PROGRAMS FOR FIRST-TIME DRINKING-AND-DRIVING OFFENDERS

The objective of these programs, which have operated since 1978, is to supplement the general preventive effect of fines and the revocation of an offender's driving license by a special preventive measure. The programs aim to convey knowledge and to change attitudes concerning drinking and driving. In addition, the participants are motivated to prove that they have succeeded in overcoming their deficiencies because successful completion of the program can have positive legal consequences in the form of a shortened period of license revocation (Hebenstreit et al. 1978, 1982; Zabel 1985).

At present there are four different program models available, based on behavioral, individual, and eclectic approaches. Information on the structure, organization, and sponsorship of these program models is given in table 4.9. The programs are carried out by specially trained traffic psychologists (Hebenstreit et al. 1981, 1982).

The driver improvement programs for first-time drinking-and-driving offenders have steadily increased in number, though at different rates in the various regions. In past years about 4,000 first-time offenders attended such programs each year, which is very low compared with about 140,000 first-time drinking-and-driving offenders apprehended annually. This small proportion of participation may reflect the marginal acceptance of such programs by the courts because judges are entirely free to decide on the legal impact of program participation.

More recently, much has been published about the extent to which courts take program participation into account in assessing driver competence following a drinking-and-driving offense (Zabel 1981, 1985; Gebhardt 1981; Arbeitskreis 1981; Janiszewski 1981; Legat 1981; Landgericht Heilbronn 1982; Evangelische Akademie Bad Boll 1982; Schultz 1982). Consequently, there appears to be a growing tendency to place greater weight on the certificate of program participation. This is also reflected in efforts made by the federal states to encourage a larger number of persons to take part in programs for first-time drinking-and-driving offenders by paving the way for legislation reducing the minimum legal period of license revocation.

The judges' fundamental concern is shown by the following question: Is the introduction of driver improvement programs compatible with the purpose of license revocation (Legat 1985)? In this connection it should be noted that judges, according to German law, are expressly obliged to protect the public from drunken drivers. This is ensured best by license revocation. In that sense, a driver improvement program can only be regarded as an additional safety measure rather than as a substitute (Schultz 1982; Legat 1985).

It is expected that the longer-term effects of the programs for first-time drinking-and-driving offenders will be better known at the end of 1987. However, the data presently available from regional evaluation studies already reveal a clear reduction in the relapse rate for program participants compared with the general rate for first-time offenders during the first twenty-four months (Stephan 1984, 1985, 1986; Justizminister Baden-Württemberg 1981; Bussman and Gerhardt 1984). Previous experience has shown that the quality of programs depends heavily upon the training of program leaders and on the adequacy of assessment procedures for selecting suitable offenders for program participation (Stephan 1985; Hebenstreit et al. 1981, 1982).

Table 4.9. Structure, Organization, and Distribution of Driver Improvement Programs for First-time Drinking-and-Driving Offenders in the Federal Republic of Germany

Program model	Organization			Methods
	Sponsor/Organizer	Schedule and duration	Number of participants	
ALFA	Gesellschaft für Ausbildung, Fortbildung und Nachschulung im Strassenverkehr, Köln	entrance examination and four sessions of 120 minutes each over a period of four weeks	approximately 10	group discussions; brief lectures, if necessary, to convey new knowledge; use of task and information sheets; homework
Hamburg '79	Institut für Gruppenforschung, Hamburg	entrance examination; two sessions per week; in all 21 sessions of 45 minutes each	8–10	group discussions concentrating on particular subjects; role-playing; discussion of new aspects; program monitoring on video screen; homework
LEER-E	Technischer Überwachungsverein, Hannover; Technischer Überwachungsverein, Bayern	entrance examination; six group sessions of two hours each; follow-up sessions (two hours) and further contact by correspondence; in all two years	8	group discussions; self-observation and self-control measures and exercises; techniques to modify behavior; information material; homework
Mainz '77	various TÜVs (technical inspection agencies)	entrance examination; 6 sessions of two hours each over a period of three weeks	8–10	group discussions; techniques to modify behavior; self-control methods; information material; homework

Improvement Programs for Drivers with Several Drinking-and-Driving Convictions

Successful participation in a program can lead to the restoration of the driving license in cases in which traffic authorities doubted the driver's competence due to the drinking-and-driving offense. This procedure has been established by the highest federal and state authorities during the model experiment and its legality has been confirmed by the administrative courts (Hebenstreit et al. 1982).

In addition to integrating the programs into the existing administrative system, the success of improvement programs is mainly due to their content, organization, and supervision (Hebenstreit et al. 1981, 1982). The key elements of the various program models are summarized in table 4.10. At present, there are about 150 trained psychologists directing programs of the three models mentioned. In addition to the regular meetings of program leaders, a variety of methods to supervise program leaders and provide further training have been applied, such as analysis of video recording of program units, program sessions given jointly by two program leaders with subsequent discussion of the observations made, and analysis of program statistics. Studies on the effectiveness of the techniques and instruments employed will provide the basis for developing guidelines for future supervision.

Due to intensive teamwork in small groups, all three treatment models for repeat offenders (individual approach, behavioristic approach, LEER model) have shown some success in helping program participants to address their personal problems in dealing with drinking and driving. Preliminary evaluation studies on the program models indicate positive changes in drinking habits, control of alcohol consumption and avoidance of occasions when alcohol will be consumed, and in the capacity for self-criticism of driving skills (Hebenstreit et al. 1981, 1982; Winkler 1982).

In addition, driver improvement programs also produce a clear reduction in the recidivism rate. This has been confirmed in a monitoring period of nineteen months following the program participation based on a comparison of 1,583 program participants with 1,533 drivers with several previous drinking-and-driving convictions but whose licenses were renewed without program attendance because their competence as drivers was not seriously in doubt. Even though the program participants had received negative medical and psychological reports, they displayed a lower relapse rate (3.3 percent)

Table 4.10. Structure, Organization, and Distribution of Improvement Programs for Drivers with Several Previous Drinking-and-Driving Convictions in the Federal Republic of Germany

Program model	Organization			Methods
	Sponsor/Organizer	Schedule and duration	Number of participants	
Individual approach	Gesellschaft für Ausbildung, Fortbildung und Nachschulung im Strassenverkehr, e.V., Köln; Technischer Überwachungsverein, Rhineland	13 double periods (6.5 hours of session over four weekends) distributed over a period of four or seven weeks	10 at most	life-style analysis; group discussions; information on the risks inherent in alcohol consumption; task sheets; information material; homework
Behavioristic approach	various TÜVs (technical inspection agencies)	four-week period of self-observation and registration; six sessions (in all 14 hours)	8 at most	group discussions combined with role-playing; analysis of behavior; setting up of individual behavioral targets; self-observation and control measures and exercises; homework
LEER-model	various TÜVs (technical inspection agencies)	12-week period of self-observation and control; follow-up survey a year after program completion; final session (2 hours) two years after program completion	8 at most	group discussions; analysis of drinking behavior; information on drinking and road safety; self-observation and control measures and exercises; methods to modify behavior; homework

than the drivers in the control group (6.7 percent) (Hebenstreit et al. 1981, 1982; Winkler 1982). A final assessment of the success of the program models will, however, be possible only when the full thirty-six-month monitoring period is over.

The sponsors/organizers of driver improvement programs have kept traffic authorities well informed on the organization and evaluation of programs carried out in their jurisdiction. A survey of fourteen traffic authorities undertaken in 1982 revealed that driver improvement programs are basically regarded as helpful in the decision for license renewal. After overcoming the usual difficulties following the introduction of new measures, no major problems have been reported by the administrative authorities. This is also borne out by the high rate of licenses renewed for successful program participants, amounting to 97.1 percent in a regional sample (Winkler 1982).

5. Perspectives

The evaluation studies on driver improvement programs have provided new insights that were not anticipated at the outset. Participants' realistic descriptions of the causes and consequences of undetected drinking-and-driving offenses were particularly revealing on how to approach the problem of undetected cases. Furthermore, important information on the diagnosis of driver ability, the implementation of safety campaigns, and the personal consequences of a drinking-and-driving conviction should also be derived from further study of the participants.

Present efforts in the Federal Republic of Germany toward a more systematic integration of driver improvement programs into the existing legal and administrative framework seem to provide a more promising route to traffic safety in the medium term than do demands for radical changes in sanctions (Winkler 1982). Driver improvement programs can already be considered as making an important and irreplaceable contribution to road safety in the Federal Republic of Germany. However, they cannot be seen as a substitute for legal sanctions and measures.

Driver improvement programs will be effective only as a functioning part of an overall system of measures providing information, support, and feedback. Efficient police control here plays as eminently an important role as does an efficient central system to register offensive road-use behavior. From the perspective of life-long learning, driver improvement programs can have very little effect compared with the lessons that are taught daily through the consequences of active law enforcement on the nation's highways (Winkler 1985).

One further element for a broader program of prevention centers on the sociopolitics of alcohol control, for there is some evidence that the rate of drinking-and-driving offenses tends to increase with the consumption of alcohol by a society (Norström 1983). Driver improvement is essentially a concept addressing the individual. But, consistent with an emerging emphasis in the United States (Mosher 1983), consideration should also be given to the establishment of prevention policies that attempt to influence the social conditions that promote drinking-and-driving offenses (Winkler 1985).

Because driver improvement programs deal with the further training and social reintegration of adult offenders, greater efforts should be made to draw upon the experience acquired in the field of adult education in the training of program leaders and the optimization of program models. What driver improvement programs basically offer is a second chance for adult socialization toward more responsible behavior (Hebenstreit et al. 1982; Winkler 1985).

In conclusion, let us consider once more the effectiveness of police controls, legislative, and educational measures. Deductions from learning theory and research on general prevention have revealed that police actions tend to be more effective than severe sanctions because sanctions generally come too late to have strong psychological effects upon motivation. The law itself is generally still further removed as an influence upon behavior. Previous experience has shown that short-term effects, such as temporary restraint, can be assumed to result from legislative measures. However, once a law is introduced, it is crucially important to examine the quality of its application and execution. And, thus, we come full circle to the control measures of the police and traffic authorities.

Why then are countermeasures often ineffective in the medium term? This brief outline of reasons may provide perspectives for future research.

Cultural Perspective

Alcohol as a drug has been known in the Western world for thousands of years and intensively consumed for centuries. However, until quite recently, hardly any society has succeeded in integrating alcohol consumption into innocuous patterns of behavior by neutralizing the risks associated with its consumption.

Social customs as part of the culture as a whole are slow in changing—often it takes centuries before a change is accomplished. Recent efforts in the fields of legal sociology suggest that an adequate comprehension of the effect of laws can be expected only if they are understood as part of a sociocultural tradition rooted in the structure of economy and society (Kerner 1985). In this connection the social pressures of being caught and the moral disapproval of the offense play an important role.

The motor vehicle has been in use for about one hundred years, and on a widespread basis only about forty years. In the Federal Republic of Germany it has seriously affected the lifestyles of not more than two generations. The process of social reorientation to change dominant attitudes and to practice new behavior modes of drinking-and-driving control will presumably be long and difficult.

Formal and Informal Sanctions

In view of the complicated structure of social control in its entirety, a solution to the problem may be sought by concentrating on primary prevention. Primary prevention, however, can hardly be achieved in the short term by formal judicial methods of social control (Kerner 1985). Driving under the influence of alcohol still is generally regarded as normal behavior and a petty or pardonable offense. Nevertheless, there are some encouraging signs that it is being more negatively assessed in recent years. Most drivers (95 to 98 percent) today probably remain below the legal BAC limit of 80 mg/100 ml. The percentage of drunken drivers caught and sentenced is, however, very low—according to recent surveys not higher than 2 percent (Kerner 1985). A denser network of police controls would probably not increase the "yield" of undetected offenders much beyond the present level. Likewise, stiffer sentences would probably have little effect because studies of chronic offenders point to the presence of deeply rooted personality factors that can only be successfully addressed by more fundamental personal and social influences.

Technical and Procedural Improvements

A considerable percentage of legitimate sanctions cannot be imposed owing to the failure rates of breath and blood tests (false negatives). Improved equipment and a more stringent standardization of on-scene application might increase the rate of convictions noticeably.

With respect to the preventive effect on the individual, however, the mere fact of being caught by the police may suffice to achieve the essential sanctioning effect intended by learning theory, despite the absence of further consequences.

Youthful Offender

The increase in the number of drinking-and-driving offenses among young drivers has been particularly high and adds considerably to the risk factors of adventurousness and lack of driving experience which are typical of the young. There are two reasons why the possibilities of influencing this development are rather limited: First, recent surveys revealed that juvenile alcoholism is generally on the increase (Gebauer 1980; Kerner 1985; Persy 1985), and second, juvenile involvement in road traffic accidents, in particular, has reached frightening proportions in recent years (Heinrich and Hundhausen 1982). In light of these trends, the following combination of measures appears to be appropriate: the use of a probationary driving license for novice drivers, instruction in "alcohol avoidance strategies" as part of driver education, and finally, publicity actions and safety campaigns in schools and companies on a continuous basis.

Public Education and Police Controls

Control and sanctioning have to be integrated still more effectively into a broad concept of educational measures and safety campaigns that are repeated on a continuous basis for combating the disastrous combination of drinking and driving.

Furthermore, special local police surveillance activities should be reported on television, over the radio, and in the press. Finally, following the Dutch practice, random alcohol tests should be legalized in the Federal Republic of Germany in order to determine the BAC-level distribution among motorists and to conduct methodologically sound evaluation studies on safety measures.

PART
3   The American Context

5 The Control of Drinking-Driving in the United States: A Period in Transition?

Joseph R. Gusfield

The story is told that when Adam and Eve were driven out of the Garden of Eden Eve berated her man for their Fall. Having enjoyed the bliss of innocence and plenty they were now suffering the indignities of climate and meager clothing in the environment of a cruel Nature. Adam attempted to assuage her bitterness by remarking, "After all, my dear, we are in a period of transition." Are we now in a period of transition in the control of drinking-driving such that our previous conceptions and conclusions may be passé and limited in their worth?

This question serves as the focal point for this chapter on American controls on drinking and driving, particularly the movements, policies, and legislation that have emerged in the past six to ten years. It is my contention in this chapter that several trends, both independent of and yet also related to each other and to drinking-driving, have converged in the past decade. Although a definitive assessment of their effects is premature, they are too significant in their potential to be ignored in this discussion.

My interest in alcohol issues began in the early 1950s and my specific interest developed in drinking and driving in the early 1970s. Although alcohol issues and drinking-driving were more noticeable in public discussion in the 1970s than in earlier periods, they continued to have a low priority on the agenda of public issues. The past decade, and especially the past seven years, has witnessed a dramatic increase in the salience of alcohol issues, including drinking-driving, in the communications media, in legislatures, and in judicial and law enforcement circles. Drinking-driving has become the focus around which alcohol and traffic safety issues are approached.

Heightened awareness of the drinking-driving problem has been translated into legislation and law enforcement policies. For the first time since repeal of Prohibition (1933) there has been a flood of new legislation placing restrictions on the availability and conditions of

109

sale of alcoholic beverages. Many states have increased the punishment for violating driving under the influence of alcohol (DUI) laws and made apprehension and conviction of offenders easier. A highly visible and active anti-DUI movement has emerged, and the resulting attention to DUI prompted its transition from a minor issue to a major national problem.

The trends and movements responsible for this transition each contributed different perspectives on DUI as a public problem. Public problems can, and often are, conceptualized in different ways by different groups. These diverse frames or perspectives confer different levels of importance to the condition of DUI, often favor different governmental policies, and represent different attitudes toward the problem and its possible amelioration (Spector and Kitsuse 1977; Gusfield 1981a).

Three of these perspectives will be discussed. First, this chapter addresses the "auto safety" perspective, which considers drinking as one among a number of other elements in controlling traffic. The other factors include the design and construction of roads, the use of seat belts, the number of miles driven, and, especially, the manufacture of safer automobiles. The emphasis of the automobile safety perspective in the past two decades has been on automobile design, rather than on the condition of the motorist. The second perspective views drinking and drunkenness as public health concerns within the more general problem of the use of alcoholic substances. In recent years the focus among alcohol and health professionals has been away from emphasis on the person as a victim of alcoholism who needs medical treatment toward prevention of a variety of alcohol problems through policies that affect institutions and environment.

A third orientation is toward drinking-driving as a specific and unique problem. This perspective largely involves a moral dimension: drivers who were drinking and cause accidents and deaths are viewed as more morally reprehensible than those drivers who for other reasons, such as carelessness, fatigue, defective machinery, or automobile design, cause accidents and deaths. Justice and retribution play a significant role in this perspective. Punishing the drinking driver is essential for justice as well as to deter others. The most notable reason for the acceptance of this approach has been the recent emergence of an organized anti-DUI movement in such associations as MADD (Mothers Against Drunk Drivers), RID (Remove Intoxicated Drivers), and SADD (Students Against Drunk Drivers).

The important changes in recent years in government policies toward drinking and driving are related to the emergence of a community of professionals who deal with alcohol problems, a community of recovering alcoholics, and the sharply increased role of the federal government in alcohol problems and automobile safety. However, it is my contention that the most significant changes have resulted from the organized movements that believe drinking-driving is a serious criminal act and deserves a more severe punishment.

Each of the perspectives outlined above may be in conflict with others, may support each other, or may be indifferent and unaffected by any other. I contend that, with some qualifications, they have emerged in confluence and cooperation. This chapter first describes each of these in their historical development and then analyzes their influence on drinking and driving by examining recent changes in legislation, patterns of alcohol consumption, and death rates from automobile accidents, and specifically, from DUI-related automobile accidents. This chapter concludes with an assessment of the possible future of the changes that have occurred in the recent decade.

The Limits of DUI Research

At the outset of this inquiry several towering impediments to a clear response to my initial question must be addressed. These arise from a number of different sources among which the following are significant: the limited character of the available data; the complex interactions between variables; and the historical period in which this chapter is written, along with the diversity of meanings and perspectives within which the subject is itself characterized and the public problem posed.

The Limited Character of DUI Data

Almost all scholarly DUI studies are dependent, in one way or another, on official records of enforcement agencies, coroners' statistics, and local, state, and federal agencies. This has two consequences. First, the vast amount of behavior constituting the events of drinking and driving go undetected and unreported and thus are outside the ken of most published studies. This difficulty, which Ross refers to as the "dark figure" problem, must be kept in mind (Ross 1984b). There is a cultural and social organization in which the daily events of DUI are situated, to support and/or resist DUI. This unofficial, informal, and interactive "society" may itself be in process of change. Although our meager knowledge of this "dark side" to DUI studies is important, for the purpose of this chapter this problem needs only to be noted.[1]

Second, DUI data is problematic because official records are often misleading or lacking in completeness and methodological utility. They are the outcomes of social organizations for which disinterested research skills and methodological competence are often lacking (Kitsuse and Cicourel 1963; Cicourel 1968; Gusfield 1981).

The Complex Interaction of the Variables

The key index in determining DUI events is the blood alcohol level (BAL) in connection with some variable that distinguishes an unwelcome event, such as arrest or accident or death. Both the measurement of the BAL and the outcome, the dependent variable, are subject to severe limitations, not only of sampling, but also of the confluence of elements that interact to produce the outcome.

One example of confounding circumstances involves DUI fatalities and young drivers. Young people (aged sixteen to twenty-five) are disproportionately represented among the automobile fatalities who were found to have been drinking above the legal limit, 0.10 in most states. However, among other confounding elements, young people have less experience with drinking or driving, are more likely than older people to drive in the nighttime and on weekends, and are more likely to suffer automobile fatalities when sober than are older people. They are more likely than other older drinking drivers to come to the attention of authorities. The appearance of alcohol is not a complete explanation of the differences between age groups in automobile fatalities or even DUI fatalities (Carlson 1973; Zylman 1968a, 1973; Gusfield 1985).

The Present Historical Period

Whether the trends observed over the past few years will continue and with what results is still uncertain. The reported studies and statistics are one to two years behind the present writing of this chapter (January 1987). By the time this chapter is published it may be so out of date as to mar its value as a description or assessment of legal and social controls.

Since the late 1930s, and especially since the 1960s, DUI has been the object of thousands of studies, many aimed at evaluating the effects of official controls or countermeasures. Despite all this sound and fury, the significance is only slightly more than in Shakespeare's time. Our knowledge is meager, incomplete, and often misleading. This chapter cannot produce certainty but it can identify the issues that deter clarity and consistency about the control of DUI.

DUI: The Perspective of Safe Transportation

At a recent conference on DUI, Frank Haight, editor of the journal *Accident Analysis and Prevention,* summed up one view of automobile safety: "It is probably fair to say that the transportation community now regards accidents as an unfortunate, but unavoidable, price to pay for the enormous benefits of road transportation" (Haight 1985, 14–15).

Whatever the validity of that remark, it does point to a conflict between widespread use of the automobile and traffic safety. In its present form, as in the past, the automobile is an inherently "dangerous instrument." Efforts at establishing control over the automobile by government and others have frequently been torn between the goals of speedier, less expensive traffic flow and interest in preventing the deaths, injuries, and property losses associated with accidents. Haight's statement suggests that there are limits to how much safety we can buy without diminishing automobile use.

Driving is a ubiquitous event in the United States. Most adults have driver's licenses and use them. In 1983 65 percent of Americans of *all ages* had a license to drive. Widespread use of the automobile and limited availablity of public transportation are a necessary background to the problems of DUI. The dependence of the American economy on driving and the relation of the automobile to consumer habits and styles of leisure are also basic data.

In the historical development of the automobile in America the major avenue of traffic control has been the building of more and better roads. Safety was a goal but of less concern than the provision of roads. In the early years of the automobile's emergence, safety did have a prominent position in government policies, particularly in legislation designed to protect nonmotorized road users and pedestrians (R. Baker 1971). The early development of a mass consumer market in the United States in the 1920s, however, prompted a shift in emphasis toward supporting traffic flow, rather than safety, as a major goal of traffic legislation.

As the automobile became increasingly common in the United States, control of traffic passed from being largely an individual matter under the direction of general rules to being the concern of the states, enforced through specific laws and specialized agencies. Speed limits changed from general principles, such as "reasonable and safe," to specific miles per hour posted along streets and highways. During the 1920s most states utilized local and county police as traffic law enforcers but added to them a new force in the form of state highway patrols (Cressey 1975).

It is comparatively recent that considerable attention has been paid to the design of safer automobiles. In the period between World War I and World War II some of the basic research on traffic safety did focus on the automobile and its design. This research, largely sponsored by the U.S. armed forces, led to such elements of automobile design as the padded dashboard, the collapsible steering wheel, and seat belts. However, the hearings on the National Highway Safety Act of 1966 revealed that the amount spent on research on automobile safety by the automobile industry was less than 0.1 percent of its profits (U.S. Congress 1968).

The reason for this lack of emphasis on automobile design was that, until the 1960s, traffic safety problems were either connected with the building of roads or seen as matters of the individual motorist responding to traffic laws. The development of the federal Department of Transportation in 1960 and the agency within it, the National Highway Traffic Safety Administration (1966), marked the appearance on a national basis of major governmental agencies directed specifically toward automobile safety. NHTSA's primary activities have been to supervise the automobile industry and mandate more safely designed automobiles. Its perspective has been toward the automobile industry rather than toward either laws or education directed at the individual motorist (Gusfield 1981a, chap. 2).

Within this perspective of the safety professional, drinking-driving laws are among a number of possible policies directed toward controlling the motorist. It is debatable that DUI laws should necessarily have primacy as a measure to provide traffic safety. The Insurance Institute for Highway Safety, reflecting the position of the late William Haddon (its director for many years and the first head of the NHTSA before that), grants much more importance to the design of the automobile and the prevention of injury as the most appropriate safety measures (Insurance Institute for Highway Safety 1986; Haddon 1972).

From this standpoint DUI is seen as a legitimate problem but not as an object for effective countermeasures. From this perspective what is to be prevented and controlled is injury and damage, whatever their source. The effect of the accident is the object of study and concern. All variables affecting safety are equally worthy of being assessed for their relation to that event and for the practicable possibilities of controlling them. The controllers are cast in the role of traffic facilitators. DUI is a facet of the problems produced by the automobile but not necessarily the best object of policies. Ralph Nader, whose writings and experiences helped the passage of the NHTSA act, once said that the aim should be to have the automobile industry produce an automobile that would be safe under the assumption that fools and drunks would drive it.

The entry of the federal government into the field of traffic safety and the attendant controls over the design of automobiles has been a major set of events in traffic safety. Localities and states, however, have jurisdiction over such matters as speed limits. In the 1970s, spurred by the oil crisis, the U.S. Congress passed legislation recommending a fifty-five mile per hour speed limit on highways. Not having direct jurisdiction in this matter, they put "teeth' into it by threatening to diminish highway funds to states that did not comply with the recommendation.

Where the traffic safety perspective and other perspectives converge is in the laws directed at controlling the motorist. Such laws include requiring obedience to posted signs and stoplights, speed limits, driver's licensing, and DUI, as well as the host of statutes that comprise the state vehicle codes. The enforcement of these laws emerged in the 1920s and exists today in substantially the same form: the use of police as agents of laws directed against the person—the motorist. This system, involving local police, traffic squads, and state highway police, operates through mechanisms of detection, arrest or citation, and punishment through fines and, in some instances, loss of license or even imprisonment. This system of deterring the driver through fear of punishment or penalty has, with one major exception (minimum age for alcohol sales), dominated public attempts to limit and control drinking and driving. It is preventive in nature, attempting to diminish the occurrence of accidents. (It should be distinguished from events that involve DUI as a felony, when injury or death has occurred.)

The automobile has become the most frequent source of relationship between police and citizens. Parking regulations are, perhaps, the most often used source of citizen citation for breach of law. There are more than ten million such citations in California alone every year (Judicial Council of California 1985). Although cases involving automobile accidents are among the most frequent source of negligence suits, and automobile theft is the third most frequently committed felony (Thomas and Hepburn 1983, 84), traffic violations remain the most frequently committed "crime" in the United States.

The quotes around crime are placed to indicate that referring to parking and "routine" traffic violations begs a significant question. Are traffic violations criminal acts? Is drinking-driving a criminal act? For the sociologist, as for many citizens, whatever may be the legal designations, the behavior of many persons may not be congruent with the legal definitions. H. Laurence Ross has coined the term "folk crime" to point to the discrepancy between a legal view of acts as crimes and a popular, public view that is opposite (Ross 1960).

No figures exist on the number of Americans who have ever committed a traffic offense or have been cited for an offense. Certainly it would be a large percentage of all drivers. Characteristically, events such as illegal parking, driving above the posted speed limits, or making a turn against posted prohibitions are not regarded by friends, spouses, relatives, or even strangers as moral derelictions in the same category as felonious assault, embezzlement, automobile theft, or even public drunkenness. Applications for employment that ask if the applicant has ever been convicted of a crime usually either specifically exempt traffic offenses or assume such. These are folk crimes; ones committed by many people or viewed by many as human acts that may be dangerous or foolish but not opening the actor to moral disapproval.

In this classification of crimes, where is DUI? In the perspective of traffic safety, laws that attempt to regulate the motorist are judged not by the moral status of the action to be controlled but by the laws' relation to automobile accidents and by their expediency as policy goals for preventing accidents and attendant damage and injury. In the detached perspective of traffic safety, the drinking driver is per se no more or less derelict than drivers who misuse roads, fail to use seat belts, or are fatigued.

DUI: The Perspective of Alcohol Use and Health

From the perspective of an interest in public health, DUI is a facet of the problems produced by beverage alcohol. The countermeasures associated with the consumption and distribution of alcohol are central in this concern. As is true of the traffic safety controllers, laws that attempt to deter the motorist from drinking or from driving are only one means among many in developing a policy to minimize drinking problems or to achieve a safer highway. It is just as logical to control the institutions that sell alcohol, to treat chronic alcoholics or "alcohol abusers," and to maintain high prices on alcohol as it is to prohibit and punish DUI as a way of promoting automobile safety. As in the transportation perspective, institutional regulation exists as an alternative to regulation of the person. However, unlike the transportation perspective, the control of alcohol has a history that makes more difficult the consideration of alcohol control policies completely apart from moral perspectives.

Drinking and drunkenness have been a far more salient political issue in American life than in most industrialized countries. With the exception of the Scandinavian nations, the United States is unusual in the degree of public concern and legislation attempting to limit the use of alcohol.[2] It is the only nation to have prohibited the sale of alcoholic beverages entirely, as it did in the passage and maintenance of Prohibition (1917–1933). The American temperance movement has a long history, commencing in the 1820s and never quite disappearing from the American public scene. Its importance for the topic of DUI lies in the meaning which alcohol has come to display among large segments of the American population and in public life.

The conflicting orientations toward alcohol that have dominated American policies since the repeal of the Prohibition amendment (1933) are revealed in two general conclusions that describe the American system until approximately 1980.

The first of these conclusions is the belief that alcohol is a "dangerous commodity." Its use is restricted by laws limiting the time, place, manner, and person of consumption. Consistently, since the early 1940s, one-third of American adults report that they do not use alcohol (Gallup 1985). No state treats alcohol or its sale or use as just another commodity. It has a particular legal status which, in every state, places some restrictions on its availability and use.

The second of these general conclusions is that drinking is an accepted custom in American society. Since repeal (1933) the public problem of alcohol has been defined largely as that of deviant drinkers who develop personal pathologies and addictions (Gusfield 1982; Beauchamp 1980). Chronic alcoholism has been defined as the major problem caused by the use of alcohol. Until recently, the treatment and prevention of alcoholism has been the primary aim of public alcohol policies. Efforts to restrict the availability of alcohol have not been increased. Neither drinking nor even drunkenness but deviant drinking has been the object of public policy.

With repeal, alcohol policy became a minor issue in American politics. Federal concern was minimal and state governments played a small role. Private organizations, such as Alcoholics Anonymous and the National Council on Alcoholism were the major "owners" of the alcohol problem in the United States. This began to change in the late 1960s with the establishment of the National Institute for Alcohol Abuse and Alcoholism, an agency of the Department of Health and Human Services. During the 1960s, organizations such as the National Council on Alcoholism, largely the outlet for recovering alcoholics, and the North American Association of Alcohol and Drug Professionals, largely the outlet for people engaged in treatment of alcoholics, were active in obtaining federal aid for treatment, research, and other programs concerned with alcohol. Their efforts were capped by the passage of legislation establishing the National Institute for Alcohol Abuse and Alcoholism in 1970. In this fashion alcohol issues became a federal responsibility for public health. Not only did this spur the development of state and county programs for alcoholism treatment, but it brought about a new climate of research and public exposure for the gamut of possible alcohol issues.

A great amount of ambivalence about alcohol exists in the American culture. Not only is there the past legacy of the political battle between "'wets" and "drys," there is also the perception of drinking as dangerous and yet accepted and appreciated. Within the movements concerned with "the alcohol problem" these ambivalences have been manifested in conceptions derived from concerns with health and those derived from moral disapproval of drunkenness. Since repeal there has been a sustained effort to define alcoholism as a disease and to bring to it less morally condemnatory attitudes than have existed in the past (Jellinek 1960). The effort to reconceptualize alcoholism as a medical rather than a moral failing has only been partially successful (Schneider 1978; Beauchamp 1980).

From the standpoint of alcohol problems, DUI is one among a variety of concerns, including public drunkenness, alcoholism, and labor force productivity. Where the traffic safety perspective focuses on the automobile, the alcohol perspective focuses on the substance of alcohol and/or the user. Within each, the person—the motorist or the drinker—is one element in the system. In some historical periods such as Prohibition, the substance has been emphasized. In others, the person, as in driver education campaigns, has been emphasized. We can express this set of alternatives as those of substance abuse or abusive substance. In the past decade alcohol policy has been moving away from a concentration on substance abuse toward a conception of abusive substance. The watchword is shifting from treatment to prevention.

During the late 1960s and through the 1970s two federal agencies— the Department of Transportation and the Department of Health, Education and Welfare—became centers of concern for drinking and driving. The problem was now open to two diverse perspectives toward DUI. One was the perspective of traffic control and traffic safety. The other was the concern for alcohol abuse, a facet of public health concerned with accidents but also with a condition of the person—alcoholism. Each represented a different constituency and a different notion of where the DUI problem was located and what significance it possessed. In terms I have used elsewhere, the ownership of the problem of DUI and its conceptualization were differently constructed (Gusfield 1981a, chap. 2).

The countermeasures associated with the consumption and distribution of alcohol are central in a concern for prevention. As is true of the traffic safety controllers, laws that attempt to deter the motorist from drinking or from driving are only one means among many in developing a policy to minimize drinking problems or to achieve a safer highway. It is just as logical to control the institutions that sell alcohol, to treat chronic alcoholics or "alcohol abusers," and to maintain high prices on alcohol as it is to prohibit and punish DUI. During the 1970s these policies, aimed at prevention of a variety of alcohol problems, assumed great importance in the research and policy fields. They came to supplement, and perhaps even supplant, the previous emphasis on alcoholism as the major alcohol problem and treatment as the major recommended policy (Moore and Gerstein 1981; Gusfield 1982).

DUI: The Perspective of Morality and Justice

In one of his essays on punishment, H. L. A. Hart points out that while different behaviors may result in the same consequences, they do not possess the same moral status and thus do not admit to the justice of similar punishments. The Ming vase, he writes, is just as broken as a result of carelessness as of vandalism but punishing each act equally would be offensive to the moral sense of most people.

From this perspective DUI has the status of a morally condemned act. It differs from other traffic offenses such as speeding, making an illegal turn, or even reckless driving. In most states it is a misdemeanor punishable by a jail sentence. In cases in which an injury has occurred, the DUI motorist is guilty of a felony.

Over the 165 years of antialcohol agitation in the United States, health has by no means been a major concern of the movements. The moral disapproval of drinking and drunkenness has played a major role, especially in the movements led by the Protestant churches that culminated in Prohibition (Gusfield 1963). In much of the research and the public discussion of alcohol there exists what James Collins has called the "malevolent assumption"—the assumption that whenever drinking is associated with an unwelcome event, it is the cause of that event (Collins 1982, 152–206).

The moral condemnation of the drinking driver has achieved a wide consensus in society, and has been translated into DUI legislation. Intuitively the belief has existed widely that drinking and driving is risky. Even though the issue of DUI has had a low place on the agenda of public problems, public discussion has seldom included a pro-DUI position. District attorneys and other public officials have continuously made public statements that supported the unique, moral excoriation of the drinking driver. Drinking-driving has a moral connotation that other sources of traffic danger lack. The image of the drinking driver is that of the "killer drunk" whose intoxication is immoral because he threatens "innocent" individuals. His behavior is villainous and those he puts at risk are his victims: passengers, pedestrians, and other motorists.

Within the drama of the drinking driver, the issue of punishment has been the focus of much public comment. The moral status of the drinking driver and the search for punishment are clear in this typical public statement in a Buffalo, New York, newspaper in 1976: "As a result of a total breakdown in law enforcement and the district attorney's 'game plan' an estimated 6,000 drunk drivers will be poured back onto Erie County streets—the majority of them unpunished and with little incentive for rehabilitation" (quoted in Gusfield, 1981a, 139).

I cannot read statements such as these without a sense of the moral indignation in which the image of the drinking driver is enveloped. Such statements are seldom made about speeding or drivers whose autos are in need of repair. This attitude is by no means recent in the public denunciation of the DUI offender. He (most often) is described as drunk, rather than under the influence; as delinquent, rather than careless; and as deserving punishment rather than penalty. In the arenas of public talk and action DUI has had the status of more than a traffic offense, more than a folk crime.

Who is being protected by DUI laws? From some perspectives, especially the transportation safety view, the drinking driver is victim of his actions as is the other driver or pedestrian involved in an accident. From other perspectives, certainly the moral view, it is the "innocent" pedestrian, passenger, or driver whose sobriety gives support to a claim of victimization.

There is a decided contrast between the moral indignation that has been characteristic of public statements about drinking-driving and the detached analysis of the traffic safety or alcohol problems "expert." In a substantial manner these groups talk past each other. They represent different conceptual domains and policy priorities. Although they may agree on DUI legislation, they differ profoundly on the significance they attribute to it and in the emotions that they express.

Control of the Drinking Driver in the 1970s

After World War II two processes began to develop that provided for a changed climate toward the control of alcohol and drinking-driving in the United States. One was the development of a technology that made police detection of drinking drivers more practicable. The other, occurring in the 1960s, was the growth of a research and policy community concerned with alcohol issues and supported by the federal government. There are sharp limits to the impact of each of these on drinking-and-driving behavior in the United States. Neither has succeeded in placing alcohol problems high on the public agenda.

Quite early in the history of the American automobile DUI was seen as a danger to safety. California passed its first DUI law in 1911. However, this intuitive belief in the danger of mixing driving and drinking was not backed by scientific research nor were such laws capable of ready enforcement until a technology for detection of drinking-driving was perfected.

By the 1930s, methods existed to test the blood alcohol level and, with the invention of the breathalyzer in the 1930s, a fast and accurate instrument of detection enabled police to substantiate claims. Before that, detecting DUI depended on observational evidence that made prosecution difficult and hazardous (Zylman 1968b). The first scientific research into the effects of alcohol on driving did not occur until the 1930s (Holcomb 1938; H. E. Heise 1934). Not until the early 1960s did a body of research emerge to support the intuitive claim that drinking is positively related to automobile accidents and deaths (Gusfield 1981a, chaps. 2, 3; U.S. Congress 1968).

As with traffic controls, the entry of the federal government into the drinking-driving arena is of fundamental importance. The first major report on DUI is that of the NHTSA to Congress in 1968 (U.S. Congress 1968). This was mandated under the NHTSA act passed in 1966. Much of the vast research conducted in the United States on DUI in the past two decades is supported by either the Department of Transportation or the National Institute of Alcohol Abuse and Alcoholism.

Since the mid-1960s police units specializing in apprehension of DUI offenders have appeared in a number of American cities. The Department of Transportation underwrote the Alcohol Safety Action Projects (ASAP) to diminish accidents and deaths through an experiment in increased enforcement in the 1970s. The program provided funds to state agencies to increase enforcement of DUI laws. Comparison of deaths involving DUI motorists on a before-after basis were then compared to similar data from non-ASAP states. The results of the ASAP study, though much debated, were at best inconclusive, at worst negative. There was no clear evidence that the projects succeeded in reducing accidents or deaths resulting from DUI (Zador 1976).

The ASAP projects were largely efforts to increase enforcement through more and better trained police. Similar efforts to increase enforcement through special units of police specializing in DUI law enforcement have yielded similar results in studies. Increased arrests for DUI have not been followed by a decrease in automobile deaths nor by a decrease in those deaths resulting from DUI (Zylman 1975; Gusfield 1972).

Prosecuting attorneys and judges have had available to them a repertoire of consequences for DUI from which they might choose in whole or in part. Judges might elect from a stipulated range of fines, might impose a jail sentence to be executed or suspended, or might recommend to the Department of Motor Vehicles that the offender's driving license be suspended or revoked for a period of time. As a stipulation for suspension of study, the judge might impose many kinds of conditions on the offender, such as writing the judge a letter every week, not drinking, attending Alcoholics Anonymous meetings, or even performing publicly needed work in lieu of going to jail. One alternative, which is commented on below, has been the practice of requiring attendance at special classes on drinking problems for both first offenders and recidivists.

Again the research results have been both ambiguous and inconclusive. Studies of enforcement in the 1970s have substantiated H. Laurence Ross's results from his study of the British Breathalyzer Act of 1973. In the first flush of publicity, deaths from DUI appear to decrease, but after a while (a year in the Ross study) enforcement becomes marred by legal limitations posed by procedural challenges and enforcement becomes lax. In the American studies, prior to the recent wave of alcohol and DUI concerns in the late 1970s, jail sentences were rarely meted out. Those that were often were suspended. Even license suspension or revocation was not the usual course of sentencing. A fine, approximately $150 to $300, was typical. Even the license suspension or revocation appeared to have limited results. Studies showed that one-third of all licensees drove without licenses anyway (Coppin and van Oldenbeek 1965). A study of San Diego County showed no difference between deaths due to DUI before and after establishment of a special DUI squad (Gusfield 1972).

Typically, as with many crimes, courts utilized less restrictive and stringent punishments than were available to them (Feeley 1979). The large amount of DUI arrests and the threat of trial was a perfect setting for plea bargaining. Whatever the public display of a consensus that drinking-driving was a "serious" crime, in the behavior of police, attorneys, and courts it was scarcely more than a traffic offense with a much higher fine.

This discrepancy between the public drama of criminal violation and the routine enforcement of a minor offense characterizes the DUI situation in the United States toward the end of the 1970s (Ross 1982; Gusfield 1981a). There is rationality in the attitude of many drinkers whose experience has indicated that the risk of accident or arrest at any time is not great. Although the chance of an accident has been estimated at about three times greater when DUI than when not, the probability of any single trip being interrupted by accident or arrest has been estimated as less than one in one thousand (Summers and Harris 1978; Beitel et al. 1975).

The second process—the growth of an alcohol research and policy community—affected the definition and policy discussion of alcohol issues. In the early 1970s the federal government assumed a role in alcohol issues on a large scale for the first time since Prohibition. Although it did so out of the interest in treatment of alcoholism, the research and policy community began to focus attention on preventive measures using tax policy, communications, and laws governing the sale and availability of alcohol. Spurred by activities and research in other countries as well as the antismoking campaigns, the professional community turned its attention to policies other than treatment of alcoholics and to alcohol problems other than alcoholism (Gusfield 1982; Moore and Gerstein 1981). Such concerns remained in the confines of the professional community of alcohol scholars and agency officials. DUI remained a minor problem in the American public arena. Alcoholism occupied the center of the small stage in the small theater of the public problem of drinking.

MADD: Dramatizing the "Killer Drunk" and His Victims

In May of 1980 Cari Lightner, a thirteen-year-old girl, was struck and killed while walking on the sidewalk by an automobile driven by a driver who was DUI and who had been arrested a few days before on a DUI charge. Her mother, Candy Lightner, sought, at first unsuccessfully, to arouse government action for new DUI legislation. She did gain the attention of journalists, however, and by the end of 1980 had brought about a California Governor's Task Force on Drinking-Driving and launched a movement that changed the national climate of attention to public problems of alcohol and drinking-driving. She called her organization MADD, an acronym for Mothers Against Drunk Drivers.

MADD was followed by other organizations directed toward a stricter policy of punishment of drinking drivers. Together they have created a new movement that has given a dramatic form to an issue that had been dormant in American life. The very name, MADD, presents the symbols that carry an expressive imagery. "Mothers" puts the issue in a framework of violence against children. "Against" provides an emotional sense of battle and of enemies. "Drunk drivers" provides an image of the DUI as socially irresponsible and out of self-control. This is the "killer drunk" who constitutes the villain of the story.

MADD has brought to the public arena the emotional and dramatic expression of the public as victim. It drew its membership from many who had either been injured or had family members injured or killed in a DUI event (Reinerman 1985; Weed 1985). In moving the issue of DUI into a higher place of public concern, MADD, RID (Remove Intoxicated Drivers), and SADD (Students Against Drunk Drivers) presented the issue of DUI as one of justice and retribution, of bringing the DUI to a deserved punishment and, through this, deterring others. The materials of the movement are filled with accounts of people killed or injured by drinking drivers and the minor punishment imposed on such drivers. As a MADD newsletter put it in 1982: "MADD is the voice of the victim" (MADD 1982, 1).

This capacity to characterize DUI as a drama of villains and victims has produced a moral fervor that moved the problem from its shadowy existence into the light of public mobilization. Lightner maintained that hers was an effort "to get the dirty secret out." In this the media of communications were influential. A television dramatization of Candy Lightner's tragedy and her efforts to move government and the courts to action gave the movement a great help. It enabled the movement to identify all drinking drivers with the "killer drunk."

Emerging in the late 1970s and early 1980s these organizations have had a catalytic effect on the problem of DUI and, as a by-product, on the public control of alcohol. Much of the effort of this movement has gone into the passage and enforcement of more severe DUI laws. Especially is this the case with per se laws and more determinate sentences. In California, for example, the DUI laws were changed in 1982 to make a BAL of .10 for motorists per se illegal. Prior to that, the BAL was evidence of DUI but was rebuttable. Now a forty-eight-hour jail sentence became mandatory on all convicted DUI offenders. A number of states have passed similar changes in DUI laws.

But the movement has had other consequences. It helped bring about the first National Commission Against Drunk Driving, which sparked a move toward increasing the minimum age of legal sale of alcohol. Many American states had made it illegal to sell alcohol to persons below the age of twenty-one, others to lower ages, but none below eighteen. With the age of voting uniformly dropped to eighteen, many states had lowered the minimum age of drinking (Wechsler 1980). Supported by studies of increased automobile casualties among the young, the commission had recommended a return to a higher minimum age. Again the federal government attached such recommendations to the distribution of state highway funds and many states have raised their minimum age.

The movement has not been without support, from government as well as private sources. The federal government has provided grants to help the anti-DUI organizations (MADD 1982). Although it may have drawn some adherents from the reputed increase in "tough" policies toward crime, the movement has not shown an interest in other areas of law enforcement or in crime in general.

Nor have the anti-DUI organizations displayed great interest in the social control of alcohol. Although they have supported some legislation to control the sale of alcohol, such as limits on price discounts of individual drinks (the "happy hour" custom), they have not embraced the prevention programs that have constituted the "new temperance movement." The drinking-driver and DUI laws have remained the focus of the movement (Ungerleider and Bloch 1986).

With the emergence of the anti-DUI movement, both DUI and the social control of alcohol have undergone a rapid and widespread change. The movement did not emerge in a vacuum. A public consensus about the evil of DUI has existed for several decades in the United States, even though muted and immobilized. The developments of the 1970s had built a research and policy community that, even though relatively limited in power, could be utilized in the new atmosphere of public concern. Nevertheless the ability of the movement to provide a symbolism, an imagery, and a dramatic focus was a potent catalyst.

The "New Temperance Movement": A Period in Transition?

After decades of quiescence, DUI has come out of the cold and is now a "hot" issue, high on the agenda of public attention. In that sense DUI is in process of change in the public consciousness and the political arena. So too is a wide spectrum of anti-alcohol preventive measures. Is it all sound and fury, signifying very little alteration of behavior, by drinkers or by law enforcement agencies or both? New legislation is enacted but its effectiveness is not assured by its passage. Symbolic and ritualistic public acts have an importance but in this chapter my interest is in the more literal implications of the new era, or what I and others have come to call "the new temperance movement."

What is occurring is the effects of several separate trends and movements that have become mutually supportive. The anti-DUI movements have galvanized the activities and provided additional support to efforts of traffic safety policy and anti-alcohol programs. In turn these have affected DUI. Within this general series of actions there are indications of a change in American health habits emerging independently of public control efforts and affecting the use of alcohol. It is too early to pronounce an assessment of these activities on DUI. However, there has been a long-run decline in automobile deaths and a more distinct possibility of a decline in the rate of DUI-involved deaths than has been true of past decades in the United States.

Alcohol Control and Consumption

MADD and other anti-DUI organizations have frequently declared they are not movements to restore Prohibition nor are they opposed to drinking. Their support for measures to raise the minimum age for sale of alcohol has been defended solely as an anti-DUI policy. Yet in raising the issue of DUI, the movement has given an impetus to the turn toward prevention that had been developing in the 1970s.

The emphasis of MADD and the other organizations is on the drinking-driver and punishment as deterrent and as justice. Yet a whole series of measures are under consideration and to some extent passed that involve a wider effort to create a less conducive atmosphere to drinking by the general public. Not only has the minimum age of sale been raised while the voting age has been lowered but other measures to limit the sale and use of alcohol are on the public agenda. Measures to limit the "happy hours" (lowered prices for drinks during the cocktail hours), to shorten hours of sale, to make bars and even hosts liable for DUI damages, to curtail advertising of alcoholic beverages, to provide health warnings on bottled goods, and to limit outlets through zoning are all under active public discussion and, in some instances, have been both the object and the outcome of serious legislative debate.

The model for these efforts, in the discussion circles of alcohol policy groups, is the success of the public health campaign against the use of cigarettes. It unites the moral fervor of the anti-DUI concerns with the public health interests of government agencies and a public seemingly more attuned to health issues than in previous generations.

There is some evidence of a decline in alcohol consumption in recent years in the United States as reported by the beverage alcohol industry (*Johnson's Liquor Handbook* 1986) and on sales tax and receipts (U.S. Department of Health and Human Services 1986). During the decade of the 1970s per capita alcohol consumption of the population aged fourteen and over increased. However, almost all of that increase came from the greater use of beer and wine. Whiskies only increased by 1 percent and, since the late 1970s, have steadily declined in use. The use of wine appears to have hit a plateau. Beer, which accounts for half of the alcohol consumed, had also hit a plateau in use. In the past year for which statistics are available (1985), per capita beer use dropped for the first time in many years. It would appear that the ascending curve of alcohol consumption characteristic in the 1970s is at an end.

Is the United States becoming a nation of more moderate drinkers than was the case two decades ago? It is playful to speculate on the possible reasons for such a trend. The growing health consciousness and the turn of medicine toward prevention rather than treatment may be among the noncontrol sources of such a trend. The grass-roots movements may play a role but moderation appeared even before the movement made headlines.

However, a degree of caution must be kept in mind before the funeral of John Barleycorn is arranged. First, the trends are most recent and the bulk of the decline in absolute alcohol consumption has come in the use of whiskies. There have been peaks and troughs in the midst of general trendlines before and it will take a few more years to indicate if anything long-lasting is at work. But the second caveat is more significant. We do not have any clear conception of the relation between total consumption and alcohol problems other than cirrhosis of the liver. It is not the amount consumed but the clustering of consumption in the form of drunkenness or DUI events that is vital to DUI. There are almost no studies that have attempted to measure the relation of total consumption of alcohol to the number of such events.[3]

Enforcement of DUI Laws

Death from DUI is a conclusion established by a variety of data affected by imperfect systems of records gathering. All automobile fatalities are not routinely tested for BAL in all jurisdictions. Even when the effort is made there are limitations. In some instances there is too great a time gap between the accident and the death; in some the condition of the corpse is such that a BAL is unobtainable. Age and general condition of health and access to emergency hospital services affect the death or recovery of accident victims. The use or nonuse of safety belts affects the event of fatality. Suicides are not always distinguishable from accidental deaths. All of these variables appear differentially related to alcohol involvement. Because all these variables are changing through time the conclusions drawn from before and after DUI death rates are inconclusive about the deterrent or nondeterrent effects of increased punishments.

Records and statistics of DUI deaths are distorted by the differential effectiveness of state and local agencies in gathering such data. The Fatal Accident Reporting Service of the U.S. Department of Transportation represents the most uniform source of data on automobile deaths for the entire country. It came into existence only in 1977. Until last year, only fifteen states in the United States had succeeded in testing more than eighty percent of motorists killed in automobile accidents (Fell 1982). More than 50 percent of all motorist deaths in the United States were unexamined for BAL in 1984. BAL tests of surviving drivers are even less often performed or reported. There is also an analysis of the FARS evidence to suggest that the testing and reporting procedures are biased in a manner that inflates the degree of DUI among automobile fatalities (Voas 1984b).

Moreover, it is highly important to recognize the "malevolence assumption" in much of the literature, both academic and popular, about DUI. This is the assumption that the fault of the accident is attributable to the driver, and only to one of the drivers and, if alcohol was present in one of the drivers, his or her driving was responsible for the accident. I know of only one study that made an effort to test this assumption. It found the drinking driver responsible in 60 percent of the cases when one of the drivers was DUI (Boston University School of Law–Medicine Institute 1969). Such studies, of course, necessarily do not take into account such features as road conditions, age and condition of cars, time of day or night. Such features act in combination with other conditions, such as the motorist, in determining the final event.

Consider the high rates of DUI deaths for young males (ages sixteen to twenty-five). Even if other elements were equal, such as drinking amounts, young men would still show high rates of DUI death. First, young men are disproportionately likely to be involved in any kind of automobile accident. Second, young men have less experience with drinking and with driving than older men. Both of these increase the likelihood of young men appearing in the list of DUI automobile fatalities. Third, as discussed above, young men are more likely than older men to drive at night when, for all groups, fatal automobile accidents are more likely.

Despite all the difficulties of obtaining definitive conclusions about the relation between drinking-driving and accidents, one generalization has remained fixed. The conclusion of the classic 1964 study of Grand Rapids by Robert Borkenstein and his associates has been confirmed in many places and in many studies: driving under the influence of alcohol increases the risk of accident and increasing amounts of alcohol increase the risk further. This is the bedrock foundation of DUI policy, whatever the degree of risk involved.

Yet, whatever research may show concerning alcohol use and accident risk, we must place this knowledge in context. Automobile deaths result from a number of considerations, one of which is DUI. They are affected by the total amount of driving, which may fluctuate. They are affected by the general safety of automobile design, which has been changing. For many years, for whatever reasons, the United States had the lowest rate of automobile fatalities per miles driven and per autos owned. At the same time, it had the highest absolute number of automobile deaths in the world and a total number of automobile fatalities that was rising continuously over twenty years (R. Baker 1971; S. Baker et al. 1984). The low rates indicated the decreased possibility that any single driving event would result in an accident. The high absolute figures represented the increased driving in the country.

Second, although this is conjectural, DUI appears to have some relation to the total consumption of alcohol. Studies of states in which the minimum age was lowered and then raised compared with control states do indicate that DUI fatalities among the young have declined (Wechsler 1980; Cook 1981; Wagenaar 1981; Williams 1986).

All of these variables—consumption habits, DUI laws, automobile use, and automobile condition—are occurring in a period of heightened public discussion and awareness of DUI to which DUI laws and movements have themselves contributed. It would be a better course to diminish the concern for a causal analysis of the deterrent effects of DUI laws and consider the historical question of the impact of the total set of events on DUI. What has happened to deaths of motorists who were tested at above .10 since the emergence of the new temperance movement?

There have been several studies of the enforcement of new, tougher DUI laws as well as of their effectiveness in diminishing automobile accidents and fatalities. Studies of enforcement do indicate a general increase in arrests for DUI in American states. The very limited use of jail sentences and/or license suspension and revocation does appear to have ended but the new-era approaches to sentencing have also not resulted in a high degree of jail sentences for first offenses. An analysis of the courts of Alameda County, California, found that of every thousand arrests, half were of recidivists. Of 840 charged, 720 were convicted. Very few cases (eight) were convicted by trial. Of the seven hundred sentenced only one hundred actually served a straight weekend jail term. Most were fined; many (385) had their license suspended or revoked. Of the 330 sentenced to jail, 230 were given weekend work for public activities or given a work furlough. The majority were forced to attend a DUI school or given treatment for alcoholism (Klein 1985).

Although these descriptions do indicate an increase in "severity" of punishment, they also indicate the limited character of that increase. While the DUI schools may diminish recidivism they do not appear to have much effect on accident and death occurrences (Speiglman 1985). License suspension or revocation appears to be a more effective measure, even though as much as a third of those whose licenses are restricted may nevertheless continue to drive.

In a careful study of the impact of the new (1982) California DUI law on injury accident and deaths, Hilton reports that the decline in such deaths in 1982 was no greater than the decline in non-alcohol-related automobile deaths. However, not only was the decline in alcohol-related events more marked in injury accidents but the deaths involving DUI were significantly greater in the first nine months of the second year of enforcement of the new law, contrary to earlier experiences and Ross's studies (Hilton 1984). Hilton's study suggests the difficulty in relating an outcome—automobile death—to a specific independent variable—new DUI laws.

Deaths from DUI

From the perspective of traffic safety, do DUI laws ensure a safer traffic environment for the potential drinking driver or for the sober driver? Here we must examine automobile fatalities as the result of a multiplicity of elements, only one of which is contained in DUI. I have pointed out the multi-causal character of traffic safety as well as the multiple causes that go into accidents even when DUI is present. Deaths from automobiles increased steadily in the United States since the advent of the mass-produced automobile. With the exception of the war years (1941–45) there was no steady and dramatic decline in numbers of motor vehicle deaths until 1973 and the oil crisis (S. Baker et al. 1984, 216). During the same period the American rate of automobile fatalities per automobile owned and per miles driven continued to decline (R. Baker 1971; S. Baker et al. 1984, 215). The paradox is explained by one of the major features of automobile accidents and deaths—the extent to which they are a function of the amount of driving.

Although 54,589 lives were lost in the United States in 1972, the peak year for traffic death, since then the figure has dropped steadily, despite increases in the total population, in automobile ownership, and in licensed drivers, and during periods of increased travel. In 1985 it was 43,555. Similarly the death rate per one hundred million miles traveled dropped from the 1966 rate of 5.72 to the 1985 rate of 2.47 (Insurance Institute for Highway Safety 1986). While numbers of automobile deaths have fluctuated between 1973 and 1985, the general trend has been that of decline (Partya 1983; Fell 1982). The decrease in automobile deaths was especially marked between 1973 and 1974, during the oil crisis, and between 1981 and 1982, during the recession. It rose again in 1983 and 1984 but it has not returned to earlier levels as in 1972. Whatever the implications of the anti-DUI movements on automobile deaths, it cannot be said that they alone have been responsible for a dramatic change in automobile fatalities, since that change began well before the current wave. Have the current waves of DUI legislation had any effect on automobile deaths?

It is difficult to account for the decrease in automobile deaths in the United States in any easy fashion. The diminished driving after the oil crisis and during the recession of 1980–82 appears to have affected total deaths but it cannot have affected deaths per miles driven. Agencies appear to read into the changes whatever fits their existing missions and perspectives. Organizations like MADD and law enforcement agencies attribute it to law and law enforcement. The Insurance Institute for Highway Safety attributes it to the National Highway Traffic Safety Administration and concern for better safety standards in automobile design. Public health authorities attribute it to a more health-conscious public.

The Fatal Accident Reporting Service of the U.S. Department of Transportation has been amassing statistics on automobile accidents since 1977. They have also gathered reports on BAL levels of drivers involved in fatal accidents, although the testing of the surviving driver in a fatal accident is both sporadic and sparse. In the latest such study only 14 percent of surviving drivers were tested for BAL. Drivers killed in crashes were tested only in approximately 50 percent of the cases. However, analysis of the fifteen states with "good" reporting (80 percent or more) of fatally injured drivers does show a decrease in the percentage of drivers who tested above .10. During the long-run decline in automobile deaths the DUI percentage had remained fairly stable, but in the past four years it appears to have declined steadily. Until 1984 the decline was small. The last report available, from 1984, indicates a significant decrease, however.

Consider the following data from the Fatal Accident Reporting Service on the percentage of fatalities, tested in the "good" fifteen reporting states, who had a BAL of 0.10 or above (National Highway Traffic Safety Administration, 1986f):

Percent of Driver Fatalities in Total Automobile
Deaths in Fifteen Selected States, 1980–84

Year	Total Fatalities	Total Driver Fatalities	% Driver Fatalities DUI
1980	51,091	28,816	50
1981	49,301	28,200	49
1982	43,945	24,690	48
1983	42,584	24,138	46
1984	44,241	25,582	43

Whether or not the decline of 1983–84 will continue remains to be seen. So much is happening to improve automobile safety and to diminish consumption of alcohol, especially among the young, that it is too early to have any conclusion about the relative role of increased severity of punishment in affecting a decrease in automobile fatalities. The results of the past few years are suggestive of a diminution in alcohol-involved automobile fatalities greater than the general decrease, whatever the causal mechanisms at work. During this writing, the Insurance Institute for Highway Safety reported a University of Michigan national roadside survey showing a drop in percent of drivers DUI from 4.9 in 1973 to 3.1 in 1986 (Insurance Institute for Highway Safety 1986, 4). Such roadside surveys, however, have some significant problems in interpretation.[4]

It would appear that whatever are the implications of increased severity of DUI laws they are a part of the total processes affecting the downward trend in automobile deaths. To what degree they are effective through a heightened consciousness about alcohol use or automobile safety or through direct deterrence based on fear of punishment is a question that at present eludes our answering.

The occurence of alcohol-related problem behavior seems to be diminishing but it is much too early to pronounce that the issue has been settled.

Conclusion

The current period of DUI control in the United States is unique in the history of the past fifty years. In intensity, in scope, and in effects, it may be having a decided influence on American behavior. Such an assessment is made with considerable reservation, given the short time the new legislation has existed, the limitations of data, and the few studies completed and available. The DUI movement, although itself of considerable importance, is both affected by and affects the wider new temperance movement. The institutional and cultural context of drinking in America may be undergoing changes in the direction of less consumption of alcohol.

The safety of driving has also undergone change in the past decade. Despite increased use of automobiles, the death rate has been sharply and steadily reduced and many fewer passengers, pedestrians, and drivers, sober or DUI, have died from automobile accidents.

But the reduction in DUI is not simply a reflection of the general control of laws and/or the operation of traffic safety controls. The movement toward severe punishment of drinking drivers has been a leading element in the changing character of the American drinking context, whatever may be the direct effects of such legislation. The expanded and focused attention on the moral drama of drinking-driving has been the most vital force at work in the changed nature of drinking-driving in the United States. How these effects may have been attained is also problematic.

This is not to deny the importance of federal entry into both the traffic safety and the alcohol policy arenas. But alone it was unable to dramatize a situation into fault and blame and victimization. It was unable to add an emotional anger sufficient to offset the long-existing public blandness and apathy toward automobile danger, injury, and death.

It is possible that the drinking public may discover the difficulties police and courts have in enforcing DUI laws. They may assert the validity of H. L. Ross's findings that after an initial period of publicity, DUI behavior will be reasserted at a customary level (Ross 1973, 1982). The difficulties created by expanded court dockets and limited jail facilities have led to greater dependence on diversionary programs of alcohol education and treatment and to voluntary service in lieu of jail (Spieglman 1985). As a group, arrested drinking drivers are a more stable part of the labor force and more "middle class" than other criminal offenders. This too makes "toughness" less politically practicable.

Yet the period since 1980 is not the same as the 1970s. The new temperance movement, itself partially a product of the DUI movement, has given a new saliency to control of drinking in American public life. Perhaps the saliency given to youth as the central actors in the DUI drama is a means of achieving compromise between the organizational and political concerns of the courts and police, on one hand, and the demands of the citizens' movements on the other. Young people have achieved a status as a separate group in American life, a source of both concern and fear, a new form of the "dangerous class" in America (Gusfield 1986, chap. 8). Further, they are also a relatively weak political group. As I noted above, a logical conclusion from the safety studies would extend the minimum drinking age to twenty-five and exclude all women from such legislation. The political impossibility of such measures is evident.

Another possibility for the solution to existing and potential conflicts over DUI remains at the inaugural stage only. For at least fifteen years, Japanese and American technicians have been studying possible ways to control DUI technologically. Such an intervention will be placed in use in several American cities on a trial basis (Los Angeles Times 1987). Used only with recidivists, this device locks the ignition system of an automobile and can only be unlocked when the attached breathalyzer indicates the driver is sufficiently sober. The device will cost several hundred dollars to be installed, and the offender, in most cases, must bear the cost.

6 The Legal Context in the United States

Michael D. Laurence

Anti-drunken driving strategies in the United States have always involved the legal process, primarily the criminal justice system, as the best avenue for reducing drunken driving behavior. Despite the increasing public awareness of the drunken driving problem and increased reliance on penal sanctions, however, little attention has been paid to how the United States form of governmental power sharing and the constitutional constraints on government authority influence the types of policies available.

Ignorance of how these two distinctive features of the American legal system affect drunken driving control strategies has produced some confusion and friction over government responsibility for the several elements that coalesce into a unified drunk driving strategy. Moreover, an understanding of the interaction among the various government actors and the limitations contained in the U.S. Constitution is essential to the formulation and evaluation of innovative policies. Thus, this chapter attempts to provide some broad perspectives on these two features of U.S. policy-making and their influence on drunken driving countermeasures.

In addition to enhancing an understanding of drunk driving decision-making, this inquiry yields important insights for other social concerns. Examining the operation of criminal justice in the context of a single substantive issue is a valuable method of developing perspectives on federalism and constitutional constraints in practice. The perspectives gained by examining these features of the American system for a single subject, such as drunken driving, provide a coherent way to attain specificity and a sensitivity to institutional context that are not always apparent in more general discussions of the criminal justice system process.

This chapter has benefited significantly from the creativity and guidance of Professor Franklin Zimring, director of the Earl Warren Legal Institute.

This chapter identifies who the policymakers are, describes how drunken driving laws evolve, and explains how the Constitution shapes those laws. In particular, it examines how federalism and the Bill of Rights in the U.S. Constitution each influence government attempts to control the drinking driver. The chapter thus serves as an introduction both to drunken driving law enforcement in the American context and to some distinctive features of criminal justice generally in the United States.

Dynamics of a Federal System

Levels of Authority in the Federal System

The American form of federalism has produced a decentralized system of drunken driving policy-making. For the most part, individual jurisdictions, primarily the states, determine criminal policy in general and the legal response to drunken driving in particular. The United States thus has fifty-one state policies—one for each of the states and one for the District of Columbia—a federal policy for federal jurisdictions, and countless local policies for each of the thousands of cities, counties, and boroughs.

Decentralized decision making occurs because drunken driving combines two elements of traditionally state and local political concerns: criminal law and regulation of automobiles and traffic. Unlike governmental structures found in most other countries, in the United States the primary locus of criminal justice decision making and policy formation is not the national government. Instead, the states establish criminal justice policy.[1] Moreover, states traditionally have had primary responsibility for formulating traffic safety policy.[2] State control of traffic safety began with the advent of the automobile, which because of its increased speed and dangerousness required that society take greater responsibility for regulating transportation. The initial responsibility for this function rested with local jurisdictions, and in the early 1900s cities enacted widely varying traffic regulations, some of which even prohibited automobiles.

When the automobile proved to be a permanent part of American society, state governments recognized the need to eliminate these inconsistent and restrictive local regulations. State legislation, therefore, was enacted to ensure intrastate uniformity. Although state-level laws and regulations were a logical response, state-level enforcement of those rules was not. For the most part, local law enforcement agencies enforced the state's criminal laws. This pattern of criminal justice administration was also used with regulations designed to promote traffic safety. Thus, state legislatures enacted comprehensive vehicle codes in the early 1900s, but local law enforcement agencies remained responsible for enforcing the laws. With the exception of a greater federal influence and the presence of state highway patrols, these roles continue today.

Table 6.1 illustrates the current division of political decision making regarding drunken driving in the United States. The three levels of government—federal, state, and local—are categorized in terms of their influence on the differing aspects of traffic safety and drunken driving policy. Each of the various policies is the primary responsibility of one level of government. Primary responsibility denotes control over the formulation, implementation, or funding of the policy. In addition, many areas of concern involve other levels of government in a secondary role, either in assisting the primary governmental sector directly or indirectly or by being responsible for a certain aspect of the larger policy.

The federal government and the states share responsibility for road construction and design, which are significant factors in traffic fatalities and drunken driving accidents. The federal government's primary-actor status stems from its funding of interstate highway projects. The federal government's influence, which began to emerge around the same time that automobiles started to have a major effect on transportation, manifests itself in road design and traffic safety planning. Beginning in the early 1900s and continuing throughout this century, the federal government has underwritten substantial portions of highway construction. To quality for federal assistance, states must submit plans and specifications for the highway projects to the federal government for approval. The secretary of transportation currently examines the state plans for, among other things, compliance with national "geometric and construction standards."[3]

Individual states, however, directly control intrastate road construction, with the federal government and local authorities playing a secondary role. National standards developed for interstate highways have a significant, though indirect, influence over intrastate road design and construction. State highway agencies use information acquired from federal highway projects regarding material use, highway safety features, and accident reduction techniques in designing non–federally funded roads. In addition, the federal government provides some grants for these projects. Local governments often participate in intrastate road construction projects by sharing planning responsibilities with the state government.

By contrast to road design and construction, regulating drivers and driving behavior has a much greater local dimension. Individual states maintain licensing authority over their drivers. State governments specify eligibility requirements for operator's licenses and establish procedures for obtaining licenses. State legislatures also create and regulate the state licensing authority, promulgate standards for suspending or revoking licenses, and determine the level of deference to be given to the licensing authority's decisions. In these matters, neither the federal government nor the local governments have any significant influence.

Similarly, design and enactment of traffic laws are mainly the responsibility of state governments. States' regulatory authority in traffic safety matters emanates from their proprietary interest over public roads and from their police power, which permits states to protect the health, safety, and general welfare of their residents. State governments have exercised this power by establishing extensive motor vehicle codes that regulate motorist behavior. Local governments have a secondary role in traffic law development by implementing the state's broad policies. For example, a state legislature promulgates the general rule that a driver must stop at all red traffic lights; however, the legislature does not determine the location of traffic signals. This responsibility has been delegated to local officials.

Although the state government determines the structure and content of traffic laws, local authorities are the agents for enforcing those laws. Each state has some type of statewide policing authority to enforce traffic laws on interstate highways and to coordinate statewide law enforcement investigations. But local authorities—the county sheriffs and local police officers—principally determine which drivers will face traffic law sanctions.

As Table 6.1 illustrates, a similar pattern of enactment and enforcement applies to anti–drunken driving policy development. Drunken driving strategies are primarily designed at the state level, but with significant influence from other levels of government. In general, drunken driving laws are enacted at the state level—for example, laws that define the prohibited conduct. In addition, state officials design broad law enforcement policies—such as permitting the use of chemical tests to determine blood or breath alcohol concentrations—with local jurisdictions playing a secondary role. The

Table 6.1. A Legacy of Federalism: Locus of Responsibilities for Traffic Safety
and Drunken Driving Policy Development and Enforcement

Policy	Federal	State	Local
Road building (interstate)	P	S	---
Road building (other)	S	P	S
Driver's licensing	---	P	---
Traffic law development (general)	*	P	S
Traffic law enforcement	*	S	P
Drunken driving definitions	S	P	---
Drunken driving law enforcement policy development	S	P	S
Drunken driving law enforcement	*	S	P
Drunken driving prosecutorial responsibilities	*	---	P
Drunken driving penalties	S	P	S
Drunken driving punishment imposition	*	---	P
Accident compensation law	*	P	---
Alcohol availability policy	S	P	S

P = Primary role
S = Secondary role
--- = no significant role
* = Primary role for federal jurisdictions only

federal government has a significant secondary influence in drunken driving policy development because of its recent efforts, through financial incentives, to encourage the states to adopt certain drunken driving policies. The growing federal influence is examined in depth later in this chapter.

Local officials are responsible for implementing the criminal punishments for drunken driving. The state legislature establishes the level of intoxication that constitutes being "under the influence" as well as prescribing the law enforcement tools that will be used to determine that level of intoxication (in most cases, a breath, blood, or urine test). But the county sheriff or city police officer decides whether to stop a driver suspected of drunken driving, whether to administer tests to determine intoxication, and whether to arrest the individual.

When an offender enters the criminal justice system, prosecutorial decisions about whether to proceed, what charges to file, and how to handle the case, including whether the offender will be permitted to plea bargain or to enter a diversion program are all local concerns. If the offender pleads guilty or no contest to a charge or is found guilty, the local judge is responsible for imposing sentence within the range of sentences established by the state legislature. Some state legislatures recently have attempted to remove some local prosecutorial and judicial discretion by statute. For example, the California legislature has sought to discourage plea bargaining by requiring the prosecution to state the reasons for dismissing a drunken driving charge or reducing the severity of the charge.[4] Moreover, judicial discretion has been severely curtailed in California by mandatory sentencing provisions.[5]

Table 6.1 includes two government policies that are not usually considered as responses to drunken driving fatalities and accidents: traffic accident compensation law and alcohol availability policies. Traffic accident compensation law consists of civil law tort recovery schemes. Such policies as liability of third parties to those injured in drunken driving accidents (for example, dram shop laws) and punitive damages against drunken drivers are important considerations in formulating anti–drunken driving measures. These policies are created at the state level, either through legislation or judicial interpretation.

Alcohol availability policies, generally developed at the state level with secondary influence from both the federal government and local governments, include the minimum legal drinking age, location of alcohol sellers, time restrictions on sales, taxation on alcohol, and even the type of alcohol that may be sold in jurisdictions. Most of these policies are governed by the state legislature or delegated to the state's alcohol beverage control board, an administrative agency. However, the federal government exercises some influence in this area in two respects. First, the federal government began taxing alcohol as a source of revenue in 1794.[6] Some anti–drunken driving organizations recently have urged increases in the federal alcohol tax as a means to reduce alcohol-related accidents.[7] The theory behind this effort is that as the price of alcohol increases, consumption declines, leading to a corresponding reduction in drunken driving. Second, the federal government recently has encouraged raising of the minimum legal drinking age by threatening highway funding reductions to those states with minimum drinking ages under twenty-one years.

Local governments regulate alcohol availability policies in several respects. First, many states have delegated to county and city governments the power to determine some of these policies, including whether alcohol may be sold in the jurisdiction. Second, local zoning ordinances determine the placement of retail stores and drinking establishments. Thus, although the states continue to be the primary architects of alcohol availability policies, this responsibility is shared among all levels of government.

State governments are the primary developers of anti-drunken driving policies, with local governments playing a secondary, though important, role. By contrast, in the area of law enforcement the roles are reversed: the local governments are the primary actors with the states having a secondary influence. These shared responsibilities, however, do not fully account for the emerging trend of federal involvement in drunken driving policy formation.

The Growing Federal Presence

The federal government's influence over traffic safety and drunken driving policy in this country developed in several stages. In the first stage, the federal government had very little influence because the states and local governments exclusively regulated motorist behavior and automobile use. The second stage consisted of the federal government controlling federal projects, such as interstate highway construction, or areas of particular federal concern, such as interstate commercial carriers. In the third stage, the federal government attempted to facilitate multistate efforts by approving interstate compacts among the states and by establishing information-sharing programs. The final, and current, stage consists of the federal government directly influencing state policies through funding incentives.

The evolution of the federal presence in drunken driving policy formation has not corresponded to any revisions in the power of the federal government to legislate in this area. For most of this century, the U.S. Congress has three options with respect to the drunken driving problem. First, it could leave the entire matter to the states. The Supreme Court has affirmed the principle of local control when Congress has not acted:

> In the absence of national legislation covering the subject a State may rightfully prescribe uniform regulations necessary for public safety and order in respect to the operation upon its highways of all motor vehicles—those moving in interstate commerce as well as others. . . .[8]

This was Congress' primary policy in the traffic safety area for the first six decades of this century.

As a second option the federal government could dominate drunken driving policy and completely preempt state decision making and control in this area. Congress has long had the authority to establish national rules for traffic safety and drunken driving policy. In the late 1930s, the Supreme Court held that the commerce clause of the U.S. Constitution permitted Congress to enact national legislation to regulate any conduct that had a direct or indirect impact on commerce between the states.[9] This broad interpretation of the commerce power has permitted Congress to regulate a wide variety of "local" concerns.

Thus, Congress conceivably could enact a national drunken driving law, and even create a national police force to enforce it. Given the current distribution of criminal justice responsibility and fiscal constraints, however, this scenario is highly unlikely.

Third, Congress could permit the states to retain primary control of drunken driving policy, while encouraging or requiring the states to initiate certain policies. Under this approach, the federal role would serve as a guide for policy direction for the states, establish minimum standards of enforcement and prohibition, and provide fiscal incentives for federally favored policies. By and large, this has been the federal government's role since the mid-1960s.

Table 6.2 depicts the development over time of the federal government's influence in road construction, traffic safety, and drunken driving policy. As the table indicates, the federal government's role in developing or guiding states' traffic regulations has become a visible force only in recent decades.

The federal influence in the first half of this century on states' traffic safety policy generally and drunken driving policy specifically was slight. The earliest federal influence appeared with the Federal-Aid Road Act of 1916, which appropriated federal monies for joint federal–state highway and "rural post road" projects. To qualify for funding under the act, states were required to maintain a state highway agency and submit highway plans to the secretary of agriculture for approval. The secretary of agriculture was "authorized to make rules and regulations for carrying out the provisions."[10] Despite these controls over state planning, the influence remained modest because federal funding comprised only a small portion of total highway expenditures.

Federal involvement in highway planning and construction increased steadily over the next few decades. In an effort to provide employment during the depression, the federal government expanded assistance in the 1930s to include funding for secondary and city roads. "The 1930's also marked the beginning of what was to

Table 6.2. Major Federal Traffic Safety and Drunken Driving Policy Initiatives

	Highway design and construction	Traffic safety	Drunken driving policy
1916	Federal-Aid Road Act of 1916 authorized funding for rural post road construction projects; required states to create highway agencies and required states to submit plans to secretary of agriculture		
1921	Federal-Aid Act of 1921 designated two types of federally-funded highway projects (interstate and intercounty); federal share of projects limited to 50 percent		
1931–1936	Emergency Public Works Construction Projects Authorized		
1944	Federal Aid Highway Act of 1944 created the National System of Interstate and Defense Highways		
1946		President's Highway Safety Conference	
1954		White House Conference on Highway Safety	
1956	Federal Aid Highway Act of 1956 required comprehensive Highway Safety Study to be conducted by the Bureau of Public Roads; authorized for the first time a long-range plan to complete the National System		
1958		Beamer Resolution of 1958 permitted states to create interstate compacts to enhance traffic safety	
1960		Congress establishes the National Driver Register federal-state co-operative exchange of records of license cancellations, suspensions, and denials	

1958   Federal Aid Highway Act of 1958 recodified the 40 statutes enacted by Congress since 1916

1965   Federal Aid Highway Act Appropriations contained additional $5 billion for federal share of revised estimate for completing Interstate System and additional design standards

1966   Motor Vehicle and Traffic Safety Act of 1966 regulated vehicle design and vehicle safety

1966   Highway Safety Act of 1966 established certain regulations governing road design and maintenance, driver licensing and education, and traffic safety measures

1967   Secretary of Transportation issues first thirteen National Uniform Standards for State Safety Programs

1967   Secretary of Transportation issues Standard #8 of the National Uniform Standards for State Highway Safety Programs that required each state to utilize chemical tests for determining BAC levels and enact BAC limits of no greater than .10%

1970   National Highway Safety Administration institutes Alcohol Safety Action Program

1974   Emergency Highway Energy Conservation Act required Secretary of Transportation to withhold federal highway funding from states with maximum speed limits in excess of 55 mph

1978   Surface Transportation Assistance Act of 1978 contained 5-year authorization to complete Interstate System

1982   Presidential Commission on Drunk Driving created

1982   Alcohol Traffic Safety Act of 1982 established a three-year program to provide grants to states enacting minimum penalties and mandatory sentences for repeat offenders

1984   Highway Safety Amendments required withholding of federal highway funding from any state with a drinking age of less than twenty-one years

become a broad Federal-aid program of research, planning, and engineering studies, commencing with the statewide highway planning surveys, which have produced a continuing supply of data on highways and their use to serve as a factual foundation for highway planning [for the next] three decades."[11]

Federal funding of construction projects, and thereby federal influence, dramatically increased in the post–World War II era. The Federal-Aid Highway Act of 1944, which authorized $1.5 billion for construction projects over three years, established the National System of Interstate and Defense Highways. Later, Congress in the Federal-Aid Highway Acts of 1956 and 1958 authorized almost $26 billion for construction of the system, with the federal government providing 90 percent of construction funds. Federal funding continues to be a crucial aspect of highway construction: in 1980 federal funds amounted to $6.43 billion, or 65 percent, of the $9.87 billion worth of highway construction contracts awarded.[12]

Beginning in the 1950s, Congress, recognizing the increasing complexity of traffic safety, sought to encourage uniform traffic laws and cooperation among the states without direct federal intervention. Through the use of compacts between the states and joint federal-state projects, Congress attempted to facilitate multistate cooperation and control of traffic safety problems. In 1958, Congress passed the Beamer Resolution, which authorized the states "to negotiate and enter into compacts for the purpose of promoting highway traffic safety."[13] In 1960, Congress established the National Driver Register, a federal-state cooperative effort to exchange records of license cancellation, suspension, and denial. Although states continue to participate in various compacts and the National Driver Register, these efforts by themselves have not been considered effective measures in managing traffic safety problems.

The national character and seriousness of traffic safety problems prompted Congress to enact the Highway Safety Act of 1966 and the Motor Vehicle and Traffic Safety Act of 1966. The Highway Safety Act empowered the secretary of transportation to promulgate safety standards for the states to follow:

> Each state [shall] have a highway safety program approved by the Secretary designed to reduce traffic accidents and death, injuries, and property damage resulting therefrom. Such programs shall be in accordance with uniform standards promulgated by the Secretary.[14]

To induce the states to comply with the newly created standards, Congress authorized the secretary to withhold federal highway funds from any state not adopting the standards.[15]

The secretary of transportation officially promulgated the new standards in 1967, including the first federal drunken driving standards. Standard Number Eight—entitled "Alcohol in Relation to Highway Safety"—required each state to "develop and implement a program to achieve a reduction in those traffic accidents arising in whole or in part from persons driving under the influence of alcohol." More specifically, such a program must include (1) use of chemical tests to determine blood alcohol concentrations; (2) establishment of blood alcohol limits of no greater than .10 percent, by weight; (3) enactment of an implied consent law for those arrested for driving while intoxicated or under the influence of alcohol; (4) use of quantitative alcohol tests for all traffic accident fatalities and drivers involved in fatal crashes; and (5) enactment of procedures for administering blood alcohol concentration tests.[16]

The states' substantial compliance with the standards illustrates Congress's financial power to "encourage" the enactment of federally endorsed traffic safety standards. Although the practice of threatening funding reductions began with the first federal highway appropriation in the early 1900s, Congress greatly expanded the use of financial incentives in the mid-1960s with the passage of the Highway Safety Act. In 1974, the oil shortage prompted Congress to enact legislation requiring the secretary of transportation to withhold federal highway aid funding from states with maximum speed limits in excess of fifty-five miles per hour.[17]

Congress has successfully used financial incentives to persuade states to enact specific legislation or programs addressing the drunken driving problem. Some states viewed the 1967 standards and the threats of highway funding reductions as intrusive on their sovereign function. Nonetheless, they complied with the new standards in order to participate in highway construction projects. For example, by 1971 all states had followed the standards' requirement that they enact a specified blood alcohol concentration level as part of the drunken driving law. However, it was not until 1981 that all states adopted the specific standard of a 0.10 or lower level.[18]

Congress has also used financial "carrots" to promote certain drunken driving policies by underwriting specific programs. In 1970, the National Highway Traffic Safety Administration instituted the federally funded Alcohol Safety Action Projects (ASAP), which established thirty-five experimental projects throughout the nation. These pilot programs were designed to provide a test environment for the many different methods of curbing drunken driving. The theory underlying the program was that the states would then implement those measures that proved to be successful.

More recently, the Alcohol Traffic Safety Act of 1982 established a three-year program to provide grants from the Highway Trust Fund to states that adopted certain anti–drunken driving measures.[19] To qualify for the grants, a state must (1) provide at least a ninety-day license suspension for a driver committing an alcohol-related offense and at least a one-year suspension for repeat offenders; (2) enact mandatory minimum sentences of at least two days' imprisonment or ten days' community service for offenders convicted of driving while intoxicated more than once in any five-year period; (3) presume that a blood alcohol level concentration of .10 percent, by weight, is conclusive evidence of guilt; and (4) increase enforcement and publicity of enforcement efforts. Many states accepted federal funding and the attached conditions to finance their increased anti-drunken driving enforcement efforts.

The recent minimum legal drinking age controversy illustrates the process by which the federal government may influence state policymaking. The controversy began with studies that found an overrepresentation of younger drivers in alcohol-related accidents. Anti–drunken driving groups quickly asserted that this overrepresentation was caused by the fact that between 1970 and 1975 twenty-nine states had lowered the drinking age from twenty-one. Stalled in their attempts to persuade state legislatures to raise drinking ages, these groups turned to the federal government.

The federal government first attempted to induce states to address voluntarily the problem of young drinking drivers. In 1983 the Presidential Commission on Drunk Driving recommended that states enact a uniform drinking age of twenty-one years.[20] This approach proved ineffective: although twenty-three states considered raising the drinking age to twenty-one after the recommendation was made, only four had done so by June 1984.[21]

The federal government then resorted to more coercive measures. In 1984 Congress enacted legislation requiring highway funding reductions for any state with a drinking age under twenty-one years. States soon began to return to the twenty-one-year age limit. At the end of 1984, fourteen of the states that had lowered the drinking age in the 1970s had raised it to twenty-one.[22] By the end of 1986, all but eight states had followed the suggestion of Congress. And even these eight states may raise their minimum drinking ages to twenty-one after the Supreme Court upheld the power of Congress to condition highway funding in this manner.[23]

This history of governmental responses to the drunken driving problem reveals a clear trend toward increased federal decision making. Although states continue to retain primary control over drunken driving policy, a greater infusion of federal influence in this area has occurred in the past two decades. Congress, with promises of grants or threats of funding reductions, has taken an active role in formulating broad drunken driving policies and in encouraging the states to adopt them.

Diffusion and Uniformity in State Level Policies

Despite the growing federal influence, state governments retain significant control over traffic safety and drunken driving policy in this country. In recent years all states have revised and strengthened their drunken driving laws. These revisions include: enacting per se laws, which criminalize driving with a blood alcohol concentration above a specified limit, regardless of impairment; expanding the types of enforcement options available, such as permitting drunken driving roadblocks and use of breath testing devices; and mandating treatment or counseling programs for those convicted of drunken driving. In addition, all states have increased the criminal penalties for those convicted of drunken driving.

Although the individual states are the principal architects of the revised drunken driving laws, in many instances they have not developed the governmental responses in isolation. Policy innovation results from many different levels, including the federal government through the ASAPs or other model programs, other states' pilot projects, and traffic safety experts. The thirty-five ASAP programs conducted throughout the nation in the mid-1970s developed several models for combating drunken driving. In addition, policies frequently develop based on academic findings and theories.

States implement developed policies in a variety of patterns. The primary method that states employ for implementing novel policies is ad hoc adoption of other states' new policies, particularly if the new policies' effectiveness has been demonstrated. A more formal approach involves incorporating provisions of the Uniform Vehicle Code, which has been adopted, at least in part, by all fifty states.

Creation of the Uniform Vehicle Code began in 1924, when the United States secretary of commerce, Herbert Hoover, convened a conference of state representatives and organizations concerned with traffic safety. The conference, later named the National Committee on Uniform Traffic Laws and Ordinances, recognized that the myriad of laws existing throughout the states created chaos; the conference proposed a Uniform Vehicle Code as a solution and approved a draft of the code in 1926.

Despite the federal government's initial sponsorship, the movement toward uniformity in traffic laws was seen as a proper task of the states through voluntary cooperative action.[24] Since the mid-1960s, however, the federal government has encouraged adoption of the Uniform Vehicle Code's Rules of the Road provisions. The secretary of transportation's Standard Number Six, promulgated under the authority of the National Highway Safety Act, requires each state to "develop and implement a program to achieve uniformity of traffic codes and laws throughout the State." Each state's program must be designed "to achieve uniform rules of the road in all of its jurisdictions" and "make the State's codified rules of the road consistent with similar plans of other states."[25]

The Uniform Vehicle Code models its provisions on existing state laws; it "deals with existing, tested laws and makes no attempt to go beyond that point."[26] For example, in 1939 Indiana enacted the first state law defining driving under the influence in terms of blood alcohol concentration. The Indiana legislation provided that a blood alcohol concentration of .15 percent, by weight, was presumptive evidence of guilt; a blood alcohol concentration of .05 percent or less was presumptive evidence of nonguilt; and a blood alcohol concentration of between .05 and .15 percent could be used as supporting evidence of guilt.[27] The Uniform Vehicle Code adopted the Indiana format in 1944, and incorporated these specific blood alcohol concentrations as part of its definition of drunken driving.[28] In turn, the Uniform Vehicle Code was used as a model by many states to enact their own blood alcohol concentration definitions of drunken driving; by 1958, some thirty states had enacted similar BAC limits as part of their anti–drunken driving policies.[29]

Policy adoption may also result from the federal government's endorsement of certain measures. As described in the previous section, the federal government uses financial grants as well as threats of highway funding reductions as incentives for states to enact specified drunken driving laws.

An excellent illustration of drunken driving policy innovation and adoption in practice is the development and spread of the "implied consent" law. In 1953, New York enacted the first implied consent law, which provided that any "person who operates a motor vehicle . . . in this state shall be deemed to have given his consent to a chemical test . . . for the purpose of determining the alcoholic content of his blood."[30] Although other states were slow in adopting this novel method of enforcing anti–drunken driving laws, the concept soon began to attract national attention. In 1962, an implied consent provision was added to the Uniform Vehicle Code.[31] In 1982, the federal government used funding grants to encourage states without implied consent provisions to enact them. Through informal adoption, inclusion in the Uniform Vehicle Code, and encouragement by the federal government, all states currently have some form of the implied consent law.[32]

The Future of Decentralized Policy-making

The United States continues to rely on individual states to enact the government response to drunken driving, although we are moving closer to a "national" system than ever before. With the rising federal presence in this area, the obvious question is how much longer will we have a decentralized form of governmental responsibility.

The evolution of drunken driving policy in the nation appears to have had profound effects on federalism. Although states retain primary responsibility for criminal law and traffic policy, the trend in recent years for federal intervention has changed traditional notions of responsibility. Indeed, drunken driving is one topic that has fostered the idea of a national criminal justice policy, one that does not evolve from state level structures, but rather from the national government. In few areas of criminal justice concern does this movement toward nationalization appear as pronounced in recent years as it does with drunken driving policies. Interestingly, this movement has occurred during the years that President Reagan and his administration are actively attempting to return decision making in many other areas of government operations to the states.

More than many other phenomena, drunken driving has created a new federalism in criminal justice. With the recognition by the federal government in the 1960s of the state governments' failure to control drunken driving came a new type of federal intervention.

The traditional federal regulatory scheme—direct regulation with federally enforceable laws that restrict personal behavior—was not employed. There are no general federal laws that punish individuals who drive drunk. Rather, a different type of regulatory scheme was attempted, one that employed "incentives"—threats of highway funding cutoffs—for states to enact very specific policies to combat drunken driving. And despite the Reagan administration's stated commitment to return power to the states, in the single area of drunken driving the federal government seems to be taking an even more active role in regulating and dictating to the states the appropriate form of governmental response.

This approach to government regulation has had significant effects on drunken driving policy. The rise of federal influence corresponds with a growing concentration of anti–drunken driving policy in a few areas: all states employ some version of an implied consent law, drunken driving definitions incorporating specific BAC levels (usually .10 percent), minimum penalties for offenders, and license suspensions or revocations.

The trend toward greater uniformity in drunk driving countermeasures may have profound policy implications. The decentralized system of government, which characterized earlier drunken driving policy-making, provided many advantages with respect to policy innovation, adoption, and adaptation to specific local needs. In many instances, state leaders enacted legislation that they believed to be appropriate for their particular state. The differing levels of governmental action permitted several laboratories for experimentation. And often decision making on a smaller scale allowed implementation of novel policies that have been successful in other areas.

Whether the recent concentration of policy presents a more effective approach to the problem remains to be seen. Moreover, the ramifications of the federal government's role in actively, but indirectly, creating "national" criminal law cannot be assessed at this time. The precedent may have been established for greater federal control of state policy in other areas. Or we may simply be witnessing an isolated occurrence of federal intervention.

Constitutional Considerations

As the preceding account reveals, current anti–drunken driving efforts focus on using the criminal justice system as the principal method of reducing this dangerous behavior. The increased emphasis in recent years on the penal sanctions makes it all the more important to understand the limits of the criminal justice system. One of the most significant constraining influences on governmental power to legislate social controls is the United States Constitution, or, more precisely, the Bill of Rights. The U.S. Supreme Court's expansion in the 1960s of the scope and coverage of constitutional protections—primarily those contained in the Bill of Rights—continues to influence criminal justice policy-making, including enactment of drunken driving countermeasures.

Constitutional Provisions that Affect Anti–Drunken Driving Strategies

This section provides a brief review of some constitutional concerns implicated by using the legal process to combat drunken driving. Among the constitutional provisions that affect drunken driving policy-making are the guarantee of due process, the prohibition against unreasonable searches and seizures, the privilege against self-incrimination, and the guarantees of the right to counsel and the right to a jury trial.

Table 6.3 provides a rough outline of the constitutional rights affected by drunken driving countermeasures. State and federal policymakers must consider constitutional limitations when considering legislation to ensure that government policies maintain the proper balance between the state and the defendant. If legislators ignore or are not cognizant of constitutional concerns, judicial protection of individual rights may thwart any effectiveness to be gained from the new policy. In the extreme, entire legislative strategies may be invalidated because they conflict with a constitutional right. In other instances, the Constitution may require that charges against a particular defendant be dismissed or that certain evidence be excluded from the subsequent prosecution. An understanding of constitutional rights is thus important in drafting anti–drunken driving measures that best serve society's needs and protect individual rights.

DUE PROCESS RESTRICTIONS ON VAGUENESS AND STATUTORY REACH

The due process clauses contained in the Fifth and Fourteenth Amendments must be considered when legislators draft criminal statutes designed to curb the drinking driver. The Constitution requires that a statute "define the criminal offense with sufficient

Table 6.3. Constitutional Doctrines and Drunken Driving Policy

Constitutional provision	Drunk driving policy affected
Due process	1. Summary adjudication of drunk driving offenders 2. Per se legislation 3. Forced chemical tests 4. License revocation and suspension 5. Use of inaccurate testing equipment
Probable cause and reasonableness requirements for searches	1. Random roadblocks/stops 2. Random breath tests
Privilege against self-incrimination	1. Implied consent laws
Guarantee of the right to counsel	1. Summary adjudication of drunk driving offenders 2. Interrogation of drivers 3. Implied consent laws

definiteness that ordinary people can understand what conduct is prohibited and in a manner that does not encourage arbitrary and discriminatory enforcement."[33] The reasons for this requirement are twofold. First, it is a matter of fundamental fairness that individuals have fair notice that they are engaging in criminal conduct. Moreover, this fair notice requirement serves utilitarian interests; the law's objective of preventing unlawful conduct cannot be fulfilled if ordinary citizens are unaware that such conduct is prohibited. Second, legislation must not permit arbitrary enforcement; a statute that employs overly broad and vague definitions of prohibited conduct provides a vehicle for discriminatory enforcement. Thus, courts will invalidate a statute that fails to provide the required specificity as being too vague.[34]

Although the vagueness doctrine encompasses all anti–drunken driving policies, it primarily applies to laws defining drunken driving. For example, opponents of per se laws—laws that punish a driver whose blood alcohol concentration exceeds a prescribed limit—claim that they fail to provide fair warning of what conduct is prohibited. Unlike the traditional "under the influence" laws, per se laws do not punish the driver's impaired condition; rather they criminalize driving with a specified blood alcohol level regardless of whether the individual's driving ability is impaired. Thus, a driver must determine not whether he or she is "under the influence" or capable of safely operating a vehicle, but rather whether his or her blood alcohol level exceeds the statutory limit, usually .10 percent. Critics of per se laws contend that such determinations are impossible for the ordinary driver; only by actually submitting to a blood or breath alcohol test will an individual know whether he or she has exceeded the legal limit.[35]

Courts have uniformly rejected this challenge to the per se laws on several doctrinal grounds.[36] The first category of reasons that courts reject vagueness challenges to per se laws reflects notions of judicial restraint and deference to the legislative function. Courts reason that accepting these challenges would impose unworkable statutory requirements on legislators. Accepting this challenge to per se laws would require invalidating a whole host of criminal statutes that involve after-the-fact inquiries, such as a jury's rejection of a self-defense claim based on its determination that the defendant's actions were unreasonable. Courts are also reluctant to "second-guess" legislative judgments, based on the theory that the legislature is the proper arena for political or technical line-drawing. Courts that reject the challenges on this ground assert that the question is not whether the per se law is vague, but whether the per se limit—usually .10 percent—sufficiently identifies a recognizably impaired condition in most individuals. At some level of blood alcohol concentration all individuals are incapable of safely operating a vehicle. Courts conclude that legislatures are in the best position to determine what that level is.[37]

A second category of reasons for rejecting vagueness challenges to per se laws centers around the conclusion that drinking individuals have fair notice that they have violated the law. A major justification for upholding per se laws is that the individual has sufficient warning that at some point he or she will exceed the amount allowed: "The very fact that he has consumed a quantity of alcohol should notify a person of ordinary intelligence that he is in jeopardy of violating the statute."[38] Courts point to widespread publicity and the availability of charts that calculate rough estimations of blood alcohol concentrations as providing adequate guidance for avoiding per se law violations.

Finally, some courts contend that the critics' challenge does not actually implicate the vagueness doctrine at all. "Vagueness" challenges to per se laws do not really argue that the statutory language is too vague; on the contrary, critics of these laws are actually arguing that the prohibitions are too exact.

In addition to defining the prohibited conduct adequately, state legislatures must be concerned with maintaining the proper balance in criminal statutes. A primary tenet of our criminal justice system is that the government must prove guilt beyond a reasonable doubt, as the Supreme Court in *In re Winship* explained: "Lest there remain any doubt about the constitutional stature of the reasonable-doubt standard, we explicitly hold that the Due Process Clause protects the accused against conviction except upon proof beyond a reasonable doubt of *every fact* necessary to constitute the crime with which he is charged."[39]

Among the implications of this standard of proof are restrictions on the state's use of "presumptions" in criminal cases. A presumption is a legal device that, after the factfinder in a case determines the existence of certain basic facts, allows the state to determine the legal conclusions that may be drawn from those facts. Although the legal terminology is confusing, people use presumptions in everyday activities: if we walk out of our homes, see clouds in the sky and water on the ground, we "presume" that it has rained even though we did not witness that event. The same reasoning process applies to the government's use of presumptions: when reasonable people would not differ on the conclusions to be drawn from a set of facts, the state may presume that legal conclusion.

There are two types of legal presumptions: permissive and mandatory.[40] A permissive presumption is one by which the factfinder is permitted, but not required, to draw a conclusion from a given fact. Courts have upheld permissive presumptions because they do not shift the burden from the state to the defendant: permissive presumptions do not "curtail[] the factfinder's freedom to assess the evidence independently," and thus such presumptions are constitutional unless "under the facts of the case there is no rational way the trier could make this connection."[41]

Mandatory presumptions are more troublesome because they require a factfinder to draw certain conclusions once it has established the existence of specified facts or a set of facts. This type of mandatory presumption completely removes from the factfinder the discretion of drawing legal conclusions. Other types of mandatory presumptions may simply shift to the defendant the burden of producing counterinferences once certain facts have been established.

The Supreme Court has held that because mandatory presumptions shift the burden of proof to the defendant or may altogether foreclose any evidence demonstrating counterinferences the state is required to demonstrate that the "evidence necessary to invoke the inference" be sufficient for a "rational jury to find the inferred fact beyond a reasonable doubt."[42] Should the conclusion fail the reasonable doubt test courts will invalidate the statute because it creates a nonrebuttable presumption: "This court has held more than once that a statute creating a presumption which operates to deny a fair opportunity to rebut it violates the due process clause of the Fourteenth Amendment."[43] Thus, a statute is invalid "when the presumption is not necessarily or universally true in fact, and the State has reasonable alternative means of making the crucial determination."[44]

Presumptions are an important component of drunken driving countermeasures. In particular, the various per se laws employ several variations of presumptions. Most states give a BAC of .10 percent or above some presumption: either as conclusive evidence that the driver is impaired, or as proof of a separate crime of driving with a BAC of .10 percent or above.

Several courts have addressed the question of whether per se statutes sufficiently protect the defendant's right of proof of guilt beyond a reasonable doubt. The first step in this inquiry is to determine the character of the presumption. In many cases, the per se laws relieve prosecutors of the burden of demonstrating impairment in driving ability by allowing them to declare that a BAC of .10 percent or above is per se evidence of impairment. This presumption appears to be a mandatory presumption, one that must be reviewed according to the reasonable doubt standard. At least one court has upheld such a statutory construction, holding that a rational individual would conclude that the driver was impaired beyond a reasonable doubt.[45] Interestingly, other courts have labeled this type of presumption as permissive and have upheld the statutes using the less stringent rational relationship test.[46]

Most courts have held that per se statutes do not establish a "conclusive presumption" of guilt on the intoxication element of drunken driving. Instead, these courts find that the per se laws establish a separate and distinct offense.[47] Thus, evidence of a BAC above .10 percent is not used to presume impairment, but, rather, it is proof of one element of the crime.

Regardless of which method the courts use to uphold the per se statutes, the prosecution must still prove the elements of the crime beyond a reasonable doubt. Thus, the state must prove beyond a reasonable doubt that the defendant's blood alcohol concentration exceeded the legal limit. This burden may include proving the accuracy of the testing equipment.[48]

Another presumption relevant to drunken driving countermeasures is that used in converting breath alcohol analysis to blood alcohol content. Most states derive BACs from converting the alcohol content in breath samples by way of a conversion formula.[49] To effect the conversion, the standard formula multiplies the alcohol concentration in the breath by a constant to ascertain the alcohol concentration in the blood. Some critics argue that the result obtained by such extrapolation cannot meet the "beyond a reasonable doubt" standard: the constant cannot be accurate for every individual, and the degree of error is so great that it cannot be said that the results of the conversion formula prove beyond a reasonable doubt that the defendant's blood alcohol concentration exceeded the prescribed limit. Thus far, courts have rejected this argument, although without providing much reasoning. In addition, some states have eliminated the conversion problem by drafting statutes using breath alcohol concentration to define the prohibited conduct.

RESTRICTIONS ON ADJUDICATION PROCEDURES: DUE PROCESS AND COROLLARY CONSTITUTIONAL PROTECTIONS

An important constitutional concern affecting anti–drunken driving strategies is whether the state's procedures adequately safeguard constitutionally "protected" interests when it takes action against an individual. The due process clause provides that an individual is entitled to a certain minimum of "process" before the state may legitimately affect a protected property or liberty interest. A state must provide an individual the opportunity to be heard "at a meaningful time and in a meaningful manner."[50] This "procedural" aspect of due process operates as an institutional restraint on arbitrary government power or erroneous decision-making by protecting the right of the individual to present reasons why the state's action should not be taken.

Procedural due process requirements depend on the interest affected and the circumstances surrounding the state's actions. Courts employ a two-step approach to determine whether the state's procedures comply with constitutional requirements. First, they determine whether the state's action impinges on constitutionally protected interests. The Constitution recognizes liberty and property as protected interests, on which a government may not infringe without satisfying procedural due process requirements. If the state's action concerns matters outside of the zone of protected interests, then procedural due process is not implicated.

After ascertaining that the state's actions affect a protected interest, the second step is to decide whether the state's procedures were sufficient. The Supreme Court uses a balancing formula to determine "what process is due to protect against erroneous deprivation" of a protected interest.[51] This test involves balancing the nature of and effect on the interest, the risk of erroneous deprivation caused by the state's procedures, the alternative procedures available, and the government's interest and impairment caused by the additional procedures.[52] If the individual's interest is significant and substantially affected, or if the risk of erroneous deprivation is substantial, or if the state's interest in the summary procedures is minimal, the Constitution requires that the state provide a hearing prior to taking the action.

Procedural due process is of primary concern to state strategies that revoke or suspend a driver's license. Although driver's license suspensions and revocations are characterized as "civil" proceedings—as opposed to criminal actions—and thus are not subject to criminal procedures and protections, they nonetheless may not be made without regard for due process.[53] For many years, most courts assumed that driving was a privilege, and not a right, and could be regulated at will by the state.[54] More recently, however, courts have recognized that once the state allows everyone who qualifies to obtain a license, and then confers a license on an individual, that individual has a protected property interest in that license.[55] Therefore, a state must provide some opportunity for a hearing when it seeks to revoke or suspend a license. The question that remained was whether the Constitution required the state to provide an opportunity for a hearing prior to the suspension or revocation, or whether the hearing could take place some time thereafter.

The United States Supreme Court in reviewing state schemes for enforcing implied consent laws has held that the due process clause does not require presuspension hearings. In *Mackey v. Montrym,* the Court upheld the constitutionality of a Massachusetts statute that mandated driver's license suspension for refusing to submit to a breath test and did not provide for a presuspension hearing. The Court applied the balancing formula to the Massachusetts statute and held that the postsuspension hearing provision was sufficient.[56]

The Court first determines the weight to accord the individual's interest by examining three factors: "1) the duration of the revocation; 2) the availability of hardship relief; and 3) the availability of prompt post-revocation review."[57] The Court concluded that, although the individual's interest in operating a vehicle is substantial, the relatively short duration of the suspension, the availability of relief in cases of hardship, and the prompt postsuspension hearing available mitigated against assigning a great weight to that interest.

The Court then assessed the probability of erroneous deprivation of licenses generally. The Massachusetts statute provided for license suspension prior to having a hearing based upon affidavits of two police officers that the driver refused to consent to a chemical test. The Court concluded that, under these circumstances, the risk of wrongful deprivation was slight:

> In summary, we conclude . . . that the risk of error inherent in the presuspension procedures chosen by the legislature is not so substantial in itself as to require us to depart from the "ordinary principle" that "something less than an evidentiary hearing is sufficient prior to adverse administrative action". . . . We fail to see how reliability would be materially enhanced by mandating the presuspension "hearing".[58]

The third part of the balancing formula involved balancing the "state's interests served by the summary procedures used, as well as the administrative and fiscal burdens, if any, that would result from the substitute procedures sought."[59] The *Montrym* Court noted that states have a substantial interest in preventing drunken driving and that summary license suspension of those refusing to take a breath test significantly advances that interest. It therefore concluded that the Massachusetts prehearing license suspension policy did not violate the due process clause.

A corollary constitutional issue is a defendant's right to present a defense in criminal proceedings. This constitutional protection, derived from the due process clause and the Sixth Amendment, includes the rights to present witnesses on one's behalf, to cross-examine the state's witnesses, and to obtain exculpatory evidence from the prosecution. The Supreme Court explained that the right to present a defense includes access to evidence held by the state:

> Under the Due Process Clause of the Fourteenth Amendment, criminal prosecutions must comport with prevailing notions of fundamental fairness. We have long interpreted this standard of fairness to require that criminal defendants be afforded a meaningful opportunity to present a complete defense. To safeguard this right, the Court has developed "what might loosely be called the area of constitutionally guaranteed access to evidence."[60]

This right is implicated in drunk driving prosecutions when the state attempts to introduce chemical test results derived from an individual's breath or blood sample taken at the time of arrest. Defense attorneys have attempted to obtain the remainder of the breath or blood samples to perform independent tests. Unfortunately, in most instances the sample had been discarded shortly after the police conducted the test. In these cases, defense attorneys claim that their clients were denied access to this material evidence—and therefore were unable to perform independent tests—and thus the state's test results should be "suppressed."

Decisions by state courts in the 1970s and early 1980s were divided over the issue of whether the police must retain the defendant's breath or blood sample. Many courts held that defendants have a due process right to conduct an independent examination of the breath or blood sample. Under this theory, if the police discarded the sample prior to trial—as is usually the case—then the chemical test results must be excluded from the trial.[61] Most courts, however, held that when the test samples were not destroyed in bad faith or for the purpose of hindering the defense or when the defendant could not demonstrate that the test sample was material to the defense, the test results were admissible.[62]

The Supreme Court resolved the issue for the purposes of the U.S. Constitution in 1984. It held in *California v. Trombetta* that the due process clause does not require the state to retain breath samples in order to use chemical test results at trial. The state has the duty to preserve evidence when it has "apparent exculpatory value" and cannot be obtained by alternative means. The Court concluded that because the police had destroyed the breath sample in good faith and the defendant had numerous methods for impeaching the test results, unavailability of the test sample did not constitute a denial of the defendant's due process right to present a defense.[63]

The Constitution's guarantees of procedural fairness and the right to be heard and present a defense constrain policymakers in formulating drunken driving countermeasures. However, careful drafting of drunken driving legislation should avoid most constitutional problems.

THE FOURTH ADMENDMENT'S PROHIBITION AGAINST UNREASONABLE SEARCHES AND SEIZURES

The Fourth Amendment protects "the right of the people to be secure in their persons, houses, papers and effects against unreasonable searches and seizures."[64] It requires that a search or seizure occur only pursuant to a warrant and that any search or seizure be accompanied by probable cause.[65] The "exclusionary rule" prohibits the use of evidence seized in violation of these requirements in subsequent criminal prosecutions. Such evidence may include statements made by the individual seized or evidence obtained by way of nonconforming searches.

The Fourth Amendment's stringent requirement that a warrant be obtained prior to conducting any search or seizure has been relaxed when exigent circumstances are present. The courts have held that the special circumstances involved in the context of traffic safety—impracticality of obtaining a warrant and the ease of escape—usually justify excusing the warrant requirement for such law enforcement.[66] Therefore, police officers need not obtain a warrant to stop a vehicle when they have probable cause to believe that a law has been violated.

By contrast, the probable cause component of the Fourth Amendment presents a greater concern to officials enforcing drunken driving laws. Courts frequently review whether certain police activities require probable cause and what constitutes probable cause. There are four drunken driving law enforcement circumstances that implicate search and seizure issues: stopping the vehicle, administering a field sobriety test, formally arresting a driver, and requiring a breath or blood test. All of these intrusions involve varying degrees of suspicion or cause before they may be undertaken by police.

Under traditional interpretations of the Fourth Amendment, law enforcement stops of motor vehicles in most circumstances are constitutionally permissible only when the officer has probable cause to believe that a crime has been committed.[67] Probable cause exists " 'if the facts and circumstances before the officer are such as to warrant a man of prudence and caution in believing that the offense has been committed' " by the person subject to the search or seizure.[68] However, several exceptions to the probable cause requirement have been used to justify automobile stops without the presence of probable cause.

Probable cause is not required for brief investigative stops based on "reasonable suspicion." The Supreme Court in *Terry v. Ohio* stated that an officer may detain an individual for a brief investigation if the officer has "reasonable suspicion," grounded in "specific and articulable facts," that the person is about to commit or has committed a crime.[69] In addition, the officer is entitled to conduct a limited search of the suspect's outer clothing to ensure that he or she is not armed. Some courts have extended the *Terry* situation to automobile stops, in which the officers have reasonable suspicion to believe that criminal activity is occurring.[70]

A second exception to the probable cause requirement is the administrative inspection search. The Supreme Court has held that administrative officials may conduct routine building inspections to enforce health and safety codes if the inspections are authorized by administrative warrant.[71] The Court has permitted administrative inspections without probable cause because the inspections have a long history of judicial and public acceptance; there is "unanimous agreement among experts" that inspections are the only effective way to enforce health and safety codes; inspections are not personal; and the inspections are not aimed at discovering evidence of a crime.

The Supreme Court in dicta implied that, under the administrative exception to the Fourth Amendment, law enforcement officers without probable cause or reasonable suspicion may stop individuals to check for possession of driver's licenses and vehicle registration as long as the stops are not conducted in an arbitrary manner.[72] Some state and lower federal courts have upheld automobile stops initially conducted for the purpose of license or registration inspections.[73] In most cases, police officers are required to have only some justification to stop an individual.

The primary law enforcement policy that is affected by the Fourth Amendment's probable cause requirement concerns the use of random roadblocks. Critics of drunken driving roadblocks contend that they are an unconstitutional infringement on protected Fourth Amendment values because the police seize individuals without the requisite probable cause.[74] Court challenges to the legality of this law enforcement technique have received mixed results. Some courts, employing the Fourth Amendment balancing test, have upheld the constitutionality of roadblocks against such challenges.[75] Some courts, although concluding that roadblocks are not per se violations of the Fourth Amendment, have promulgated specific guidelines for their use.[76] Other courts have held that the roadblocks are unconstitutional.[77]

Once an individual has been lawfully stopped, a police officer may lawfully request that the driver complete a field sobriety test—a battery of functional tests to determine alcohol impairment in many circumstances. Courts have held that the presence of alcohol containers in the vehicle,[78] the intoxicated appearance of the driver, an admission of drinking, driving erratically or in violation of motor vehicle laws, or the presence of a strong alcohol odor on the driver all support a request to complete a field sobriety test. Probable cause to arrest for drunken driving includes traffic violations or failure to complete successfully the field sobriety test.[79]

The Fourth Amendment applies to drunk driving law enforcement strategies, but its effect appears to be minimal. Exceptions to the warrant requirement and relaxed requirements of cause needed to search and seize a suspected drunk driver have reduced the difficulty that police officers might otherwise confront in most stops of individual drivers. On the other hand, the Fourth Amendment's more significant influence might be its effect on anti-drunken driving detection techniques—specifically on the use of sobriety checkpoints.

PRIVILEGE AGAINST SELF-INCRIMINATION

The Fifth Amendment provides that no person "shall be compelled in any criminal case to be a witness against himself." It prohibits a state from requiring a person to produce "evidence of a testimonial or communicative nature."[80] The key to determining the scope of the protection, however, is ascertaining whether the evidence sought by the state is "testimonial":

> [T]he prohibition of compelling a man in a criminal court to be a witness against himself is a prohibition of the use of physical or moral compulsion to exhort communications from him, not an exclusion of his body as evidence when it may be material.[81]

The Supreme Court in *Schmerber v. California* decided whether the forced taking of a blood sample from an unconscious driver violated the Constitution. The Court held that it did not because the evidence derived from the test was physical evidence rather than testimonial. Thus, the right against self-incrimination was not implicated.[82]

The Court in *South Dakota v. Neville* addressed whether the admission of evidence that the driver refused to submit to a breath test violated the prohibition against self-incrimination. Holding that the Constitution was not violated, the Court first noted that the refusal constitutes a physical and not a communicative act.[83] However, the Court rested its decision on the ground that refusal to submit to the test did not involve impermissible coercion. The nature of the test was characterized as "safe, painless, and commonplace," and the state could have coerced the test, according to the Court's previous decision in *Schmerber*.[84]

CRITICAL STAGES AND THE RIGHT TO COUNSEL

The Constitution provides the right to counsel in varying degrees. The most common protection derives from the Sixth Amendment. The Sixth Amendment guarantees the accused a right to counsel at all "critical stages" of a criminal prosecution. Thus, if the accused cannot afford counsel, the government must provide counsel.

The second form of the right to counsel is much broader in scope but does not require that the state provide counsel to those who cannot afford it. This right to counsel derives from the Fourteenth Amendment's due process clause and it provides that a person may consult with an attorney prior to making important legal decisions, even though technically the individual may not have even been arrested.

The right to counsel is important to drunken driving policy primarily in the area of law enforcement strategies and techniques. For example, the question has been raised whether an individual stopped by police has the right to seek the advice of counsel prior to submitting to a blood alcohol test. Most courts have held that the individual does not have a Sixth Amendment right—that is, the right to have counsel appointed and present—at the time the test is administered.[85] However, courts are divided over whether the due process clause requires the police to allow the individual to consult with an attorney. Some have held that it does, if such consultation would not interfere with test accuracy.[86] Other courts have held that there is no such right.[87]

Drunken Driving's Effect on the Constitution

The Bill of Rights contained in the U.S. Constitution significantly influences the adoption and implementation of anti–drunken driving strategies. From the initial legislation to the sentencing of the individual, the Constitution guides, directs, prescribes, and limits governmental decision making and authority. However, the influence has not been entirely unidirectional: over and above the apparent and strong influence that constitutional doctrine has on drunken driving policy-making, drunken driving has had a significant influence on the way courts interpret the Constitution.

Traffic regulation has long influenced constitutional doctrine. This may be partially explained as a response to the increasing mobility of our society as well as our apparent difficulties in addressing the law enforcement problems created by that increased mobility.

One example of this influence is the automobile's effect on the scope and coverage of search and seizure doctrine. The "automobile exception" to the warrant requirement, announced in *Carroll v. United States,* permits a warrantless search when "it is not practicable to secure a warrant because the vehicle can be quickly moved out of the locality or jurisdiction in which the warrant must be sought."[88] Ironically, the *Carroll* case involved a search for liquor by prohibition agents. A growing number of courts are relying on this exigent circumstance rationale and the seriousness of the problem to justify drunken driving roadblocks. The same influence may be observed in the judicial interpretation of the vagueness doctrine and the right against self-incrimination. In both of these areas, the courts have retreated from more protective interpretations to accommodate the widespread anti–drunken driving strategies. Constitutional experts disagree over whether the current interpretations are legitimate or reasonable. But few will deny that the perceived seriousness of the problem has played a role in formulating the new approaches.

Conclusion

This chapter has examined two unique influences on drunken driving countermeasures: policy-making within the U.S. federal system and the limitations placed on the government by the Bill of Rights contained in the U.S. Constitution. Although everyone agrees that drunken driving should be eradicated, a formulation of effective governmental responses must take these two influences into account. Moreover, we should recognize the effect that drunken driving has had on our federal system of government and the protections guaranteed by the Constitution.

Traditional Methods of Control

7 The Effects of Changes in Availability of Alcoholic Beverages

Ragnar Hauge

Introduction

Drinking and driving defines itself as a combination of two elements—drinking alcohol and driving a motor vehicle. In countries under Muslim law where alcohol use is prohibited—and the prohibition is effective—drinking and driving will be nonexistent. The same is the case in countries where motor vehicles are not used. Although it may be difficult to find such countries today, one need not go very far back in history to find examples.

Because these two elements are crucial, it should be possible to reduce drinking and driving by reducing alcohol consumption or the use of motor vehicles, or both, and some examples confirm this. The oil embargo in 1973, which resulted in a dramatic decrease in oil export from the Gulf States to the Western world, led to severe restrictions on the use of gasoline in many countries. Some countries prohibited the use of private cars on Sundays, with the result that drinking-and-driving offenses declined to a minimum. The experience during World War II affords another example. Owing to reductions in the import of alcoholic beverages and restrictions against using grain or potatoes for the production of beer and spirits, alcohol consumption, especially in many countries in Northern Europe, decreased significantly. This, in combination with scarcity of cars and gasoline, led to a dramatic decrease in drinking and driving.

In practical politics, however, there have been few or no measures against the consumption of alcohol or the driving of motor vehicles that are deliberately aimed at reducing drunken driving. Admittedly, in many countries measures imposing restrictions on car driving have been introduced. High taxes on gasoline are one example of this; the subsidizing of public passenger transportation is another. But these measures have been justified on the grounds of financial policy, regional development policy, or social welfare policy. Measures restricting the consumption of alcohol are also very common, for example, in the form of taxes on alcoholic beverages, compulsory licenses for the sale of alcohol, and monopoly provisions. But these measures also are justified on grounds other than the restriction of drunken driving.

Measures against drunken driving instead have been directed against the combination of driving a car after having drunk alcohol and not against each of these two elements separately. Information campaigns have been used in attempts to persuade people to abstain from driving when they have been drinking or from drinking when they are going to drive. Penal provisions have been introduced in attempts to deter potential drunken drivers, and intensive police surveillance has been used as a means of increasing the risk of apprehension. Finally, efforts have been made to prevent those who have been caught drinking and driving from repeating their offenses by subjecting them to treatment measures.

In the course of the last couple of decades, however, certain changes have occurred. Over large parts of the world there has been a marked increase in the consumption of alcohol. Both in the United States and the United Kingdom the consumption of alcohol per inhabitant has approximately doubled since the middle of the 1950s, and in West Germany, the Scandinavian countries, and many other places the increase has been even greater (Produktschap voor Gestilleerde Dranken 1985). At the same time studies demonstrate that increased mortality and a long series of chronic injuries to health are directly linked to the consumption of alcohol (Sundby 1967; Lelbach 1974; Pequignot, Tuyns, and Berta 1978; Skog 1980). In addition, alcohol consumption has been implicated in a number of other social problems such as violence, public drunkenness, financial problems, and the like, even though cultural factors also play a major part (Mäkelä 1978; Hauge and Irgens-Jensen 1986).

The increased knowledge of the harmful results of high alcohol consumption naturally leads to the question of whether introducing social policies to control alcohol consumption may limit the harm. The theory underlying this question has, however, been met with counterarguments. Even if one succeeded in reducing the consumption of alcohol among the majority of people, it cannot be taken for granted that one would also thereby reduce the harm caused by alcohol. The majority of people have a comparatively moderate consumption of alcohol, which does not lead to particularly harmful effects. Consequently, if they reduced their consumption of alcohol, it would have little effect. Because alcohol-related problems of health and social behavior are primarily due to very high levels of personal consumption, no control measure will succeed unless it affects the behavior of heavy drinkers. Some contend that the heavy drinker's consumption of alcohol will be little influenced by measures directed at the general population. Even if it becomes more difficult to obtain alcohol, heavy drinkers will be willing to incur the extra trouble and the extra costs required to maintain their consumption rather than to reduce it. If this is correct, then such general measures aimed at restricting the supply of alcohol will be of marginal significance.

More recently, however, it has been thought possible to show that a reduction in the total consumption of alcohol in the population will also lead to a reduction of consumption among heavy drinkers. This point of view was first advanced by Ledermann (1956), and has subsequently been further developed by others engaged in alcohol research, especially by a group of researchers from Canada, Finland, Norway, the United Kingdom, and the United States sponsored by the World Health Organization (Bruun et al. 1975).

This view has been derived from studies of the drinking habits prevailing in different countries. These studies demonstrate that if one classified all alcohol consumers in a population on the quantity of alcohol consumed, one will find a specific distribution curve. Even if one could theoretically envisage an even distribution of consumption, in the sense that all drank about the same amount—or a normal distribution with, on the one hand, a group that drank little and, on the other hand, another group that drank a lot, and with the great majority in between—this is nevertheless not the pattern one finds. Instead there is a very uneven distribution, in which the majority of the population has a very modest consumption of alcohol, whereas a small part of the population is responsible for a disproportionately large part of the total consumption.

The same consumption curve is observed in diverse cultures, regardless of cultural differences in the absolute volume of alcohol consumption. It is found in countries in which alcohol, most often in the form of wine, forms an integral part of the general diet, as in many of the wine-producing countries in Southern Europe. And it is found in countries in which the consumption of alcohol, often in the form of large quantities of spirits, is linked to social intercourse at the weekend, as is the case in many population groups in Northern Europe and North America. In other words, there does seem to be a general distribution model for the consumption of alcohol despite the differences that otherwise exist as regards such consumption.

This means that if alcohol consumption of a population is altered, the percentage of heavy drinkers will also be altered. An increase in the total national consumption will regularly lead to an increase in all consumer groups, both among those who previously drank little and among those who drank a lot; as moderate drinkers increase their consumption, they eventually cross the threshold for reclassification and the percentage of heavy drinkers will consequently rise. Conversely, a decrease in total consumption will lead to a decrease in all consumer groups (Skog 1983).

Because the percentage of heavy drinkers will be altered in step with total consumption, it also follows that the harmful effects will likewise be altered. The connection between total consumption and the percentage of heavy drinkers on the one hand, and between heavy drinkers and harmful effects on the other, therefore implies a connection between total consumption and the extent of harmful effects.

The empirical connection between changes in the total consumption and changes in the harmful effects is apparent in mortality rates for cirrhosis of the liver (Seeley 1960; Ledermann 1956; Popham 1970). Subsequently, the relationship has also been demonstrated in mortality rates for other types of alcohol-related diseases (Skog 1985).

The fact that changes in total consumption seemingly affect all consumer groups, including heavy drinkers, suggests that alcohol-related traffic injuries may be decreased through a reduction in total consumption. Even though drunken driving is relatively widespread in large groups of the population, certain groups are more likely than others to be involved in alcohol-related traffic accidents. A long series of studies has shown that the chances of being involved in a traffic accident increase greatly as the blood alcohol concentration (BAC) increases. Among Norwegian drivers, for instance, the risk of being killed in a traffic accident is five times greater for a driver with a BAC between 1.0 and 1.5 promille than for a driver between 0.5 and 1.0 promille (100 milligrams of alcohol per 100 milliliters of blood). With a BAC between 1.5 and 2.0 promille, the risk is twenty-five times greater, and with a BAC over 2.0 promille the chances are one hundred times greater (Andenaes and Sørensen 1979).

The fact that accident risk increases as the BAC increases means that heavy drinkers represent the major threat to traffic safety. About half of those arrested for drunken driving in the Scandinavian countries have a BAC of over 1.5 promille. It is not, however, just a matter of chance that anyone drinks so much. A BAC of such dimensions will be achieved virtually only by persons with a long history of heavy consumption. And among the remaining half there are very few who have a BAC of under 1.0 promille (Nordisk Trafiksikkerheds Råd 1984).

Other types of data also confirm that a large percentage of those arrested for drunken driving have a very high level of alcohol consumption. Around one-third of those who are arrested for drunken driving in Scandinavia have been previously convicted of drunken driving (Nordisk Trafiksikkerheds Råd 1984). Studies of the so-called biological indicators of high alcohol consumption, primarily the level of GGT (gamma glutamyl-transferase), have found that in Finland 18 percent (Pikkarainen and Penttila 1981) and in Norway 21 percent (Gjerde et al. 1986) of drunken drivers have increased GGT activities. Especially among drunken drivers aged thirty years or more, the percentage with increased GGT activities is great—and in the Norwegian study this was the case with one-third.

Reducing the total consumption in the population should therefore also have the effect of reducing traffic accidents. This is to be expected partly because all consumers would lower their consumption and therefore less often drive with a BAC or more often drive with a lower BAC than they would otherwise have had. But because those driving with a low BAC do not have a particularly high accident risk, this would not mean much for the bulk of consumers. The major gains would be obtained because those drivers with a high consumption pattern also would reduce their consumption.

Theory and practice are, however, often two different things. The question of what actually happens with drunken driving and traffic accidents when the total consumption is altered is therefore an open question, to which only empirical data can give an answer. In what follows we shall therefore take a closer look at some studies that have attempted to highlight this question.

The Connection between Total Consumption and Drunken Driving

An obvious way of testing the connection between total consumption, drunken driving, and traffic accidents is through time-series analysis. If a relationship exists, then total consumption and traffic accidents will follow a more or less parallel course of development over time.

A study in Norway investigated the relationship between total consumption, persons convicted of drunken driving, and drivers of motor vehicles killed or injured from 1948 to 1979 (Hauge 1982). The reason for choosing drivers who were killed or injured was that among these drivers the percentage under the influence of alcohol is especially high. Figure 7.1 shows that course of development in the three variables. To obtain a uniform measure the data are converted to index values in which the year 1970 is equated with 100.

As appears from the figure, an approximately parallel course of development seems to have occurred: from the beginning of the 1950s, the consumption of alcohol, the number of drunken drivers convicted, and the number of drivers of motor vehicles killed or injured have all increased steadily. This is also the case after 1970 for the relationship between the consumption of alcohol and the number of drunken drivers convicted, whereas the covariation between alcohol consumption and the number of drivers of motor vehicles killed or injured seems partly to have been ruptured. In spite of an increase in alcohol consumption and an increase in the number of persons convicted for drunken driving, the number of drivers killed or injured stabilized in the first half of the 1970s. The main impression for the entire period seen as a whole is, however,

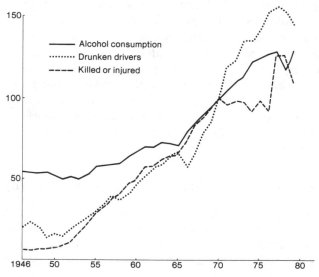

Fig. 7.1. Alcohol consumption, persons convicted of drunken driving, and drivers of motor vehicles killed or injured in Norway, 1946–1980 (1970 = 100).

that there is a marked connection between the three variables. This appears quite clearly if we calculate the covariations statistically. The correlation coefficient for alcohol consumption and persons convicted of drunken driving is 0.99, and for alcohol consumption and drivers killed or injured it is 0.93.

A statistical covariation tells us nothing, however, about the causal connection, and one cannot therefore draw the conclusion that the increase in the total consumption of alcohol is responsible for the increase in drunken driving and traffic accidents. Another possible explanation of the increase is the fact that the number of motor vehicles has greatly increased since the war. As appears from figure 7.2, a very high correlation also exists between the development in the number of motor vehicles and the numbers of drunken drivers and drivers killed or injured, respectively. The correlation coefficient is 0.98 for both the number of motor vehicles and the number of drivers killed or injured.

There are several possible interpretations of this configuration. One possibility is, of course, that the increase in alcohol consumption is the real causal factor, while the connection between the damage figures and the number of motor vehicles is spurious, that is, not an expression of any real causal connection. Such a spurious

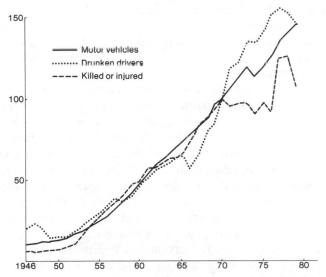

Fig. 7.2. Motor vehicles, persons convicted of drunken driving, and drivers of motor vehicles killed or injured in Norway, 1946–1980 (1970 = 100).

correlation may, for example, arise from the fact that both the increase in the consumption of alcohol and the increase in the number of motor vehicles are results of growing affluence since World War II. As both these increases have a common causal background in the economic development, there is a high degree of correspondence between them—the correlation coefficient is equal to 0.98. Both of them will therefore tend to have a high correlation with the damage figures, even though the increase in the consumption of alcohol is the real causal factor. In the same way one could, however, argue that the increase in motor vehicles is the real causal factor.

A third possibility is that both the consumption of alcohol and the number of motor vehicles can have a spurious correlation with the damage variables. It is a well-known problem in connection with the study of time series that two or more phenomena can co-vary over shorter or longer periods even though they have nothing at all to do with each other. Although it may sound a bit far-fetched, one could, for example, argue that the increase in drunken driving is primarily an expression of a change in attitude among the population, and that this change in attitude is independent of the change in drinking habits and the number of motor vehicles. This theoretical possibility is particularly present when the time series for these phenomena contain long-term trends, as in this case.

In principle, then, it cannot be excluded that the covariation of both the number of motor vehicles and the consumption of alcohol with the damage variables is fortuitous. The question is, therefore, whether on the basis of the available data one can say anything about which of these interpretations is correct.

If there is a causal relationship between the dependent variable (conviction for drunken driving or the number of car drivers killed or injured) and the independent variables (the consumption of alcohol and the number of motor vehicles), this should be evidenced by the fact that even short-term changes in the consumption of alcohol or the number of motor vehicles should correspond to changes in drunken driving or in accidents. For example, if motor vehicles increased 3 percent one year, alcohol consumption increased 1 percent, and accidents increased 4 percent, this would suggest stronger influence of motor vehicles than of alcohol consumption upon accidents for that year. There are several advantages connected with observing annual changes instead of long-term trends. First, one obtains a certain degree of protection against spurious correlations because the degree of change varies relatively unsystematically from year to year. Consequently, one will be able to study whether the dependent and the independent variables actually increase or diminish in step with each other, as the hypothesis of a causal connection would require. Correlation coefficients based on the long-term trend, on the other hand, reveal only the obvious relation that all the variables covary and tell us little about whether the covariations occur simultaneously.

Another advantage is that the covariation between the two independent variables becomes less when we look at the data showing changes than when we look at the data showing the long-term effect. In fact, the correlation between alcohol consumption and number of vehicles declines to 0.08. This eliminates the identification problem involved in deciding which of the two factors is of importance for the dependent variables if only one of them has a causal effect, or in deciding the relative importance of each if both have a causal effect.

When the linear correlations between annual change scores were calculated, the correlation between alcohol consumption and drunken drivers was 0.17, and between alcohol consumption and drivers killed or injured was 0.14. Neither of these is significant. As regards the number of motor vehicles, the corresponding correlation coefficients were 0.45 and 0.33, respectively. The first is highly significant ($p > .001$) and the second just missed significance ($p = .06$). (When the change scores were subjected to a logarithmic transformation, the correlation coefficients involving alcohol consumption were now 0.13 and 0.10 and, thus, were still not significant. For the number of motor vehicles, however, the figures were 0.51 and 0.48, respectively, and both were significant beyond the .001 level.)

If any conclusion is to be drawn from this, it must be that it is not possible to demonstrate any connection between the total consumption of alcohol and the number of persons convicted of drunken driving or the number of motor-vehicle drivers killed or injured in Norway during the period 1946–1979. Before firm conclusions may be drawn, the apparent connection must be related to other changes that have taken place during this period, especially the increase in the number of motor vehicles.

A similar analysis of Danish data covering 1930–1983 showed the same result (Thoresen and Petersen 1986). When an analysis was made of the covariations between alcohol consumption on the one hand and traffic accidents and personal injuries and deaths, respectively, on the other, no clear relationships emerged.

Skog (1985) has analyzed Norwegian data further with more advanced statistical techniques. Nevertheless, it was not possible to prove any connection. He could, however, show that the power of the statistical tests is limited, and that even reasonably strong relations would be difficult to verify statistically. His conclusion is that the data are inadequate for deciding whether or not the increasing consumption has led to an increase in traffic accidents.

Liquor Store Strikes and Drinking and Driving

On September 19, 1978, workers at Norway's state-operated Wine and Spirits Monopoly embarked upon a strike lasting nine weeks. Because sole selling rights for wines and spirits are vested in the monopoly, the result was a complete standstill in deliveries of wine and spirits to the monopoly's retail outlets and to licensed premises. At most retail outlets existing stocks were largely sold out in the first three weeks of the strike. On October 16 most retail outlets closed, and for six weeks, to November 27—one week after the strike was called off—retail sales of wines and spirits in Norway were virtually nonexistent.

This is illustrated by figure 7.3, which shows retail sales at monopoly outlets during the strike and in the weeks immediately preceding and succeeding it compared with retail sales in same period the year before. Before the strike actually commenced, a tendency to hoard wines and spirits was evident, but the stocks thus accumulated were insufficient to offset the decline in supplies during the strike. Immediately after the outlets reopened, sales increased, but the rise was remarkably moderate compared with what many people had expected considering the length of the strike. Sometime after the strike, and up to Christmas, sales were no different from what they had been in earlier years.

Throughout the strike, beer was sold as usual in ordinary grocery stores with a special permit. During the strike an increase in beer consumption probably made up for about 20 percent of the drop in sales of wine and spirits. Moreover, close to 10 percent of the drop was probably offset by increased purchases from the Swedish monopoly's outlets just across the border. At two of these outlets sales were five times higher than normal during the closing weeks of the strike. Customs officials reported that legal importation and smuggling of alcohol by people coming from abroad by plane and boat rose sharply, as did sales of the ingredients for homemade wine.

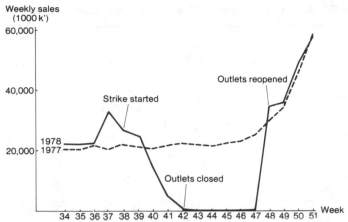

Fig. 7.3. Sales at State Wine and Spirits Monopoly outlets, weeks 34–51 (1977 and 1978).

Surveys based on interviews suggest that, in addition, there was an upswing in the production and consumption of illicitly distilled spirits. Furthermore, it must be assumed that many people were able to draw on stocks of wine and spirits which they had had at home before the strike. Although exact figures are unobtainable, it is reasonable to suppose that at least 40 to 50 percent of the decline was compensated by alcohol obtained through other channels. This would suggest that, in terms of pure alcohol, the decrease in consumption during the strike averaged up to 20 to 30 percent—rather less at the start, rather more toward the end (Horverak 1983).

Prompted by the strike, the National Institute for Alcohol Research embarked upon several related projects. Statistics were compiled on drunkenness, crime, venereal disease, casualty clinic intakes, absence from work, and commitments to various types of institutions for alcoholic patients in the weeks immediately preceding, during, and following the strike and in the corresponding weeks the year before.

A comparison of the five weeks of the strike when alcohol consumption was at its low with the same period the preceding year found a sharp decline in cases of public drunkenness during the strike. This is illustrated in table 7.1, which also shows a more significant decrease during the strike period than during the nonstrike period in the number of cases reported to the police of domestic disturbances and acts of violence against the person.

To examine the connection between drunken driving and the change in overall consumption resulting from the strike, three measures

Table 7.1. Reports to the Police 1977 and 1978 (Strike Year)

Reports of	1977	1978	Percentage change 1977–1978
Drunkenness			
Strike	1415	849	− 40.0
Nonstrike	1763	1877	+ 6.4
Domestic disturbances			
Strike	406	315	− 22.4
Nonstrike	476	487	+ 2.3
Acts of violence against the person			
Strike	136	115	− 15.4
Nonstrike	170	175	+ 2.9

Note: Strike period: Weeks 42–46; Nonstrike period: Weeks 34–36, 49–51.

were employed. As a measure of road accidents in general, information was obtained on claims made to one of the country's principal insurance companies. From the Central Bureau of Statistics, information was procured on accidents resulting in personal injuries or in drivers killed and injured. Finally, figures were gathered on the number of blood specimens sent to the National Institute of Forensic Toxicology, the central processing laboratory for blood alcohol analysis in Norway (Hauge and Irgens-Jensen 1980). Figure 7.4 illustrates the weekly trends in road accidents reported to the insurance company. No appreciable changes appear to have occurred during the 1978 strike, neither compared with the weeks immediately preceding and succeeding it, nor compared with the same periods the following year.

But what about accidents in which drivers were killed or injured? Other studies have shown that alcohol is a contributory factor in a comparatively large number of such accidents. It would therefore be reasonable to suppose that any decline in alcohol consumption would be reflected more strongly in accidents of this type than in less serious accidents.

Figure 7.5 reveals a more or less parallel trend in serious accidents for the year in which the strike took place (1978) and the previous year, apart from an extra-high peak in week forty-seven of the strike year, when the strike ended. This could be taken to mean that people let themselves go more than usual. In light of the appreciable weekly fluctuations that are a general feature of these accident statistics,

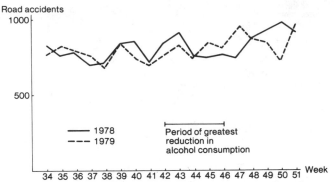

Fig. 7.4. Road accidents reported to a major insurance company, weeks 34–51 (1978 and 1979).

however, one cannot rule out the possibility that this peak occurred by chance. That the strike does not appear to have resulted in a reduction in the number of drivers killed or injured is also borne out in that the number of drivers killed or injured fell from 1977 to 1978 by 14.2 percent during the strike period and by 14.9 percent during the nonstrike period.

Figure 7.6 illustrates the number of blood specimens submitted to the National Institute of Forensic Toxicology in the weeks under review in 1978, the strike year, and the previous year. The number is perceptibly lower in 1978, and the difference appears to be particularly marked during the strike. In the strike period the number of specimens sent in fell from 1,197 to 989 in 1978, a drop of 17.4 percent, and in the nonstrike period it fell only .7 percent, from 1,332 to 1,323. This could mean that the strike led to the taking of fewer

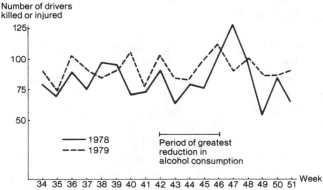

Fig. 7.5. Number of motor-vehicle drivers killed and injured, weeks 34–51 (1977 and 1978).

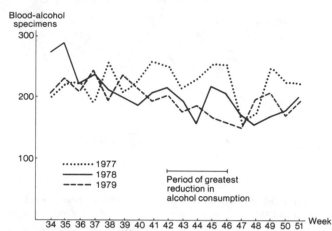

Fig. 7.6. Blood alcohol specimens received for analysis by the National Institute of Forensic Toxicology, Oslo, weeks 34–51 (1977, 1978, and 1979).

specimens than usual. However, if we compare the strike year with the following year, no corresponding difference is discernible; if anything, such a difference as there is points in the opposite direction. In fact, from 1978 to 1979 the number of blood specimens submitted for analysis in the strike period fell by 10.7 percent, and in the nonstrike period by 8.7 percent, suggesting that the number submitted during the strike period was greater in the year the strike occurred than might have been expected.

Summing up, it may be said that if we consider the five weeks during the strike when alcohol consumption was at its lowest level, there does not appear to have been any drop in the number of accident claims or in the number of drivers killed and injured on the roads. The picture is less clear with regard to blood samples submitted for analysis, but here too it is not possible to speak of a definite drop. In general, then, it appears that it is impossible to pinpoint any decline during the strike corresponding to the very considerable dip in, for example, reported cases of drunkenness.

How do these Norwegian results compare with those of other countries that have experienced liquor strikes? In the spring of 1972 a strike closed the retail outlets of the Finnish Alcohol Monopoly. It resulted in a substantial reduction in alcohol consumption, despite the fact that licensed premises and sales of light beers were not affected. During the strike, arrests for drunkenness decreased to about one-half of the normal number. A comparison between the strike month and the same month the year before and the year after showed that during the strike cases of drunken driving fell by 10 to

15 percent (Karaharju and Stjernvall 1974; Mäkelä 1974). However, in view of considerable monthly fluctuations, part of this drop may be explained by chance circumstances, and it has been claimed that the reduction in drunken driving due to the strike was practically negligible. This is explained by the fact that driving under the influence of drink in Finland is largely associated with visits to bars and restaurants; and, as has been noted, such places were unaffected by the strike and continued to serve alcoholic beverages (Takala 1973).

The effects of an alcohol strike in Sweden in 1963 were in many respects analogous to the Finnish experience. The impact of the Swedish strike on retail sales made itself felt gradually, and slowly tapered off, so that as an experimental situation the strike period was less clear-cut than in the Finnish case. However, when the strike was at its height, arrests for drunkenness in Stockholm were approximately half of prestrike figures. At the same time, though, only a slight reduction in the incidence of drunken driving was found (Andreasson and Bonnichsen 1965).

By and large, the conclusions drawn from the Swedish and Finnish studies accord with those arrived at in Norway—that is, public drunkenness was substantially reduced and the reduced availability of alcohol led to a reduction in alcohol consumption among certain categories of heavy drinkers. With regard to drunk driving, however, the changes appear to have been on a far more modest scale. Finally, it may be mentioned that these Scandinavian experiences are similar to what happened during two liquor strikes in Canada in 1975 (Smart 1976).

The Effects of Saturday Closing

In 1983 a decision was made to introduce Saturday closing for the State Wine and Spirits Monopoly shops in Norway. The reason for the decision was the desire to reduce the harmful effects of alcohol consumption. Because there was some doubt whether this measure would have the intended effect, it was at the same time decided that Saturday closing should be implemented on a trial basis in 1984. The results of this test period were to be evaluated by the National Institute for Alcohol Research, and on this basis it would be decided whether the system of Saturday closing should be made permanent.

For a more sensitive assessment of Saturday closing, six pairs of towns were selected for comparison. The towns in each pair were of roughly equal size; they were situated in the same part of the country and relatively far away from other towns with State Wine and Spirits Monopoly outlets. For each pair it was decided by drawing lots that in one of the towns the monopoly outlets should remain open on Saturdays, whereas in the other town (as was the case with the rest of the country) the outlets should be closed. Because the results of the study had to be available early in the autumn of 1984 when the government was to decide whether the system should be made permanent, the study period only covered the first half of 1984.

When Saturday closing came into force at the beginning of 1984, a long series of different sorts of data was obtained. Data concerning the sales in the monopoly outlets showed that in the experimental towns the sales of wine and spirits measured in liters of pure alcohol declined by 1.3 percent compared with the corresponding period in the previous year, whereas in the control towns it increased by 1.5 percent. In other words, the difference between the towns was found to be relatively modest because Saturday closing in the experimental towns led to increased sales on the other days. At the same time, there was a certain tendency toward an increase in the sale of beer—which was not covered by the Saturday closing—in the experimental towns than in the control towns. On the whole, this means that Saturday closing had a very limited significance for the total consumption (Nordlund 1984).

If one looks at individual days, however, the situation is different. In the experimental towns there was no opportunity to buy wine and spirits on Saturdays, and the effects, if any, should therefore primarily manifest themselves on Saturdays. In the first half of the year, for example, the number of persons detained for drunkenness compared with the corresponding period in the previous year declined by 5.1 percent on Saturdays (to Sunday morning) in the experimental towns with Saturday closing, whereas it increased by 10.8 percent in the control towns with Saturday opening. But the results were, nevertheless, not unambiguously positive. Even though the number of persons detained for drunkenness declined on Saturdays in the experimental towns, it increased on the other days. When one thus looks at all the days as a whole the difference between the two sets of towns was minimal—in the first half of 1984 the number of persons detained for drunkenness in the experimental towns declined by 7.5 percent compared with the first half of 1983, whereas in the control towns it declined by 7.9 percent. In other words, Saturday closing, as in the case of sales, seemed to have led only to a shifting from Saturdays to other days of the week and not to any real decrease (Hauge and Nordlie 1984).

To discover the effect on drunken driving, data were obtained concerning the number of drivers of motor vehicles who were subjected to blood tests because they were suspected of drunken driving. In the experimental towns the number of blood tests increased by 3.8 percent on Saturdays in the first half of 1984 compared with the first half of 1983, while in the control towns there was an increase of 3.3 percent. The conclusion consequently was that it was not possible to prove any clear effects of Saturday closing upon drunken driving (Irgens-Jensen 1984).

Discussion and Conclusions

The hypothesis that there is a connection between overall alcohol consumption and harmful effects also implies that, other things being equal, if alcohol consumption increases in a population, the percentage of motor-vehicle drivers driving under the influence of drink should increase accordingly. Since drunken driving is a contributory factor in many road accidents—and, in particular, in many in which the driver is killed or seriously injured—one would expect that, if alcohol consumption increases, the number of serious road accidents would also increase. Conversely, a drop in overall consumption would result in a reduction in the number of drunken drivers, and as a consequence, in the number of accidents.

The results of the studies in this review do not, however, seem to support this hypothesis. First, the reduced availability of alcohol during the period when the employees of the State Wine and Spirits Monopoly were on strike did not result in any demonstrable drop in the number of drunken drivers or in the number of road accidents. And the closing of the liquor shops on Saturdays was not followed by a drop in the number of drunken drivers on Saturdays overnight to Sundays.

One reason may be that strikes only mean a short-term reduction in the availability of alcohol. Most people manage to sustain their consumption of alcohol at a normal level all through the strike by drawing on their home supply, by making their own wine or liquor, by bringing alcohol from abroad, and by other means. The same applies to Saturday closing. For most people it simply means shifting their purchases from Saturdays to other days.

However, this demands a certain measure of initiative, reasonable financial resources, and possibilities of keeping a stock of alcohol. Certain groups of people, for example, skid-row alcoholics, may have had difficulty in sustaining their alcohol consumption in such ways.

There is evidence to suggest that this was indeed the case. According to a questionnaire survey comprising a representative sample of the adult Norwegian population, only about 10 percent of those queried reported that they consumed less alcohol during the strike. Separate studies of heavy drinkers at detoxification centers indicated that there was a greater reduction in this group's consumption of alcohol, both during the strike (Horverak 1983) and on Saturdays in towns where the liquor shops were closed. This seems to correspond to the reduction in public drunkenness during the strike. As mentioned earlier, similar results were found in connection with the liquor store strikes in Finland and Sweden, and in a study of Saturday closing at the Swedish Alcohol Monopoly (Olsson and Wickstrøm 1984).

Since relatively few people with grave drinking problems, like skid-row residents, are in a position to own or drive a motor vehicle, a drop in their consumption would probably not notably effect the incidence of road accidents and drunken driving. If, at the same time, it is assumed that alcohol consumption among the bulk of the adult population remained more or less unchanged during the strike and on Saturdays, this may explain why the effect of the strike was not particularly marked in terms of road accidents and acts of drunken driving.

Nevertheless, this cannot fully explain why the great increase in the consumption of alcohol in Norway and Denmark, as in most other countries, in the postwar period has not produced demonstrable effects as regards drunken driving and traffic accidents. Admittedly the number has greatly increased, but this increase seems to a high degree to be relatable to the increase in the number of motor vehicles and other possible factors rather than to the increase in alcohol consumption.

One obvious explanation may be that the lack of connection is due to cultural factors, where the penal provision and people's attitude to drunken driving enter in as central variables. It is a common feature of the Scandinavian countries, from which most of the studies referred to above are derived, that they have introduced permanent and relatively low BAC limits, and that from an international point of view violations of the drunken driving provision are severely punished. At the same time there is a high degree of acceptance of the statutory provisions and of the view that drunken driving is objectionable (Carstensen et al. 1978). The result of this is that there is reason to believe that large groups of the population will in practically every situation abstain from driving after drinking. At any rate, as far as Norway is concerned, this seems to be the case (Snortum, Hauge, and Berger 1986). This means that even if the consumption of alcohol increases, in that people drink more often or drink more on every drinking occasion, the risk of being involved in drunken driving is nevertheless not increased because they abstain from driving after drinking. The increase in the total consumption for which these people are responsible will therefore not occasion any increase in drunken driving.

If such factors as the penal provisions and the attitudes to drunken driving are conclusive, one would think that the effects of changes in total consumption would be different in countries with different penal systems and different attitudes. In countries where the population has small objections to drunken driving, and it is virtually exclusively the need for transport that decides whether one drives after drinking or not, there is reason to believe that drunken driving and accidents as a result of drunken driving will be far more affected by the total consumption in the population.

8 Deterrence of Alcohol-impaired Driving: An Effect in Search of a Cause

John R. Snortum

Historically, there has been little depth (Borkenstein 1985) or durability (Douglass 1982) of American commitment to reducing alcohol-impaired driving. However, the current control effort in the United States shows signs of outliving the lifespan that would be projected from past cycles of political activism and apathy. After a noteworthy federal investment in the Alcohol Safety Action Programs in the 1970s (National Highway Traffic Safety Administration 1979a), the usual decline of public interest was cut short by the astonishing surge of political influence by grass-roots organizations such as RID and MADD in support of stronger deterrence policies. As a result, from 1981 to 1985, state legislatures passed 478 new laws amidst rising expectations about the prospects for controlling the alcohol-impaired driver (National Commission Against Drunk Driving 1985).

Nevertheless, evaluations of the effects of increased legal threat in the United States and throughout the world have not been encouraging (Ross 1982, 1984a, 1985a). Such studies have rather consistently shown only temporary reductions in alcohol-impaired driving following the introduction of tougher laws or increased enforcement. The strict drinking-driving laws developed in Scandinavia have provided a model for legislation in many other countries. For this reason, it was particularly surprising that research on the introduction of

This review was supported in part by a grant from the Law and Social Sciences Program of the National Science Foundation. Special thanks are due to the following for their constructive criticisms of the manuscript: Ross Homel, Macquarie University, North Ryde, Australia; Thomas W. Mangione, Center for Survey Research, Boston; Michael Laurence, Fellow, Earl Warren Legal Institute, University of California, Berkeley; Franklin E. Zimring, Earl Warren Legal Institute, University of California, Berkeley.

per se laws in Norway and Sweden revealed *no* deterrent effects—not even a temporary reduction (Ross 1975). Thus, Ross concluded:

> There is no adequate proof for the proposition that the Scandinavian *per se* laws deter people from drinking and driving. Belief that such proof exists can be termed "the Scandinavian myth." The real basis for the belief is primarily folklore and anecdote. (Ross 1975, 308)

In those countries where temporary reductions in drinking-driving casualties were found, the results were more parsimoniously explained as the effects of publicity surrounding the introduction of controversial policies. Ross was, therefore, drawn to the rather pessimistic conclusion that "deterrence-based policies are questionable in the long run. No such policies have been scientifically demonstrated to work over time under conditions achieved in any jurisdiction" (Ross 1982, 111). It is crucial to note that Ross (1982, 8–9) carefully restricted his review to the effects of *simple deterrence,* which he identified as "the short-term component of general deterrence. . . . This focus is not intended to deny the existence of the long-term components. However, their attainment is expected to be a function of the adequacy and persistence of the short-term threat, which thus become a prior concern." Furthermore, in the interest of scientific caution, Ross preferred to emphasize studies which applied interrupted time-series analysis in testing the effects of legal changes because this method circumvents some of the problems of causal inference which plague correlational methods.

In an earlier review of Norwegian and Swedish evidence on deterrence (Snortum 1984a), it was suggested that Ross's (1975) assessment of Scandinavian drinking-driving policy was essentially correct within the framework of his methods and assumptions. However, it resulted in an imbalanced overview because he applied an unnecessarily narrow definition of "deterrence" (simple deterrence) and of "science" (causal analysis).

> Ross's standard of causal proof is a useful scientific ideal which promotes constructive dissatisfaction with the state of current knowledge and prods researchers to improve their methods for isolating the effects of critical variables. However, if this standard is used as the pivotal guide for policy review, it may result in a serious underestimation of the information at hand and lead to conclusions which seem to pit science against common sense. Between the extremes of causal proof and "speculation and intro-

spection" lies a huge storehouse of information about alcohol-impaired driving that has been accumulating since the turn of the century. The evidence is patchy, varying in quality, but improving over time. Legislators cannot wait until all the data are in nor wait for social scientists to test their models when the conditions happen to be ideal. As practitioners of the art of the possible, they do not ask for certain proof but only for an informed judgment about the weight of current findings—the circumstantial evidence. (Snortum 1984a, 14–15).

In decades past, the effectiveness of deterrence efforts was, more or less, assumed to be self-evident. Now after several years of sophisticated assessments, we have come to expect the opposite—that tough new programs will fail or will deliver only temporary gains. Even though this pattern of findings has been replicated with discouraging consistency throughout the world, there are now two bodies of "indirect" evidence that stable deterrence may be less elusive than we have been led to believe.

First, there is "circumstantial evidence" that Norway and Sweden have derived substantial benefits from strong formal and informal sanctions against drunk driving. Compared to the United States, Norway and Sweden exhibit somewhat lower rates of alcohol impairment among fatally injured drivers and much lower rates of impairment in roadside breath testing (Snortum 1984a, 1984b). Furthermore, compared to American drivers (Snortum, Hauge, and Berger 1986), Norwegian drivers demonstrated clearer knowledge of local drinking-driving laws, claimed stronger moral agreement with the law, and reported more tangible steps to reduce drinking in situations that require driving. The second body of evidence indicates important reductions in alcohol-impaired driving among American drivers over time. Extrapolations from the Fatal Accident Reporting System indicate that, between 1980 and 1985, there has been a steady decline in the proportion of fatally injured drivers who were intoxicated at .10 percent BAC or more (Fell 1985; Fell and Klein 1986). This decline is consistent with roadside breath testing data from eighteen police jurisdictions showing a 51 percent reduction in the proportion of drivers who were at or above .10 percent BAC in 1985 compared to 1973 (Wolfe 1986a).

Such findings place researchers and reviewers in an interesting conflict. "Something good" seems to have happened, but we cannot isolate the cause. In light of the many "successful" policies and programs which have been subsequently debunked by careful scholarship, we are well advised to be alert for extraneous influences which may produce results which mascarade as program effects. Ross's requirement (1982) that we identify the causal linkage between law and behavior has obvious merit in protecting against false attributions of effect for legal interventions. However, there are also risks in casting too narrow a methodological net in policy analysis because we may fail to give credit to life-saving programs that work in more subtle or more complex ways than anticipated.

The present review, then, will apply broader definitions of "deterrence" and "evidence" than were applied in Ross's earlier reviews (1982, 1984a, 1985a). In particular, this paper will attempt to advance the following goals: (1) to provide a simple schematic overview of several models of social control as they apply to special segments of the driving population; (2) to review some of the principal findings on the effectiveness of special deterrence, simple deterrence, and general prevention; (3) to explore some points of interaction between formal and informal sanctions; and (4) to suggest some issues for future research.

Because of the wide range of topics to be covered within a limited number of pages, it should be understood that this is not an exhaustive review of the literature on drinking-driving control. Other reviews offer a more intensive survey of special topics (e.g., Ross 1984a; Voas 1986a) or a more comprehensive survey of general topics (e.g., Jones and Joscelyn 1978; National Highway Traffic Safety Administration 1985a). As an orientation to some of the issues which lie ahead, current research is interpreted as showing that: (1) there are grounds for guarded optimism about the prospects for durable deterrence of drunk driving among a large proportion of the general drinking population; (2) a research focus on chronic drinking-driving offenders may blind us to important changes in compliance rates among marginal offenders; (3) a better understanding of the contextual influence of "moral climate" within a culture might help to resolve some of the inconsistencies within the quasi-experimental literature on deterrence; and (4) the principal challenge for researchers in the next decade will be to develop more sensitive measures for assessing the effects of "technical adjustments" to current drinking-driving laws.

I. Models of Social Control

In order to preserve the widest possible latitude in discussing the relationship between law and behavior, this review will employ the general definition of deterrence offered by Gibbs (1975, 2): "*Deterrence* can be thought of as the omission of an act as a response to the perceived risk and fear of punishment for *contrary* behavior." The value of this definition is that, by leaving the form of the punishment or the identity of the punisher unspecified, it allows for the operation of other social forces that are an outgrowth of legal sanctions or that interact with legal sanctions.

Figure 8.1 provides an overview of three general sources of social control, including the effect of formal sanctions (special deterrence), the effect of the *threat* of formal sanctions (general deterrence), and the effect of informal sanctions (social norms). An additional base layer of historical and cultural influences is shown in figure 8.1 as a reminder that broader contextual influences may either facilitate or inhibit the functioning of formal sanctions. Column One identifies the group which is most commonly targeted by selected tactics of social control. Column Three lists some general social processes which parallel these control theories on a continuum of coerciveness and also provides some examples of programs which implement elements of relevant control theories.

Because the concepts listed in figure 8.1 are not "pure" concepts which form mutually exclusive categories, one should not ascribe too much precision to the vertical placement of terms. For example, one could easily make the case that sobriety checkpoints are *intrusive* as well as *intimidating*, or that the checkpoints may very well serve for detecting violations by offenders with prior convictions as well as by offenders who have never been caught. Nevertheless, on balance, it is fair to say that convicted offenders are vulnerable to more intrusive control of their lives than undetected offenders and that undetected offenders constitute a larger proportion of offenders targeted by sobriety checkpoints than convicted offenders. In this respect, it would be better to imagine figure 8.1 as a color chart in which horizontal rows of color shade imperceptibly into one another.

Indeed, the chief function of this integrative scheme will be to demonstrate the conceptual hazards of attempting to review a single model of social control in isolation from others because they form an interdependent network. The strength or weakness of one element within the control structure may affect others (Andenaes 1974, 1975). For example, if jail is the legal sanction for drunk driving, then the deterrent threat of the law is weakened if the penalty is not actually imposed upon convicted offenders (a top-down influence in figure 1). Conversely, a heavy penalty, such as a jail term, is less likely to be

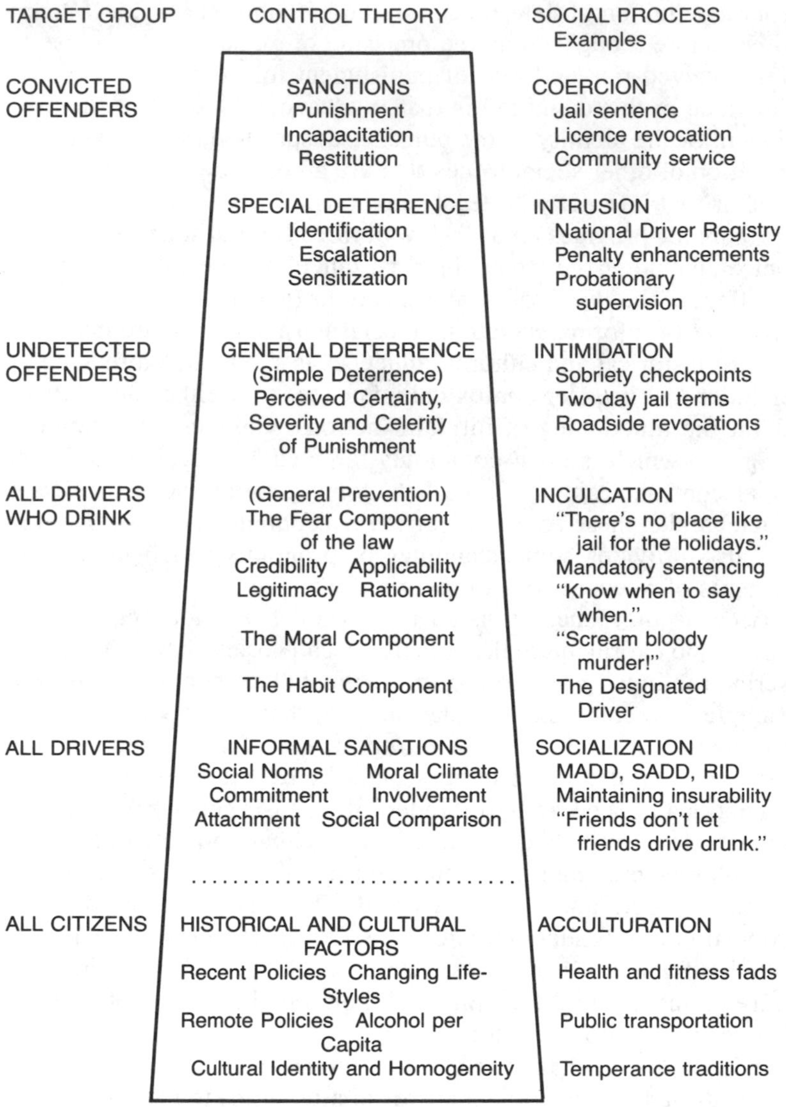

TARGET GROUP	CONTROL THEORY	SOCIAL PROCESS Examples
CONVICTED OFFENDERS	SANCTIONS Punishment Incapacitation Restitution	COERCION Jail sentence Licence revocation Community service
	SPECIAL DETERRENCE Identification Escalation Sensitization	INTRUSION National Driver Registry Penalty enhancements Probationary supervision
UNDETECTED OFFENDERS	GENERAL DETERRENCE (Simple Deterrence) Perceived Certainty, Severity and Celerity of Punishment	INTIMIDATION Sobriety checkpoints Two-day jail terms Roadside revocations
ALL DRIVERS WHO DRINK	(General Prevention) The Fear Component of the law Credibility Applicability Legitimacy Rationality The Moral Component The Habit Component	INCULCATION "There's no place like jail for the holidays." Mandatory sentencing "Know when to say when." "Scream bloody murder!" The Designated Driver
ALL DRIVERS	INFORMAL SANCTIONS Social Norms Moral Climate Commitment Involvement Attachment Social Comparison	SOCIALIZATION MADD, SADD, RID Maintaining insurability "Friends don't let friends drive drunk."
ALL CITIZENS	HISTORICAL AND CULTURAL FACTORS Recent Policies Changing Life-Styles Remote Policies Alcohol per Capita Cultural Identity and Homogeneity	ACCULTURATION Health and fitness fads Public transportation Temperance traditions

Fig. 8.1. The continuum of coerciveness from formal to informal control of drunk driving.

adjudged if the drinking-driving law does not enjoy broad public support (bottom up). Such interactions make it more difficult to be confident that law can be treated as a simple, independent variable. For example, the apparent effects of strict laws may, in fact, be due to the hidden influence of the strong moral indignation which gave rise to the law in the first place.

A review by Vingilis and Mann (1985) suggests still another reason for maintaining a broad conceptual sweep; there may be an interaction effect between the psychosocial type of offender and the type of countermeasure employed. The various control theories, shown in figure 8.1, are not all competing on a "level field." The difficulty of the deterrence task increases enormously with each vertical step among the target groups. For example, self-report surveys of drivers in Sweden (Norström 1978), Canada (Wilson and Jonah 1985), and the United States (Berger and Snortum 1985, 1986) have revealed distinctive social and attitudinal characteristics among drinking-driving violators which seem to make them more resistant to deterrence efforts. They were generally younger, unmarried males who drive more than average and drink more than average. Compared to other drivers, impaired drivers were less likely to believe that alcohol-impaired driving is wrong, physically dangerous, or legally risky, and they were more likely to claim a circle of friends who share their beliefs. Furthermore, within any group of self-reported violators, one can expect great individual differences in the frequency of violations and in the level of intoxication per event (Wilson and Jonah 1985; Snortum and Berger 1986).

Because drinking-driving violations are widespread and police apprehension rates are very low, there is a natural tendency for arrested drivers to feel embittered as arbitrary victims of "bad luck." However, Wilson and Jonah (undated) found that convicted impaired drivers differed in some respects from impaired drivers who have never been caught. The convicted drivers tended to drive more, consumed more drinks on the last occasion, and were higher on personality characteristics of depression and assaultiveness. Other research (Donovan et al. 1985) reveals close similarities between DUI offenders and "high-risk" drivers (with a history of nonalcohol-related violations) on personality characteristics of hostility, thrill-seeking, and depression. As further testimony to the array of problem behaviors which may be associated with alcohol-impaired driving, a significant proportion of DUI offenders have been shown to be "problem drinkers," and as a group they tend to show a consumption pattern that falls midway between control groups of non-drinkers and alcoholics (Vingilis 1983a).

The most vivid evidence that arrested drivers are not just a random sample of the general driving population comes from a criminal record search of 1,406 DUI cases in Massachusetts (Argeriou,

McCarty, and Blacker 1985). It was discovered that 27 percent had previous DUI arrests and 51 percent had been arraigned on criminal charges other than DUI. Within the full sample, 19 percent had been charged with crimes against persons, 29 percent with property crimes, and 34 percent with public order crimes, such as disorderly conduct, carrying a concealed weapon, and family abuse. Looking only at those drivers with prior DUI arrests, it was found that 68 percent had other kinds of criminal arrests. In short, DUI offenders tend to manifest a host of problems in impulse control and they have strong lifestyle commitments to social activities involving heavy drinking. Therefore, it is to be expected that deterrence gains will be hard won with this group.

It is apparent from figure 8.1 that the most recalcitrant offenders tend to be subjected to the most coercive kinds of tactics. While this is, no doubt, necessary, Zimring and Hawkins (1973) suggest that coercive restraints upon one's freedom of action may generate *psychological reactance,* whereby forbidden behavior actually becomes more highly desired. Thus, as offenders become increasingly antagonistic toward law enforcement, they may gain special satisfaction in finding ways to "beat the system," for example, by acquiring multiple licenses or by sharing "intelligence" on the likely times and places of sobriety checkpoints.

A. Formal Social Control

1. SPECIAL DETERRENCE

Although the sanctioning process may have important symbolic value for society at large, the concept of *special deterrence* is exclusively concerned with the direct effect of formal sanctions in preventing recidivism by the individual offender. Ideally, sanctions alone should be enough to sensitize the offender to the risks of further violations. However, because of high recidivism rates, it is common legislative practice to raise the stakes so that a second offense is met with a stronger penalty than the first. This, of course, requires an extensive record system so that the first offender will be properly "marked" for special sanctions upon the next conviction. Other sensitization procedures include probationary supervision or mandatory participation in community programs in lieu of stronger sanctions.[1]

There is relatively little evidence on the effects of penal sanctions. The available evidence suggests that, with one exception (Compton

1986b), incarceration appears to be either ineffective or counter-productive (Voas 1986a). Nevertheless, Voas (1986a, 65) suggests that "it would be a mistake to reject the use of incarceration on the basis of current evidence, if for no other reason than that the expanded use of the sanction in the United States will generate new evidence bearing on the issue."

It is generally assumed that imprisonment anchors the punitive extreme on the scale of sanctions for drunk driving. Indeed, an informal survey of Americans (Little 1971) showed the strongest aversion to "going to jail for a short time," followed by having one's picture in the paper, one-year license suspension, fine, and traffic school. However, there are probably individual and cultural differences in the meaning of sanctions and, furthermore, the relative rankings could, no doubt, be affected by increasing the relative "cost" attached to particular sanctions.

Middendorf (1985, 9) observed that many West German drivers would rather go to prison than lose their driving license. His explanation highlights the potential interaction between formal and informal sanctions: "If someone serves a prison sentence, those outside his immediate family need not know anything about it; but if he cannot drive his motor vehicle, the fact is immediately apparent to a large number of people and particularly to his co-workers." Middendorf's impressions square with a Norwegian survey in which people were asked to specify the amount of money that they would be willing to pay in order to avoid the two standard penalties for drunk driving (Bratholm and Hauge 1974). While only 11 percent of the sample were willing to pay as much as 3,000 Nkr. in order to avoid a twenty-one-day prison sentence, 28 percent would pay the amount in order to avoid a two-year license suspension. When Homel (1986) asked Australian DUI offenders to specify whether two weeks in prison or a six-month disqualification was the harsher penalty, he obtained the same fifty-fifty split shown earlier by Dutch DUI offenders in response to this question (Buikhuisen 1969). Both studies also demonstrated that disqualification was generally preferred by white collar workers, while incarceration was preferred by people who were most dependent on an automobile in their daily work.

There is a growing body of evidence in support of licensing actions as an effective drinking-driving countermeasure. In a pivotal study, Hagen (1978) identified drivers who escaped the usual mandatory suspension or revocation by virtue of having their prior DUI charges declared unconstitutional. These drivers were matched on gender and prior offences with similar drivers who had received the standard license withdrawal. In tracking survival rates over a six-year period, licensing action produced a significant suppression of DUI rearrests for about forty-two months and a reduction of crash rates for about forty-eight months. This effect went well beyond what would have been expected from incapacitation alone, for it was estimated that at least 70 percent of the cases involved only a twelve-month suspension rather than a thirty-six-month revocation.

Further insight into the "workings" of licensing controls was provided by anonymous surveys of suspended-revoked drivers (Williams, Hagen, and McConnell 1984). The results suggest that the term *incapacitation* should be applied to licensing actions in only a relative sense. Approximately 65 percent of drivers with a twelve-month suspension continued to drive, as did 75 percent of those with a thirty-six-month revocation. However, even among those who admitted driving, about two-thirds claimed some decrease in the amount of their driving and 29 percent reported as much as a 75 percent decrease. Furthermore, 85 percent claimed to limit their driving mainly between 6 A.M. and 6 P.M., and 66 percent felt that they drove more carefully than when they had their license. In short, this "sounds like" special deterrence (even though it is only *marginal* rather than *absolute* in degree).

There is some scattered evidence that alcohol-abuse treatment programs may be slightly more effective than licensing action in reducing alcohol-related driving violations (Peck, Sadler, and Perrine 1985a). Nevertheless, the bulk of the evidence indicates lower recidivism for multiple offenders subjected to licensing action than to treatment. Sadler and Perrine (1984) interpret the advantage of licensing action as being largely due to reduced driving exposure and driving more carefully. These effects are augmented by the practical considerations that a significant proportion of suspended-revoked drivers simply fail to meet the stipulated requirement to prove insurability as a condition for license reinstatement (Peck, Sadler, and Perrine 1985a). (In this sense, treatment groups are placed in a disadvantageous position in "survival" comparisons with licensing action groups, for many of the drivers in the licensing action group have simply been forced off the road by financial and bureaucratic obstacles to reinstatement.) In sum, convicted offenders are a highly recalcitrant group but, nevertheless, there is preliminary evidence that a small proportion are affected by some combination of special deterrence, incapacitation, and bureaucratic heavy-handedness.

2. GENERAL DETERRENCE

There is broad agreement that the so-called "dark figure" of undetected drunken driving is extremely high. While there are, of course, no reliable measures of hidden crime, the ratio of reported arrests to actual violations may be as high as 1/2000 in the United States (National Highway Traffic Safety Administration 1979a). Given the small proportion of offenders who are subjected to sanctions and given the limited effectiveness of special deterrence, it is clear that dramatic reductions in impaired driving will not occur unless means are found to deter violations within the general driving population. The concept of *general deterrence* is actually multidimensional and it is important to note that the term may cover either more (Andenaes 1952, 1977) or less (Ross 1982) ground than is commonly understood.

a) Simple deterrence: short-term components

If legal threat is the unifying thread of all deterrence theories, then *simple deterrence* is the purest form of the theory because legal threat is presumed to be both a necessary and sufficient cause of deterrence.

> In the simple model of deterrence, the reaction is a very specific one—comparing *this* crime with *this* penalty for one particular moment—and the results of this episode of weighing the pros and cons of lawbreaking do not alter the individual's personality, or sense of right and wrong, or general propensity to obey the law. If the individual is to be kept law-abiding, the process of simple deterrence must confront him at every turn—making each form of forbidden conduct a risk not worth taking. (Zimring 1971, 3)

The three principal facets of legal threat are commonly identified as perceived *certainty, severity,* and *celerity* of punishment (Gibbs 1975; Ross 1982). Thus, policymakers may attempt to influence these perceptions by passing laws which increase the probability of detection, the amount of the penalty, or the swiftness of punishment. Much of the current interest in evaluating deterrent effects from drinking-driving legislation can be traced to Ross's (1973) classic study of the British Road Safety Act of 1967. In order to aid police detection and documentation of offenses, the new law permitted officers to administer a preliminary breath test to all drivers who were involved in accidents or traffic violations or who provided other cause for suspicion of intoxication. To increase the probability of conviction, the law specified an absolute limit of .08 percent BAC as providing conclusive evidence of guilt, per se, without having to prove faulty driving. Based upon sanctions previously established, conviction led to a loss of driving privileges for one year. The law was highly controversial and the surge of associated publicity helped to increase public awareness of the change. Fatal and serious-injury crashes on weekend nights plunged sharply upon introduction of the new law, but gradually eroded over the next several months. Ross attributed the initial effect to the exaggerated perception of risk created by the publicity—a perception which could not be maintained when the objective risk of arrest remained very small.

Ross (1982) noted a similar pattern of temporary effects following legislation setting per se limits or expanding police opportunities for breath or blood alcohol testing in France (Ross, McCleary, and Epperlein 1982), New Zealand (Hurst 1978), Canada (Carr, Goldberg, and Farbar 1975), and the Netherlands (Noordzij 1977). Most of this legislation was modeled after laws which were pioneered in Scandinavia. But, ironically, Ross's (1975) analysis of archival crash records in Norway and Sweden failed to show even temporary reductions following the introduction of per se laws.

Far less causal analysis has been conducted on the effects of increased severity of sanctions upon deterrence but most of the evidence is not encouraging. Ross (1975) could not discern a reliable effect from doubling the maximum prison sentence in Finland from two years to four years in 1950. Conversely, after Denmark and Finland *reduced* sentence lengths, Ross, Klette, and McCleary (1984) could not detect a consistent pattern of *increased* casualties.

A recent Canadian study (Vingilis et al. 1985) offered a rare opportunity to test the effects of increased celerity of sanctions. Police in Ontario were authorized to initiate an immediate twelve-hour license suspension for any driver who registered .05 percent BAC in roadside breath testing. Time-series analysis suggested that, if there was any effect at all, it was slight and temporary.

Because legislative changes may be too subtle to be noticed, too technical to be understood, or too poorly implemented to be effective, it is possible that highly focused law enforcement "campaigns" would offer a better opportunity to observe simple deterrence in operation. From the array of studies reviewed by Ross (1982, 1984a, 1985a), it appears to be difficult to reduce offense rates by increased law enforcement activity, but it can be done—at least for short periods. For example, in the now-famous "Cheshire blitz" in Cheshire

County, England (Ross 1977), the chief constable instituted a one-month program of mandatory breath testing for all drivers involved in accidents or traffic offenses. The campaign generated a storm of public controversy but also yielded more than a ten-fold increase in breath testing compared to the same month in the previous year. Ross's time-series analysis revealed a significant reduction in crash injuries during that month and a nearly significant reduction in total late-night crashes which appeared to operate for as long as a month after the intervention.

More recently, Sykes (1984) reported beneficial effects from a five-month program of concentrated patrol in a fifteen-square-block area in Superior, Wisconsin. This target area encompassed only 15 percent of the city but it accounted for 48 percent of all accidents and contained 62 percent of the city's eighty-five bars and nightclubs. Accident rates within the target area decreased during the specific hours and days of concentrated patrol even though total accident rates in the target area increased slightly.

Using very different research methods, Votey (1978, 1979, 1982) employed econometric modeling to demonstrate the relationship between increased law enforcement activities and decreased fatal accidents in Norway and Sweden. While he reported an inverse relationship between accident probabilities and prison sentences served in Sweden, the more consistent finding from Votey's Scandinavian research suggests an inhibiting effect from licensing actions.

Not every enforcement campaign succeeds in driving down accident rates. The National Highway Traffic Safety Administration (1979b) supported thirty-five Alcohol Safety Action Projects throughout the United States in the early 1970s. After considerable methodological debate about the impact of this increased enforcement activity, it was finally concluded that significant reductions in nighttime accidents were achieved in twelve of these sites, that is, in about one out of three programs. In general, it appeared to be easier to demonstrate accident reductions in sites with a stable rather than expanding population and in sites with a relatively high base rate of nighttime fatal crashes, thereby allowing more room for improvement. While there was no simple relationship between DUI arrest rates and crash reductions, there was some evidence that higher enforcement levels had beneficial effects within those "ideal" sites with low population growth and high initial nighttime crash rates.

Despite the many intervening years of experience with enforcement campaigns since the Alcohol Safety Action Projects, the formula for guaranteed success still seems elusive. Wolfe and O'Day (1984) evaluated the first thirty-eight months of work by a special alcohol enforcement team in Oakland County, Michigan. While the program showed a reduction of alcohol-related accidents over base-line rates, the Oakland County rate was almost identical to the av-erage decline shown for the rest of the state. In contrast to the temporal pattern of accident reductions in Superior, Wisconsin (Sykes 1984), the accident rates in Oakland County showed less reduction during the enforcement team hours than during the rest of the week.

Other disappointing results were recently obtained from evalua-tions of sobriety checkpoint operations in Canada and the United States. Self-report surveys revealed no differences in drinking-driv-ing violations for target counties versus control counties in Maryland and Delaware (Williams and Lund 1984) and no difference in self-reports or alcohol-related accidents before and after a roadblock blitz in British Columbia (Mercer 1985b). Mercer (473) asks: "How could a month-long blitz that utilized 13,290 police hours, stopped 265,455 vehicles, and cost at least a half million dollars in police time, have failed to reduce drinking-driving?" Mercer (474) answers: "There is compelling evidence that police drinking-driving road-check activity will have little effect on reducing drinking-driving accidents without the public being made aware of this activity through substantial media support." If the success of law enforcement cam-paigns depends more upon the image than the substance of threat and if this image is largely in the hands of the press, then it is understandable that the police may have difficulty in producing re-liable results. Law enforcement campaigns will, undoubtedly, con-tinue to play an essential role in the total mix of deterrence tactics. However, their limitations are as apparent as their advantages. Law enforcement campaigns can be effective but, paraphrasing Zimring's definition of simple deterrence, these tactics seem to succeed in deterring only *this* crime, at *this* time, in *this* place.

Before generalizing too broadly about short-term effects, it is noteworthy that two recent tests of simple deterrence from legis-lative changes (one in the United States and one in Australia) have demonstrated somewhat more stable gains than is commonly re-ported in the literature. In 1981, Maine introduced a complex pack-age of laws which not only increased the penalties for drunk driving, but also increased the probability of conviction (Hingson et al. 1986). By downgrading lesser forms of intoxicated driving from a criminal offense to a civil offense, the evidence needed for conviction was reduced from "guilt beyond a reasonable doubt" to "a preponderance of evidence."[2] The next year, 1982, Massachusetts increased the severity of sanctions but did not include provisions for increased probability of conviction.

In the first year following the Maine legislation, telephone surveys revealed that drivers in Maine held stronger beliefs than those in Massachusetts that they would be caught, convicted, and punished. In 1982, following the Massachusetts legislation, there was an increase in the proportion of Massachusetts drivers who believed that they would be caught and punished, but no significant increase in the proportion who believed that they would be convicted. The attitudes of Maine drivers remained constant over the two-year period. Moreover, during the first postlaw year, Maine experienced a 33 percent decline in fatal crashes. This was somewhat greater than the decline for the same year in Massachusetts (24 percent) and was significantly greater than the decline for the other New England states (16 percent). While these gains were still intact during the second postlaw year in Maine, the fatal crash rates had returned to the prelaw baseline by the third year.

The introduction of strict enforcement procedures in New South Wales in 1982 appears to have resulted in an even longer suppression of crash rates. Homel (1986) reported a 23 percent reduction in fatal crashes during the first thirty-two months following the introduction of random breath testing. Implementation was vigorous. During the first twelve months, police administered almost one million breath tests, or one test for every three drivers. In addition, about $1 million was spent upon a publicity campaign to supplement general news sources. As was true in the Maine study, attitude surveys revealed that most of the critical features of the simple deterrence model were in place: there was high awareness of the program, drivers who had friends exposed to random breath tests had higher perceptions of arrest risk, and higher perceptions of risk were associated with stronger personal efforts to modify drinking or driving behavior toward compliance. Because this study employed a variety of methods and probed issues at many levels, it will serve to illuminate other dimensions of deterrence in later discussion.

In summary, recent findings generally continue to support Ross's (1984) generalization about the transitory nature of deterrent effects following increased legal threat. However, it may be instructive to ask the question: What is the definition of a "short-term" effect? Is it three months? One year? Two years? Perhaps those programs which have yielded *relatively* stable benefits (e.g., for a year or more) may provide important clues for further improvements in implementing the simple deterrence model.

b) General prevention: long-term components

The concept of simple deterrence is attractive to evaluation researchers because it is parsimonious and provides a straightforward framework for assessing the practical consequences of drinking-driving countermeasures. However, several writers (Andenaes 1952; Hawkins 1971; Meier and Johnson 1977; Synder 1985; Tittle 1980) have tried to alert us to the prospect of some broader dimensions of deterrence which are more difficult to operationalize but which may be equally important to the control process.

> To conceive the preventive effects of punishment as simply a matter of deterrence or intimidation is to miss the more subtle points which are fundamental; the whole thing is considerably more complex than the classical theory suggests. . . . It would be unwise to assume that because some evidence suggests that the short-term effects of change in the law are negligible that the long-term effects are also likely to be insignificant. (Hawkins 1971, 163–164, 176).

Monroe Snyder (1985) of the National Highway Traffic Safety Administration voiced similar reservations in response to a series of conference papers which reported rather disappointing effects from the introduction of legal countermeasures:

> Too much and too little have been expected from general deterrence programs; too much in the short turn, too little in the longer run. . . . General deterrence is not the total answer, but we should expect more from it than deterrence of a segment of the population. The long-term solution is the creation of a societal norm in which impaired driving or drinking and driving too closely in proximity is unacceptable. (Snyder 1985, 144)

If simple deterrence deals with the short-term component of deterrence, then what are the "long-term components" that encompass the rest of the concept of general deterrence? Because durable deterrence is presumed to depend upon the prior establishment of simple deterrence (Ross 1982), these long-term components cannot be clearly disentangled from their short-term antecedents. Classical deterrence theory emphasizes the role of the law as the "hammer" which functions through fear. Andenaes (1952, 1974, 1975, 1977) acknowledges the importance of the "fear component" of the law in producing a deterrent effect. But, in addition, he posits a socializing influence of the law which gradually engenders a change in moral outlook and promotes habitual law-abiding behavior. "From the legislator's perspective, creating moral inhibitions is of greater value than mere deterrence because the former may work even when a person need not fear detection and punishment" (Andenaes 1977, 51). He prefers the term *general prevention* over *general deterrence* as a reminder that law-abiding behavior may be driven by more complex motives than fear alone.

To those evaluation researchers who have seen how difficult it is to produce even a slight, temporary change in drinking-driving behavior, the notion of creating a new social norm must seem grandiose and implausible. Andenaes (1977) acknowledges that this moralizing effect is not inevitable but is more likely to operate when the law is perceived as reasonable, is promulgated by legitimate authority, and is impartially administered within "the machinery of justice."[3] Thus, while certainty, celerity, and severity of punishment are considered to be the cornerstones of simple deterrence, these facets of legal threat can be implemented with such integrity as to convey that the law is not only efficient and powerful (generating short-term fear) but also fair and reasonable (generating long-term respect). For example, the force of the law may be enhanced by demonstrations of its *applicability*. "Even if law enforcement agencies are capable of enforcing threats, members of an audience will not fear the imposition of consequences unless they are persuaded that the threat is meant to apply to them" (Zimring 1971, 66). In this light, when the media report that an eminent person, such as a senator or a bishop, is arrested for drunk driving, it helps to convey that the law applies to public figures in expensive cars as well as to day laborers in pickup trucks. Walker (1975, 280) elaborates a related concept which ostensibly pertains to probability of punishment but which also reveals the integrity of the "machinery of justice," *the credibility of the penalty*: "By this I mean the subjective probability not of being detected or convicted, but of receiving, if convicted, the sentence in question, and of having to undergo it in full."

If there is a greater willingness to comply with a law that is reasonable rather than arbitrary, it may be difficult to separate the "threat value" of the law from its "instructive value." Zimring (1971) suggests that the threat of punishment can offer a "a rationale for conformity." Mandatory seat belt laws provide an interesting case in point. Seat-belt use in New York State was 16 percent before implementing the new law (Rood and Kraichy 1985). Three months after enforcement began, use rates shot to 57 percent, and after nine months it had slipped to 46 percent, though still almost triple the original rate. In the first postlaw survey (three months), the predominant reason given by regular belt users was "the mandatory seat-belt law has passed." In the second postlaw survey (nine months), the predominant reason had become "safety." While "legal threat" was, no doubt, instrumental in promoting initial compliance, it is most likely that the threat was so effective because it gave people an extra reason to do what had always seemed vaguely sensible.

From the perspective of *general prevention* (Andenaes 1977), it becomes more difficult to construe law as a simple independent variable, for law is both a cause and an effect of "moral climate." Likewise, the process of moral socialization is a complex process which may require several years to take root. Such considerations help to explain why Andenaes was not disturbed by the apparent lack of effects in a causal analysis (Ross 1975) of the Scandinavian laws:

> If, as many people believe, the effect of the drunken driving legislation in Norway is due to the moral impact of the law, this is something that depends on a long-term process which would not be discernible in accident statistics. The lack of discernible effects of the law on traffic deaths therefore neither proves nor disproves anything. (Andenaes 1978, 47)

The theory of *general prevention* is not directly testable. However, two types of indirect or "circumstantial evidence" lend credence to the concept.

(1) Measures of compliance within a jurisdiction. The traditional question in criminology is: "Why do people break the law?" The traditional answer seems to be that people break the drinking-driving laws because drinking is pleasant, driving is convenient, and arrest risk is trivial—as low as one arrest in the United States per two thousand violations. Under these conditions of low risk, the converse question becomes the more interesting one: "Among people who like to drink and need to drive, why would *anybody* obey the drinking-driving laws?"

The United States tends to anchor the bottom ranks in international comparisons of undetected drunk driving (Organisation for Economic Cooperation and Development 1978; Nordisk Trafiksikkerheds Råd 1984; Snortum 1984a). In the spirit of Diogenes' search for an honest man, Snortum and Berger (1986) surveyed 1,401 American drivers in 1983 with little optimism of finding people who take tangible steps to control their drinking or driving in drinking-driving situations. Questions addressed the driver's usual drinking volume under ordinary circumstances, the mode of transportation to the last drinking occasion, the volume of alcohol consumed at this event, and the mode of transportation on the return trip. As expected, the survey revealed very high rates of drinking-driving violations. However, three types of control occurred at rates beyond chance levels: (1) people who traveled to the last drinking occasion in the role of driver showed significantly larger reductions of drinking (beyond baseline levels) than did people who traveled as a passenger; (2) there was a tendency to assign the driving role to people with low baseline levels of drinking, thus it was less of a sacrifice for them to control their drinking; and (3) drivers who drank heavily at the last occasion were more likely to relinquish the driving role on the way home than were other drivers. While one cannot rule out the possibility that these drivers were manifesting the usual short-term reponse to a short-term enforcement campaign within particular jurisdictions, in light of the nationwide scope of the study, it seems more likely that the survey was tapping a stable pattern of control.

If it is surprising to find some evidence of stable compliance in the United States, it is even more remarkable to discover a long-term *declining trend* in drunk-driving deaths (Fell 1985). Fifteen states have contributed relatively complete data to the Fatal Accident Reporting System (FARS) since 1980. Drawing upon the FARS data from 1980 to 1984, Fell noted the following annual proportion of killed drivers who were intoxicated to the level of .10 percent BAC or greater: 50 percent, 49 percent, 48 percent, 46 percent, and 43 percent, respectively. The figures had obvious limitations as national estimates for the fifteen states were not necessarily representative and the accident statistics for the huge state of California determined approximately half of the total. As a remedy, Fell and Klein (1986) applied discriminant analysis to cases with a known BAC in order to develop a profile of driver and vehicle characteristics that might be used to estimate alcohol involvement among fatally injured drivers who had not been tested. The new national estimates on the proportion of drivers killed at .10 percent BAC or greater were slightly lower than the fifteen-state figures but, as before, they continued to show the same downward trend. These figures span 1982 through 1985 (Finkelstein 1986): 44 percent, 43 percent, 40 percent, and 38 percent, respectively. The proportion of cases with BACs from .01 to .09 remained constant at about 9 percent through these four years and the proportion of cases with no trace of alcohol in the blood increased: 47 percent, 49 percent, 51 percent, and 53 percent, respectively.

Fell and Klein (1986) provide some important clues about the people who are dropping out of the casualty statistics. The greatest reductions in· alcohol-related fatalities from 1982 to 1984 occurred for the following types of cases: *for drivers* under twenty and over thirty-four, with a valid license, with no prior DWI convictions, using seat belts, in four-door rather than two-door vehicles, and in cars rather than on motorcycles; *for accidents* that occurred during daytime rather than nighttime, during weekdays rather than weekends, and on major highways rather than local streets and that involved many vehicles in the crash rather than just one.

What does it all mean? Is this deterrence or is it the good luck of demographic shifts away from younger to older, more responsible drivers? Examining only the reduction in teenage fatalities, Fell and Klein (1986) credit the legislative action in many states that raised the drinking age to twenty-one during this period. "The reduction in the *proportion* of the teenage drivers who were drunk was more of a factor in the overall reduction and not the slight reduction in their involvement in fatal crashes overall" (17). Furthermore, they believe that most of the decline in alcohol-related fatalities for the general population was due to a combination of stricter laws, increased alcohol awareness, and increased publicity about prevention. Based upon the profile of driver-and-crash types showing the greatest improvement, it appears that the principal gains have come from social drinkers who exercise reasonable precautions during daytime activities.

Researchers at the Crime Control Institute (Irwin 1986) expressed strong reservations about Fell and Klein's estimation procedures and they urge, instead, that all states should move toward comprehensive testing of crash-involved drivers in order to obtain direct measures of BAC. Whatever the merits of these criticisms, it is interesting to note that there is independent evidence in support of a declining rate of alcohol-impaired driving in the United States. In 1986, Wolfe replicated his 1973 sampling of breath alcohol levels obtained from drivers on Friday and Saturday nights between 10 P.M. and 3 A.M. The national estimates showed a drop from 4.9 percent at or above .10 percent BAC in 1973 to 3.2 percent in 1986, a reduction of 37 percent. The proportion at or above .05 percent BAC fell from 13.5 percent to 8.3 percent, a reduction of 39 percent. Looking only at the data from eighteen police jurisdictions which were tested in both studies, the reduction at the .10 and .05 percent BAC cutting points were even stronger, 51 percent and 58 percent, respectively.

As is usually found in such surveys, male drivers registered higher BACs than did female drivers. And, given that there were more female drivers on the road on weekend nights in 1986 (26 percent of the sample) than in 1973 (16 percent), this factor contributed to the reduction in the average BAC. Nonetheless, because of the strength of the BAC differences between samples, it is Wolfe's assessment that real change has occurred. "Clearly the war has not been won, for one cannot feel very sanguine about finding that only one in seven instead of one in four drivers are potential accident hazards due to drinking. But it is pleasing to have some evidence that the drunk-driving problem is not completely intractable and that some progess is being made" (Wolfe 1986a, 4).

(2) Cross-cultural comparisons of compliance. International comparisons of alcohol impairment among the general driving population have shown a lower rate of alcohol impairment among drivers in Scandinavia compared to other countries in Western Europe and North America (Nordisk Trafiksikkerheds Råd 1984). The contrast is particularly sharp between Norway and Sweden versus the United States (Snortum 1984a). Random roadside breath alcohol surveys have shown no more than 2 percent of the drivers in Oslo and Stockholm to be above .05 percent BAC on a weekend night compared to rates of 6 to 24 percent obtained in some American cities. The Scandinavian advantage shrinks considerably in data on fatally injured drivers. Approximately one in three drivers in Norway and Sweden have been shown to have BAC levels of .05 percent or greater, compared to a ratio of about one in two at this level in the United States. It is, of course, difficult to interpret such data because they were obtained under dissimilar conditions using dissimilar measures and they are, undoubtedly, affected by a number of extralegal factors such as per capita alcohol consumption and automobile usage. Nevertheless, there is evidence that these national differences are not wholly spurious effects of these indirect influences but are largely due to the conscious decisions by drivers in handling specific situations where alcohol is available.

In his frequent travels between Norway and the United States, Andenaes was struck by the "radical difference" in attitudes toward drinking-driving situations in the two countries. In Norway, "when a man goes to a party where alcoholic drinks are likely to be served, and if he is not fortunate enough to have a wife who drives but does not drink, he will leave his car at home or he will limit his consumption to a minimum" (Andenaes 1975, 60). These observations were used to frame questions for a survey which was administered to 1,012 Norwegian drivers and 1,000 American drivers (Snortum, Hauge, and Berger 1986). Almost as if following a script, these drivers confirmed the "radical" national differences in each of the three forms of controls specified by Andenaes. Interviewees estimated the rate of compliance by other drivers at drinking occasions, using a five-point scale ("almost none," "about one-quarter," "about one-half," "about three-quarters," "almost all"); however, modal responses for Norwegians and Americans always fell at opposite extremes: (1) proportion who abstain from drinking when they are driving: in Norway, 75 percent of drivers reported "almost all"; in the United States, 60 percent reported "almost none"; (2) proportion of groups that appoint one person to remain sober for the drive home: 76 percent, "almost all" versus 42 percent, "almost none"; (3) proportion of parties where at least one person arrives by bus or taxi in order to feel free to enjoy drinks: 83 percent, "almost all" versus 63 percent, "almost none."

Norwegian and American differences in self-reported violations were somewhat less dramatic, but were consistent with the pattern reported for other drivers. Twenty-three percent of Americans admitted at least one instance of driving "while slightly intoxicated" within the previous year, compared to only 8 percent of Norwegians. Given that the Norwegian blood alcohol limit is only half that in the United States (.05 percent versus .10 percent BAC), it is interesting to note that Norwegians seemed to apply a more stringent definition of "intoxication." When asked to identify "the largest number of drinks that you personally have been able to handle and still manage to drive your car back home," the American rate for driving after consuming three or more drinks was eight times the Norwegian rate (25 percent versus 3 percent).

Considering only self-reported behavior at the last drinking occasion away from home, the average Norwegian consumed about fifty percent more alcohol than the average American. However, the pattern of consumption differed sharply according to the individual's role as driver or passenger. Norwegians who drove "to" and "from" the occasion drank far less than the American drivers, while the Norwegians who were two-way passengers drank much more than their American counterparts. Even though teetotalers were removed from this analysis, it was found that 78 percent of all Norwegian drivers "from" the last occasion abstained from alcohol at this event, compared to only 1 percent of all Norwegian nondrivers. This contrasts with abstention rates of 17 percent for American drivers and 8 percent for nondrivers. In addition, this survey of the last drinking occasion revealed much higher proportions of Norwegians than Americans who used public transportation to the last occasion and who relinquished the driving role to a substitute driver after heavy drinking.

Of course, it is impossible to isolate the cause of these effects because of the many "background" factors which could be operating. Compared to the United States, Norway is a more homogeneous culture, with stronger temperance traditions, lower per capita alcohol consumption, higher taxation on alcoholic beverages, lower levels of automobile usage, and a more complete public transportation system (Snortum 1984b). Nevertheless, as shown in table 8.1, there were a number of survey items that suggest that legal threat and moral commitment contribute to these national differences in some important way.

Norwegian drivers had a much better technical understanding of local drinking-driving laws than did their American counterparts. Norwegians were particularly knowledgeable about BAC limits, the role of per se laws, and the sanctions that would follow conviction. In contrast, Americans responded at a level of accuracy that could be obtained by random guessing among alternatives. Norwegians also showed almost universal moral disapproval of driving after consuming as many as four drinks and they were more likely than Americans to believe that their peers would also disapprove. While one might be impressed by the fact that 79 percent of Americans also registered their disapproval on this item, the remaining 21 percent of the population are crucial because they represent a disproportionate share of the heavier drinkers. Thus, disapproval was registered by 94 percent of the drivers who never drink alcoholic beverages, by 77 percent of the drivers who ordinarily drink no more than three drinks (even when not driving), and by only 47 percent of those who routinely consume four or more drinks at a sitting.

Table 8.1. Comparison of American and Norwegian Samples on Knowledge, Risk Perception, Moral Agreement, and Perceived Sanctions

	U.S. %	Norway %
Knowledge[a]:		
Knows whether BAC alone is sufficient for conviction (2 alternatives)	46	95
Knows the BAC limit in own jurisdiction (5 alternatives)	18	84
Knows the number of drinks needed for a 140-pound person to reach illegal BAC level (7 alternatives)	18	43
Knows the sentence for first offense violations (5 alternatives in the U.S. and 8 alternatives in Norway)	14	72
Knows the license suspension period for first offense violations (5 alternatives)	19	50
Moral Commitment to the Law:		
Favors random roadside breath tests by police	57	95
Morally opposed to driving after as many as four beers	79	98
Friends would disapprove driving after four beers	63	89
Favors a prison term for first offense drunk driving	52	71
Perceived Risk:		
Knows someone who has been killed or injured by a drunken driver	40	27
Believes that there is at least a 10% probability of an accident after drinking six shots of whiskey	69	71
Believes that there is at least a 10% risk of an arrest in driving after drinking six shots of whiskey	41	30
Perceived Sanctions:		
Knows someone who was arrested for drunk driving in the past year	37	22
Knows someone who served a jail term for drunk driving during the past year	15	23

[a]Questions probing accuracy of knowledge count "no response" as a "wrong" answer. All other questions exclude nonresponses from the tallies.

Comparable disapproval rates among Norwegian drivers were 97 percent, 98 percent, and 98 percent, respectively.

Perceptions of "risk" did not seem to follow a simple pattern and, surprisingly, failed to show a consistent advantage for Norway. A higher proportion of Americans claimed to know someone who was arrested for drunk driving, and Americans also tended to give higher estimates of risk of arrest. On the other hand, a higher proportion of Norwegians admitted that they had been arrested for drunk driving (6 percent versus 3 percent, not shown in table 8.1), and a higher proportion of Norwegians knew someone who had been subjected to incarceration. And, as further evidence of the complexity of risk perception, more Americans knew someone who had been killed or injured by a drunk driver but this did not seem to produce a significantly higher perception of accident risk among Americans. These findings suggest that, if the so-called preconditions for deterrence do contribute to the reported national differences in drinking-driving violations, then subjective risk of arrest may be a less critical variable than knowledge, moral commitment, and legal consequences following arrest.

B. Informal Social Control

1. CONCURRENT INFLUENCES: PEER PRESSURE

There tends to be a natural division of labor whereby researchers either evaluate the direct effects of formal countermeasures or estimate the indirect effects of informal social controls. Part of the attractiveness of *general prevention* is that Andenaes (1974) writes "as if" people live in both worlds at the same time. As general prevention gathers momentum behind a particular law, it is assumed that there will be fewer "bad examples" and more positive role models in the general population. "A successful inculcation of moral standards may result in social pressure toward acceptable behavior even for persons who have not been personally influenced by the moral message of the law " (51).

Here is where the definitional problems become critical. If "legal threat" has, somehow, been transformed into "social influence," should this material be included in a review on deterrence? There is little disagreement that more encompassing conceptions of deterrence multiply the evidential problems which were already monumental among simpler theories (Andenaes 1977; Gibbs 1975; Tittle 1980). One can appreciate why many policy analysts might simply choose to circumvent the issue by treating informal social control as "noise" that confounds the effects of legal countermeasures. Nevertheless, scattered pleas for an integrated theory of deterrence (Meier and Johnson 1977; Tittle 1980; Zimring and Hawkins 1973) seem to be gaining ground.

Meier and Johnson (1977, 293–95) object to "an uncritical acceptance of the deterrence doctrine without a corresponding theoretical rationale that is based on established principles of social influence and control. . . . The deterrence hypothesis *requires* that the multiple sources of conformity be identified; only one of these is legal threat." In even stronger terms, Tittle (1980, 5) suggests that "it is the height of academic and linguistic imperialism to claim that a symbol such as the word *deterrence* can be applied to only one situation, especially when even conventional usage allows greater flexibility."

Among the many competing theories of social influence, Hirshi's (1969) *control theory* is particularly well suited for delineating the social context within which legal threat may be effective or ineffective. The theory predicts, for example, that a person will be less likely to break the rules if he or she has strong bonds of *attachment* to individuals who would disapprove of the violation. Likewise, one would expect fewer violations among people who have a strong *commitment* to social opportunities that would be jeopardized if they were caught in the violation. Thus, one might expect that taxi drivers would have a higher than average "stake" in avoiding a drunk-driving arrest in order to protect their livelihood.

While peer pressure is a central theme in most compliance research, recent efforts to create a new drinking-driving norm through MADD and SADD provide a rare opportunity to observe such compliance pressures as an evolving process. There seem to be no systematic assessments of these programs to date; however, these two groups have received "honorable mention" in research designed to examine other issues. In a recent survey tapping awareness of roadblock testing in three eastern states, Williams and Lund (1984, 13) noted that, aside from roadblocks, "most frequently cited were the activities of Mothers Against Drunk Driving (MADD) (22 percent) and news media coverage (17 percent). The activities of MADD and Students Against Drunk Driving (SADD) were most prominently mentioned in Fairfax County.[4] In fact, MADD received more mentions in Fairfax than did roadblocks (37 percent versus 35 percent)."

The norm against drunk driving appears to be both intense and broadly based in Norway (table 8.1). The Swedish standard seems to be equally severe. In assigning crime-seriousness ratings to a variety of offenses, Swedes rated drunk driving at about the same level as armed bank robbery (Lindén and Similä 1982). This kind of "moral climate" is, undoubtedly, desirable from the standpoint of traffic safety, but it creates headaches for the researcher who is responsible for assessing the effects of new laws. "If community condemnation of certain criminal acts is strong, this may lead to lower crime rates and at the same time to a greater severity of punishment, thus creating the impression that the lower crime is due to the severity of punishment" (Andenaes 1975, 348). Similarly, once strong norms are established, it may be difficult to isolate the effects of police practice because "policing" drunk driving becomes everybody's business. Indeed, excluding drunk-driving arrests through routine accident investigations, it appears that about one out of every four drunk-driving arrests in Norway, Sweden, and Denmark originates from the general public (Nordisk Trafiksikkerheds Råd 1984).

Despite scattered efforts to promote such citizen reporting in the United States, it is not yet clear if the approach will take hold. During the first several months of operation of a Colorado hotline for reporting suspected drunk drivers, there were 21,147 calls, leading to 2,550 arrests (Curry 1983). Larson (1985) surveyed North Dakota drivers' perceptions of the REDDI (Remove Every Drunk Driver Immediately) program twenty-one months after its inception. While 26 percent were vaguely aware of the program, only 8 percent knew the 800 number for calling REDDI, and only .3 percent had actually called REDDI.

There may be greater hope for success through less punitive forms of intervention as expressed in the slogan: "Friends don't let friends drive drunk." In a 1980 survey of 1,500 American drivers, 42 percent claimed to have taken some action to prevent someone from drunk driving in the previous year (National Highway Traffic Safety Administration 1980). This proportion is an improvement over figures from the early 1970s: 1972, 16 percent; 1974, 21 percent; 1975, 39 percent; 1976, 41 percent; 1978, 37 percent; 1979, 43 percent. Among drivers interviewed in 1980, intervention tactics included: drive person home, 64 percent; took keys, 15 percent; had person stay over, 12 percent; physical restraint, 3 percent; called a taxi, 2 percent; called police, 1 percent; other, 15 percent. McKnight (1986) as well as Mann et al. (1986) have reviewed programs designed to promote peer intervention by teenagers in drinking-driving situations. Such programs commonly demonstrate short-term changes in attitudes toward control, but there is little evidence that these improved attitudes yield subsequent behavior changes toward increased self-control or increased rates of peer intervention.

There is now a large literature of attempts to "model" the influence of formal and informal sanctions upon various types of self-reported offenses (Paternoster, Saltzman, Waldo, and Chiricos 1985; Tittle 1980). Consistent with much of the quasi-experimental research on deterrence of drunk driving (Ross 1982; Voas 1986a), these correlational studies typically reveal an inverse relationship between delinquent activities and perceived risk of punishment, but only occasionally do they show a significant effect for perceived severity of sanctions (Grasmick and Bryjak 1980; Paternoster and Iovanni 1986).

Of course, the temporal ordering of variables in such causal modeling is problematic. More recent longitudinal research suggests that much of the alleged "deterrent effect" reported in earlier cross-sectional research could be better interpreted as an "experience effect" (Paternoster et al. 1983). That is, as people commit rule violations and "get away with it," they may revise their risk estimates downward. Of greater significance for the present discussion, several studies have shown a strong influence for extralegal variables linked to social control. In fact, when the statistical contributions of formal and informal sanctions have been directly compared in multivariate analyses, informal sanctions have tended to predominate (Anderson, Chiricos, and Waldo 1977; Meier and Johnson 1977; Paternoster and Iovanni 1986; Paternoster et al. 1983).

Norström (1978, 1981) developed multivariate models of self-reported drunk driving by Swedish drivers, based upon a matrix including demographic characteristics, knowledge of the law, moral agreement with the law, and perceived risk of an accident or arrest. In an unusual step, Norström also tapped two drinking-driving "opportunity variables," estimates of annual driving mileage and alcohol consumption. Using path analysis in the first study and LISREL in the second, alcohol consumption and moral agreement were the two strongest predictors, while legal knowledge and perceived risk did not contribute to either model.

Berger and Snortum (1986) applied path analysis to survey data from American drivers and, essentially, replicated the Swedish findings in showing an influence for alcohol consumption and moral agreement and no effect for arrest risk and legal knowledge. Two additional predictors, preference for beer and moral attitudes of one's friends, also made independent contributions to the model, indicating the potential significance of social norms and a "beer subculture." While these findings suggest that perceived risk of arrest is not a critical inhibitor of drunk driving, it should be noted that drivers estimated arrest risk for an anonymous driver rather than for themselves. A review by Paternoster, Saltzman, Chiricos, and Waldo (1982) showed that personalized estimates tend to be more sensitive; therefore, the absence of effect for detection risk may be a methodological artifact. In support of this interpretation, Mangione (1983) developed an effective additive model, involving a combination of peer influence and perceived detection risk, to predict illegal alcohol purchases by underage teenagers in Massachusetts.

Perhaps the most intriguing findings on the relationship between formal and informal sanctions stem from Homel's (1986) work in New South Wales. Drivers were asked to imagine a group drinking situation and to rate "how hard or easy you personally would find it to drink less alcohol than your friends." Peer pressure to drink was associated with self-reported violations and drunk driving convictions. Interestingly, peer pressure to drink was also associated with beer drinking but not with wine drinking. When asked whether the passage of the random breath-test law had made it easier or harder to resist peer pressure to drink, 40 percent found it easier and only 9 percent found it harder. Thus, while it is usually assumed that informal sanctions form the context for the operation of formal sanctions, here is an instance of the reverse pattern. In this sense, formal sanctions seemed to provide an extra "rationale for conformity" (Zimring 1971) that may have been easier to "sell" to one's peers than the rationale of safety alone. "No more for me, thanks. Those damned checkpoints, you know."

2. HISTORICAL INFLUENCES: The CULTURAL COMPONENT

Informal sanctions have been included in figure 8.1 as a legitimate part of the total deterrence scheme because they form a "second line of defense" against drunk driving; they supplement the formal system of surveillance provided by police and the formal system of punishment administered by the courts. The case could be made that still broader cultural and historical influences should also be included. For example, the new health consciousness in the United States (Reed 1985) may be contributing to lower alcohol consumption, thereby reducing drunk-driving deaths indirectly. Or, in European countries, drunk-driving deaths may be slightly suppressed by the historical forces which produced "walkable" cities and good public transportation systems. But the line has to be drawn somewhere. Because punishment mechanisms are not explicitly involved, these historical and cultural forces are included in figure 1 merely as a contextual influence.

Nevertheless, this contextual influence might be substantial. It may be one thing to be out of harmony with one's peers in a culture which emphasizes individualism and quite something else to be ostracized in a culture which emphasizes group cohesiveness (Weisz, Rothbaum, and Blackburn 1984). In a comparative study on the effects of mandatory seat-belt laws in the United States and Japan, it was found that both countries demonstrated a sharp, postlaw increase in compliance. In subsequent assessment, however, American usage rates showed the usual decline but Japanese rates remained relatively constant (Demick, et al. 1986). As a contextual note, the authors observed that "whereas a significant number of American participants voiced their concern that mandatory seat belt legislation was an invasion of privacy and an infringement on human rights, this feeling does not appear to be manifest among the Japanese" (iii). Similarly, it is possible that the strong temperance tradition in Norway and Sweden (Hauge 1978; Klette 1978) provided a particularly receptive audience for the implementation of their strict drinking-driving laws. If problem drinkers constitute a large proportion of the hard-core recalcitrant offenders, then it is also instructive to be reminded of the strong cultural differences in alcohol abuse (Muhlin 1985).

Some situations may force a head-on clash between cultural values and legal constraints. When an American man and woman are in a driving situation, it is generally observed that the man will take the wheel (Snortum, Hauge, and Berger 1986). In addition, it appears that an American man who chooses a nonalcoholic beverage is seen as *less masculine* than average, while a woman who chooses a non-alcoholic drink is seen as *more feminine* (Snortum, Kremer, and Berger 1987). Plainly, if the concept of the *designated driver* is to succeed in the United States, it will be necessary to provide a new cultural definition of masculinity that either frees men from their social obligation to drink or relieves them from their social responsibility to drive.

II. Conclusions

In earlier reviews of the Scandinavian literature, Ross (1975, 1982) and Snortum (1984a, 1984b) derived substantially different conclusions about the effectiveness of drinking-driving legislation in Norway and Sweden. The present review, based on a much wider literature, takes the same pattern. By applying a broader definition of deterrence and surveying a more eclectic range of evidence than Ross (1982, 1984a, 1985a), present findings challenge the pessimistic conclusions that "deterrence-based policies are questionable in the long run" (Ross 1982, 111).

The most encouraging evidence about the long-run durability of deterrence comes from the contrasting patterns of compliance in Norway and the United States (Snortum, Hauge, and Berger 1986) and from the steadily declining proportion of alcohol-impaired drivers in the Fatal Accident Reporting System during the past five years (Fell 1985; Fell and Klein 1986). While neither study can claim to demonstrate the causal linkage between "the omission of an act" and "the perceived risk and fear of punishment for *contrary* behavior" (Gibbs 1975, 2), the prima facie case is quite strong. Social scientists can readily identify with the wish to hold out for the highest standards of evidence and to pronounce, in concert with the great scientific skeptics, that the case is "not proved." But scientific error is a two-edged sword and lives are at stake. Can we pronounce, with equal confidence, that the enormous investment in countermeasures, during the past five years in the United States and the past fifty years in Norway, is *irrelevant* to current levels of compliance?

These comments should not be construed as a general opposition to the quasi-experimental approach itself. Interrupted time-series analysis is not free of limitations (Votey 1984b) but, under favorable conditions of implementation, it can gauge intervention effects with a clarity that is unmatched by other methods. As noted in an earlier review (Snortum 1984a, 15), "Interrupted time-series analysis or some related procedure should be attempted at every opportunity for testing the consequences of legislative change. We would prefer clear causal evidence and, wherever it appears, it should be given special weight in policy analysis." Based upon time-series evaluations of legislation in New England (Hingson et al. 1986) and Australia (Homel 1986) it is clear that there is still more to be learned from causal assessments of simple deterrence. Maine appeared to sustain its gains for a full two years before showing a loss of effects, and New South Wales, at last report, had not yet shown a decline after thirty-three months. While the decline, may, of course, occur in the future, these programs should be examined more closely for distinguishing features. Finally, it should also be acknowledged that Ross (1982, 1985a) provides a valuable service in pressing for evidence that the costs of public policy are justified by their benefits. In the political crush to "declare war on drunk drivers," it is likely that many ineffective and expensive countermeasures were included within ambitious packages of controls.

Given the need to assess the deterrent effects of new laws and to search for "excess baggage" in old laws, it may be useful to survey some of the methodological and theoretical problems which might complicate these efforts:

(1) *The machinery of justice.* Most of the studies which purport to test the effects of *law* could be more accurately described as tests of *law enforcement.* Only rarely does a law include tight provisions for ensuring the strength of its implementation. Ross (1982) notes that many of the countermeasures examined in his review were implemented so halfheartedly (e.g., breath testing in France and the United Kingdom) or for such a brief period of time (e.g., the Cheshire blitz) that it would have been unrealistic to expect them to produce stable deterrence. Reviewing the programs that seem to have yielded long-term general prevention (e.g., Norway) or relatively stable simple deterrence (e.g., Maine and New South Wales), all created a stronger objective risk of arrest than was evident among available comparison groups (the United States, Massachusetts, and South Australia). In addition, all three developed highly effective systems for prosecution and punishment. The postlaw conviction rate in Maine was over 80 percent (Hingson et al. 1986). In New South Wales, "ninety-eight percent of all positive breath analyses for which records are kept result in a court appearance . . . and ninety-nine percent of these court appearances result in a finding of guilt" (Homel 1986, 4). Likewise, a review of sanctions given to convicted drunk drivers in Norway showed that 100 percent lost their driving license and 85 percent received prison sentences, usually for longer terms than the twenty-one-day minimum (Christensen and Fosser 1980).

(2) *Moral climate.* If strong laws are imposed in the context of weak social support, they will probably fail. In his historical review of alcohol and traffic safety, Borkenstein (1985, 11) noted:

> I read over most of the papers I have written on this general subject during the past thirty years. In nearly every one of them, I state that the weakest link in attacking this problem has been public support. What we perceive as low-level action against the drunken driver is probably a direct result of lack of public support. We can inform and we can enforce and as a result change behavior through fear for a while. But when we fail to change attitude, regression is bound to occur.

Homel's (1986, 20) observations about the effectiveness of random breath testing in Australia help to dispel the notion that that law has some special *power* which is independent of social context. Victoria introduced random breath testing in 1976, but showed no decline until 1980, and this decline remains largely unexplained. South Australia introduced the practice in 1981 but still has found no reduction in fatal crashes, probably due to "low levels of enforcement and minimal publicity." New South Wales, by contrast, did not introduce the law until December 1982, but it was initiated amidst strong popular support. The residents of Sydney were asked if they agreed or disagreed with the idea of random breath testing in New South Wales. In 1973, 37 percent supported the measure. Subsequent levels were: March 1979, 70 percent; December 1981, 79 percent; December 1982, 80 percent; and March 1983, 91 percent. It is interesting that, despite the rising level of support for the law since 1973, the rate of fatal crashes remained flat until December 1982. Then, the law was introduced and, like a coiled spring ready for release, there was strong enforcement and a sharp decline in fatalities. It is worth noting (table 8.1) that this level of support far surpasses the American rate (57 percent) and approaches the Norwegian level of endorsement of random breath testing (95 percent).

(3) Tracking causality in the context of change. Culminating a series of highly sophisticated studies on perceived risk and behavior change, Paternoster et al. (1985, 430) concluded: "What is clear is that even after a decade of intensified perceptual deterrence research, very little is known about the relationship between perceptions and behavior." Time-series analysis stands on firmer ground, but, ultimately, many of the same issues arise, for example, the problem of separating the effects of law from the moral climate which gave rise to the law (Andenaes 1975) or the problem of extricating contaminating influences due to changes in "background variables," such as alcohol consumption or the economy (Votey 1984b).

One of the more subtle problems in trying to generalize from past applications to future applications of countermeasures rests on the fact that future programs will be imposed on a "different world" than was in place for the earlier interventions. First, based upon Fell and Klein's (1986) analysis of the types of drivers who were dropping out of the Fatal Accident Reporting System, we must assume that the earlier countermeasures have been "skimming the cream" from the deterrable population. Programs that might have "worked" in the past will now "work" only if they affect the hardcore offenders. Furthermore, in the face of declining national rates of alcohol-impaired driving, it may be more difficult to demonstrate intervention effects which exceed the level of regional decline. While one may comfortably conclude that a particular intervention "failed" to add an *extra* deterrent effect, can we add up such failures and conclude that there has been no impact from the array of deterrence-based laws passed in the United States since 1980?

(4) On removing "excess baggage." It will be recalled that Ross (1975) found no apparent casualty reductions following the introduction of Scandinavian per se laws. Likewise, some years later, Ross, Klette, and McCleary (1984) found no consistent worsening of casualty rates following reductions in some Scandinavian sanctions. Ostensibly, these findings support their argument for the further liberalization of Scandinavian practice. The case can, at least, be made for selective reductions. Snortum (1984c) could find no indirect evidence of distinctive deterrent advantages for the more stringent use of prison sanctions in Norway compared to Sweden. Therefore, it was suggested that Norway would sustain no serious losses by adopting the Swedish two-tier system, reserving incarceration for convicted drivers at or above .15 percent BAC. A similar conclusion was subsequently reached in a much more extensive review by Assum (1985). Votey's econometric analyses of Scandinavian accident rates do not rule out the possibility that prison sanctions may reinforce lesser penalties (Votey 1978, 1979, 1982; Votey and Shapiro 1983). However, Votey's findings indicate that licensing actions may yield more consistent and less costly reductions in alcohol-related casualties than prison sanctions.

In their review of Scandinavian practice, Ross, Klette, and McCleary (1984, 481) push the strategy of dismantlement to its ultimate conclusion. They acknowledge that the small number of violators detected in roadblocks "may testify to the success of the Scandinavian approach—in custom as well as law—in keeping the less dangerous moderate drinkers off the highway." Nevertheless, the frequent involvement of highly intoxicated drivers in Scandinavian crashes "may testify to the failure of the Scandinavian approach to remove the more deadly alcoholic from behind the wheel." In a breathtaking leap, the authors conclude: "The continued commitment of the Scandinavian countries to a criminal-law approach to the problem of drunk driving seems paradoxical in light of evidence that in these countries it is a very small and clinically identifiable fraction of the population that drinks and drives" (471). In light of the slow and costly American progress in nudging social drinkers out of the casualty statistics (Fell and Klein 1986), it seems peculiar to advocate the abrogation of the criminal-law approach *because* of its success with such drivers.

As the research on Norway illustrates, one cannot safely assume that, because the Norwegian drinking-driving laws failed to produce sharp, measurable simple deterrence (Ross 1975), they have also failed to produce general prevention (Snortum 1984a; Snortum, Hauge, and Berger 1986). Granted, one cannot separate the effects of "law and custom"; however, the circumstantial evidence for the legal-moral influence is far stronger than for the view that the Norwegians were culturally "blessed" with attitudes that would automatically make them avoid drunk driving. Quite the contrary. The more salient Scandinavian norm is that real men should "drink to get drunk." Only 15 percent of Norwegian drivers claimed to be teetotalers, compared to 38 percent of American drivers. Excluding nondrinkers, alcohol consumption for "drinkers at the last drinking occasion" was found to be 50 percent higher for Norwegians than for Americans. Bear in mind that this figure seriously understates Norwegian consumption because the estimate of average consumption included Norwegians in the driving role—most of whom drank nothing at all. With the advent of the automobile, this strong drinking norm required the invention of an equally strong counternorm, expressed in tough drinking-driving sanctions. The same pattern is taking form in Australia which, like Scandinavia, has enjoyed a reputation for hearty drinking and which is now developing strong countermeasures.

Andenaes maintains that one must adopt a long-term perspective to appreciate the concept of general prevention. "The legislation of one generation may become the morality of the next" (Andenaes 1975, 341, quoting Nigel Walker). If interrupted time-series analysis is an inadequate tool for assessing the symbolic and educational influence of the law following its *introduction,* the problems are even greater in assuming that one can cleanly test the losses that might occur after its *removal.* To exacerbate the time-lag problem, it is highly unlikely that officials will launch a campaign to publicize the removal of drinking-driving restraints. It may also be difficult to assess the effect of "downgrading" the severity of law if there is confounding of severity and credibility of a sanction. For example, is the law being strengthened or weakened if a change is made from a one-year prison sentence that is never given to a two-day sentence that is always given?

(5) Detecting incremental effects from technical adjustments to policy. Ross (1982, 17) notes that interrupted time-series analysis is

most useful "in situations in which an intervention is expected to have a short, sudden impact." For the countries discussed in this review, there will be fewer and fewer opportunities to take the bold policy initiatives which break new ground and produce dramatic effects. In jurisdictions where there is unrelenting political sentiment for control, legislators will be motivated to add new tactics on top of old in hopes of reaching sufficient "critical mass" for deterrent effectiveness. When this strategy has run its course, they will make technical adjustments to improve the returns from old tactics—improved detection methods, better records systems and more effective prosecutorial procedures. While no social scientist welcomes the methodological problems inherent in such confounded incrementalism, it would be a mistake to assume that nothing can be learned from these diffuse attempts to "ratchet-up" the system.

The greatest need is to develop more sensitive measures of change so as to avoid the premature rejection of exploratory programs that are losely implemented. While alcohol-related fatal injuries represent the most important measure of effects, the statistical rarity of these fatal crashes makes them an unstable indicator of activities within smaller jurisdictions. Furthermore, there are a number of studies which caution against excessive confidence in standard surrogate measures such as nighttime fatal crashes because deterrence may take unanticipated forms (Fell and Klein 1986; Heeren et al. 1985; Noordzij 1983). Finally, multiple measures should be employed and particular stress should be placed upon responses at the "wide end of the behavior funnel," such as the use of alternative beverages, alternate drivers, and alternate transportation.

III. Summary

The findings reviewed here were generally consistent with earlier assessments in showing that alcohol-impaired driving is highly resistant to social control. The majority of interventions failed to demonstrate deterrent gains. Nevertheless, there is scattered evidence for deterrent effects in selected programs. License actions have been shown to yield special deterrence of convicted offenders, at least to a marginal degree (Peck, Sadler, and Perrine 1985a). While simple deterrence has not proved to be the panacea that lawmakers have long sought, it appears that intensive law enforcement (Ross 1977; Sykes 1984) augmented by media support (Mercer 1985b) can deliver nontrivial, short-term benefits under optimal conditions (National Highway Traffic Safety Administration 1979b). Most intriguing, the vigorous implementation of random breath testing in New South Wales has already broken previous endurance records for deterrence effectiveness from a "get-tough" program (Homel 1986). There is much more to be learned from this program and from eventual replication efforts elsewhere. Thus, it would be premature, at this point, to assume that we have plumbed the limits of simple deterrence.

The concept of general prevention (Andenaes 1952, 1977) has been seriously neglected in previous reviews on deterrence. Certainly, drinking-and-driving behavior in Scandinavia would be badly misunderstood without the aid of a comprehensive theory which leaves room for interaction between strict legal sanctions and strong social norms (Snortum 1984a, 1984b). Compared to their American counterparts, it is clear that Norwegian drivers are more likely to know the law, endorse strong controls, and take definite steps to modify their drinking or driving behavior in drinking-driving situations (Snortum, Hauge, and Berger 1986). Furthermore, there are now three forms of evidence which indicate that long-term changes in American drinking-driving norms may be quietly occurring beneath the surface. First, the proportion of drivers who claimed to have taken some action to prevent someone from driving drunk increased from 16 percent in 1972 to 42 percent in 1980 (National Highway Traffic Safety Administration 1980). Second, the proportion of alcohol-impaired drivers (.05 percent BAC or above) sampled on weekend nights decreased from 13.5 percent in 1973 to 8.3 percent in 1986 (Wolfe 1986a). Third, and most important, the proportion of fatally injured drivers with illegal blood alcohol levels (.10 percent BAC or above) in fifteen "good-reporting" states decreased from 50 percent in 1980 to 43 percent in 1984 (Fell 1985).

The cause of these changes remains unidentified. Starting in the present and working backwards, one can at least "round up the usual suspects." Part of the reduction in alcohol-impaired driving may be due to a diffuse, deterrent influence from the assortment of laws which have recently been deployed in various combinations throughout the United States, including: per se limits, implied consent laws, preliminary breath testing, roadside revocations, sobriety checkpoints, and increased use of fines, license actions, and jail sentences (National Commission Against Drunk Driving 1985). In addition, of course, there was the pervasive influence of thousands of news stories that announced the new laws and served to educate and threaten the public about legal consequences to violators (Estep and Wallack 1985). And, what "caused" the laws and the news stories? Without fear of contradiction, one can cite the moral indignation and the political pressures generated by groups such as MADD and RID. But did it really begin there? To what extent do these groups owe their fast start to the ambitious Alcohol Safety Action Projects in the 1970s? Whatever may be the uncertainties about the effectiveness of these projects, they did serve to dramatize the high density of impaired drivers on weekend nights and to document the sorry state of court records and prosecutorial procedures. Beyond the interactive influence of these political, legal, and moral variables, one would have to credit a number of auxiliary forces, including drinking age laws, demographic shifts within the drinking population, health and fitness norms, and reductions in per capita consumption.

Finally, it should be acknowledged that while the recent drinking-driving trends in the United States have been favorable, it would be a grave error to assume that they are permanent. American drinking-driving compliance is still minimal compared to that in Norway but even these slight gains have come at considerable social cost. If the police and the public are led to believe that the whole legal-moral approach has failed (e.g., see Ross and Hughes 1986, "Getting MADD in Vain—Drunk Driving: What Not To Do"), there is the risk that the current momentum will be lost. For this reason, it is important that the present findings, for all their methodological limitations, be clearly communicated to provide provisional support that we are "on the right track."

In overview, then, all of the forms and ingredients of deterrence must be considered in one sweep in order to make a balanced judgment about the relationship between law and behavior. Such global assessments of the literature are highly subjective and, therefore, risky. However, if interpretive errors are made, it is believed that they compensate the errors made in other reviews which have been based upon a narrow band of methods and assumptions. Although the patchwork of concepts and evidence presented in this review does not constitute a theory, it does demonstrate the *need* for a theory. Future efforts toward theoretical integration will have to accommodate the following polarities: law-abiding behavior and rule-breaking behavior, short-term and long-term compliance, simple deterrence and general prevention, formal sanctions and informal sanctions, legal threat and moral persuasion, external constraints and internal inhibitions, and predispositional qualities of the offender and of the general population. In short, the position taken here is that durable deterrence *exists,* but it can only be found "by looking in the right places."

9 The Impact of Insurance and Civil Law Sanctions on Drunk Driving

James B. Jacobs

This chapter examines insurance and tort law doctrines and pro-posals to reduce drunk driving. These include measures to make civil liability easier to prove, permit punitive damages, impose in-surance surcharges, and expand liability to third parties responsible for the drunk driver's intoxication. The chapter's goal is to assess the potential and limits of private law for combating drunk driving. Section 1 examines the relationship between automobile insurance and drunk driving and analyzes proposals to use various insurance schemes to combat drunk driving. Section 2 examines drunk drivers' liability for property and personal injuries resulting from accidents. It also surveys proposed changes in tort law designed to reduce drunk driving. Such proposals include awarding punitive damages to victims of drunk drivers and expanding the scope of liability to commercial alcohol dispensers and social hosts for damages and casualties caused by customers and guests.

1. Drunk Driving and Insurance

Insurance Systems

The dominant purpose of insurance is to spread the risk of fortuitous economic loss among a large number of similarly situated individ-uals, groups, or enterprises. (See, e.g., *Globe Life and Health In-surance Co. v. Royal Drug Co.,* 1979; Keeton, 1971.) Insurance does not require an insured to be free from fault; and most insurance covers loss regardless of fault. For example, medical insurance com-pensates the insured for medical costs despite the insured's un-

The author greatly appreciates the comments of Ronald Ehrenberg, Eleanor Fox, Lewis Kornhauser, and David Leebron, and the research assistance of Fred Rush. The research was made possible by the generous support of the Filomen D'Agostino and Max E. Greenberg Research Fund of New York University School of Law.

healthy lifestyle. By contrast, automobile liability insurance has traditionally been concerned with fault: it protects the insured against the risk of being held liable for injuries caused by the negligent operation of his vehicle.

Under the traditional fault system, an automobile accident victim obtains compensation for property and personal injuries from the other driver if that person was at fault; thus a great deal of time and resources are expended in determining which driver was at fault (Smith, Lilly, and Dowling 1932, 785; O'Connell and Henderson 1976, 99–100). The fault system of automobile accident insurance was criticized because it did not compensate victims of no-fault accidents or victims of uninsured motorists (Murphy and Netherton 1959, 701–10). It sometimes provided only incomplete compensation to other victims (New York State Insurance Department 1970). In the early 1960s, there was tremendous pressure, fueled by an avalanche of academic scholarship, to revamp the entire accident law system according to no-fault liability principles. (See generally Keeton and O'Connell 1965; Blum and Kalven 1965; Ehrenzweig 1955; Calabresi 1970.)

The reform was only partially carried out. Many states did not adopt no-fault systems. Of those that did, many included significant limitations. For example, most states retained the fault system for losses above a certain threshold.

Although first-party no-fault plans have been criticized for weakening accident law's deterrent effect on irresponsible driving, it seems unlikely that many drivers will feel less inhibited about driving recklessly simply because they know that the injured party's insurance carrier, rather than their own, will cover any losses caused by an accident. (See Kornhauser 1985, n. 33.) Moreover, in theory, no-fault does not eliminate economic incentives to drive safely because the reckless driver is more likely than the careful driver to file claims for injuries to his car and its occupants and his rates will be a function of those claims. In a pure fault system a driver's insurance rates are a function of the likelihood that other people will present claims based upon the insured's driving, or, to get more complicated, on the faulty driving of the insured and others who use the insured's car.[1] In a pure no-fault first-party system, a driver's insurance rates depend upon the likelihood that the insured (or a family member) will file a claim for damage to the car and injuries to its occupants. In either case, insurance rates are affected by predictions about future accidents.

Insurance Initiatives Designed to Reduce Drunk Driving

The current anti–drunk-driving campaign includes several proposals to utilize insurance to reduce drunk driving. These proposals include revising the calculation of insurance rates to account for drunk-driving behavior, imposing a surcharge on drunk drivers, and denying drunk drivers insurance. This section analyzes these proposals.

REGULATING AUTOMOBILE INSURANCE RATES

Throughout the history of automobile insurance there has been a tension between insurance rating systems based on demographic characteristics, such as age, sex, and marital status, and those based on performance characteristics, such as amount and type of driving, number of accidents, and traffic tickets. Performance characteristics have never predominated because it is too difficult and expensive to monitor insureds' driving habits and records. Although the recent drunk driving campaign has revived interest in basing insurance rates on performance characteristics, such proposals suffer from the same problems that other reform efforts confront.

Although perfectly reasonable in theory, utilizing performance indicators to establish insurance rates would be very difficult to implement accurately and fairly. A major problem is that for most drivers, accidents are relatively rare events; even in a several-year period the majority of drivers will be accident- and claim-free.[2] The rating process is further complicated by the practice in the United States of insuring the vehicle rather than (as in England) the driver. Thus, to predict future accidents and claims, insurance companies would need to consider the joint risk presented by all of the vehicle's drivers.

There can be no scientific formula for factoring prior accident-related claims into future insurance rates. Is a claim this year predictive of future claims? Do all this year's claims, regardless of amount, fault, and years of previous claim-free driving, have the same expected impact on future claims? If a driver who has filed a claim is to be surcharged, how long should the surcharge remain in effect? The cost of collecting data to answer these questions would be extremely high.

If performance criteria are to play a role in rate setting, they must necessarily be imprecise surrogates of dangerousness, like "accidents" or traffic tickets. These indicators present substantial problems of under- and over-inclusiveness. For example, drivers who were hit by drunk drivers will legitimately object to being categorized for rate purposes with drunk drivers who caused these collisions. Drivers with fender benders will object to being grouped with drivers with head-on collisions.

Basing insurance rates on traffic convictions is even more complicated and controversial. We do not know, for example, how well a speeding ticket predicts future accidents. We surely cannot assume that a single speeding violation identifies a certain type of driver. Indeed, differences in local traffic enforcement policies will largely dictate the likelihood of receiving a traffic citation.

Similarly, the correlation between actual drunk-driving behavior and the likelihood of having a recorded conviction for drunk driving may be quite small. Vast numbers of people who have never been charged with any given traffic offense have committed the offense on one or more occasions. Moreover, apprehension for drunk driving might be negatively correlated to future drunk driving episodes. The shock of apprehension and all that follows might make the driver *less likely* to violate the law in the future.

Under-inclusiveness is a problem in setting higher insurance rates for drunk drivers. The chance of a drunk driver being apprehended is extremely small. Many drivers who have never been arrested or convicted of drunk driving have, nevertheless, driven under the influence on occasion or even regularly. Some people, classified as "non–drunk drivers," have actually been arrested for the offense, but diverted into a pretrial treatment program, or afforded plea bargains to lesser traffic offenses. It would thus seem irrational to categorize and define insurance risks according to the vagaries of criminal law enforcement and case processing.

INSURANCE SURCHARGES

Although restructuring insurance rate setting according to performance indicators involves insurmountable difficulties, surcharging drivers convicted of certain offenses is a less drastic solution. Under a surcharge policy, an insurance company assesses an additional charge for a drunk-driving conviction. Despite its apparent simplicity, there are many reasons why the insurance industry has not vigorously pursued surcharging.

Insurance companies make little effort to determine whether their insureds have been convicted of drunk driving primarily because of the high costs of collecting and analyzing criminal justice information.[3] However, the realities of automobile insurance and the structure of the insurance industry also account for the insurance companies' apparent lack of concern. Insurance companies are primarily interested in cash flow. The insurance industry makes most of its profits from its massive investments, not from maximizing the difference between premium dollars paid in and claim dollars paid out. The more cash flow and the longer the float, the more opportunity for investment and profit (Nader 1964). Understandably, insurance companies place more emphasis on investment than rate setting.[4]

Moreover, developing an accurate system to charge drunk drivers the actuarially appropriate amount may prove difficult, if not impossible. The insurance industry claims that there are no actuarial data to demonstrate that a person with a drunk driving conviction is a more dangerous future risk than a person without a drunk driving conviction. This proposition, if true, undermines many of the suppositions of drunk-driving enforcement. Further reflection, however, reveals that there are many problems in using criminal convictions for drunk driving as an operational definition of a dangerous drunk driver.

Utilizing "driving under the influence" (DUI) convictions as an indicator of "drunk drivers" would produce enormous numbers of "false negatives," people who should be classified as drunk drivers but who have eluded the classification system for one reason or another. Many drunk-driving offenses, even if detected, are not recorded as such. Defendants may plea bargain or be diverted to pretrial programs in lieu of prosecution. Often courts do not forward conviction records to the department of motor vehicles, or the department fails to record the information. When convictions are recorded, they do not normally come to the attention of the insurance companies.[5] States do not require motor vehicle departments to notify insurance companies of the insured's convictions. A few states' privacy laws bar the release of such information. Elsewhere, insurance companies learn of the existence of a DUI conviction only if the insurance broker decides to perform a check at time of renewal. In the absence of an accident, it is highly unlikely that any investigation will be undertaken.

A driver's record check requires a request to the department of motor vehicles (or to a private data base system like Equifax) for a copy of the insured's driving record. The information provided will often be incomplete. It is very unlikely, for example, that the record will include traffic convictions in other states. Furthermore, because fairness surely requires that drivers be given some opportunity to challenge the information's accuracy and relevancy, the process would be complicated and expensive.

Even if the companies did obtain reasonably accurate records of traffic offenses, major questions remain, such as how much the insured should be surcharged, what offenses justify a surcharge, how long the surcharge should last, and whether it is cost-effective for the companies to make these calculations. To answer these questions scientifically would require actuarial data on the likelihood of automobile-related claims being filed at future points in time by people with different driving records. The industry has not systematically collected such data, and it would be extremely expensive to do so. Accurate data about millions of traffic violations would have to be regularly collected and correlated against claim records. The exercise would be complicated by undetected traffic violations, failure to report accidents, and variations in criminal justice adjudications. To calculate the rate at which drunk drivers have accidents would also require estimating the frequency of drunk driving behavior, a task involving extreme uncertainties.

Practical problems explain only part of the insurance companies' reluctance to impose surcharges on drivers convicted of drunk driving. Because profits are regulated, insurance companies may have no economic incentive to surcharge drivers with traffic convictions.[6] If these drivers are made to pay more for their insurance, and if profits are already at their legal maximum, other drivers must be given a reduction. Yet, the companies cannot be sure that other drivers are being properly charged for their riskiness. Moreover, a system like this (assuming it were imposed or regulated by a state agency) would be implementing criminal law objectives at the expense of traditional insurance principles. Insurance executives resist taking such steps because of their fear that insurance rate setting increasingly will become a battleground for political interest groups seeking to implement their political and social agendas.

Despite the forces that inhibit surcharging practices, some automobile insurance rates do take limited account of driver performance under so-called Safe Driver Insurance Plans (SDIP), which increase the rates of drivers with accident or traffic violations. Under the New York version of SDIP a drunk driving conviction triggers a 75 percent increase in the insurance premium; the surcharge lasts for three years (NY Insurance Law § 2335(a)(4)). A recent New Jersey law imposes a three-year $1,000 per year insurance surcharge on anyone convicted of drunk driving (NJCRR §11:3-1.16(f)(l)(i)[1985]). The joint underwriters keep 80 percent of this surcharge. The remaining 20 percent goes to the state agency charged with coordinating and implementing the state's anti–drunk-driving campaign. Neither a percentage surcharge nor a flat "insurance fine" are based on the predicted costs of drunk driving; rather they reflect legislators' feelings about the culpability and dangerousness of drunk driving.

To the extent that an insurance surcharge is meant to punish past behavior or deter future behavior, why not increase criminal fines? One answer might be that criminal fines are difficult to collect, especially at the higher levels. Admittedly, if efficacy were the only criterion, it might be easier to impose large costs on drunk drivers indirectly through insurance than directly through fines. Nevertheless, although insurance surcharges may be easier to collect, they are not always collectable. Insurance surcharges are "voluntary" because a driver can always forgo driving, or drive a vehicle registered to somebody else (spouse, child, relative, friend); these are, of course, still costs. Unfortunately, one can also drive illegally without any insurance.

The practical problems encountered with implementing an effective surcharge program undermine the theoretical premise of such a policy. However, even if administrative difficulties could be overcome, surcharges would not pose a deterrent greater than what criminal fines could provide.

Denying Insurance Benefits to Drunk Drivers

Some anti–drunk-driving strategists advocate denying automobile insurance benefits to drunk drivers. This proposal might be analogous to the public policy that forbids insuring intentional wrongdoing; people should not be encouraged to break the law by the existence of insurance nor should people (or their beneficiaries) be permitted to profit by their own wrongs (McNeeley 1941, 26; Keeton 1971, § 5.3(f)). Nevertheless, a moment's reflection will reveal the weakness of the analogy. In jurisdictions with fault systems of automobile insurance, denying drunk drivers the benefits of their third party liability coverage would also deny recovery to many victims. Such a result would defeat a prime goal of automobile insurance—to provide adequate compensation to accident victims. To deny liability insurance coverage to drunk drivers would have the perverse effect of punishing some drunk driving victims as well as some drunk drivers. Moreover, drunk drivers are not "profiting" by receiving the benefits of the policies that they purchased.

Professor Ehrenzweig (1955) proposed a "tort fine" as a way of denying drunk drivers the economic insulation of insurance without imposing hardship on injured parties. Under his scheme, states would establish a fund whose managers could seek civil recovery on behalf of the fund from a driver engaged in "criminally negligent behavior." The amount of this recovery, like a criminal fine, would be measured by the defendant's fault and financial resources, rather than by the victim's loss. The plaintiff fund could collect twice, once from the liability insurer and once from the insured. Thus, the crash victim would be assured compensation, and the fund could pierce the insurance veil to punish this offender and deter others. Professor Ehrenzweig argued that this proposal would provide better deterrence than traditional tort law, because left to their own devices some drunk driving victims would not sue or would not sue with sufficient vigor.

The Ehrenzweig tort fine proposal has some uncertainties. First, the marginal deterrent effect is questionable. Second, the administrative costs might exceed revenues. Third, courts might invalidate the plan on the ground that, in effect, it imposes criminal sanctions without the protection of criminal procedures. If it is sensible to impose larger fines on drivers, why not simply increase criminal fines?

Another proposal involves denying first party insurance benefits to drunk drivers (Fileding 1977). A drunk driver who crashed into a tree injuring himself and destroying his automobile could be denied any recovery. Though the consequences seem harsh, the policy has been justified on general deterrence grounds: if drivers know that they will not be compensated in the event they hurt themselves while driving under the influence, they will not drive under the influence.

Several states have adopted this policy. New York's no-fault automobile liability scheme prevents a drunk driver from recovering any benefits if it can be proved beyond a reasonable doubt that the driver was intoxicated and that the intoxication caused the injuries (NY Insurance Law § 672[2]). Whether the intent of the law is actually carried out is another matter. Insurance companies' efforts to withhold benefits in such cases may end up before sympathetic arbitrators, who are reluctant to withhold insurance benefits from automobile casualties.[7]

The general deterrence rationale for such a policy is dubious. If the threat of personal injury itself is insufficient to deter the drunk driver, the threat of denying insurance benefits in the event of an accident is unlikely to be effective, particularly when most drivers are covered by medical insurance. Perhaps deterrence advocates might propose the next logical step: deny medical insurance coverage to drunk drivers. Indeed, why not carry this strategy to the limits of its logic and deny medical care itself!

Each of the proposed changes in insurance schemes aimed at curbing drunk driving appears to suffer from substantial problems. Several of the proposals violate insurance principles or would require revamping the insurance industry. More important, the proposals would probably be ineffective deterrents to drunk driving.

2. Drunk Driving as Tortious Behavior

Tort law generally provides that a person who willfully or negligently injures another person must compensate the victim for losses and pain and suffering. Negligence is the failure to adhere to the standard of care that a reasonable person in the same situation would exercise (Prosser and Keeton 1984, 169). Drunk driving is obviously negligent behavior; the reasonable person does not drive while intoxicated, thereby exposing himself and others to risk of injury. Moreover, driving under the influence of alcohol or drugs is illegal, and thus many courts treat such behavior as "negligence per se" (Prosser and Keeton 1984).

The current anti–drunk-driving campaign has begun to focus more attention on tort law as a means of reducing drunk driving. Changes in tort law in recent years include defining drunk driving for negligence purposes as driving with blood alcohol concentrations in violation of state per se laws, awarding punitive or exemplary damages against drunk drivers, and expanding the scope of liability of parties other than the actual driver.

Defining Drunk Driving for the Purposes of Tort Law

Defining drunk driving for purposes of tort law in past decades proved to be a difficult task. Civil standards basically paralleled definitions contained in criminal statutes. The traditional benchmarks of drunk driving—"driving under the influence of alcohol" or "driving while intoxicated"—were nebulous standards that did not readily lend themselves to concrete definitions.[8]

Drunk driving definitions became simplified when states began adopting criminal statutes that defined drunk driving in terms of a specified blood alcohol concentration (BAC) and made driving with BACs above the limit, usually .10 percent, a per se violation. Using a .10 percent per se standard in civil negligence cases raises some problems. The majority of drivers are impaired at a BAC of .10 percent; however, some drivers are not. Negligence per se has different implications in different jurisdictions. In some jurisdictions it means that negligence is conclusively proved; in others, it means prima facie negligence or only "mere evidence" of a breached duty (Prosser and Keeton 1984, 200–202). At least one court has held that a BAC of .10 percent, although admissible in evidence, does not create a presumption of intoxication (*Burke v. Angies, Inc.* 1985).

Intoxication short of BAC of .10 percent is not necessarily non-negligent. Judges might be inclined to permit a jury to consider evidence of *any* alcohol consumption under the theory that the amount of alcohol goes to the weight of the evidence, and not to its admissibility. In today's anti–drunk-driving climate, there is a danger that a tort defendant who can be shown to have imbibed any alcohol prior to driving will be presumed negligent and responsible for any traffic accident in which he is involved.[9]

Mobilizing tort law as a means of curbing drunk driving seems misguided. Tort law is a less complete system of punishment and deterrence than criminal law, which punishes drunk driving whether or not it results in injury or property loss. Furthermore, in any given case there may be a poor fit between the driver's culpability and the extent of the damage caused. The criminal law prohibiting drunk driving expresses a societal judgment that there should be no driving under the influence. A drunk driver can be justly punished regardless of whether he was driving dangerously on a particular occasion, and the punishment cannot be blunted by insurance. The amount of punishment can be calibrated to culpability rather than to what may be fortuitous property or personal injury.

Punitive Damages

When a tortfeasor's behavior transcends mere carelessness, reaching the level of wanton and malicious conduct, the plaintiff may recover punitive or exemplary damages in addition to compensatory damages (Restatement [Second] of Torts § 908).[10] Punitive damages have been criticized by scholars and jurists for providing victims undeserved windfalls and imposing freakish punishments on the tortfeasor. (See *American Surety Co. of New York v. Gold* [1966].) In addition, if the risk of punitive damages is insurable, punishment does not fall on the tortfeasor; instead, there is a tax on the entire population of automobile insureds.

When juries are asked to consider punitive damages, they have complete discretion to decide on the amount.[11] The jury is permitted to take into account the defendant's culpability and wealth, and awards can vary from one dollar to millions of dollars depending upon a particular jury's assessment or whim. However, judges retain the authority to reduce extravagant awards.

Although states are divided on the availability of punitive damages against drunk drivers, the trend is in favor of allowing them.[12] Proponents of punitive damages believe that these exemplary punishments will deter future drunk drivers. The California Supreme Court explained this rationale in its landmark decision, *Taylor v. Superior Court* (1979):

> The allowance of punitive damages in such cases may well be appropriate because of another reason, namely to deter similar conduct, the "incalculable cost" of which is well documented. Section 3294 (the California punitive damages provision) expressly provides that punitive damages may be recovered "for sake of example." The applicable principle was well expressed in a recent Oregon case upholding an award of punitive damages against a drunk driver. "The fact of common knowledge that the drunk driver is the cause of so many of the more serious automobile accidents is strong evidence in itself to support the need for *all possible means of deterring* persons from driving automobiles after drinking, including exposure to awards or punitive damages in the event of accidents." (980) (emphasis in original) (footnote omitted)

One can sympathize with the California Court's inclination *to do something* to suppress drunk driving, but, as Justice Clark's stinging dissent points out, permitting drunk driving victims to collect punitive damages will not affect the incidence of this behavior; deterrence will not be operative for the reasons previously discussed (*Id.* at 901 [Clark, J. dissenting]). Moreover, imposing punitive damages may have some unfair and distortive effects on our tort law system. A jury might label any drunk or drinking driver "willful, wanton, and reckless" and award punitive damages regardless of the defendant's actual driving behavior and the victim's injuries. Punitive damages, in part dependent upon the defendant's wealth, amount to a retributive sanction, albeit meted out in the context of accident law rather than criminal law. The same result could be better achieved by increasing the range of criminal fines available in drunk driving cases, and permitting sentencing judges to calibrate fines to defendants' culpability and dangerousness. Criminal fines accrue to the state, for the good of all citizens (and can be earmarked for anti–drunk-driving programs), while punitive damages constitute a windfall for a victim. In *Bielski v. Schulze* (1962), the Wisconsin Supreme Court stated:

> We recognize that the abolition of gross negligence does away with the basis for punitive damages in negligence cases. But punitive damages are given, not to compensate the plaintiff for his injury, but to punish and deter the tortfeasor . . . and were acquired by gross negligence as accoutrements of intentional torts. Willful and intentional torts still exist, but should not be confused with negligence. The protection of the public from such conduct or from reckless, wanton, or willful conduct is best served by the criminal law of the state.

Another issue is whether insurance covers and should cover punitive damages arising from a drunk-driving incident. (See Schumaier and McKinsey 1986.) Automobile insurance contracts are ambiguous on the question (see Note, *Dickinson Law Review* 1980, 233). In the mid-1970s, the Insurance Service Office drafted a uniform exclusion of punitive damages provision, but it did not gain industry acceptance (see Burrell and Young 1978, 10–11). The majority of courts construe uniform net loss clauses of insurance policies to cover awards of punitive damages (*Id.* at 221, 224; Schumaier and McKinsey 1986, 70). Some courts, however, on public policy grounds refuse to allow insurance coverage because it undercuts the rationale for punitive damages (Prosser and Keeton 1984, 13).

If automobile insurance covers punitive damages, any potential deterrent effect is greatly weakened: instead of drunk drivers being held liable for exemplary punishment, insurance companies pay the award and pass the loss along to all insured motorists in the form of higher rates. When a drunk driver wantonly injures someone, all automobile insureds are taxed and the victim receives a windfall. Therefore, as the Fifth Circuit has explained, there is strong reason to make punitive damages uninsurable:

If that person were permitted to shift the burden to an insurance
company, punitive damages would serve no useful purpose. . . .
In actual fact, of course, and considering the extent to which the
public is insured, the burden would ultimately come to rest not on
the insurance companies but on the public, since the added liability
to the insurance companies would be passed along to the premium
payers. Society would be punishing itself for the wrong committed
by the insured. (*Northwestern National Casualty Co. v. McNulty*
1962, 440–41)

On the other hand, making punitive damages uninsurable also
raises grave problems. Insurance provides security against losses,
injuries, and catastrophes. If punitive damages arising from drunk
driving are uninsurable, people will be uncertain about what would
happen if they have an accident after consuming alcohol. All of us
would be exposed, without insurance coverage, to the whim and
caprice of juries that might try to make their own statement about
the "evils of the drunk-driving problem." Not only would "drunks"
be vulnerable to devastating financial losses, so would anyone whom
a jury sitting years after the event might brand a "drunk (or otherwise reckless) driver." This could include anyone who had had
anything to drink, or even a person falsely accused of having been
under the influence of alcohol. Such unpredictable liability would
be similar to a law that provided anyone convicted of drunk driving
(or injuring someone as a result of drunk driving) should be fined
any amount of money.

Proponents of liberal punitive damage award policies might respond to these objections by arguing that persons desiring to avoid
the possibility of uninsured punitive damage awards could do so by
not driving drunk. This argument is unsatisfactory for several reasons. If all of us acted responsibly and competently all the time, we
would not need much of the insurance we now have. It is because
we sometimes act negligently, or might be found to have so acted,
that we purchase insurance. A normally responsible person might,
for any number of reasons, operate a vehicle under the influence of
alcohol on a particular occasion. It seems reasonable for a person
to insure against that possibility and the possibility that it will lead
to an accident, no matter how remote.

Awarding punitive damages might also produce other counter-
productive consequences. If a jury found that the defendant's drunken behavior warranted punitive damages, the insurer might refuse
to cover compensatory awards against the insured on the ground

that he acted wantonly, willfully, and maliciously. If this argument were successful, the usefulness of punitive damages to victims would be negated.

Civil Liability of Alcohol Dispensers

Because it is so difficult to change the behavior of drunk drivers, perhaps greater success in reducing drunk driving could be achieved by trying to influence the behavior of those who dispense alcoholic beverages to people who ultimately become drunk drivers. Several anti–drunk-driving proposals include imposing tort duties on commercial dispensers and social hosts who serve alcohol to the drivers. Commercial dispensers include liquor stores, roadside bars, and restaurants. Social hosts range from intimate party givers to fraternities.

CIVIL LIABILITY FOR COMMERCIAL DISPENSERS OF ALCOHOL

At common law, third party dispensers of alcoholic beverages were not liable for injuries and deaths caused by their drunk customers (Johnson 1962; Keenan 1973). The person who did the drinking and caused the subsequent injury constituted an intervening cause that superseded the dispenser's causal contribution.

Over the years, particularly during Prohibition, many states passed dram shop acts, making liquor dispensers jointly liable for their intoxicated customers' torts. These laws vary in some respects.[13] Some even permit an intoxicated person who injures himself to sue the person who served him (e.g., *Christiansen v. Campbell* 1985). Some dram shop laws appear to impose strict liability (Note, *North Dakota Law Review* 1983, 450–51). All the victim needs to show is that a liquor store or tavern sold alcohol to an intoxicated person who subsequently caused injury. Some statutes permit punitive damages (see, e.g., *Pfeifer v. Cooperstone Restaurant and Lounge* 1985; Ala. Code § 6-5-71 [1975]; Me. Rev. Stat. Ann. tit. 17, § 2002 [1983]).

Unsurprisingly, commercial alcohol dispensers have always opposed dram shop laws, arguing that drinkers (at least adults) should be held responsible for their own actions and that dispensers should not be required to function as law enforcement officials. After World War II, under pressure from bars and taverns, many dram shop statutes were repealed (Comment, *Cal. Western L. Rev.* 1982, 108). In the last decade, however, the trend has reversed. Several legislatures have enacted new dram shop acts,[14] and several state courts have imposed dram shop liability through common law (see, e.g., *Corrigan v. United States* 1984; *Sorenson v. Jarvis* 1984) by finding that liquor dispensers have a duty of care to the general public, or they have inferred such a duty from criminal statutes prohibiting liquor sales to intoxicated patrons.[15] The federal government has encouraged states to adopt some form of dram shop liability by conditioning, in part, supplemental highway funding upon passage of a dram shop law. Counterpressure by the liquor industry remains very strong, however, and state legislators have reversed several aggressive court decisions establishing dram shop liability (see, e.g., S.D. Comp. Laws Ann. § 35-4-78 [1985]).

Courts that established dram shop liability have been motivated by concern about the magnitude of the drunk-driving problem. For example, the Supreme Court of New Mexico, in establishing common law dram shop liability in 1982, stated:

> In light of the use of automobiles and the increasing frequency of accidents involving drunk drivers, we hold that the consequences of serving liquor to an intoxicated person whom the server knows or could have known is driving a car, is reasonably foreseeable. (*Lopez v. Maez* 1982, 1276)

In a similar vein, the South Dakota Supreme Court stated:

> We take judicial notice that since *Griffin* was decided, alcohol has been involved in 50.8% of this state's traffic fatalities from 1976 to 1981; in 1981 alone, 62% of South Dakota's traffic fatalities were alcohol related. This tragic waste of life prompts us to review our conclusion in *Griffin*. If the legislature does not concur . . . it is the prerogative of the legislature to so assert. (*Walz v. City of Hudson* 1982, 122)[16]

The theory underlying dram shop liability is that the threat of such liability would encourage alcohol dispensers to monitor their customers' drinking behavior. Such a thesis, however, assumes that dispensers are able to recognize those customers who pose a significant accident risk to others.

How much care can and should we expect from bartenders, waiters, and waitresses, many of whom are young people not long in the liquor business?[17] Can we expect that they be able to determine what it means to be "intoxicated," and identify customers who have reached this state?[18] The determination is by no means simple, as a recent study by Dr. Peter Nathan, a Rutgers University researcher, concluded:

The study included social drinkers, bartenders, and police officers who were evaluated on their ability to determine whether individuals were drunk. The study indicated that all three of the subject groups studied . . . correctly judged levels of intoxication only twenty-five percent of the time. The accuracy of the ratings by the three groups deteriorated when intoxication increased. . . . The study concludes that the *Zane* decision [99 N.J. Super 196 (1961)]—that whether a man is sober or intoxicated is a matter of common observation not requiring special knowledge or skill—is clearly in error. . . . Whether a person is sober or intoxicated is not a matter of common observation: rather it requires special skill and special training. (Reported in 2 *Dram Shop and Alcohol Reporter* 1984 (3):1–2)

In a crowded bar, a bartender will have little opportunity to keep track of any particular patron's consumption. Indeed, he or she may have no way of knowing whether the patron had done any drinking before entering the bar, how long he intends to stay, or how much he has eaten. Monitoring consumption is further complicated by the common practice of purchasing rounds of drinks for several people, and of groups sharing communal pitchers of beer. Servers may have no way of identifying the drivers.[19] Moreover, if customers are not cut off from drinking until they are identified as intoxicated it may be too late to prevent drunk driving.

No doubt bars could do more to refrain from serving the stereotypical drunkard. However, the vast majority of customers, including heavy drinkers, do not fall into this category. It will be awkward, to say the least, for bartenders to police their customers, interrogate "suspicious" patrons about their consumption, and require some sort of sobriety test before bringing the next drink.

Taverns, bars, and even many restaurants are in the business of selling alcoholic beverages. Profits depend upon creating an attractive atmosphere in which to drink. The goal is not to encourage long evenings of quiet conversation over two alcoholic drinks and several sodas. The best customers are the big drinkers; many run up huge bar tabs. It is highly unrealistic to expect most liquor establishments to police themselves. As Gusfield, Rasmussen, and Kotarba (1984, 55) note in their ethnographic study of bar culture:

Asked about the responsibility or obligation of the drinking place toward the patron, the bouncers at That Place and the bartender at the Hermitage absolve themselves of concern by using what one might call the ideology of adulthood, asserting that although most drinkers can manage themselves at drinking with competence, adults also possess the liberty and license to be incompetent. Incompetence is not the responsibility of management because the customers are adults and "a person who is old enough to drink is old enough to take care of himself after he stops drinking."

Laws regulating size of drinks[20] and prohibiting happy hours and two-for-one nights (e.g., Massachusetts, 204 C.M.R. § 4:03 [1984]) may be of marginal help in controlling excessive drinking a little, but it is hardly likely that bar culture can be radically reconstituted.[21]

Moreover, dram shop liability will not produce a significant deterrent effect unless there is a significant threat that such suits will be brought. Drunk-driving victims may not sue alcohol dispensers unless the drunk driver has sufficient insurance to cover the victim's injuries. Moreover, the existence of a secondary pocket will not make any difference, unless it is a deep pocket. Normally (but not always, as in the case of large hotel chains) there will be no point in suing unless there is liability insurance.

Nevertheless, injured victims can be expected, with increasing frequency, to sue bars, taverns, and restaurants as well as injury-causing drunk drivers. Even if the drunk driver's insurance is adequate, the liquor dispenser may be held as a joint tortfeasor. The law does not require exhausting the drunk driver's insurance before dipping into the liquor dispenser's.

Will bars and taverns be able to purchase dram shop liability insurance, and will they desire to do so? Apparently, the market for it has developed slowly, if at all; Minnesota's Insurance Department has required the insurance industry to offer this type of insurance. Even if such insurance is available, some percentage of liquor dispensers may not be able to afford it, or may choose to do without it, believing that without insurance they are unlikely to be attractive tort targets. States may be led to consider requiring liability insurance as a prerequisite to being granted a liquor license.[22] In that event, we return to the dilemma discussed previously: insurance provides compensation for victims, but it undercuts the deterrent value of the threat of civil liability.

CIVIL LIABILITY FOR SOCIAL HOSTS

So far we have been talking about taverns and bars, where we suspect many drunk drivers become intoxicated. We know that people also get drunk at private parties. If this were the heart of the problem, we might have more cause for optimism. At small parties, at least, the hosts are in a position to know how much their guests have consumed, their condition at the time of departure, and their means of getting home. They do not have an economic incentive to encourage alcohol consumption; in fact, their economic incentives are just the reverse. Perhaps imposing civil liability on social hosts for the drunk-driving accidents of their guests would motivate hosts to police drinking at their parties.

Not all parties are of the intimate sort envisioned in the preceding paragraph. Some are fraternity parties, or huge company bashes, or weddings, or wakes, or team celebrations. At these gatherings, an open bar may leave drinkers free to consume as much alcohol as they wish. At such parties, it would be hard to hold any person responsible for a guest's intoxication. If blame is appropriate, it is for structuring a situation where, without supervision, guests can become intoxicated. If party givers were required to monitor and supervise their guests' alcohol consumption, social life would have to be radically restructured.

Historically, dram shop liability did not extend to social hosts, perhaps reflecting the view that social hosts cannot be expected to police the behavior of their guests, and that to establish such liability would be too disruptive of social relations. Moreover, imposing social host liability might result in the loss of the defendant's personal assets and home (see Graham 1979). Social hosts, unlike commercial dispensers, have no way of passing along the cost of litigation, damages, and insurance.

Today there is a great deal of interest in extending dram shop–type liability to social hosts, particularly to employers and large party givers, and to those who serve liquor to minors. In 1972, both the Minnesota (*Ross v. Ross* 1972) and Iowa Supreme Courts (*Williams v. Kleinesrud* 1972) expanded liability to social hosts, but both states' legislatures thereafter amended their laws to exclude social hosts (Minn. Stat. Ann. § 340.95 [1980]; Iowa Code Ann. § 123.95 [1980]) The Iowa Supreme Court reinstated social host liability under a negligence per se theory, based on the Iowa Alcohol Control Act (*Clark v. Mincks* 1985). New York imposes criminal liability on commercial and social hosts who sell or serve alcohol to minors (N.Y. Alcoholic Beverage Control Law § 65[1]).

The most successful nonvendor suits have been brought against employers who have served already intoxicated employees at company parties and picnics. Typically, these cases are brought under theories of negligence per se based on violations of the liquor control acts, rather than on common law or dram shop act theories. Most, if not all, of the successful cases have involved employers serving alcohol to minors (see, e.g., *Congini v. Petersville Valve Co.* 1983; *Brokett v. Kitchen Boyd Motor Co.* 1972; *Brauttan v. Herron* 1974; *Thaut v. Finley* 1973). Three recent cases have extended the employer rule to adult employees. *Chastin v. Litton Systems, Inc.* (1984) and *Halligan v. Pupo* (1984) imposed third party liability by the usual criminal violation/negligence per se route. However, the Minnesota court in *Meany v. Newell* (1984) took a different approach. Citing the special relationship between an employer and employee at common law, it held that the company owed a heightened duty of care to the drunk employee (see Restatement [Second] of Torts § 317). Thus, to serve more liquor to an already intoxicated employee constituted a breach of duty and gave rise to a direct negligence action.

Recently, the New Jersey Supreme Court issued a controversial and highly visible decision imposing tort liability on social hosts who knowingly serve intoxicated guests who ultimately cause injury.[23] In *Kelly v. Gwinnell*, the court said:

> We imposed this duty on the host to the third party because we believe that the policy considerations served by imposition far outweigh those asserted in opposition. While we recognize the concern that our ruling will interfere with accepted standards of social behavior; will intrude on and somewhat diminish the enjoyment, relaxation, and camaraderie that accompanies social gatherings at which alcohol is served; and that such gatherings and social relationships are not simply tangential benefits of a civilized society but are regarded by many as important, we believe that the added assurance of just compensation to the victims of drunk driving as well as the added deterrent effect of the rule on such driving outweigh the importance of those other values. . . . Indeed, we believe that given society's extreme concern about drunk driving, any change in social behavior resulting from the rule will be regarded ultimately as neutral at the very least, and not as a change for the very worse; but that in any event if there will be a loss, it is well worth the gain. (1984, 438)

The scope of a New Jersey social host's liability is unclear. The New Jersey Supreme Court noted that the defendant was a social host who *knowingly* served his guest thirteen drinks in a short period of time. The court also stated that to prevail, the plaintiff would have to prove that the host knew that the guest would subsequently be driving. Further, it limited its holding to the situation in which the host directly served the guest. Thus, this decision does not open the way for suits by victims of drivers who become inebriated at large gatherings where hosts are uninvolved and unaware of each guest's consumption (*Kelly, supra,* at 560).[24]

Two other courts have adopted social host liability since *Kelly.* In *Clarke v. Mincks* (1985), the Iowa Supreme Court held that social hosts may be civilly liable for accidents caused by serving guests who were already intoxicated. *Clarke* did not add anything to the theory of liability expressed in *Kelly,* but it is a notable decision in at least one respect. The Iowa legislature previously had reversed an Iowa Supreme Court decision (*Williams v. Klemesrud* 1972) that imposed social host liability under the dram shop act. The Iowa Supreme Court's latest decision constitutes a reversal of the legislature's reversal, indicating the court's intense desire to reduce drunk driving.

In *Ashlock v. Norris* (1985), an Indiana intermediate court of appeals held that a bar patron who procured drinks for another customer who was already intoxicated could be held liable for third party injuries. *Ashlock* illuminates an often-overlooked distinction between vendor and nonvendor liability. The defendant was not a social host, but a drinking buddy, buying a round for his friends. The plaintiffs sued both the bar as server and the patron as host. Thus the court divorced liability from the defendant's status as a server—an identity crucial to liability in *Kelly.* However, since the *Ashlock* court's novel theory has not yet been reviewed by the Indiana Supreme Court, it is too soon to say whether it indicates further extension of civil liability to those involved in drinking episodes.

How likely is it that such a civil liability rule will reduce drunk-driving accidents? Admittedly, social hosts at intimate dinner parties are in a better position than commercial dispensers to monitor their guests' drinking, but it may prove no easy matter to gauge guests' consumption and capacity, nor will all social hosts have the interpersonal skills necessary to stop their friends, clients, bosses, and family members from drinking too much before driving. Some hosts might, of course, decide to stop serving liquor or to serve less of it.

Once again, much will depend upon the availability of liability insurance. Comprehensive personal injury and some homeowner policies cover social host liability, but only to policy limits.[25] Many insureds will no doubt increase these coverages to protect themselves against the risk of catastrophic loss. Others, no doubt, out of ignorance or risk-preference, will not seek to insure themselves against this type of potential liability. Perhaps, if insurance companies perceive a demand for social host insurance, they will attempt to market it as a standard part of the homeowner's package.

Conclusion

The mobilization of tort and insurance law to deter drunk drivers and those in some way responsible for their behavior is an understandable impulse of the current drive against drunk driving. There is reason to believe, however, that punishment and deterrence through civil law are particularly unsuited to those problems. Although tort law may well have a deterrent role to play in other contexts, it is unlikely to have much effect when the behavior is dangerous to those who engage in it, and when the decision processes tend not to be deliberative. In any case, the tort law is, at best, a very imperfect system of punishment and deterrence because it only applies when damage occurs, and its effects are significantly blunted by insurance.

Although the various tort and insurance law initiatives discussed in the chapter may not add much to our overall social control efforts against drunk driving, one might ask whether, even if they add just a little marginal deterrence, they are not worthwhile. Here the answer is more complicated, and perhaps depends upon each particular initiative. Anti–drunk-driving strategists should be cautious about jeopardizing other goals of civil law, most importantly providing full assistance to victims of automobile "accidents," but also doing justice to defendants in tort suits. The basic constituents of tort and insurance law should not be swept aside without serious consideration of the consequences.

10 Programs to Change Individual Behavior: Education and Rehabilitation in the Prevention of Drinking and Driving

Robert E. Mann, Evelyn R. Vingilis, and Kathryn Stewart

The seriousness of the drinking-driving crash problem has resulted in major efforts being expended in the social control of the drinking driver. Although the principal attempt to control the drinking-driving problem has been through compulsory (legal) controls, related and perhaps increasingly important countermeasure approaches have employed voluntary controls (education and rehabilitation). As in compulsory controls where legal countermeasures can impact either on the nonoffending population through general deterrence or on the offending population through specific deterrence, so too education and rehabilitation countermeasures tend to target the nonoffending and offending populations, respectively. In addition, rehabilitation is unusual in that it brings treatment into the legal realm usually occupied by punitive sanctions. However, in a social control framework, education and rehabilitation are similar in that they aim to change the behavior of individuals through more or less direct attempts to influence these individuals, rather than through efforts to alter the legal or social environment. Within this context, these countermeasures share much with, and draw heavily from, efforts to deal with other problems society faces, in particular other problems of substance abuse. On the other hand, the problem of drinking and driving is unique in many respects, and so the parallels cannot be complete.

Interest in education and rehabilitation as drinking-driving countermeasures is not recent (cf. Heise 1955; Glatt 1963); with the repeal of prohibition laws in North America, advertisements against drinking and driving began to appear (Mosley 1955). The initiation of blood and breath testing among samples of drivers killed or injured in accidents revealed many with extremely high blood alcohol levels

We wish to thank Mrs. D. Lindholm for her excellent help in the preparation of this manuscript. The views expressed in this chapter are those of the authors and do not necessarily reflect those of the Addiction Research Foundation.

(e.g., Lucas, Kalow, McColl, Griffith, and Smith 1955), leading to studies suggesting high proportions of problem drinkers or alcoholics in the drinking-driving population (Schmidt and Smart 1959a) and to suggestions that treatment or rehabilitation may be an important drinking-driving countermeasure (Schmidt and Smart 1959b). Along with early efforts to introduce driver education and alcohol education programs in the schools came the inclusion of educational materials on drinking and driving (Linton 1955).

With increasing awareness of the magnitude of the drinking-driving problem, the 1960s witnessed the beginnings of large-scale efforts to implement countermeasures in some jurisdictions, for example, the introduction of per se laws in Great Britain and Canada. However, early evaluation of these countermeasures revealed effects that were either small, transitory, or both (e.g., Ross 1982). This surprising (to some) finding resulted in an increase in the emphasis on the evaluation of drinking-driving countermeasures. Thus, meaningful evaluation of education and rehabilitation countermeasures did not begin to appear until the late 1960s, although these programs had been in existence earlier.

This chapter reviews educational and rehabilitative countermeasures. Our purpose is not to provide an exhaustive summary of the literature, since such reviews have recently appeared (e.g., Klitzner, Blasinsky, Marshall, and Paquet 1985; Mann, Leigh, Vingilis, and De Genova 1983; Mann, Vingilis, Leigh, Anglin, and Blefgen 1986; McKnight 1986; Peck, Sadler, and Perrine 1985a). Instead, we intend to address the issues raised by these programs and to consider the role of these programs within the larger framework of countermeasures. First, we consider briefly the guiding principles of voluntary social control. Second, we review the current findings and the methodological problems in assessing school-based education programs. Then, we provide a similar review of rehabilitation programs. Finally, we examine the role of education and rehabilitation within the larger context of prevention of alcohol-related traffic injuries and fatalities.

Guiding Principles of Voluntary Social Control

Underlying all education and rehabilitation programs seems to be the assumption, as in classical deterrence theory, of a "rational man" in which knowledge is viewed as fundamental to the decision-making process of behavior choice. Thus, the knowledge of drinking-driving issues is perceived as an important component in appropriate driving behavior formation or behavior change. The philosophy seems to be that once an individual becomes aware of the dangers involved in drinking and driving, he or she will be less likely to combine the two behaviors. In sum, knowledge of the issues and consequences of drinking and driving is considered a necessary, but most likely not a sufficient, condition for the formation of sober driving behavior or drinking-driving behavior change.

The issues regarding what other variables, if any, are required to influence behavior have been the subject of research in psychology and communications for nearly half a century. Current attempts to influence the behavior of individuals or groups have arisen, in part, from the assumptions based on this research about the processes of persuasion or influence. Prevention programs, be they primary (education) or secondary (rehabilitation), vary in the extent to which these assumptions are made explicit and incorporated into formal models.

The historical trend in the development of models of influence has been toward increasing degrees of complexity and comprehensiveness beginning with the simplistic "one-step" model to the multistep process involving a number of variables and phases (Addiction Research Foundation 1981).

Parallel developments in the discipline of social psychology led to efforts to comprehend the linkages between changes in knowledge, attitude, and behavior. Various information-processing models of attitude change have formed the basis for much of current social-psychological theorizing about human communication and have identified several independent, dependent, and intermediate variables in the influence process. However, considerable debate still exists over the relative emphasis of the differing variables and about the linkages between communication input, changes of belief or attitude, and behavioral outcomes (Addiction Research Foundation 1981; Flay, Di Tecco, and Schlegel 1980; McGuire 1974).

School-based Education Programs

In North America, Australia, and Europe, many schools are implementing drinking-driving prevention programs. School-based education programs are primary prevention strategies. Primary prevention attempts to reduce the incidence of new cases of a public health problem in the population. Primary prevention strategies try to divert or dissuade a large proportion of society who are potential drinking-drivers from undertaking such a behavior. These objectives are met by the legal approach (general deterrence) and/or by the education approach which involves strategies such as the use of classroom instruction on drinking-driving in schools, driver education programs, and similar environments.

While drinking-driving components have long formed part of alcohol and drug education programs (Milgram 1975), they are now receiving increasing time in the curricula of high schools, colleges, and universities, and even the primary grades. The interest in school-based alcohol and traffic safety programs seems to be the result of three converging influences: (1) the movement for alcohol and drug education in the schools; (2) the movement for traffic safety education; and (3) the growing awareness of drinking and driving as a major public health problem, particularly among youth (Mann et al. 1986). These programs hold the dual promise of reducing the tragic alcohol-crash problem among youth (Mayhew, Warren, Simpson, and Haas 1981; Vegega 1984), and of shaping the attitudes and behaviors of new generations of drivers when they are most amenable to influence (Bishop 1973; Organization for Economic Cooperation and Development 1975; Waller 1968).

A large variety of programs have developed, drawing heavily on experience with alcohol and drug education efforts. In a study of 133 drinking and driving prevention programs for youth in the United States, a number of common conceptual orientations were identified, among the most common being increased alternatives (e.g., alcohol-free parties, responsible hosting), improved life skills (e.g., decision-making skills, self-esteem building, values clarification), increased peer pressure resistance skills, and alteration of peer and community norms (Klitzner et al. 1985). Examination of the formats in which these content areas are contained suggests three didactic orientations that they have in common with alcohol and drug education (Mann et al. 1986). The first is the information approach. According to this approach, provision of the relevant information will lead to appropriate changes in knowledge, attitude, and behavior. Such programs involve traditional classroom techniques including lectures and audiovisual presentations. The second approach considers affective processes as important links to behavioral change. These programs either seek to arouse affect, such as fear, through presentations of accident scenes, etc., or to stimulate affective involvement through student participation, values clarification, and analysis of decision-making processes. The third approach employs one of the variants of learning theory as a basis for program development. These programs employ principles derived from learning theory to provide the skills and responses necessary to avoid drinking and driving (cf. Braucht and Braucht 1984; Goodstadt 1978; Durell and Bukoski 1984). Although these three orientations seem to describe well the programs that have been evaluated, it should be noted much overlap occurs. Thus, for example, affect-based and behavior-based programs provide information as well (e.g., McKnight and McPherson 1986).

Effectiveness of School-based Education Programs

A small number of evaluations of these programs have appeared in recent years. For purposes of this review, studies involving one or more experimental groups and a control group (randomly or non-randomly chosen) have been selected. Except where otherwise noted, these programs required two to five classroom periods to present, and were carried out in a secondary school setting; assignment to programs was on a nonrandom basis.

INFORMATION-BASED PROGRAMS

Three studies have examined the impact on students of information-based programs. Turnauer (1973) found that exposure to an information program had no effects on attitudes immediately following the program or three weeks later when compared to controls. Jenkins (1970) compared the effects of a traditional lecture-oriented information program with an enriched information program—supplemented with audiovisual aids—and found that the enriched program resulted in significantly greater posttest knowledge scores than did the traditional program. Hames and Petrucelli (1980) examined the impact of a 3 1/2-minute informational film immediately following the film and after a follow-up of four months. When compared to a randomly chosen control group, individuals who saw the film scored significantly higher on posttest and follow-up knowledge measures, particularly if a "reinforcing" test was given immediately after the film.

AFFECT-BASED PROGRAMS

Most of the research in this area has examined the impact of affect-based (in particular, affective involvement) programs. Turnauer

(1973), in the previously described study, also included an affective involvement program. The affective involvement program, but not the information program or the control program, had a significant positive effect on attitudes immediately following the program and three weeks later. Subsequently, several studies have replicated the finding that these types of programs have positive effects on knowledge and attitude measures immediately following the program (Malfetti, Simon, and Homer 1977; McKnight, Preusser, Psotka, Katz, and Edwards 1979; Masten 1979; Albert and Simpson 1985). One study has found that these benefits are maintained over an eight-week follow-up interval (Malfetti et al. 1977), while another found no differences between groups after sixteen weeks (McKnight et al. 1979).

Only one study has examined the impact of affective arousal procedures. Kohn, Goodstadt, Cook, Sheppard, and Chan (1982) compared the effects of a twenty-minute drinking-driving film in which affective arousal (threat) had been manipulated (low, medium, and high) through varying depictions of the consequences of an accident. Students were randomly assigned to one of the three threat conditions or a control condition. All three threat conditions had a positive effect on knowledge immediately following the film but not six months later. In addition, the low and high threat conditions had significant negative effects on attitudes immediately following the film, that is, more permissive attitudes to impaired driving.

BEHAVIOR-BASED PROGRAMS

One study has examined the impact of a behavior-based program. McKnight and McPherson (1986) developed a nine-hour program designed to teach students to intervene in the drinking-driving behaviors of peers, and compared its effects to those of an affective involvement program. Both programs had a significant positive impact on knowledge immediately and two to six months later. As well, both programs had a positive impact on self-reported intervention behaviors immediately, but only the students in the behavioral program maintained these gains over the follow-up interval.

SUMMARY OF EFFECTIVENESS

It seems that nearly all programs evaluated so far have beneficial effects on knowledge or attitudes, at least in the short term. However, at least for some programs, these effects seem to dissipate with time. Although only a small number of studies permit comparisons of programs based on different orientations, the literature to this point suggests that behavior-based programs may have the greatest net positive effects, followed by affective involvement programs, informational programs, and affective arousal programs, in that order. Thus, the results reported so far are very encouraging. However, it is important to point out that no information is available on the ultimate test of efficacy: the impact these programs have on the actual drinking-driving behavior of the participants.

Issues in Development, Evaluation, and Implementation

As stated above, the analysis of program results suggests that these programs could have promise for reducing the drinking-driving problem. However, before these results can be uncritically accepted, important issues must be considered. This section discusses issues in program evaluation, and then considers program implementation and development.

EVALUATION ISSUES

The large number of educational programs that have been implemented and their widely varying content and format should provide considerable information about the effectiveness of different approaches. Unfortunately, very few of these programs are evaluated and many of the evaluations which are carried out do not even achieve minimal levels of methodological or conceptual adequacy. In Klitzner et al.'s (1985) review of 133 programs, only twenty were found to have evaluations which adequately assessed the validity of the programmatic approach adopted. Without adequate evaluations, valuable opportunities for learning about educational efforts are being lost.

Since evaluations provide the measures of success, and since evaluation procedures can influence the apparent results of programs independent of their actual reports, it is important that evaluation procedures be employed that permit accurate measurements. Many methodological strengths are apparent in this literature, including the use of large sample sizes (e.g., Malfetti et al. 1977; Hames and Petrucelli 1980), and the development of measures of outcome with good psychometric properties (e.g., Malfetti et al. 1977; McKnight et al. 1979). However, there are methodological concerns which suggest that care be taken in interpreting available results.

The most important concern is the choice of measure of outcome. All of the studies described here employed some measure of knowledge and/or attitude to assess program impact; a few studies (McKnight et al. 1979; Kohn et al. 1982; Albert and Simpson 1985; McKnight and McPherson 1986) employed some self-reports of behavior as well. The choice of measures of impact seems to reflect didactic orientation, that is, information programs measure knowledge gains, affective involvement programs measure attitude changes, and so forth. These choices are sensible when viewed in terms of the hypothesized underlying process of behavior change, for example, increases in knowledge result in changes in attitudes which in turn lead to changes in behavior. However, the validity of such models can be questioned, and their assumptions have been criticized (Braucht and Braucht 1984; Goodstadt 1978). Furthermore, related research indicates that it cannot be assumed that changes in knowledge, attitudes, or even self-reported behavior will be reflected in actual behavior or on measures of traffic safety (Mann et al. 1983; McGuire 1974). Thus, it is now important to assess the impact of these programs on traffic safety measures; in the absence of such data it is not possible to say that the beneficial changes in knowledge and attitudes observed will be translated to traffic safety gains.

Two other evaluation issues should be mentioned. First, only a small number of these evaluations have employed random assignment (Hames and Petrucelli 1980; Kohn et al. 1982; McKnight and McPherson 1986). While random assignment can be difficult to accomplish in the context of these programs, it adds substantially to the strength of observed results. Second, follow-up beyond immediate program impact often is not performed. Estimations of sustained program impact are essential for evaluations of effectiveness.

The importance of rigorous evaluation procedures is underscored by experiences in evaluating alcohol and drug education programs. These programs sometimes reveal paradoxical results, that is, students exposed to programs report more favorable attitudes toward, or more use of, alcohol and/or drugs (e.g., Stuart 1974). Goodstadt (1980) and Schaps, DiBartolo, Moskowitz, Palley, and Churgin (1981) reviewed the literature and suggested that paradoxical or adverse results seem to occur in studies employing less rigorous research designs. Thus, it is important to use the most powerful evaluation procedures in order to guard against these anomalous findings.

PROGRAM IMPLEMENTATION AND DEVELOPMENT ISSUES

School-based alcohol and traffic safety programs are being implemented in a variety of contexts, for example, in health education classes, in alcohol and drug education classes, and in compulsory driver education classes. While the place in the curriculum where the program is placed often depends on factors unique to each school, studies of driver education illustrate that the context of implementation may have important traffic safety effects.

Many schools have introduced driver education courses; in some areas these driver education courses are compulsory for all students approaching the age of licensure. Shaoul (1975) evaluated a compulsory driver education course in Great Britain; the results indicated that the group assigned to the course subsequently had more accidents than a control group. Shaoul (1975) suggested that this result was due to higher numbers of students in the driver education condition than in the control condition subsequently obtaining a driver's license. Later research (Robertson 1980; Robertson and Zador 1979) supported the hypothesis that compulsory driver education for adolescents increased the likelihood of licensing and exposure to traffic hazards. Recently, Lund, Williams, and Zador (1986) reexamined the results of a large-sample randomized evaluation of compulsory driver education for adolescents (Stock, Weaver, Ray, Brink, and Sadoff 1983). The original report found that compulsory driver education resulted in a short-term reduction in numbers of accidents per licensed driver. However, the reanalysis by Lund et al. (1986) confirmed Shaoul's (1975) original observation that, as a group, the students receiving compulsory driver education had more total accidents and violations since more of them subsequently obtained a driver's license. Thus, the context in which alcohol and traffic safety programs are implemented may have an important influence on their net effects.

The issue of quality of implementation is extremely important. No program, however well designed, can be expected to have optimal effectiveness unless implementation is strong. In Klitzner's review, several serious implementation problems were found to be common. In particular, program operation was found to be inconsistent and level of participation was often low. The data suggested that with intensive staff training, a much higher quality of program implementation was possible (Klitzner et al. 1985).

As regards the future development of these programs, this review suggests that those programs which have been evaluated are based on a limited number of models of behavior. Programs based on other models exist (Klitzner et al. 1985; Vegega 1984), but have not been evaluated. Recent research is leading to a more comprehensive understanding of the behavior problems of adolescence in general, and the relationships among youth, alcohol, and traffic safety in particular (e.g., Jessor and Jessor 1977; Mann, Vingilis, Adlaf, Kijewski, and De Genova, 1985; Mayhew et al. 1981; Vingilis 1981). This research should eventually result in more powerful models upon which programs can be based (cf. Jessor and Jessor 1977; Ajzen and Fishbein 1980). At this point, most programs seem to be aimed at the individual level. However, promising models do exist with the goal of bringing about changes in peer values and behavior and in community attitudes (Klitzner et al. 1985).As well, the development of programs can exploit serendipitous research findings. McKnight (1986) provides an excellent example in describing how the observation that adolescents seem willing to intervene for the safety of others (McKnight et al. 1979) led to the development of an alcohol and traffic safety program to encourage this behavior (McKnight and McPherson 1986).

These programs, then, hold a great deal of promise. Initial evaluations reveal generally positive effects. It seems likely that even more powerful programs will be developed in the near future. However, these positive aspects must be balanced against the fact that, as yet, their impact on traffic safety is unknown.

Rehabilitation Programs

Rehabilitation programs are strategies for secondary prevention. Secondary prevention attempts to reduce the prevalence of cases of a public health problem in the population. Secondary prevention in the field of drinking-driving refers to reducing recidivism. Strategies for reducing recidivism can be legal through punitive sanctions (specific deterrence) and/or rehabilitative through education and treatment programs.

A brief glance at the provision of rehabilitation programs for convicted drinking drivers in Western nations reveals great disparities. In some jurisdictions (for example, California and Alberta) programs are widely available and are mandated by law; in other jurisdictions (for example, Ontario) they are available on a more or less haphazard basis; and in yet other jurisdictions (for example, Norway) few, if any, programs exist. These discrepancies in program availability

reflect many things, including differences in laws and legal philoso-
phies, the availability of funds to support such programs, and, perhaps most importantly, differences of opinion on the effectiveness
of these programs.

Aside from these considerations, there are many difficulties involved in introducing rehabilitation programs for drinking drivers,
which are compounded when attempts are made to evaluate these
programs. In general, the use of rehabilitation in the legal or corrections field has been an issue of contention; some argue that the
purpose of the legal and corrections systems is to punish, not treat,
convicted offenders. Others contend that the limited resources available to combat the drinking-driving problem are best placed in areas
other than rehabilitation, for example, prevention and deterrence.
If, in spite of these issues, programs are still implemented, elements
or features of both the health and legal systems can act to inhibit
program efficacy and impede evaluation. Both systems have, as a
mandate, the classification of individuals and assignment to an appropriate course of action, be it imprisonment, treatment, or some
other alternative. The work required to implement a program involves often substantial efforts to arrange appropriate referral or
assignment procedures. Once these procedures have been implemented, it is often extremely difficult to introduce changes. Individuals involved in the legal and health systems in the classification
and assignment of individuals (for example, judges) have this diversion of people to appropriate outcomes as their mandate. Understandably, efforts to alter or limit this discretionary power often
meet with difficulty, particularly when attempts to create/employ a
control group for evaluation purposes are involved (e.g., Blumenthal
and Ross 1973). For some studies, it has been necessary to enact
laws permitting the use of a control condition (e.g., Reis 1983).

These and other problems have created many instances where
the results of evaluations of rehabilitation programs must be viewed
with caution (Mann et al. 1983). Thus, our knowledge of the impact
of these programs has important limitations. However, there are
many significant strengths in the work that has been done. For example, in comparison to work in related areas, particularly the treatment literature on alcohol problems, recent evaluations of
rehabilitation programs for convicted drinking drivers are notable
for methodological strengths such as large sample sizes, length of
follow-up interval, use of objective measures of outcome, and use
of random assignment to conditions, among others. These strengths

have made it possible to begin to outline with some certainty the effectiveness of various types of programs.

Effectiveness of Rehabilitation Programs

In an earlier review (Mann et al. 1983) we examined the impact of education- and treatment-oriented programs on three types of outcome measures: (1) knowledge and attitudes; (2) drinking behavior and lifestyle; and (3) traffic safety measures, primarily drinking-driving recidivism. Both quasi-experimental and experimental studies were included. The results suggested that these programs have a beneficial effect on knowledge and attitudes, and that some programs have a beneficial effect on traffic safety measures, by reducing recidivism. Of interest was the observation that no beneficial impact on drinking behavior or lifestyle had as yet been reported.

With regard to effects on traffic safety measures, it did not at that time seem possible to say with any certainty under what conditions programs would have beneficial effects. In reexamining this literature, in particular more recent studies employing experimental designs with random assignment, some coherence is appearing. To achieve the greatest amount of coherence, it seems important to consider, first, comparisons of rehabilitation with punitive sanctions, and second, evaluations of different forms of rehabilitation with different types of offenders.

COMPARISONS OF REHABILITATION WITH PUNITIVE SANCTIONS

Rehabilitation programs and punitive sanctions have often been seen as mutually exclusive sanctions for convicted drinking drivers. Major arguments for rehabilitation programs have been that they provide an alternative to punitive sanctions that does not have adverse socio-economic effects—for example, job loss due to license disqualification—and that can offer important benefits to the individual and to society—reduction in recidivism due to decreased alcohol problems (Hall 1977). This perspective—coupled with the fact that the role of rehabilitation programs in the legal process has been unclear, leading in many cases to situations where courts will not assign individuals to programs unless they have indicated a desire to attend—has resulted in many jurisdictions in the use of waived sanctions, especially license suspension, as an incentive to enter programs.

In many experimental or quasi-experimental evaluations of rehabilitation, the experimental group consists of individuals who have entered programs with some form of reduced or waived license suspension, while the control group consists of individuals whose license has been suspended for a longer period. Thus, in these studies, the comparison in effect is not between a treatment and a control condition, but between two "treatment" conditions. This literature has recently been reviewed in detail by Peck et al. (1985) and will be discussed only briefly here.

In nearly all of these studies, either no significant differences on traffic safety measures were found, or else program participants had significantly worse driving records (especially increased nonalcohol-related crashes and violations) than individuals given license suspensions only (Hagen, Williams, and McConnell 1979; Popkin, Li, Lacey, Stewart, and Waller 1983; Preusser, Ulmer, and Adams 1976; Sadler and Perrine 1984; Salzberg and Klingberg 1982). These differences appear to be due primarily to driving exposure factors; when differences in amount of time with a valid license are taken into account, they tend to disappear (Preusser et al. 1976), although the benefits due to license suspension may extend beyond the period of suspension (Hagen et al. 1979). The evidence suggests, however, that individuals assigned to rehabilitation programs may have fewer alcohol-related violations and crashes (Sadler and Perrine 1984).

Little is known about the comparative impact of rehabilitation and other sanctions such as fines and imprisonment. In fact, only a small number of quasi-experimental studies have examined the effects of sanctions themselves. Homel (1980) found that larger fines were associated with lower recidivism. However, he also reported that longer jail terms were associated with increased recidivism. In support of the latter observation, Sherman, Gartin, Doi, and Miller (1986) reported that jailed drinking drivers had significantly more driving violations than those not incarcerated. As well, Salzberg and Paulsrude (1984) reported that the imposition of increased penalties (including mandatory jail sentences) for drinking-driving convictions in Washington State was associated with no change in the likelihood of accidents or violations among those convicted, although accident rates did decrease among a general population sample. However, Falkowski (1986) found that imposition of jail sentences decreased nighttime accidents. In the only study which compared the impact of jail and rehabilitation, Caghan (1976) found, not surprisingly, that offenders assigned to a brief educational program with or without a jail sentence showed significantly more improvement in knowledge and attitudes than offenders assigned to jail alone.

Thus, substitution of rehabilitation for license suspension cannot be supported on traffic safety grounds. License suspensions appear to have important traffic safety benefits that rehabilitation programs should supplement, not replace (Mann et al. 1983; Peck et al. 1985). Whether or not rehabilitation programs should be substituted for other forms of sanctions to obtain traffic safety benefits remains an unanswered question.

EFFECTIVENESS OF REHABILITATION WHEN OFFENDER TYPE AND
PROGRAM TYPE ARE CONSIDERED

Many evaluations of rehabilitative countermeasures have found no impact, or even adverse impact, on traffic safety indices. However, in many cases the effects of rehabilitation were confounded by license suspension differences (as described above) or by other differences between treated and "control" groups such as different levels of drinking problems or prior convictions for drinking-driving (e.g., Anderson and Merrick 1980). Much of the data from the Alcohol Safety Action Projects (ASAP) conducted in the United States in the early 1970s were subject to these difficulties (Nichols, Weinstein, Ellingstad, Struckman-Johnson, and Reis 1981). More recent studies have employed true experimental designs to examine the impact of rehabilitation, and these will be considered here.

There are large variations in the types of rehabilitation programs employed with convicted drinking drivers, ranging from simple provision of reading materials (Swenson, Struckman-Johnson, Ellingstad, Clay, and Nichols 1981) to long-term treatment of alcohol problems (Reis 1983). Within this range of programs, three major types can be discerned: (1) educative, (2) short-term structured treatment, and (3) long-term individually oriented treatment. The purpose of educative programs is to provide information on alcohol effects, drinking driving laws, signs of problem drinking, and safe driving practices, and to enable program participants to devise strategies and make decisions to prevent further impaired driving. The Phoenix program (Malfetti and Winter 1980) has served as a prototype for many educative efforts. In Phoenix-style programs, offenders typically attend a series of four to eight meetings lasting approximately two hours each. In these meetings, information on alcohol effects, drinking and driving, and identifying problem drinking is provided through lectures, films, and group discussion. Other educative programs may simply provide reading materials to participants (Swenson et al. 1981) or may involve participants in closed-course driving sessions (McGuire 1978). In short-term structured treatment programs, assumptions are made about the type of problem that results in drinking-driving behavior, and a short program to alleviate the problem is devised. Typically, such programs have emphasized social skills or assertiveness training (e.g., Holden 1983). Long-term individually oriented treatment programs typically focus on reducing the alcohol problems offenders experience. As well, these programs often include alcohol education, assessment (and referral) for other problems, and some form of supervisory component like probation (e.g., Holden 1983; Reis 1983).

Even within this framework, however, programs may vary considerably in format and content. For example, some programs are structured as short but intensive experiences which isolate offenders from the outside world for a short time and immerse them in the educational and assessment material (e.g. Siegal 1982). Others emphasize briefer contacts over a long period of time. Programs can also vary in their emphasis, with some programs focusing primarily on the traffic safety aspects of drinking-driving, some focusing on alcohol problems and alcoholism as the major cause of drinking-driving, and still others emphasizing other types of life skills such as assertiveness (Pacific Institute 1985).

A survey of the literature on offender types reveals that convicted drinking drivers are a very heterogeneous group (e.g., Donovan and Marlatt 1982; Vingilis 1983). Research over the past decade has suggested that convicted drinking drivers seem to have personality problems, alcohol problems, and/or driving problems (Donovan and Marlatt 1982; Mercer 1985; Simpson 1977). In fact, some researchers suggest that convicted drinking drivers are "impaired problem drivers" not "problem impaired drivers" (Mercer 1985; Simpson 1977). However, this heterogeneity has received little attention in the design of rehabilitation programs. One offender type that can, at present, be related in a meaningful way to outcome in different programs is alcohol problem level. Low alcohol problem level offenders are defined, in different studies, as first offenders (e.g., Reis 1983) or on the basis of a limited number of criteria including scores on a measure of alcohol problems such as the Mortimer-Filkins test (Mortimer, Filkins, and Lower 1971), numbers of previous offences, and arrest blood alcohol level (e.g., Landrum, Miles, Neff, Pritchard, Roebuck, Wells-Parker, and Windham 1982). High alcohol problem level offenders are defined as multiple offenders or, again, on the basis of a limited number of criteria.

Several experimental evaluations of the traffic safety impact of educational programs with low alcohol problem level offenders have been performed. Blount, Reis, and Chappell (1983) found that offenders exposed to a Phoenix-style program had significantly fewer DUI rearrests than those simply given reading materials. Reis (1983) compared first offenders assigned to a Phoenix-model program with those assigned to a no-program control condition and with those assigned to a home-study program. Program participants demonstrated significantly less recidivism over 1,260 days of follow-up than the control group; however, they did not differ from the home-study group, who also showed significantly less recidivism than the controls. Essex and Weinerth (1982) compared the recidivism rates of first offenders randomly assigned to a Phoenix-model program or a no-program control group.Individuals assigned to the program had significantly fewer drinking-driving rearrests twelve months but not eighteen months later. These positive results must be tempered by the observations of Holden (1983) and Landrum et al. (1982). These investigators found no significant differences in recidivism rate be tween individuals assigned to Phoenix-model programs and those assigned to control conditions.

Three experimental studies have examined the impact of educative programs on high alcohol problem level offenders. Vingilis, Adlaf, and Chung (1981) compared seventy multiple offenders assigned to a Phoenix-style program to sixty-one multiple offenders not assigned to the program. Over forty-two months of follow-up, no significant differences in recidivism rates were observed. In studies with larger sample sizes, Holden (1983) and Landrum et al. (1982) replicated this observation. However, Nichols et al. (1981), in an analysis of the results of the multisite Short-Term Rehabilitation (STR) study, found significant reductions in recidivism fifteen, sixteen, and seventeen months after arrest for individuals assigned to an educational program. This difference was due to two of the four sites that had small-group, interaction-oriented programs, which may be more similar to treatment than other educational programs.

No experimental studies have examined the impact of short-term rigid format programs with low alcohol problem individuals. However, two studies have examined the impact of these programs on high problem populations. Nichols et al. (1981), as part of the STR study, compared a thirty-two-hour, structured therapy called Power Motivation Training (PMT), which included "experiential exercises on risk-taking, goal-setting and interpersonal communication during stressful situations" (Swenson et al. 1981), with control conditions.

PMT participants had significantly worse levels of recidivism than controls over the eighteen-month follow-up period. Holden (1983) compared the traffic safety effectiveness of education plus treatment, one year of probationary supervision, and a combination of education/treatment and probationary supervision with a control group for problem drinker first offenders. Education consisted of a Phoenix-model program and treatment consisted of group assertiveness training for eight 1½-hour sessions. No beneficial effects of treatment on recidivism were observed.

Two studies have examined the impact of long-term programs oriented to individual needs for low alcohol problem offenders. Landrum et al. (1982) compared rearrest rates of offenders assigned to an education program, one year of probation, and education plus probation to a control condition. Lower rearrest rates, over twenty-four months of follow-up, for individuals assigned to probation plus education compared to the other three groups reached marginal levels of significance (p values between .05 and .07), although these differences had disappeared by the thirty-six-month follow-up. However, Holden (1983), in an evaluation of very similar rehabilitation modalities, found no significant traffic safety impact of the probation plus education condition when compared to controls.

Several experimental evaluations of the impact of long-term, individually oriented programs on high alcohol problem offenders have been reported. Reis (1983) compared recidivism rates of multiple offenders assigned to one year of eclectic group educational counseling/therapy (some of these individuals also received Antabuse), to brief, biweekly, individual contacts for one year, or to a no-treatment control group. Over nine hundred days of follow-up, the group therapy participants had significantly less recidivism than controls; the biweekly contact group also had less recidivism than controls, though the difference was not significant. Blount et al. (1983) compared the traffic safety effectiveness of bibliotherapy, a Phoenix-model educational program, and the educational program plus referral to five months of group therapy. In eighteen months of follow-up, no significant differences in recidivism were observed between groups; however, when individuals who dropped out of the programs were excluded, individuals assigned to the educational program plus group therapy had significantly less recidivism than either of the other two conditions. Nichols et al. (1981) reported on the evaluation of the STR study, in which possible problem drinkers were assigned to group therapy or control conditions. Group therapy participants had significantly less recidivism than controls in one of the eighteen months of follow-up. Holden (1983) found that offenders assigned to probation supervision with or without education and therapy had significantly fewer rearrests for offenses other than drinking-driving over two years of follow-up than a control group or a group provided with education and therapy alone. However, Landrum et al. (1982), comparing similar groups, found no significant differences in outcome.

Table 10.1 summarizes the research discussed above, and a comparison of studies reporting positive and negative effects for the different categories suggests what programs work for what types of people. For offenders with low alcohol problem levels, education programs appear to have a traffic safety benefit; there is as yet insufficient research with other types of programs to suggest how they will influence this group. For high alcohol problem offenders, long-term, individually oriented treatment programs appear to have traffic safety benefits. However, alcohol education and short-term, rigid-format treatment programs seem to have few traffic safety benefits, and may even exacerbate recidivism.

The basis for classification of program and offender types presented here is very crude, and thus the summary presented in the table should be treated with a certain amount of skepticism. However, the studies presented in the table have important methodological strengths—random assignment, large samples, long follow-up periods. Thus, what may be emerging from these studies is a set of preliminary guidelines to assist in developing programs with maximum traffic safety benefits.

In rehabilitative programs as in educational programs the issue of quality of implementation is very important. Rehabilitative programs are implemented in a wide variety of settings by staff with widely varying characteristics and skill levels. Programs must often deal with unwilling participants who are involved only to fulfill legal requirements and who may resist any kind of meaningful engagement in the program process. Thus, high-quality implementation is difficult to achieve. Evaluations of program effectiveness often do not include measures of quality of implementation and it is possible that some outcomes may be due to poor implementation rather than to inherent weaknesses in program models (Pacific Institute 1986).

Summary and Speculations

It appears that, under certain conditions, rehabilitation programs for convicted drinking drivers can have traffic safety benefits. The first, and most important, condition is that these programs not be

Table 10.1. Results of Drinking-Driver Rehabilitation Programs when Program and Offender Types are Considered

Program Impact	"Low-Problem" Offenders			"High-Problem" Offenders		
	Alcohol Education	Short-Term, Rigid-Format Treatment	Long-Term, Individually Oriented Treatment	Alcohol Education	Short-Term, Rigid-Format Treatment	Long-Term, Individually Oriented Treatment
Impact on recidivism not detectable or adverse	Holden 1983 Landrum et al. 1982		Holden 1983	Blount et al. 1983 Landrum et al. 1982 Vingilis et al. 1981	Holden 1983 Nichols et al. 1978	Landrum et al. 1982
Beneficial impact on recidivism	Blount et al. 1983 Essex and Weinerth 1982 Reis 1983		Landrum et al. 1982	Nichols et al. 1978		Blount et al. 1983 Holden 1983 Nichols et al. 1978 Reis 1983

used to replace license suspensions, which have important traffic safety benefits of their own. The second condition seems to be that offenders be assigned to appropriate types of programs. There are, as well, areas in which program improvement might occur.

Studies of drinking-driving offenders are unanimous in concluding that the population is a heterogeneous one (Barnes, Landrum, Cosby, and Snow 1986; Donovan and Marlatt 1983; Vingilis 1983). As well, drinking and driving occurs in many different environments, and these environments differ for different people (Snow, Cunningham, and Barnes 1985; Vingilis and Mann 1986). Efforts to take these differences into account in designing rehabilitation programs have, as yet, been minimal; typically, offenders are viewed, as described earlier, as having low or high levels of alcohol problems. However, research demonstrates that many additional factors are associated with the risk of impaired driving and accidents (e.g., Donovan and Marlatt 1983; Mann, Vingilis, Anglin, Suurvali, Poudrier, and Vaga in press; Barnes et al. 1986). It seems possible to design programs which can be tailored to the needs and problems of the individual (Vasquez 1986), or to introduce comprehensive assessments linked to several different types of programs (Siegal 1986). Evidence suggests that such approaches may improve traffic safety benefits (Siegal 1986).

Education and Rehabilitation in the Larger Context of Social Control

Any efforts to control a social and public health problem such as the alcohol-crash problem must consider the nature of the problem: is the problem one for which the person is primarily responsible, is it one for which the environment is primarily responsible, or does the problem result from some interplay of both person and environment? Efforts to control the drinking-driving problem have typically emphasized either the person, for example, through education and rehabilitation, or the environment, for example, through implementing stricter laws, or controlling alcohol availability. Typically, countermeasures based on a single approach are limited in their impact (e.g., Ross 1981; Landrum et al. 1982), leading to suggestions that the particular control efforts involved be abandoned and resources be channeled in more promising directions.

An analysis of the alcohol-crash problem suggests that it results from both the individual and the environment, both independently and interactively (Mann and Vingilis 1985; Mosher 1985; Snortum, this volume; Vingilis and Mann 1986; Waller 1985). Thus, counter-measure approaches must seek to understand the independent and interactive influences of both personal factors and environmental factors. The relevant research supports the contention that both types of factors must be included to understand and ameliorate the problem.

One example which supports the need for this interactive approach comes from literature on the influence of alcohol on youth. Research demonstrates that young people are overrepresented in alcohol-related crashes at lower blood alcohol levels (Simpson 1985), leading to the suggestion that they are less tolerant to, or somehow more influenced by, low levels of alcohol. However, laboratory studies of psychomotor impairment demonstrate that young people are in fact less influenced by lower doses of alcohol than older individuals (Vogel-Sprott and Barrett 1984). Thus, it seems that the impact of alcohol on different people depends upon the environment in which those people find themselves, and a single-factor approach to this problem would be inadequate.

This perspective suggests, at a minimum, that the most effective way to combat a complex social problem like drinking and driving is to introduce a set of complementary person-based and environment-based countermeasures; otherwise, only a part of the problem is addressed. For example, recent studies of the alcohol-crash problem and of apprehended drinking drivers in countries which have strengthened laws and police detection abilities (for example, with random breath testing) suggest that individuals with few or no alcohol problems are deterred, but individuals who are heavy or problem drinkers are still on the roads and involved in unacceptably high numbers of accidents (Dunbar, Pikkarainen, and Penttila in press; Glad 1985). In these instances, introduction of countermeasures aimed at the person (education and rehabilitation) could be associated with further important reductions in the alcohol crash problem.

Education programs for youth can serve as an important meeting place for person-oriented and environment-oriented efforts. Many of these programs are designed not only to change the behavior of young people at immediate risk of drinking and driving, but also to bring about long-term changes in peer group and community norms (Klitzner et al. 1985). These programs may be effective in molding the attitudes of young people who will influence social attitudes, and thus environmental factors such as laws, for many years to come.

Under ideal conditions, effective primary prevention methods such as education programs would eliminate the need for secondary prevention. As yet, primary prevention techniques are imperfect, and secondary prevention methods such as rehabilitation programs are needed. However, reliance upon the voluntary social control methods of education and rehabilitation alone cannot be recommended; nor can reliance upon such measures as stricter laws, alcohol control, and improved vehicle or road design alone. Instead, it seems probable that truly effective social control of drinking and driving will make judicious use of both education and rehabilitation, in addition to other measures.

11 The Economic Perspective on Controlling the Drunken Driver

Harold L. Votey, Jr.

The economist's objective in analyzing any social phenomenon is to learn more about the economic aspects of the phenomenon to develop policies for social improvement. In recent years economists have become involved in studying an increasingly broad range of social issues. Although it may seem removed from the more usual subject matter of economics, drunken driving has consequences that make it imperative that methods such as those used by economists be applied. This follows simply because it has been well established that drunken driving imposes immense costs on society and any measures applied to reduce those costs require resources that must be diverted from other beneficial uses. How scarce resources should be allocated among alternative uses is, after all, the most fundamental question that economists address.

There are two aspects of the methodology of economics that are particularly relevant to the issue of reducing social losses to drunken driving. One is the fundamental approach to analysis that allows for practical definitions of "best" policies and points the way to the sorts of investigations that potentially reveal available policy choices. The second is the nature of the statistical methodology, until recently largely unique to the discipline of economics, developed to respond to the questions that must be answered if "best" policies are to become reality. For these statements to make sense one must understand the problem solving approach underlying most of what economists do.

To explain the economist's perspective and method in greater detail, this chapter proceeds from a theoretical basis for an approach that is consistent with achieving best policies to illustration of the details of analyses that have the potential for achieving them. Finally, the literature is reviewed briefly to provide the reader with an appraisal of the progress made in reaching "best" objectives and what is required to complete the task.

The first task of the paper is to explain the economic paradigm and how it attempts to resolve issues such as those relating to the drunken driver. The implementation of the paradigm is essentially a three-stage process and each step is explained and considered in turn. As the reader will see, there is nothing magical about using such a paradigm. It is simply a formalization of what sensible people do when they apply logic to the solution of any important personal problem. However, proceeding through the steps in a logical sequence helps to clarify what the appropriate steps should be for achieving best policies.

The second objective is to discuss the method economists typically use to view a problem so that critical aspects are not overlooked. This is the implementation stage of applying the paradigm. The illustration of optimal decision-making in dealing with the drunken driver progresses through each of the three successive stages with some discussion of method at each stage. An attempt has been made to deal with some of the criticisms of these methods as the exposition proceeds.

The third task undertaken is a brief review of progress that has been made thus far in using the paradigm for obtaining answers regarding optimal policy choices for reducing the social costs of drunken driving. The search for optimal policy choices is far from complete and one objective of discussion is to reveal this lack of completeness.

The ultimate objective should be, not to convince others that they should become economists, but to convince them that they should view the paradigm as a generic approach to improved problem solving for most social issues.

The Economic Paradigm and Drunken Driving Policy-Making

The Economic Paradigm Defined

Perhaps one of the most perceptive analyses of the economist's viewpoint and motivation for becoming involved in a wide variety of social issues has been done by Reuven Brenner (1980). The question of motivation had already been reviewed rather carefully in an interesting article by Coase (1978) who viewed much of this movement beyond the traditional interests of economists into "contiguous disciplines" as a kind of predatory process. In his view, the expansion was made possible in part because methods common to economics could be used profitably to study a wider range of issues. Brenner focuses on what is different about the economic approach. He argues that the key difference lies in the very nature of the study of economics that tends to integrate elemental aspects of a problem into a framework that permits logical decision-making. His perception is that social science generally is a maturing field and draws a parallel to maturation of scientific thought in the natural sciences. In his view, what economists have to contribute to this process is a paradigm that, presently, is unique to economics. He argues that predictions made by the economic approach are more consistent with the facts than are the predictions of other social science theories.

Neither Coase nor Brenner predict that economists will take over the analysis of a wider range of social issues. Rather, as Brenner puts it, social science, as a field, will gain in maturity by adopting useful attributes of what has previously been unique to the method of economics.

The paradigm that Brenner refers to, interestingly, derives from the theorizing of the Utilitarians whose writings form the basis for classical criminological theory as well as for modern economic decision theory. An elemental aspect of the paradigm is that it supplies a uniform framework for analyzing phenomena that are central to important social objectives. The empirical testing associated with evaluating theories within this framework clarifies the key social issues and the decisions upon which resolutions of those issues will logically depend. The objective is always social optimization and it is important to cast this objective in a framework that can be accepted generally without debate.

As an example, I will assert that the logical objective with respect to crime is to minimize the social costs of crime. What this means in terms of society's resources is that, if we reduce the social costs of crime, we have greater resources available for more desirable uses. Within such a framework, we may wish to debate the definitions of costs—surely most people's notions of purely monetary costs are not adequate for our purpose. But the notion of accounting for all costs and benefits, including psychic ones, helps us to focus on the appropriate objective. Although this paragraph began by asserting that social cost minimization is the appropriate objective, most people will accept it as eminently reasonable.

This framework helps us to perceive that there are important interdependencies among critical elements of the problem, something that natural scientists avoid in evaluating cause and effect by laboratory techniques. Natural scientists understood full well that confounding forces could invalidate efforts at empirical validation of fundamental theories and that ignoring key interactions could invalidate policy efforts as well. This is a point made long ago in another context when John Muir stated: "When we try to pick out anything by itself, we find it attached to everything else in the Universe." The economic paradigm forces us to recognize such interactions in social science research and policy prescription.

A seeming stumbling point with the economist's paradigm is the fundamental premise that the actors in any given system will act rationally. This appears to be a crucial element of the arguments against the economist's approach. Some have argued that a theory based on rationality cannot possibly lead to useful conclusions or policy because a substantial amount of illegal behavior seems to be undertaken irrationally. A number of responses need to be made to this position. First, an appropriate social response does not depend upon *all* actors behaving rationally, but only on there being a sufficient number doing so for useful outcomes to be achieved. In conducting empirical validations of theory, it is obvious that in some cases such validations will not be forthcoming if rational behavior is nonexistent. The appropriate testing of hypotheses will, in effect, be testing the hypothesis of rationality.

Second, if for some aspects of the problem, rationality is absent, this is not in itself a reason to discard the economic approach. It is perfectly appropriate to develop integrated models of response to a social problem in which some behavior can be taken as random and the process modeled accordingly. There will still be a rational policy for control. What is crucial is that the paradigm prevail and that social objectives still form the basis for policy within a framework where key interactions are not ignored.

To move from the more abstract level of Reuven Brenner's discussion to the case at hand, an illustration may prove helpful to the reader. The illustration is purposely an oversimplification of the problem. The intent is not to convince the reader that all solutions are simple if we can reduce essential elements of the problem to a simple figure, but to provide an unambiguous illustration of a principle in an uncomplicated example.

An Illustration

In applying the economic paradigm to the problem of drunken driving I intend to take a narrow view of the problem, by limiting the discussion to the damages or expected damages directly attributable to driving while impaired by alcohol or drugs. For the purpose of this discussion I want to take the position that we would not be concerned with drinking and driving if no one were likely to be injured by the behavior. In such a simplified view, the only direct costs of drunken driving are those to victims: death, personal injury, or property damage. Let us also assume that drunken driving is controllable by some set of social measures. Under such circumstances, there will be an optimum social position that is not at a zero level of drunken driving but one below the level it would be if controls were absent.

Figure 11.1 illustrates the essential elements of the argument. On the horizontal axis the aggregate level of drunken driving is represented, increasing as one moves from the origin (0) to the right. On the vertical axis costs are represented rising from zero at the origin. Thus, any point on the figure represents a level of costs associated with a particular level of drunken driving. We presume that social costs related to drunken driving rise as drunken driving increases. We represent that aspect of costs by line 0V which assumes that all costs—death, injury, and property damage—rise proportionately to the level of drunken driving.

We can also plot the relationship between costs for controlling drunken driving and its incidence. In the extreme, consider the case in which there is a known population of drunken drivers. As we put increasing numbers of them in jail for a given period, the costs rise. But, at the same time, the amount of drunken driving will diminish. This relationship can be illustrated by the line CC that shows that at lower levels of expenditure for control there will be a higher incidence of drunken driving. The curve is drawn with diminishing slope (in absolute value) to suggest that, for any control effort, there are likely to be diminishing returns in reducing the behavior as expenditures are increased. For example, as we increase police officers to seek out drunken drivers from a given pool of drivers, the added law enforcement personnel have an increasingly difficult time finding additional drunken drivers as fewer remain out of jail. This same curve would be appropriate to represent a case in which deterrence works through the threat of jail to prevent potential drinking drivers from becoming actual drinking drivers.

Plotting these two elements of cost provides the total social costs associated with any particular level of drunken driving. It will be simply the level of costs to victims measured on curve 0V that are associated with any particular level of drunken driving, plus the costs of control from curve CC at that same level of drunken driving. For example, the level of social costs of drunken driving at level D

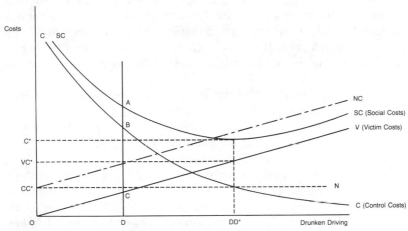

Fig. 11.1. The social cost minimization process for drunken driving.

will be costs to victims (CD) plus those for control (BD) which add to AD. The social cost curve (SC), defined in this manner, represents the vertical summation for every level of drunken driving of the values represented by curves 0V and CC.

We can see that, under the circumstances depicted, there is an optimal level of drunken driving shown in figure 11.1. Perhaps it is more intuitive to think in terms of an optimal level of control at level C*, the low point of social costs DD*, at which victim costs will amount to VC* and control costs to CC*. We conclude that the level of drunken driving DD* is optimal because efforts to reduce the behavior further will result in added social costs that exceed the marginal benefits of accident reduction.

One should understand that, if the behavior is not controllable, there will be no downward sloping relationship between control costs and the level of drunken driving looking like CC. If amount CC* is spent for control and it has no effect, as for example by spending funds on educational programs that are totally ignored by all persons who drink, a control cost curve would be generated that looks like CC*N. In this case, total social costs would be represented by CC*NC. Under such circumstances, the optimal solution with respect to efforts at control would be to spend nothing for control, pushing the total social cost curve downward to coincide with 0V, leaving the level of drunken driving to be determined by behavior that is uncontrolled.

From this illustration, we can see that the paradigm provides guidance as to the correct policy decision. Whether or not to impose control depends on whether the behavior, in fact, is controllable by some social measure. If it is not, no expenditure for control is justified on the basis of minimizing costs associated with drunken driving.[1]

An essential point is that, whether a behavior is controllable is an empirical question and, until that question is answered, the paradigm is powerless to provide useful answers to the policy question. To formulate policy in the absence of answers to this empirical question risks wasting social resources.

There is a further point in connection with the economic paradigm that needs to be made explicit. That is, one cannot determine the correct control position unless one is capable of evaluating alternatives. For example, it would be pointless to argue, even if drunken driving is controllable, that it is always appropriate to apply a particular control measure. That decision depends upon the correct valuation of alternatives. The question of value is a second empirical question and it may be more difficult to answer than the question of controllability. It cannot be answered arbitrarily, because the correct answer depends upon the values held by those persons who will be paying the costs, both for control measures and as victims, if the solution is to be justified as a social measure.

The Economic Paradigm Applied

When one undertakes to apply the economic paradigm, it is appropriate to separate its elements into three steps:
1. Specifying the possible or feasible states of the world.
2. Valuing each of these alternatives.
3. Optimizing, that is, simply selecting the best among all feasible options.
If one can achieve steps 1 and 2, the answer to the third will generally be self-evident.

If one accepts the logic of the paradigm and reviews the research relating to drunken driving, one conclusion stands out immediately: most research has not proceeded beyond the first step of the paradigm. In fact, many people would argue that the issue of controllability has not been resolved. However, even resolving the controllability issue is not sufficient to complete the first stage of the paradigm.

In fairness to many who argue against specific kinds of control for drunken driving, it must be pointed out that usually their arguments are based on the belief that controllability is not possible with the specific measure they oppose. Their position with respect to the paradigm is correct *if* they are correct on the issue of controllability, because controllability is a necessary justification for imposing any control measure.

There are two further aspects of the defining of feasible alternatives that need to be understood. One is that, even if a behavior is controllable by a particular measure, the level of the behavior may depend upon the level of control effort. It is important to have some idea as to the degree of controllability at different operating levels for a particular measure if one is to select a "best" solution. The second point is that other control measures may work as well, or better, or add to the effectiveness of the first control measure. No arbitrary selection of a policy mix is likely to produce best results unless these factors are known. Such logic does not, of course, deter policymakers from establishing a combination of policy based on other grounds. Some attendees at the Tenth International Conference on Alcohol, Drugs and Traffic Safety recently argued for a balanced strategy comprised of law enforcement actions against drivers, education of drivers, and controls on alcohol. This type of approach may indeed be appropriate, but, to date, little analysis has gone into the logic behind any particular blend of policy. "Balance" as defined in this way is, at best, a political concept rather than an attempt to achieve a scientifically determined "best" policy.

The first point—regarding the correct level of control—is illustrated directly in figure 11.1 by level DD*. The appropriate criteria for the level of operation of a particular control measure are perhaps better understood by referring to a second diagram, figure 11.2. Here the analysis is formulated directly in a benefit/cost framework so that the feasible alternatives are stated in terms of value, thus taking account of both the first and second steps of the paradigm. This was also implicit in figure 11.1, but we will see that in figure 11.2 an important difference is that the correct solution can be viewed in relation to the benefit/cost ratio, a measure commonly used to evaluate social policy alternatives.

In figure 11.2, the range of costs for alternative levels of a particular control effort is represented along the horizontal axis, from zero at the left, increasing to the right. Associated benefits are increasing as we move upward and are represented by the scale of the vertical axis. Any point within this space represents a level of costs and a corresponding level of benefits. Curve 0B represents a hypothetical example of associated costs and benefits of some control

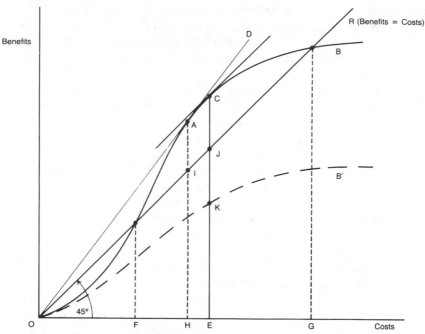

Fig. 11.2. Benefits, costs, and alternative candidates for "best" policy.

effort. For example, this might represent a situation in which the only damage caused by drunken drivers was property damages. Savings associated with jailing drunken drivers would be indicated on the vertical axis and the associated costs of putting drivers in jail would be represented on the horizontal axis. Curve 0B is drawn to represent a case in which at low levels of operation there are increasing returns but as control levels increase there are diminishing returns, perhaps as drivers who drink and drive less frequently are caught and jailed. The line drawn at a forty-five-degree angle to the horizontal axis is the locus of all points at which benefits are exactly equal to costs.

To relate these concepts more generally to the control of drunken driving, one could think of movements that increase costs as being in the direction of increased control effort. That is, the scale of the effort would be registered as a cost along the horizontal axis. If the benefits were only lives saved, the vertical axis could be calibrated simply in terms of lives and would need not be a monetary scale. If, however, the benefits include injuries prevented and a reduction of costs of damage, to property, then the benefits must be denominated in some measure that can equate values for injuries and damages as well as deaths. Thus, for most analyses, we need to determine monetary equivalents for such damages, including justifiable psychic costs.

The first point that one might make, if the curve representing associated benefits and costs is like 0B, is that there will be positive benefits at all levels of operation from cost level F to G. That is, all the values on 0B lying between cost levels F and G lie above the line 0R at which benefits exactly equal costs. The highest attainable benefit/cost ratio will be represented by line 0D that just touches the benefit/cost curve at A with scale of operation H. Clearly, the situation at A (cost level H) is superior to one at the same scale of operations as H with benefit/cost curve 0B′ because, for the latter curve, costs everywhere exceed benefits. But from society's perspective, point A is not the best. Net benefits to society are greater at C, with net benefits measured by CJ at a scale of operations E. This follows because CJ is greater than AI. The correct solution is that at which the contribution to benefits, at the margin, is exactly equal to the contribution of costs. That point is at C because, for either an increase in the scale of operations by some small move to the right of C, or for a decrease in the scale of operations by a move to the left of C, net benefits, the vertical distance between lines 0B and 0R, will be diminished. Note that the slope of curve 0B at point C is exactly the same as that for line 0R, thus satisfying the marginal costs equal marginal benefits condition for optimality.

The logic of such a choice should be clear. If there are diminishing returns to an activity, and there is a range in which that activity can be conducted at a social profit, one would want to expand the activity up to the point at which the addition to benefits exactly equals the addition to costs, thus extracting the maximum of potential net benefits. But there is another consideration as well. Our analysis in figure 11.2 presumes only a single control alternative. If there were two mutually exclusive control alternatives and limited resources so that we could choose one or the other, we would choose the one with the maximum net benefits. However, choosing the correct policy is an empirical question.

The point of all of this is that, although proving the ineffectiveness of a control measure is sufficient to dismiss it as inappropriate, demonstrating that it does work in a physical sense is not a sufficient justification for invoking it to the exclusion of other measures. We need to take into account the second and third steps of the paradigm: valuation and finally the choice among feasible successful strategies.

Establishing the Feasible Range of Options

Evaluative efforts that are incapable of leading to policy improvements aptly provide the rationale for seeking methods that yield the required information. The economist prefers to combine the objective of evaluation with that of modeling a system or process. Nonparametric evaluative techniques that do less do not yield the information necessary for policy improvement except in the limiting case in which it can be decisively demonstrated that a policy has no effect or an undesirable effect. Should either be true, it would be inappropriate to continue the clearly ineffective policy.

A further, and perhaps obvious, point regarding combining evaluation analyses with estimation of key parameters is that evaluative studies are costly and if savings can be achieved by avoiding duplication in processing data and estimation it should be done. Because estimation of such parameters facilitates effective hypothesis testing of controllability, the obvious choice of method is the one that achieves both goals simultaneously.

The Policy Choice

The discussion to this point has made it obvious that most policies to control drunken driving seem to have been made in a knowledge vacuum. Because most research has failed to complete Stage 1 in the economic paradigm, we are not in a position even to specify the range of feasible alternatives. One might think that this is a sufficient basis to argue that no policy should be invoked at all. Such an argument, however, lacks *any* logical support because there are costs to doing nothing. Failing to invoke control measures may be more costly on balance than invoking less than the best out of ignorance as to what is best.

In the past, society has primarily based drunken driving policies on intuition and faith. It is unlikely that policy mixes chosen in such a manner are optimal. But one cannot argue on any scientific basis that abandoning a policy is better unless it provides no benefit, something that has not been well demonstrated for any popular policy at this stage of scientific progress among the social sciences. An important question is: How can society obtain sufficient information to establish policy based on an informed judgment? To respond to this question, it is useful to consider the methodology that points the way toward the needed answers.

Evaluation Methodology

Modeling the Control Problem

To be able to operate correctly within an optimization paradigm based on social cost minimization, it is important to begin with a model of the process that clearly relates potential costs and benefits. One needs not only to be able to discern cause and effect, one must be able to understand the process of regulating the system to achieve a particular level of costs and benefits.

A schematic diagram of a simplified version of such a process is displayed in figure 11.3. As depicted, there are two elements of social costs: those arising out of accidents and those associated with re- source allocations for accident control. There are a number of ex- ogenous influences on the process. Among these will be the body of law, transport demand, weather, the number of vehicles, vehicle mix, road quality, and, for the moment, let us include resources for control. The number of vehicles is not actually shown in the figure but it interacts with the level of driving, both normal and drunken, to determine jointly traffic density for a given network of roads. All of these exogenous factors are likely to vary over time and across jurisdictions. Implicit in the diagram are two classes of actors: driv- ers and the authorities concerned with minimizing social costs who will make the resource-allocating decisions. As the figure is drawn, the level of driving by all drivers interacts with weather, vehicle mix, and road quality to cause accidents. Law enforcement moderates the process to the extent that it affects the level of drunken driving. It may also affect how sober drivers use care in obeying speed laws and other safety measures, an effect not included in the diagram. Law enforcement may also be used to regulate alcohol consumption, also not shown. Law enforcement activity is jointly determined by the allocation of resources to it and the body of law.

As one can readily see, to replicate the conditions of the natural science laboratory in any social experiment to reduce accidents, one will have to hold constant all forces except those affected directly by the experiment. If we wish to evaluate an effect of a change in statutes, say by enacting a per se law, we must assume other ex- ogenous factors remain constant, for example, enforcement levels do not change, the extent and mix of sanctions do not change, and even that, over the evaluation period, weather factors are not so

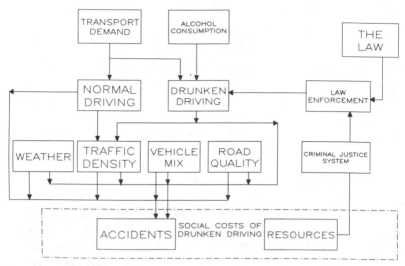

Fig. 11.3. Accidents and the process of control.

unusual as to influence the outcome abnormally. Implementing such a law has great appeal for policymakers because the implementation of the law, if effective, would seem to be essentially costless. If we examine only an accident time series following the implementation of a per se law to estimate the effect, however, consider how much we must assume to be unchanged. Tests on long time-series data conducted in a format that considers only an accident series certainly must strain credulity. This is because neither the policymaker nor the evaluator can safely expect no other changes to take place.

To conduct a serious evaluation requires a methodology that can provide ways to standardize for the factors that may vary along with the target series, in this case, accidents. There is no single approach that will be infallible for addressing this problem, but some methods used by econometricians to monitor complex social systems have many of the needed attributes. I refer to the simultaneous systems analysis most often applied in time-series form to monitor the behavior of macroeconomic systems.

Some very simple models have been tested for dealing with the problems of drunken driving. A model that goes much beyond the limitations of the interrupted time-series formulation often used to evaluate measures to reduce accidents need not be very complex.

Much of what is depicted in figure 11.3 can be captured by a three-equation, partially recursive system. Consider a model in which the law is presumed to remain fixed and sentencing standards do not vary. Any resources applied to control drunken driving are injected in the form of increased law enforcement activity. Even if driving demand is not invariant and other factors such as vehicle mix and road quality change, the situation can be described by the three equation system that follows:

The first necessary relation is one to capture the initial effect of added resources for enforcement:

$$CR = f(DD, L), \tag{1}$$

in which the ratio of convictions to the level of drunken driving is CR, a measure of enforcement effectiveness. The level of drunken driving is DD, and law enforcement resources are indexed by L. One might expect that law effectiveness will increase as more resources (L) are made available, and it will tend to diminish as the load on the system of violations (DD) increases. Behavior can be captured by the relation

$$DD = d(CR, ALC, . . .), \tag{2}$$

that is, drunken driving responds to the expected probability of apprehension and conviction and to the anticipated desire to drive while intoxicated that will be related to the general level of alcohol consumption and other things. One would predict that, if drunken driving is controllable, a rise in law enforcement effectiveness (CR) will tend to reduce it, and a rise in alcohol consumption among the population (ALC) will tend to exacerbate the problem. Note that each of these relations feeds into the other to determine jointly an equilibrium level of drunken driving (DD) and law enforcement effectiveness (CR). Accident levels follow recursively from this equilibrium:

$$AC = a(DD, VM, RQ, TD, KD, . . .), \tag{3}$$

that is, accident levels or rates are a function of the level of drunken driving and the general likelihood of accidents, which also will be influenced by vehicle mix (VM), road quality (RQ), traffic density (TD), distance driven (KD), and so forth.

Such a model may seem complex and has been criticized for being so, but it certainly incorporates most of what a simple interrupted time-series model neglects and it can effectively evaluate marginal changes in enforcement over time as well as the effect of a "blitz" (a one-time increase or a short period of intense enforcement). Furthermore, such a model will yield the estimates of parameters required to implement adequately the first step of the paradigm. That is, the relationship between changes in the resources input (L) and the target, accidents (AC), can readily be worked out. There is a problem with the direct estimation of such a model in that we do not directly observe the level of drunken driving. However, equation (2) can be substituted into equations (1) and (3) so that the required parameters can be estimated within a framework in which drunken driving levels and law enforcement effectiveness are determined jointly.

Modeling Limitations and Remedies

There have been vigorous criticisms of the results obtained by such simple models. Some critics have pointed to the well-known study by Blumstein, Cohen, and Nagin (1978) for the National Academy of Sciences that attempted to evaluate a number of econometric studies of felony crime. The authors employed the talents of Franklin Fisher, a distinguished econometrician, to add credibility to their case. The study made a number of very valid points regarding existing studies. One of these related to the techniques required for "identification" of key parameters of the system. Another relates to the problems associated with assuming resources are exogenous as pictured in figure 3. The fact that the probability of conviction incorporates in its denominator the level of offenses that is also on the right hand side of equation (1) and on the opposite side of equation (2) leads to potential biases. There were other criticisms of the method, but these three are sufficient to typify the nature of the critique. These were all valid criticisms of existing studies and, without reinvestigation of the same data, it would have been impossible to determine the extent to which results in such studies were biased. Many critics who less than fully understood the techniques assumed that these criticisms rendered the techniques themselves invalid.

In fact, virtually all of the criticisms can be effectively dealt with in properly designed studies. The identification problem exists when all the variables chosen to be regarded as exogenous are contemporary with the dependent variables. In many cases it has been found that individuals' perceptions of arrest probabilities depend more on earlier arrest behavior than on current behavior. The problem of using conviction probabilities as explanatory variables in which the denominator is the same as the dependent variable can be corrected by a simple algebraic reformulation of the estimating relationship.

Resources can be treated as endogenous variables to get around the third criticism. The Blumstein et al. critique performed a useful service and forced investigators to be more careful. It would be a mistake, however, to regard their criticism as an argument to justify discarding economic methodologies in favor of more primitive techniques. As thorough an investigation of other statistical methods probably would reveal that most can be criticized for the implicit assumptions required for their appropriate application and often violated by a particular evaluative study. One would hope that such valid criticism would lead to technological advance rather than reaction.

There are a number of steps that have been taken to address the very useful National Academy criticisms and a number of methodological advances that are worth noting. The key to effective analysis of the drunken driving problem is to begin with a conceptual model that accurately describes the process to be modeled. A step in the right direction might be to progress from figure 11.3 to figure 11.4, which incorporates several additional relevant factors. For example, the possible effect of accidents on the allocation of resources to the criminal justice system or to the entire technology of transport can be included. This takes account of one of the criticisms of Blumstein et al. as well as the potential effects of additional potential endogeneity that we discuss in what follows. The mix of sanctions can be considered. Variations in court policies need not be neglected. There may be aspects of accident control not falling within the jurisdiction of the criminal justice system that are relevant as well. One point that follows from an understanding of the economic approach is that alternative measures to reduce accidents may have a greater payoff than law enforcement. For example, requiring vehicles to be safer may save more lives than threatening to arrest drunken drivers. Airbags or seat belts may have a greater beneficial impact than longer jail sentences. Better roads may reduce the likelihood of all accidents. To consider the relative merits of such alternative measures requires that an evaluative model contain their effects.

Although it is easy to include some of these forces in figure 11.4, it is more difficult to do so in a statistical sense. The statistical problem conceptually is not difficult, but the problem may be in acquiring data appropriate for statistical evaluation. Good evaluative studies of drunken driving will not be possible unless additional data sources are developed.

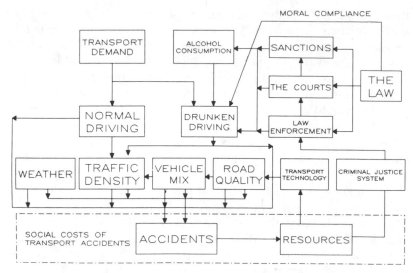

Fig. 11.4. Accidents as an element of the social cost of transport.

Some questions can only be answered with more insightful modeling. For example, many investigators believe that some effects of the law are largely independent of the threat of sanctions. It is felt that many persons will obey the law simply because it is moral to do so. It is easy to draw a line from "The law" to "Drunken driving" and to label it "Moral compliance" as is done in figure 11.4. It is another thing to be able to model such a force statistically. Yet there is considerable evidence, as the reader should be aware by now, that the force of moral beliefs may play an independent role.

Moral compliance belongs in this modeling process in an important way because we should learn whether there is a real trade-off in costs between simply establishing the moral imperative by creating a law that many will respond to on moral grounds and the more costly approach of enforcing the law by the imposition of apprehension and sanctions. A critical question is whether moral compliance is reinforced by the deterrence effect of law enforcement or is an effect that stands alone. A related question is whether moral compliance, the threat of sanctions, and, for that matter, incapacitation effects work best on the same individuals or, as appears likely, on different subsets of the population.

Assuming we can successfully model the process of generating accidents completely enough to evaluate the impacts of alternative accident control measures, we still must complete the rest of the economic paradigm. The first stage will have been satisfied—the relevant and alternative states of the world will have been identified. We still need to choose among them.

The Question of Value

The second step of the paradigm is valuation. On the control side, valuation for the most part is relatively easy. Most of the required data are determined and the appropriate information is recorded for later use in the analysis. A major difficulty is that there is only vague information on costs on the victim side. Although we have seen periodic evidence compiling the staggering cost of automobile accidents or of those attributable to drunken driving, we need more precise information. If one hundred accidents are prevented, we need estimates on how many would have been fatal, the number that would have involved serious injuries, and the extent that motorists would suffer substantial property losses. Not only do we need to know the incidence of such things, we will need to be able to place a monetary value on them.

There have been some advances along this front. Jones-Lee's *The Value of Life* (1976) is a masterful effort to record the evidence of the author's and others' research on the appropriate values that should be used for policy decisions. His later work, cited in Maycock (1986), advances still further our notions of how to value human life for decision-making purposes. Nonetheless, there will continue to be considerable debate because the range of the estimates is very large, from an early estimate (1956) of $25,000 to Jones-Lee's most recent estimate (1985) of $2,100,000.

The cost of accidents when serious injuries are involved has been estimated rather carefully in Hartunian, Smart, and Thompson (1981). Although their results will be debated by those who would make alternative critical assumptions, they have provided us with an excellent data source from which one can place some bounds around the range of relevant costs. Consequently, decision makers will be in a far stronger position to render sensible policy judgments. These data coupled with sound data on the costs and relative effectiveness of control measures should help policymakers to choose among a wide range of measures to reduce life- and health-threatening impairments.

Optimization

Once decision makers have a set of values for each of the classes of accidents and can predict the distribution among these accident classes associated with a particular control alternative, they are in a position to compare marginal benefits to the marginal costs of a change in policy. With this kind of information on alternatives and their valuation, policymakers could have a much clearer range of choices with respect to efforts for accident control. This would be true not only with respect to controlling drunken drivers but also with respect to alternative measures to reduce deaths and injuries.

This is not to suggest that the path to better policy is easy or the rewards immediate. The important point is that achieving better outcomes will require evaluators to develop and adopt methods aimed at achieving objectives that would not have been regarded as conceivable two or three decades ago. This will require a willingness to reject inadequate methods in favor of those with greater promise. This is the process Reuven Brenner has described of striving toward the maturity of the social sciences as a discipline.

Economic Evaluations of Drunken Driving Controls

Thus far, this paper has described an ideal and a method as it might relate to the question of drunken driving. Even those who fully accept the logic of the paradigm have the right to ask: How far has this method of evaluation really moved us toward sound policy prescription? To that end, it makes sense to discuss some of the evidence. That evidence relates primarily to Scandinavia, with some reference to England and Wales, simply because I know of no data set for the United States or another country adequately compiled to support a model such as that presented here.

For Norway and Sweden there have been a number of estimations of essentially the simplified model presented here. Most of these have been discussed in Votey (1984a). Useful results have been obtained both from time-series and cross-section data. Some have used pooled cross-section–time-series data. Invariably, they support the hypothesis that resources devoted to apprehending drunken drivers reduce accident levels below what they would otherwise have been. Using a variety of tests with a common method establishes fairly well that replication has not generated a huge body of counter examples to the hypothesis of effectiveness. Inevitably, the statistical results have been found to be significant based on the test statistics generated by the estimates. Limited testing, using estimated parameters to forecast beyond the data base for estimation, has tended to reinforce the credibility of this approach. This is perhaps the most demanding test of any model. In a variety of ways, the more telling criticisms of Blumstein et al. have been responded to.

In the process of striving to generate new answers on the effectiveness of control measures and to dispute tests based on inappropriate or inadequate methods, much has been achieved in advancing to the use of more effective statistical methods. For example, multiwave panel studies (Greenberg 1979) or, equivalently in the language of econometrics, pooled cross-section—time-series analyses have been used to deal with the identification problem. By using such models, presumably the arbitrariness of crucial identifying restrictions can be avoided, if it can be assumed that an individual's subjective probability of apprehension and cost of sanctions is derived from earlier observations. Although this seems to be a reasonable presumption, there is some evidence, for example, Votey and Shapiro (1983), based on distributed lag estimation with monthly data, that appropriate lags are considerably less than that required to fit the annual data generally available for estimating multiwave panel models.

Another notable advance has been the development of vastly improved techniques for time-series data analysis. The development of auto-regressive integrated moving average (ARIMA) techniques has immeasurably improved our ability to test hypotheses relating to time series and to generate accurate forecasts, an important aspect of the first step of the paradigm. However, these techniques, as generally utilized, have some of the limitations of the interrupted time-series technique in that formulations generally deal with univariate or, at best, bivariate series. Such formulations are not well suited to modeling the complexities of a process such as that illustrated in figure 3. There have, however, been recent advances in the use of ARIMA methods to evaluate multivariate relationships. Examples are Phillips and Ray (1982, 1983) and Phillips, Ray, and Votey (1984). This latter technique has the advantage that, when used to identify deterrence effects, it does not suffer from the criticism of Blumstein et al. that identification requires the apparently arbitrary selection of variables excluded from some of the estimating relations.

One difficulty with this technique is that it is not an easy one to implement. It requires a high degree of statistical expertise, and considerable skill and judgment in processing the data to satisfy the assumptions under which the estimation is conducted. A part of this is the choice of appropriate techniques for deseasonalizing and de-trending the data.

The principle underlying this technique is that it isolates systematic relations between the dependent and explanatory variables unrelated to seasonal variation and trend. One difficulty is that some explanatory variables are themselves very seasonal because of the nature of the behavior generating them. Deseasonalizing will tend to remove these effects along with unrelated seasonal variation. The consequence may be that some explanatory power of key variables is overlooked, that is, variables may appear to have no significant influence when, in fact, they critically affect the outcome. For this reason, an investigator must be very careful to understand the nature of the influences that generate a data series so that the interpretation of statistical tests is not in error. Filtering out the effects of some variables in this manner probably will not affect the forecasting power of the model, but will lead to an understatement of the power of key variables. This multivariate ARIMA technique has been used quite satisfactorily to isolate the effects of the British Road Safety Act of 1967. It revealed initial accident reductions of essentially the same magnitude as those found by Ross (1973), and it forecasts exceptionally well for a full twenty-four months beyond the data base for estimation. It denies Ross's assertion, which was not based on any true hypothesis test, that the effect of the British Road Safety Act simply died out over time, by suggesting instead the alternative hypothesis that other factors have changed to overshadow the effects of the Road Safety Act.

The latter result is consistent with a study (Votey 1984b), using the simulation of a model essentially like that of figures 11.3 and 11.4, with parameters approximately correct for Norway, to evaluate the effect on the accident series of a significant intervention at the midpoint of a series. After roughly twelve periods the effect, still present, appears to have worn off. A major point of these studies was to illustrate the perils of using simplistic interrupted time-series evaluations to study effects of interventions on long time series.

Another approach to studying potential deterrence effects with time-series data to avoid the identification problem has been that of Votey and Shapiro (1983). In that study, a distributed lag formulation is used to capture the influences of past law enforcement actions that presumably affect the subjective probability of apprehension. Once more, for Swedish monthly accident data, a significant effect of control efforts is isolated, continuing to support the contention that the enforcement of Swedish laws against drunken driving reduces accident levels to below what they would otherwise have been.

The data that generated the aggregate series used for this last study can also be used in another form to examine individual behavior. A model has been tested by Shapiro and Votey (1984) that postulates a learning effect associated with prior arrests and convictions. The model allows for the likelihood that subjective probabilities of arrest depend on more than current objective probabilities and, in fact, models the process of individuals formulating subjective probabilities. It accounts for the influence of law enforcement resources and for variations in sanctions across jurisdictions and over time. The model allows for the likelihood that behavior varies with the individual characteristics of drivers. Its implementation in statistical analysis supports the hypothesis of a learning effect associated with prior exposure to the law such that first and second arrests tend to reduce the likelihood of further arrests, but for those with more lengthy records, one can expect continuing violations.

Some progress has been made in incorporating the effect of moral compliance into models that can simultaneously consider other influences on individual behavior. The theoretical modeling of the problem has been advanced in Shapiro and Votey (1987). Empirical investigation with individual data for other kinds of offenses that pits moral influences against others that affect criminal behavior, including specific deterrence, is reported in Phillips and Votey (1987). Unfortunately, the data that will be required to investigate this issue for drunken driving have yet to be collected.

A number of points can be made from these results. One is that a widening menu of statistical methods is being applied to questions generated by the debate over the controllability of drunken driving. Although dissent continues on the issue of controllability by the enforcement of laws, I think it is safe to say that Scandinavian and other laws have had at least some control effect. Many of these studies go further in providing parameter estimates that can be used to implement the first stage of the economic paradigm.

This is not to suggest that such results are unchallengeable. All of them can be criticized on one ground or another. It would be difficult to conceive of a statistical test that can fully satisfy all of the assumptions required to analyze so complex an issue. All of the results are likely to incorporate some degree of bias. Nonetheless, by now, for an impressive list of tests, each with its test statistics peculiar to its own methods, results indicate a control effect. These results have been strengthened by replication with alternative time-series and cross-section data. In many cases the validity of results has been supported by forecasting techniques. The challenge at this point is not to conduct more tests of the deterrence or control hypothesis, but to improve techniques so that parameter estimates can be used with greater effectiveness to spell out alternatives and generate more acceptable information for prescribing the direction of policy change.

There also are other questions that need to be answered. Much needs to be done to choose among control methods. This means that alternative sanctions need to be evaluated in a consistent framework in which one can be truly matched against another. An initial effort to do this in the case of Swedish sanctions is Votey and Shapiro (1983). That study partially answers the questions implicit in figure 11.2 by estimating benefit-cost ratios for sanctions that include fines, jail, and driver's license withdrawal. In general, all sanctions are found to be cost-effective, but considerably more needs to be learned before one could prescribe a best mix of sanctions. It may be difficult to do so with the current Swedish data because of the high degree of uniformity in sentencing in that country, thus generating series in which there is little variance in sentencing patterns to relate to subsequent offense levels among the general population or among previously sentenced offenders. Of particular concern in the case of Scandinavia is the high social cost of the present sentencing policy. Long jail terms for first offenders, typically three weeks in Norway and thirty days in Sweden, impose high costs both on society at large and on offenders. The fact that jail sentences appear to be cost-effective does not alter the possibility that some alternative sanction mix involving substantial fines might be superior. If successful, such a policy would reduce the public's burden of supporting the long jail terms and, as an added benefit, would transfer much of the burden to the offender who would pay the fine. Thus, both the objectives of minimization of the social cost and a redistribution of income that most citizens would find desirable would be the consequence.

Conclusions

The approach presented should not be thought limited to situations in which there has been a change in the law, in enforcement intensity, or in sanctions against violators. Nor should we limit our focus to drunken drivers. The target, after all, is unnecessary deaths and injuries. The problem may be equally complex if one is evaluating the effects of a highway improvement or the completion of an alternative mode of transportation and these are reasonable alternatives to criminal justice measures to save lives. More generally, the ultimate objective of any of these activities is improvement in the level of safe transportation services supplied. The obvious way to measure that is by its complement: accidents relative to the level of services provided. Any change in the overall delivery system will likely affect the level of safe transportation and, because the change is never undertaken in a true experimental environment, measurement of the productivity of the change must be conducted in such a manner as to isolate the effect in question, purified of the influence of other concomitant changes. The point is both that any sort of policy change can be evaluated within such a conceptual framework and that any major change in contributing factors must be accounted for in evaluating the impacts, if the analysis is to be useful for policy prescription.

It should be obvious that the main stumbling block to achieving cost-effective measures is the process of estimation. It is this measure of cause and effect that is the fundamental and essential input to linking costs and benefits. The same sort of calculation would be required if the policy variable were sentence length and resources to law enforcement were assumed invariant. And, of course, if the measures of key parameters of the system we model are statistically insignificant then the cost/benefit calculations are as well and there is no possibility of policy fine-tuning to attain an optimum level of control.

The present state of accident modeling and/or economics does not facilitate generating a simple formula for such tools as the non-linear benefit curve like that illustrated by 0B in figure 11.2. Nor can a limited set of points on such a curve be readily plotted. Alternative methodologies applied to accident modeling should make possible the calculation of the costs and benefits of a particular policy in the vicinity of the current level of operation, however, and hence the calculation of marginal benefits and costs within narrow limits. To be able to make such a determination is of immense significance, and certainly a start toward achieving substantial progress in improving policy.

Not only is effective accident modeling the key to improved policy, but the form of the modeling itself is critical. The methodology must be such that we can accurately calibrate the link between control inputs and accidents. And the stakes are high, if existing estimates of the value of life are to be believed—that is, the average of a number of careful estimates exceeds $560,000—then obviously it would be important to know that on the average we could save one life by, say, one thousand extra hours of highway patrol, but it would be more important to know whether we could increase patrols by one hundred thousand hours and save one hundred lives before diminishing returns set in and the added costs of this extra effort exceeded the added benefits. It is not clear that existing methods and data will always provide easy calculations of the first set of numbers, let alone the second, but the task need not be regarded as insurmountable.

This is not intended as an argument for any particular scheme or methodology for obtaining the necessary information for implementing the paradigm. Econometric techniques provide several alternative methods, but, faced with the challenge, any discipline has the potential for generating a methodology to yield this information. The paradigm lies in the public domain. If researchers are not trying to attain the paradigm's objectives for each activity in which significant numbers of deaths and injuries could be prevented, they have set their sights too low, and the public will be the losers.

Innovations in Social Control

12 Drinking-Driving Intervention Strategies: A Person-Situation-Behavior Framework

E. Scott Geller and Galen R. Lehman

Effective social control of excessive alcohol consumption and drunken driving requires, in part, an analysis of drinking and driving as target behaviors that can be changed within specific environmental contexts. However, several factors that complicate a behavior-environment assessment should be taken into account when designing interventions to decrease drinking and driving. First, the effects of alcohol on behavior must be considered because drinking-and-driving decisions are apt to be influenced by the amount of alcohol consumed. Second, drinking behavior patterns that have become well established may be difficult to change unless more rewarding alternative behaviors are available. Third, feedback regarding the level of alcohol impairment may be rendered less effective or even counterproductive to preventing driving under the influence (DUI) if the drinkers interpret the information as a contest or game.

Drinking and DUI behaviors, whether controlled or uncontrolled, intentional or unintentional, are responses made by individuals. Therefore, insights into effective DUI countermeasures may come from increasing the knowledge about those persons who drink excessively. This chapter reviews the role of several personal variables in DUI, including age, gender, attitudes, and beliefs, and briefly addresses the extent to which alcoholism and alcohol abuse augment the DUI problem.

The drinking environment is another critical factor that cannot be ignored in a complete analysis of the complex problem of drinking and driving. An environmental assessment requires that drinking behavior be systematically observed in various settings (for example,

The research by Geller and his students reviewed in this chapter was supported, in part, by grants from the Alcoholic Beverage Medical Research Foundation of the Johns Hopkins University School of Medicine, Anheuser-Busch Companies, and the Societal Analysis Department of General Motors Research Laboratories. The authors gratefully acknowledge the helpful comments of Nason W. Russ.

parties and bars) and studied as a function of specific environmental (or stimulus) variables. Unfortunately, this type of research is relatively infrequent in the drinking-and-driving domain. This chapter reviews the study of certain environmental factors at college parties, including (1) the labeling of beer kegs, (2) the availability of low-alcohol beer, and (3) methods of providing feedback to individuals regarding their blood alcohol concentration. In addition, the naturalistic assessment of alcohol consumption in bar settings has yielded important information regarding the influence of a "happy hour," the availability of beer by the pitcher, and the size of drinking groups.

Among the most significant determinants of alcohol consumption and DUI is the behavior of the beverage server. Some investigators have sought to determine whether servers can be trained to use intervention techniques that will effectively reduce their patrons' risk of DUI. Systematic evaluation, refinement, and implementation of server intervention programs on a large scale have the potential to yield the most rapid and successful progress toward the social control of drinking and driving. This chapter highlights the beginning of this promising area of applied research.

Theoretical views of problematic social behavior have emphasized the interaction between drinking persons and drinking environments, which is the prime theme of this chapter. For example, Jessor and Jessor (1975) proposed a "problem behavior theory" (PBT) to account for the occurrence or nonoccurrence of a problem behavior such as excessive alcohol consumption. The PBT approach includes three explanatory systems: personality, perceived environment, and behavior. The interactions among the variables within these three systems produce patterns that may predict an individual's tendency to engage in problem behavior. Applying this model to a longitudinal study of adolescents, the Jessors found evidence of a significant relationship between onset of drinking beverage alcohol and a certain pattern of personality, perceived environment, and behavior.

Schlegel, d'Avernas, and Manske (1984) replicated the Jessors' work and extended their analysis to the next step on a "continuum of drinking behavior." Their results showed that PBT could be used to identify variables accounting for 42 percent of the variance among regular drinkers' transition from controlled to uncontrolled levels of alcohol consumption.

The measured factors within the three PBT systems that significantly predicted both the onset of drinking among adolescents (Jessor and Jessor 1975) and later transition to uncontrolled drinking

(Schlegel et al. 1984) were: (1) personality—the individual's attitude toward drinking alcohol, reported intention to drink alcohol, attitude toward deviance from social norms, and religiosity; (2) perceived environment—a friend's approval of one's attitude toward drinking, and peer controls (for example, if your friends disapproved of your behavior would they try to stop you?); and (3) behavior—church attendance and drug use. The significant relationships were all in the direction one would expect. For example, an adolescent at risk for uncontrolled or excessive alcohol consumption (and DUI) is one whose attitudes toward drinking are positive and consistent with his or her peer group, and who smokes marijuana and rarely if ever attends church.

The research employing the PBT model illustrates the importance of person and environmental factors in understanding the occurrence of excessive alcohol consumption and drunken driving, and in developing a comprehensive approach toward reducing drinking and driving. Within this framework, this chapter reviews research primarily from the sociobehavioral literature that relates to the social control of alcohol-impaired driving. From this perspective, it is first important to define the target behaviors (drinking and driving) and examine some parameters relevant to the development and evaluation of intervention strategies.

Drinking Behavior and DUI

The Effect of Alcohol

Alcohol's principal influence in the blood is on the central nervous system. The first effect is to reduce tension, release inhibitions, and produce a mild feeling of euphoria. These symptoms may lead to the misconception that alcohol is a stimulant; however, alcohol actually has a depressant effect on nerve cells. As the level of alcohol in the blood increases, bodily functions progressively deteriorate. Alcohol symptoms due to central nervous system depression include impairment of motor skills, vision, and hearing. Alcohol consumption also causes loss of attention, blunted judgment, staggering gait, sleepiness, and decreased ability to learn (Winek 1983). However, not all people are similarly affected at the same blood alcohol concentration (BAC) level due to a phenomenon termed "tolerance." Thus, an individual's specific social behaviors during alcohol consumption are difficult to predict.

Two types of tolerance to alcohol have been identified: chronic and acute. Chronic tolerance occurs in heavy drinkers and among chronic alcoholics, in which the degree of impairment for a given BAC is less than for a moderate or light drinker. Acute tolerance, called the Mellanby Effect, develops during a drinking session and relates to a noticeable performance impairment while BAC is rising. An hour or so later, the individual may show somewhat less impairment even though BAC is at the same level (Chesher 1985). Despite acute tolerance, the correlation between BAC and impairment remains significant.

Behavior Patterns

Several distinct patterns of alcohol drinking have been identified that discriminate between those who DUI and those who do not. Vingilis (1983) concluded that high risk, drinking drivers are overrepresented as heavy/frequent alcohol consumers, problem drinkers, and alcoholics. Borkenstein, Crowther, Shumate, Ziel, and Zylman (1964) found that drivers with BACs of .08 and higher were also likely to report that they habitually have six or more drinks at a setting. Further, those excessive drinkers who DUI are much more likely to obtain their drinks from licensed alcohol establishments than from the home of a friend or relative, or from their own home (O'Donnell 1985). Moreover, high risk, drinking drivers are generally deviant on many psychosocial measures (Donovan and Marlatt 1982; Donovan, Marlatt, and Salzberg 1983; Vingilis 1983; Wilson and Jonah 1985). Consequently, much drunken driving may simply be one manifestation of a general pattern of deviant behavior.

Alcohol-Impairment Feedback

Some have argued that drinkers are often unaware of their alcohol impairment, and that receiving personal feedback about one's BAC may reduce the probability of alcohol-impaired driving (e.g., Geller, Altomari, and Russ 1984; Geller and Russ 1986). Feedback regarding a drinker's level of alcohol impairment can be readily available at bar and party settings in the form of (a) a BAC chart called a "nomogram"; (b) a breath alcohol test that can be self-administered; or (c) through one's performance on certain "field sobriety tests."

BAC Nomograms.

Using body weight and the number of drinks consumed within two hours, one can use normative values to estimate BAC. For example, a 120-pound individual who consumes four twelve-ounce beers in two hours could have a maximum BAC of .10 percent (U.S. DOT 1979). Nomograms have been printed on key chains and bar napkins, and have been widely distributed as part of some anti–drunk-driving campaigns, but they are imprecise. Although these scales were derived from carefully controlled laboratory studies with calculations based on an "average" individual, O'Neill, Williams, and Dubowski (1983) demonstrated that the actual range of BACs for a given weight and within a certain time period can vary greatly. Thus, nomograms may lead individuals to over- or underestimate their BAC substantially (Waller 1986). In the case of underestimation, nomograms may actually be a menace to DUI prevention. Therefore, it has been suggested that nomograms be removed from circulation and a better index of alcohol impairment be developed (Dubowski 1984).

Self-Testing BAC Meters

Picton (1979) concluded that minimal user effort is required to obtain accurate BAC measurements from the relatively inexpensive, portable BAC meters. Such devices can be purchased, borrowed, or made available in drinking establishments to provide immediate, individualized BAC feedback for guiding individuals in their drinking-driving decisions. However, research assessing the utility of BAC meters has not been completely favorable (e.g., Calvert-Boyanowsky and Boyanowsky 1980; Oats 1976; Picton 1979; Vayda and Crespi 1981). For example, in a field study with drinking-and-driving information provided to bar patrons, Oats (1976) reported that subjects who received BAC feedback were no more likely to use the public transportation services (that is, taxi or bus) than were nonparticipants.

In a DUI alcohol education and prevention program for first and multiple offenders, Sobell, Vanderspek, and Saltman (1980) provided subjects with personal BAC meters to be used before operating their vehicles. At the conclusion of the program, 50 percent of the multiple offenders responded on a questionnaire that they used the device to determine if they were legally drunk. Only one of the ten subjects whose BAC level exceeded .10 percent reported driving. In addition, eighty-two of ninety-two first-time offenders and seventy-eight of ninety-nine multiple offenders indicated that they would use a feed-back device even if they had to pay $1.00 per test.

Due to the unique characteristics of their subject pool, it is difficult to generalize the results of the Sobell et al. study. Clearly, convicted DUI offenders have a high motivation to avoid future arrests, and therefore may be more likely than the general public to use a self-monitoring feedback device. In addition, most of the data were obtained by self-report questionnaires rather than from actual observation of behavior.

Calvert-Boyanowsky and Boyanowsky (1980) placed blood alcohol screening devices in several bars in British Columbia to determine whether BAC feedback affected subsequent DUI of bar patrons. They administered questionnaires to study subsequent driving plans of those individuals who volunteered to take the breath test. The patron's decisions about subsequent driving were assessed by self-report and unobtrusive observation of a patron's mode of transportation upon leaving the tavern. The authors concluded that, although breath testing was popular, knowledge of BAC did not deter the majority of alcohol-impaired subjects from driving.

Vayda and Crespi (1981) argued that even if BAC feedback monitors were shown to reduce DUI substantially, widespread application of these devices will depend on the level of public acceptance. To assess public acceptance, these authors conducted focus groups, administered questionnaires, and held meetings with special interest groups. Results from this undertaking revealed general skepticism and nonreceptivity toward BAC meters. Many respondents judged the feedback concept as ineffective for people who drink and drive, because self-monitoring requires a high degree of rational decision making. Others felt that the BAC feedback devices would be used primarily by people who are already responsible about their drinking and driving. Those individuals who actually need the BAC feedback would not use the machine, or would choose not to heed its warning.

A further concern expressed frequently was that BAC monitors might actually exacerbate drinking because drinkers may view the feedback as a game score rather than information to prevent DUI. Support for this notion was observed in a study by Harwood (1984) that was conducted at a university fraternity party. During the party, students urged other students to obtain higher BAC levels. Some students cheered wildly as "players" successively increased their BAC levels. In the Harwood study, however, a self-selection sampling bias may have accounted for the significantly greater beer consumption among those partiers who requested BAC feedback.

FIELD SOBRIETY TESTS

Given that alcohol adversely affects performance along several dimensions, including reaction time and standing steadiness (e.g., see Carpenter 1962 for a review), Geller and Russ (1986) argued that behavioral tests of impairment might be useful in a social context for determining a person's level of intoxication. The validity of this thesis was studied by asking students at college beer parties to participate in simple behavioral tasks that might indicate their level of alcohol impairment (Geller and Russ 1986; Russ and Geller 1986). These tests were modified from laboratory studies and were designed to be easily administered and scored. For example, subjects were asked to catch a ruler as it dropped between their thumb and forefinger. The number of inches that it fell was used as an indication of reaction time. The subjects were also asked to participate in a five-step, progressive body-balance task. Participants were given points for maintaining their balance at each increasingly difficult level of the task.

Performance on both the ruler-drop and body-balance tasks contributed significantly to the prediction of actual BAC. Many subjects reported that poor performance on these tasks would dissuade them from driving. However, such favorable reaction to the field sobriety tests decreased as the participant's BAC increased. More research is needed to investigate how simple performance tests can be used to convince alcohol-impaired individuals not to drive. Indeed, field sobriety tests may be more valid than BAC as an index of performance deficits related to driving (Johnson 1983). Furthermore, simple field sobriety tests could be administered by party hosts, drink servers, or friends in order to increase the respondents' awareness of the debilitating effects of excessive alcohol consumption.

The Drinking Person

One approach to understanding the problem of alcohol-impaired driving has focused on describing the personal characteristics of those who drink excessive amounts of alcohol and then drive (e.g., Wilson and Jonah 1985). Knowledge about the person who drinks and drives should guide the design of more effective programs and direct countermeasures toward those who are at the highest risk of DUI. Reviews of such work have been written by Donovan, Marlatt, and Salzberg (1983) and Vingilis (1983). Here we only briefly review findings related to age, gender, and attitudes, and describe the relationship of some interpersonal factors to alcohol consumption.

Age of the Drinker

A great deal of attention to the drunk-driving problem has focused on the issue of age. In fact, much of the research aimed at developing interventions to decrease alcohol-impaired driving has targeted teenagers and college students. Education programs to increase alcohol awareness have been developed specifically for young persons. One example is Alcohol Peer Intervention (API) developed by the National Public Services Research Institute (1984). The goal of API is not only to educate young people about how drinking raises a driver's risk of being involved in accidents, but also to provide students with the necessary intervention skills and confidence for preventing a friend from excessive drinking and DUI.

A primary legal approach to preventing drunken driving has been to enact legislation that increases the minimum age at which persons can purchase and consume beverage alcohol. This effort is based on the statistic that drivers between the ages of sixteen and twenty-four are disproportionately involved in fatal vehicle crashes both as drivers and passengers (Williams 1985). The U.S. Department of Transportation reported drivers in this age category have the highest rates of accidents per mile traveled and per licensed driver (Fell 1984). In fact, sixteen through twenty-four year olds as a group represent 20 percent of all licensed drivers and account for the same relative percent of miles traveled, yet they are involved in more than 40 percent of all the fatal DUI accidents (Fell 1984).

Several factors contribute to the over-involvement of youth in alcohol-related crashes. Teenagers have had relatively little experience with drinking alcohol, with driving, and with drinking and driving (Williams, Lund, and Preusser in press). Teenagers are also susceptible to detrimental peer influence and may exhibit negative reactions to parental advice (Russ and Geller 1985). The Insurance Institute for Highway Safety (1984) surveyed over 46,000 high school students from across the United States and found that by age seventeen, nearly half of the males and one-third of the females reported driving after drinking alcoholic beverages at least once in the past month.

The archival data examined by Farris, Malone, and Lilliefors (1976) indicated that after eighteen and nineteen year olds consumed alcohol in *any* amount, their relative probability of a crash was four to nine times higher than for older drivers. This observation is supported by an analysis of 29,000 records in the Fatal Accident Reporting System (FARS) which showed that 25 percent of teenage drinkers and drivers involved in fatal crashes had BACs greater than zero but less than .10, compared to 15 percent of drivers aged twenty to twenty-nine and 16 percent of those thirty and older (Voas and Fell 1984).

Despite the high involvement of youth in alcohol-related crashes, recent data indicated that younger drivers were substantially underrepresented among those who are arrested for DUI (Voas and Williams in press). This curious finding is not fully understood and needs further study. It may be that youthful drinking drivers are more likely to be charged with offenses other than DUI, or perhaps drivers under the age of eighteen who are arrested for DUI are charged as juvenile offenders and their records do not appear in the same statistical data bases from which the adult samples are drawn. It is also possible that the compensatory driving behavior (such as driving excessively slow and taking side streets) used by the older, more experienced drinker and driver are readily noticed by police and increase the probability of getting caught for DUI.

After age twenty-five, there appears to be an inverse relationship between driver age and fatality from DUI. For example, Fell (1984) reported that drivers aged forty-five to fifty-four represent 13.3 percent of all licensed drivers and drive about 17.6 percent of the total vehicle miles, but these drivers account for only 7.5 percent of the drinking drivers in fatal accidents.

Gender Differences

The strong and consistent gender difference in alcohol consumption and alcohol-impaired driving may reflect the influence of a variety of cultural factors. The traditional masculine role includes risk-taking, adventure-seeking, and confidence in performance skills that may increase the likelihood they will DUI even when they feel impaired. By contrast, females are often socialized to be more dependent, and less competent with respect to performance skills. As a result, in mixed-gender driving situations, males are more often cast in the role of driver, and females submit to being passengers. Moreover, males learn about alcohol earlier and from different sources than do females. Specifically, males rely more on their own experience and input from friends, whereas females tend to gather their information about alcohol from the mass media and family members (Beck in press).

From surveys administered to over 2,300 suburban high school students in the Washington, D.C. area, Beck found that adolescent males drink beer, wine, and liquor more frequently and in greater quantities than do females. Furthermore, males reported more instances of drunken behavior and DUI, partly because the males believed they were more effective than females at controlling the risks associated with drunken driving. Compared to females, males also believed risks from excessive alcohol consumption to be less serious and less likely to occur. Actually, young male drivers are more likely than females to become involved in nighttime, single vehicle accidents (Carlson 1973). This may be because fewer females are driving after midnight, and, if they are on the road, females are more likely to be passengers than drivers.

A survey of over 4,200 students from seventy-two colleges throughout the United States was conducted in 1983 and repeated in 1985 (Hanson and Engs 1986). In general, the comparison of data across the years yielded very few overall changes in the extent of drinking problems. However, there was a significant decrease from 1983 to 1985 in the proportion of male students who reported (1) driving a car after drinking, (2) driving a car after knowing they had too much to drink, (3) drinking while driving, and (4) losing a job because of drinking. On the other hand, the proportion of males who reported that they missed class because of drinking increased. There was also a decrease in the proportion of females who reported driving after drinking, or drinking while driving.

The results from another survey of 272 college students (Beck 1983) revealed a psychosocial profile of the alcohol abuser in college as a male underclassman (freshmen or sophomore) who consumes beer more often and in greater quantities than nonabusers, and who tends to drink with the intention of getting drunk. Naturalistic observation of 187 male and 66 female college students in six taverns by Geller, Russ, and Altomari (1986) supported this survey research by finding that males drank more beer and at significantly higher rates than females (a mean of 9.2 ounces per ten minutes for males compared to 5.6 ounces per ten minutes for females). This observed difference in drinking rates for males versus females is analogous to the drinking rates observed among older males and females (Cutler and Storm 1975; Reid 1978; Sommer 1965).

Some gender differences among slightly older males and females (estimated mean ages of thirty-four and twenty-nine, respectively) were identified by direct observations in a naturalistic (beer parlor) setting (Cutler and Storm 1975). Groups of women drinkers tended to include slightly more persons than did groups of male drinkers, and only 5 percent of the women drank alone compared to 25 percent of the men. Furthermore, women tended to stay in the beer parlor slightly longer. Similarly, Geller et al. (1986) found that females remained in bars significantly longer than males (an average of sixty-five minutes for females and fifty minutes for males).

With males leaving bars sooner than females, after consuming more alcohol at higher rates (Geller et al. 1986), it is not surprising that males are more apt than females to DUI (e.g., Borkenstein, Crowther, Shumate, Ziel, and Zylman 1964; Filkins, Clark, Rosenblatt, Carlson, Kerlan, and Manson 1970; Waller, King, Nielson, and Turkel 1970). For example, Borkenstein et al. (1964) reported that 88 percent of the crash-involved drinking drivers were male. Perrine, Waller, and Harris (1971) conducted roadside surveys and found that 79 percent of the vehicle drivers they interviewed were male, and 83 percent of those interviewed who were legally drunk (BAC > .10 percent) were male.

Attitudes and Beliefs

The relationship of cognitive aspects (attitudes, beliefs, intentions, and knowledge) to the drinking of alcoholic beverages and drunken driving has often been explored with questionnaires. For example, Hanson and Engs (1984) reported very little change in the drinking attitudes of students from fourteen different colleges across a span of twelve years (1970 to 1982). A later survey of over six thousand college students indicated that their attitudes toward drinking largely reflected a continuation of parental attitudes and expectations (Hanson, Engs, and Katter 1985). Beck (1981), using the Fishbein Model (Fishbein and Ajzen 1975), showed that college students' attitudes and beliefs regarding drinking could be used to predict intentions to DUI, and that intention to DUI was the best predictor of reported drinking and driving behavior.

Many DUI countermeasures are based on the assumption that changes in knowledge or attitudes result in behavior change (Zaks-Walker and Larkin 1976). Vingilis (1984), however, suggests that changes in knowledge and attitudes about alcohol and DUI do not necessarily result in concomitant changes in drinking-and-driving behaviors, and a number of studies in social psychology have supported this view (e.g., Deutscher 1966, 1973; Wicker 1969, 1971). For example, the National Highway Traffic Safety Administration's evaluation of the Alcohol Safety Action Projects (ASAP) indicated that ASAP increased knowledge and elicited beneficial changes in relevant attitudes, but did not result in a significant decrease in DUI arrests or crash involvement among the program participants (U.S. DOT 1975). Likewise, evaluations of other education and information programs designed for the general public have shown that modifications in knowledge and attitudes are not systematically related to changes in DUI (Wilde 1975).

Alcoholism and DUI

If the majority of drunken drivers are alcoholics, then intervention strategies to prevent DUI must address, if not focus on, the treatment of alcoholism. However, if the evidence suggests a substantial percentage of nonalcoholic DUI offenders, interventions should use combinations of education, legislation, and primary prevention. If a bimodal distribution of alcoholic and nonalcoholic offenders exists, then a screening process could be used to direct individuals to an appropriate intervention program.

Research results differ as to the proportion of alcoholics among the drinking-driving population. For example, Popham (1956) looked at the records of drivers charged with DUI in Toronto and found significantly more alcoholics among this group than would be expected on the basis of the number of alcoholic clinic patients in the drinking population. Other authors have reported similarly high frequencies of alcoholics among DUI offenders (e.g., Hirsch 1956; Ryan and Slater 1979; Yoder and Moore 1973). In contrast, Vingilis (1983) concluded from an extensive review of the literature that the often-cited finding that alcoholics constitute the larger percentage of alcohol-impaired drivers is not only outdated, but suffers from intractable methodological problems.

Vingilis compared the involvement of drinking drivers and alcoholics along several dimensions, including age, race, marital status, education, drinking history, and driving record. She observed that alcoholics as a group seem to be "high risk" drivers, and thus are highly represented in DUI statistics. However, she also concluded that the majority of DUI offenders are not alcoholics. Depending on the definition of "alcoholism," Vingilis estimated that only 30 to 50 percent of the drinking drivers are alcoholics. These results clearly suggest that light or "social" drinkers consume enough alcohol to put them at risk for DUI. The excessive and sporadic alcohol consumption among college students also suggests that nonalcoholics contribute substantially to the DUI problem.

The Drinking Environment

Compared to the effort devoted to understanding the alcohol drinker and driver as a person, the exploration of environmental determinants of drinking behavior in naturalistic settings has received much less attention. Yet, the environmental context within which drinking occurs moderates the causal relationship between the drinker as an individual and alcohol-related problem behaviors. The present section reviews the relatively minimal research that examined the effect of specific environmental variables on drinking and DUI risk. Most of this field research has occurred in bars or tavern settings, although about as much alcohol consumption occurs at home and at parties or social gatherings (O'Donnell 1985), and these latter settings are places where socially responsible drinking could potentially be taught. For example, the home is the usual place for receiving one's first alcoholic beverage (Hanson, Engs, and Katter 1985), and parental reaction to such drinking behavior can certainly have a major influence on subsequent alcohol consumption.

The party or social gathering of friends and acquaintances is an ideal setting in many respects for introducing socially responsible drinking techniques. For example, such events could provide opportunities to serve low-alcohol or nonalcoholic beverages, or to administer field sobriety tests, or to make BAC feedback meters available. It is more likely that among friends, beneficial interactive discussions can naturally evolve to provide the rationale and support for appropriate server intervention, and thereby increase the probability that partiers will practice DUI-prevention strategies. Indeed, such discussions among friends may result in practical refinements of techniques for controlling drinking and driving.

The high school and college settings often represent the last chance to gather a "captive audience" for increasing group awareness of drinking and driving issues and teaching a socially responsible approach to alcohol consumption. Alcohol awareness groups based at high schools (for example, SADD) and colleges (for example, BAUCUS) have been among the most innovative and active in promoting socially responsible drinking. Thus, organizations and individuals are available at high schools and colleges to implement party-based interventions for reducing excessive alcohol consumption and preventing DUI. The field studies reviewed in this section hopefully are only the beginning of a promising research domain to define setting-specific determinants of drinking and driving.

Drinking at Parties

BEER LABELS AND STIMULUS CONTROL

Geller and his students (Geller et al. 1986; Kalsher and Geller 1987; Russ and Geller in press) have found some intriguing environment-behavior relationships from systematic observations of students' drinking behavior at university parties. The general procedure for these field studies was as follows:

1. When entering a party, subjects were informed that their drinking would be monitored, that they would be asked some drinking-related questions, and that they would be given a breath test (BAC) upon leaving the party.

2. Subjects were given a blind taste test whereby they successively sampled three two-ounce samples of different beer types (Budweiser, Bud Light, and LA), and then asked which sample they preferred to drink at the party.

3. Each subject was given a cup and an ID badge, both marked with the last four digits of their social security number.

4. Whenever a subject obtained a drink, two research assistants recorded the subject's ID number and the time. Individuals approaching the bar with more than one cup were requested to announce the ID number of the person(s) for whom they were getting beer.

5. When a subject left the party, a brief exit interview was administered and a measure of BAC was taken using an Alco-Sensor breath testing device.

6. Those with a BAC of .10 percent or greater were informed that they were above the state's legal limit of intoxication and were urged not to drive home. A member of the research team offered a free ride home to any person who wanted to use this service.

In one study (Kalsher and Geller 1987) the stimulus control (or marketing impact) of beer brand labels was clearly demonstrated. In particular, subjects' beer drinking during the party matched the results of the taste preference test only when the beer kegs were unlabeled. When beer kegs were labeled according to the three types available—Budweiser, Bud Light, and LA—drinking preferences suggested a strong influence of marketing strategies and perhaps a desire to get drunk. The low-alcohol alternative (LA) was only consumed to any great extent when the kegs were unlabeled.

Figure 12.1 depicts the cumulative number of drinks (cups of beer) consumed at two university parties, the first with the three beer kegs of Budweiser, Bud Light, and LA beer labeled as A, B, and C ("Unlabeled Party"). At a second "Labeled Party" (one month later) the three kegs were labeled according to brand name (Budweiser, Bud Light, and LA). At the Unlabeled Party (86 males and 72 females), the drinking preferences during the party matched the results of the taste preference tests obtained at the start of both parties. That is, the taste tests at both parties showed Budweiser to be most preferred, with 42.3 percent of the subjects at the Unlabeled Party and 41.0 percent at the Labeled Party selecting Budweiser. Low-alcohol beer was least preferred in the taste tests (22.6 percent at the Unlabeled Party and 23.4 percent at the Labeled Party). When the beer kegs were labeled according to brand name, the subjects

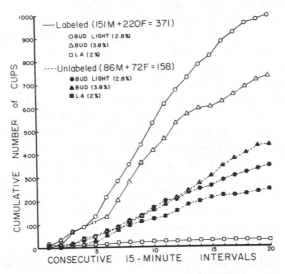

Fig. 12.1. Cumulative cups of beer consumed at two fraternity parties as a function of beer type (Budweiser, Bud Light, or LA), and of whether the beer kegs were labeled according to beer type (labeled) or were unlabeled.

(151 males and 220 females) rarely selected LA beer, and showed a significant preference for Bud Light over Bud. When separate functions were derived for male and female drinkers, the preference rankings for each gender were identical, as shown in figure 1, although males did consume significantly more beer than females.

The low popularity of LA beer at the Labeled Party may suggest a social stigma attached to ordering a low-alcohol drink. The preference for Bud Light over Budweiser at the Labeled Party implies a powerful influence of marketing strategies. Indeed, it is possible that most individuals perceive light beers as having only fewer calories and not less alcohol. Would Bud Light have been more popular than Budweiser if the kegs were labeled according to their alcohol content as well as brand name (that is, 3.8 percent alcohol for Budweiser and 2.8 percent alcohol for Bud Light)?

Low-Alcohol Beer

Making low-alcohol beer (for example, LA beer from Anheuser-Busch) available at bar and party settings represents a potential strategy for reducing alcohol impairment and DUI. However, field research by Kalsher and Geller (1987) indicates that such beneficial effects may be limited. Some individuals may be reluctant to order a low-alcohol alternative because of social pressures or because they desire to get drunk. But, what if low-alcohol beer were served at a party (perhaps near the end of the evening) without the guests being informed? Recently, Geller and his students researched this empirical question with the general party observation procedures described above (Geller, Kalsher, and Lehman 1987). At two parties both mixed drinks and beer were available at no cost to the subjects. At the start of the party, each participant was required to select one drink alternative (beer or mixed drinks) and to continue with that choice throughout the evening. For one party (64 males and 43 females), the only beer was Budweiser, whereas at the other party (70 males and 48 females) the beer served was LA. Subjects were unaware of the brand of beer being served.

In contrast to conclusions from interview research that beer drinkers get more impaired than those who consume mixed drinks (Berger and Snortum 1985), those who drank beer—either Budweiser or LA—(approximately half at each party) did *not* do so at significantly higher rates or get more impaired than those who chose mixed drinks. In fact, the rates of drinking beer and mixed drinks were quite similar across the two parties. Moreover, the BAC levels at the end of the party were significantly lower among those students who drank LA beer than for those who drank mixed drinks.

Drinking at Bars

Sommer (1969) identified several factors likely to attract a patron to a bar and influence subsequent drinking behavior, including bar location, room decor, and drink prices. The availability of recreational and entertainment activities such as watching sports on a large television screen, dancing, and live band music may also influence the risk of DUI in particular ways. Unfortunately, systematic observational studies of relationships between alcohol consumption, BAC, and various situational factors in a bar setting are essentially nonexistant and urgently needed. Thus far, the findings from field observations may not be so straightforward as some have presumed from intuition (e.g., Schaefer 1983). For example, although bar entertainment prolongs the time spent in a bar and thus increases the amount of alcohol consumed (Clark 1981; Schaefer 1983), certain activities (for example, dancing) may detract from excessive drinking and increase "sobering up" time.

Results from an investigation of 185 bars in Vancouver (Graham 1984) indicated that intoxication and aggression were related to larger seating capacity, rows of tables, no decor theme, and lower standards of furnishings and upkeep. Graham suggested that the decor and upkeep in a bar may convey a message to patrons about the kinds of behaviors expected. Other activities and general atmosphere characteristics that Graham identified as significant determinants of intoxication included the type of entertainment, availability of food, ventilation, noise, and crowding.

Happy Hour

The "happy hour" typically refers to a period of time after the workday has ended and before the evening meal. These are "off-peak" hours for most drinking establishments, and to attract a greater volume of business, some entrepreneurs provide a happy hour as a context for socializing and an opportunity to consume alcohol at bargain prices. It is noteworthy that at the time of this writing, sixteen states prohibit happy hours or other forms of sales promotion, and twenty-two additional states have such legislation pending (Waller 1986).

The effect of reduced drink prices on individual drinking patterns was explored by monitoring the same persons as they drank in experimental and natural settings (Babor, Mendelson, Uhly, and Souza 1980). In both settings, reduced prices (during happy hour) significantly increased the frequency of drinking episodes and the amount of alcohol consumed among casual and heavy drinkers. In a controlled setting (that is, the clinical research ward at the Alcohol and Drug Abuse Research Center, Harvard Medical School), Babor, Mendelson, Greenberg, and Kuehnle (1978) found that during periods of reduced drink prices, male volunteers, categorized as casual or heavy drinkers, significantly increased (by eight times) their alcohol consumption compared to a control group without a happy hour. Furthermore, the increased alcohol drinking during the happy hour was not a substitute for consumption at other times of the day. Babor et al. (1978) concluded that the patterns of drinking influenced by the happy hour (gulping drinks, massing of successive drinks, and consumption of straight drinks) are likely to be learned and repeated. The same function of lower beverage cost and increased consumption was found in the general population (Schmidt and Popham 1978).

Size of Drinking Group

Sommer (1965) was among the first to recognize the importance of conducting systematic field research to investigate drinking patterns. He observed isolated male drinkers (sitting alone) in thirty-two Edmonton beer parlors and contrasted their drinking behavior with that of drinkers in groups. He found that isolated drinkers ordered an average of 1.69 drinks, whereas individual drinkers in groups ordered 3.51 drinks. However, when the amount of time spent in the barroom was taken into account, the data suggested that the reason persons in groups drank more than isolated drinkers was not because they drank faster, but because they remained in the barroom longer. Sommer also found that isolated drinkers tended to be older (average age forty-two) than group drinkers (average age thirty-six).

These seminal findings of Sommer were replicated twenty years later by the naturalistic observation of college-aged drinkers by Geller et al. (1986). Of the 243 college students (mean age about nineteen) observed drinking beer, only 19 percent drank alone whereas 48 percent drank in pairs, 16 percent drank in triads, and 17 percent drank in groups of four or more. Students drinking in groups drank significantly more beer per individual than those drinking alone (mean of thirty-one ounces for students drinking with at least one other person compared to nineteen ounces for those drinking alone), but those drinking alone spent significantly less time in the bar (approximately thirty-nine minutes for the 45 students drinking alone, fifty-seven minutes for the 116 students in dyads, fifty-five minutes for the 40 students in triads, and sixty-eight minutes for the 42 students observed drinking in groups of four or more). Thus, the rate of beer consumption was nearly identical for those drinking alone (.49 ounces per minute) and individuals drinking with others (.48 ounces per minute).

Rosenbluth, Nathan, and Lawson (1978) also observed that male and female college students drank more beer in groups than in dyads. An intriguing finding from these field observations that requires follow-up research was that same-gender dyads showed less rapid beer consumption than mixed-gender dyads.

Foy and Smith (1978) employed a within-subject, laboratory study to demonstrate that the size of a drinking group did not influence the alcohol consumption of chronic alcoholics. It may be that drinkers with an extended history of excessive alcohol consumption have established drinking patterns that are relatively impervious to certain social factors. In other words, an interaction between personal and environmental factors is suggested such that the drinking behavior of alcoholics is less determined (or controlled) by situational factors than is the alcohol consumption of nonalcoholics.

GLASSES VERSUS PITCHERS

Geller et al. (1986) offered convincing evidence from naturalistic field observations that the sale of beer in pitchers may contribute to excessive alcohol consumption and subsequent risk for DUI. These investigators obtained systematic, reliable, and unobtrusive observations of drinking behavior at six bars that sold large quantities of beer to college students in forty-ounce pitchers, ten-ounce plastic cups, and twelve-ounce bottles. Of the 243 drinkers observed during their entire stay in a bar, 77 percent were male and 68 percent ordered their beer by the pitcher. By far, the most beer was consumed per person when it was ordered by the pitcher (mean per capita beer consumption was 10.0 ounces from cups, 15.1 ounces from bottles, and 35.2 ounces from pitchers). But rate of drinking did not vary significantly as a function of drink container because those who ordered their beer by the pitcher stayed in the bar significantly longer (mean of sixty-six minutes) than those ordering beer by the bottle (mean of thirty-four minutes) or by the glass/cup (mean of twenty-three minutes).

Follow-up research is needed to determine whether the container-consumption relationship is a cause-and-effect contingency or merely an artifact of different intentions of the drinker. In other words, do those who order a pitcher of beer intend to drink more from the outset, or is greater beer consumption from pitchers due to drinkers feeling obligated to finish its contents? One way to ascertain this information would be to have patrons estimate, upon entering the bar, the amount of beer they expect to drink, and how long they expect to stay in the bar. The expected amount and duration could later be compared to the actual amount and rate of beer consumed. The drinking patterns of those patrons who indicate their intentions should also be compared with the patterns of patrons who are not requested to provide the estimates.

THE SERVER

An especially critical aspect of the drinker's social environment is the server of alcoholic beverages. In response to dram shop laws, which permit holding tavern owners liable if they serve alcohol to an intoxicated patron who later causes an accident while DUI, servers of alcoholic beverages are receiving special training aimed at preventing their customers from DUI (Mosher 1979, 1983; Peters 1986). Most intervention training programs teach servers to identify the specific warning signs that indicate when a customer may overindulge. Then, servers learn to use a variety of tactics, including delaying alcoholic drink service, offering food, serving nonalcoholic beverages, and suggesting that the patron not drive. Some programs include the use of video vignettes and role-playing to help servers evaluate customers' behavior and to practice intervention skills.

There are a number of server intervention programs available, for example: (1) TIPS: Training for Intervention Procedures by Servers of Alcohol (six hours) developed by Morris Chafetz (1984), a member of the Presidential Commission on Drunk Driving, and used nationwide by major corporations such as Anheuser-Busch, Heublein, Miller Brewers, Mobil, Ogden Foods, and Ramada Inn; (2) TAM: Techniques in Alcohol Management (six to eight hours) funded by the Michigan Licensed Beverage Association and sponsored by the

Stroh Brewing Company (Christy 1986); (3) LAST CALL: Learning Alcohol Service Techniques for Control Against Liquor Liability (six to eight hours) which also offers advice regarding the modification of policy and environmental factors to reduce the probability of DUI (Christy 1986); (4) HEART: Help End Alcohol-Related Tragedies, implemented by the South Carolina Commission on Alcohol and Drug Abuse for both alcohol servers (two hours) and bar managers (ten hours); (5) a Management/Server Alcohol Awareness Program (3 $\frac{1}{2}$ hours) sponsored by the National Restaurant Association for preparing managers to train their service personnel (Alcohol Health and Research World 1986); (6) the Professional Beverage Server: Alcohol Server Awareness Curriculum (twelve hours) distributed out of the Wisconsin Office for Highway Safety; (7) a California Office of Traffic Safety (OTS) program implemented in more than eighty licensed establishments (Bonney 1984); and (8) a six-hour training program available from the National Highway Traffic Safety Administration (McKnight, personal communication, December 4, 1986; Vegega 1986).

There have been only two systematic evaluations of the server intervention concept (Russ and Geller 1987; Saltz 1986; Saltz in press). The Saltz evaluation compared DUI probability at two U.S. Navy enlisted clubs, one whose staff (waitresses, bartenders, food servers, security staff, and night managers) received an eighteen-hour, comprehensive server intervention program that included policy changes and situational modifications. Policy/environmental changes included, for example, having food available during all hours, assigning waitresses to specific stations, providing transportation for intoxicated patrons, and refusing or delaying the delivery of alcoholic beverages to customers at risk for DUI.

The Saltz evaluation concluded that server intervention was effective (Saltz 1986), and made "a scientifically significant difference in alcohol-related problems stemming from alcohol sales and service" (Christy 1986; 16). However, it should be noted that the dependent measures used in this evaluation did not include a direct measure of server intervention or of alcohol impairment. Specifically, the conclusions were based on interviews with customers who were asked their beverage consumption, height, weight, and gender from which BACs were estimated. Not only is it risky to rely on self-report data to access behavior change, but the fact that many patrons were alcohol-impaired adds another reason for caution in drawing conclusions from this evaluation. Indeed, Russ, Harwood, and Geller (1986) found substantial underestimation of beer consumption among partiers, especially among those with BACs greater than .05 percent. Saltz and his associates did directly observe drink consumption among patrons in the experimental and test sites, but an analysis of this data had not been completed at the time of this writing (Saltz, personal communication, January 6, 1987).

The server intervention evaluation by Russ and Geller (1987) obtained direct measures of servers' intervention behaviors and patrons' BAC levels both before and after 50 percent of the servers at two bars were trained in the TIPS program. Research assistants, who were unaware of which seventeen servers had received the training, posed as regular patrons ("pseudopatrons") and set the occasion for server intervention to occur by drinking three alcoholic beverages per hour for two consecutive hours. Using a hidden microphone, a partner taped all interactions between the server and pseudopatron and at the end of the session, measured the pseudopatron's BAC. Although the servers were told during training about the use of pseudopatrons and agreed to the evaluation, servers were unable to distinguish the pseudopatrons from regular patrons when the visits actually occurred.

The comparison of data from pseudopatrons served by trained versus untrained bar personnel revealed substantial impact of the TIPS program, at least over the short term. Specifically, the trained servers initiated significantly more interventions to reduce the probability of DUI than did untrained personnel, and the pseudopatrons served by trained personnel exhibited fewer signs of intoxication and had significantly lower BAC levels than the pseudopatrons served by untrained servers.

The fact that the servers in this study were apparently able to identify correctly some intoxication cue(s) of the pseudopatrons is inconsistent with the results from Langenbucher and Nathan (1983). These investigators showed that bartenders, police officers, and social drinkers were able to identify target individuals' level of intoxication (BACs of .00, .05, and .10 percent) only 25 percent of the time. In contrast, Teplin and Lutz (1985) showed that observers in a hospital emergency room could reliably apply an Alcohol Symptom Checklist to estimate levels of intoxication accurately. This contrary finding reveals the need for further research to determine which intoxication cue(s) servers can identify accurately in a bar setting. It may be that the cue used most often to prompt server intervention in the naturalistic setting was one that the "judges" in the Langenbucher and Nathan study did not have—the frequency and timing of personally serving the alcoholic beverages.

Implications for Social Control of Drinking and Driving

This chapter has suggested that understanding DUI and the development of effective prevention interventions requires analyzing the problem behavior, the individual, and the environmental aspects of excessive alcohol consumption and drunken driving. From a strict experimental analysis of behavior, excessive drinking and drunken driving are viewed as target behaviors that are influenced by environmental conditions which precede (antecedents) and follow (consequences) these responses. From this perspective, the antecedent conditions found to increase alcohol consumption (for example, two-for-one prices during happy hour, the sale of beer by the pitcher, and brand labels associated with a particular marketing strategy) are predictable because they provide convenience or an incentive for the drinking behavior. Similarly, the response consequence of positive reinforcement can be used to explain the facilitative effects of social attention from other drinkers. Moreover, the effectiveness of certain intervention strategies (for example, feedback from BAC meters, field sobriety tests, and server intervention techniques) on drinking and driving will depend upon the antecedent incentives and disincentives and the reinforcing or punishing consequences.

The opportunity to receive convenient feedback on one's BAC or to perform a sobriety test can increase or decrease alcohol consumption or have no effect, depending upon the antecedent and consequence conditions within the drinker's environment. If the BAC meter is a novel item in a bar or party setting, and partiers are drinking in groups providing peer attention for alcohol consumption, then BAC feedback probably will be a reinforcing consequence that will set the occasion for more drinking. Similarly, the challenge to perform well on a sobriety test while under the influence of alcohol can be an incentive to drink. Thus, peer pressure to "beat the system" may result in a drinking, feedback and performance "game" resulting in excessive alcohol consumption and DUI risk.

On the other hand, a server or party host may introduce a sobriety test or the opportunity for BAC feedback as indicators to determine whether additional drinks should be served, whether "sober-up" time is needed before driving, or whether an alternative form of transportation from the bar or party should be sought. Rewards, including social attention, should be available for those who follow the advice reflected by BAC feedback or sobriety test performance. The impact of any intervention strategy designed to prevent excessive drinking and drunken driving is critically dependent upon the social and environmental context in which that intervention is presented. Indeed, without appropriate environmental or social antecedents and consequences, an intervention will have no effect.

The role of person variables in excessive drinking and DUI, as highlighted in this chapter, further complicates the development of intervention strategies to control drinking and driving. The individual factors (for example, age, gender, attitudes, and drinking history) that predispose a person to drink excessively or DUI, make it advisable to go beyond the strict behavior analysis model when developing and implementing intervention strategies. In other words, one cannot assume that a given set of antecedent conditions (for example, incentives or disincentives) and response consequences (for example, rewards or punishments) will have the same effect across various person variables. Rather, the outcome of an intervention tactic will depend on the interactions among individual and environmental factors. Thus, interventions should be designed for particular categories of individuals. For example, interventions can be individualized by integrating a social marketing approach with a sociobehavioral analysis (cf. Geller and Nimmer 1987). From this perspective, the target population (or "market") is first partitioned into homogeneous submarkets based on common characteristics identified by a market analysis. Then, an intervention tactic for changing the problem behavior is developed by incorporating the special interests and characteristics of the identified targets. Also, information from the marketing analysis of person variables must guide the selection of methods to disseminate and promote the particular intervention procedures.

This chapter does not provide a solution to the complex problem of excessive alcohol consumption and DUI. Rather, it offers a behavior-person-environment framework within which to interpret the successes and failures of particular attempts to reduce drinking and DUI. This model might also be helpful in developing new tactics and strategies or refining existing interventions to prevent excessive alcohol consumption and drunken driving. The need to focus programmatic research on this tragic societal problem is obvious. Given the theme of this chapter, no single simple solution will work, and even "small wins" (Weick 1984) will not come easily.

13 Emerging Technologies for Controlling the Drunk Driver

Robert B. Voas

I. Introduction

We are all familiar with technology in law enforcement, from Dick Tracy's wrist radio in the 1930s to the miniature listening devices, infrared glasses, taser guns, and specially equipped police helicopters of today, which, if not in the arsenals of many of the smaller police departments, are at least a central feature of most television crime shows. There can be little doubt that advances in forensic toxicology along with extensive funding of fingerprint and computerized crime record systems have significantly influenced crime detection and law enforcement in the twentieth century. Technology has also had a major effect on the enforcement of laws against driving under the influence (DUI)[1] because of the relatively direct relationship between blood alcohol content (BAC) and driving impairment and the relative ease with which BAC can be measured. This chapter describes the role of technology in enforcing DUI laws. In addition, it overviews existing and proposed technological solutions to the drinking-driving problem outside the law enforcement area.

Technology has played a significant role in traffic safety, although most of this development has not been directly related to alcohol safety. For the most part, highway safety has been a technological rather than human enterprise. The annual number of vehicle miles driven has increased since 1945, but we have managed to hold highway deaths relatively constant (between forty and sixty thousand) through a compensating reduction in the mileage death rate. The major contributors to this rate reduction appear to have been roadway improvement (particularly the interstate system) and vehicle safety engineering (including safety belts and improved impact protection).

Engineering improvements that make the driving task easier and safer should benefit impaired as well as sober drivers. Some that benefit both, such as passive restraint systems, may be more effective with drinking drivers, because research has shown that crash-involved drinking drivers are less likely to use their safety belts. It has also been suggested that because of the tendency of drunken drivers to run off the road, wider edgelines may be particularly effective in reducing alcohol-related accidents (Ranney and Gawron 1986). This chapter, however, describes only those devices developed specifically to address the drinking-and-driving problem.

This discussion of technologies for controlling the drunk driver proceeds chronologically from the point at which drinking begins, through arrest, trial, and the application of sanctions to the offender. In the process, an attempt will be made to review technology applicable to the public as a whole, as well as to DUI suspects and DUI offenders. This discussion will include proposed technologies, which have been studied and rejected, as well as innovations that are not yet available, along with those that are currently being applied.

II. Control at the Point of Alcohol Consumption

Logically, drunken driving can be eliminated in three ways: eliminate driving, eliminate drinking, or separate drinking from driving. The first alternative is absurd to most Americans who believe that driving is essential to earning a living and living a good life. We attempt this solution only for convicted drinking drivers. We unsuccessfully tried the second alternative during Prohibition. The abstinence approach now applies only to those under age twenty-one. Most of our safety efforts have been directed, though unsuccessfully, at separating drinking from driving. This is best expressed by the National Safety Council slogan, "If you drink, don't drive."

The historic approach in the United States to prevention of alcohol problems has focused on abstinence, most notably in the temperance campaigns of the late nineteenth century and the enactment of the Volstead Act early in this century. Although that experiment with legal control ended in failure, recent public attention to the drunken driving problem has rekindled research interest in controls at the point of consumption. The enactment of age-twenty-one drinking laws has led to a number of evaluations of this countermeasure (Williams 1986). In addition, attention has turned to beverage-serving policies and server training (Mosher 1983). Beyond these social controls, there are some technological interventions that may be useful in controlling alcohol consumption or the effects of alcohol consumption.

A. Low-Alcohol Beverages

Consumption of distilled spirits in the United States has been declining in recent years. Although wine sales have increased, the growth in beer sales has slowed. At the same time, the marketing of low-alcohol or alcohol-free beers and wine coolers (mixed wine and fruit juice) has increased. The reason for this trend is unclear. It may be related to both the "health fad" that is manifest in the public's increased interest in diet and exercise, and to the increasing public concern with drunken driving and drug use. Whatever the reasons for this trend, if a significant portion of the public begins to use alcohol-free or low-alcohol substitutes instead of their normal alcoholic drinks, the number of impaired drivers should be reduced.

Several issues arise in evaluating the potential of this approach for reducing impairment. For example, it is not clear how alcohol users control their consumption. If, on the one hand, users count drinks so that the number consumed controls the total intake, low-alcohol beverages should reduce peak BAC. If, on the other hand, users drink for effect, then it should be expected that drinkers will simply consume greater quantities of a low-alcohol beverage to produce the habitual physiological and psychological changes. Early research suggested that slower consumption of alcohol and use of beer as compared to spirits would significantly lower peak BACs obtained by otherwise similar drinkers. If this were the case, the use of low-alcohol beverages might result in some lowering of peak BAC through slower alcohol consumption and slower absorption into the bloodstream. However, a recent carefully controlled study by O'Neill, Williams, and Dubowski (1983) demonstrated that speed of drinking and beverage type were relatively unimportant in determining peak BAC when the total alcohol dose was carefully controlled.

Their study of sixty-four males between the ages of twenty-one and forty showed that an alcohol dose of 1 gram per kilogram of body weight produced, as would be expected, a peak BAC twice as high as a dose of .5 gram per kilogram. However, the rate at which the alcohol was consumed—rapidly (within twenty minutes), or slowly (within forty minutes)—made little difference. Similarly, there was little difference between beer, champagne, and mixed drinks in the peak BACs produced in these drinkers.

Thus, the key determinant of the safety value of low-alcohol beverage technology appears to be the extent to which the public controls its drinking by the number of drinks as compared to the BAC itself. This technology could be counterproductive, however, if low-alcohol beverages become a tempting transition vehicle for individuals who would otherwise use alcohol only infrequently. Considerable evidence suggests that the advertising campaigns for these beverages are aimed at females who historically have consumed less alcohol than males. Clearly, we need to know more about who uses these beverages, their drinking patterns, and the extent to which the availability of these alternatives reduces or increases overall alcohol consumption.

B. Minimizing the Effects of Drinking

Once alcohol has been consumed, there are three primary methods by which the effects of this drug on the brain can be minimized: (1) slow absorption into the bloodstream, (2) block the effects of alcohol on the cortex, and (3) speed elimination of alcohol from the body.

Food in the stomach can delay absorption up to several hours and reduce peak BAC by as much as 50 percent (Lin, Weidler, Garg, and Wagner 1976; Sedman, Wilkinson, Samar, Weidler, and Wagner 1976). This phenomenon has been exploited by some entrepreneurs who have proposed substances such as fructose as blocking agents (Walls and Brownlie 1970, 21; Freifeld and Englemayer 1985). Aside from the question of whether these products contain enough carbohydrates to slow alcohol absorption significantly, the products have frequently been presented in a misleading fashion which suggests that they would be effective if taken *after* drinking—product names include "Sober Up," "Sober Up Time"—when clearly, to block absorption, the substances should be ingested *before* drinking.

Blocking alcohol's effects on the cortex has received somewhat more extensive research attention (Kolata 1986), partially because studies on alcohol's influence on brain receptors increases our knowledge of how alcohol produces the behavioral changes resulting in performance impairment. An article by Suzdak, Glowa, Crawley, Schwartz, Skolnick, and Paul (1986) reported on the antagonistic effect on alcohol produced by Imidazoben-zodiazepine (R015-4513), a derivative of the more common benzodiazepines used in tranquilizers such as Valium and Librium. There is evidence that alcohol, benzodiazepines, and barbiturates act on a common receptor in the brain (the Gaba receptor—see Kolata 1986). There is also evidence that Imidazoben-zodiazepine appears to block the behavioral effects of alcohol. This antagonist is of particular interest because it appears to be effective when taken *after* alcohol ingestion. Rats, sedated with alcohol to the point that they lie on their backs immobilized, get up and walk around within two minutes of the administration of this sobering agent.

The availability of a cortical blocking agent of this type would place highway safety and alcoholism treatment professionals in a considerable quandary. Although the availability of a sober pill that could be taken after a night of drinking but before getting into the car would obviously be an attractive safety aid, whether it would actually reduce alcohol-related accidents is unknown. Many, if not most, alcohol users drink for effect—to "relax" or to get "high." One issue, therefore, is whether a significant number of drinking drivers would be willing to "undo" the benefits of a night's drinking to reduce the risk of the drive home. More troubling is the impact that an effective antagonist would have on the legal countermeasures to drinking and driving. Most state DUI laws are based on a "per se" or presumptive BAC level. If the sober pill would restore the performance of a driver with a BAC above the legal limit (usually .10 percent) to the level he or she could achieve when sober, then the utility of a BAC test in enforcement would be severely compromised. If the high-BAC suspect claimed that he or she had taken a sober pill, would the burden of proof be on the defendant? Would it be necessary to produce a blood test to detect the use of such an alcohol antagonist to be used when the suspect claimed to have taken a sober pill? What about prosecutions under dram shop laws: Would an offer of a sobering agent by the management relieve the owners of liability for injuries caused by patrons?

Significant concerns would also arise for therapists because blocking the action of alcohol on brain receptor centers would not necessarily affect the actions of alcohol on other body systems. To the extent that the ability to sober up encouraged higher consumption, damage to the liver and other body systems could increase. Moreover, since the mechanism that produces addiction is inadequately understood, it is not clear whether a sobering agent would prevent alcoholism even if it prevented accidents. To date, these and similar issues have prevented the manufacturer of RO15-4513, Hoffmann-LaRoche, from attempting to market it as a sobering agent (Kolata 1986). The Food and Drug Administration also has resisted the marketing of sobering agents, insisting that such products (no matter what the compounds) are drugs and must be submitted for approval in accordance with standard procedures (Freifeld and Englemayer 1985).

A substance that increased the speed with which alcohol was me-
tabolized in the liver would provide a sobering agent that would not
conflict with current DUI laws. Because some very heavy drinkers
have alcohol elimination rates at least 50 to 100 percent higher than
normal, there is evidence that there may be some substance that could
facilitate elimination of ethanol. However, despite some manufacturers'
claims (Freifeld and Englemayer 1985), there appears to be no safe
drug currently available (Lemberger and Rubin 1976).

C. Consumption Limiters in Alcoholic Beverages

Disulfiram therapy (trade name Antabuse, Ayerst Laboratories) is
used to encourage abstinence in alcoholics. By increasing the ac-
cumulation of acetaldehyde (a toxic substance produced in the body
in the course of the oxidation of alcohol) Antabuse produces extremely unpleasant symptoms (flushing, headache, and nausea). The
use of disulfiram is controversial even with alcoholics and is clearly
inappropriate for the general public (Lubetkin, Rivers, and Rosenberg 1971; Marco and Marco 1980). The availability of this type of
drug has led some investigators to suggest that a tasteless, odorless
product might be added to alcohol that would have no effect at low
dose levels but, as consumption rose, would produce sufficiently
unpleasant (though not harmful) effects to prevent excessive drinking (Robertson 1981). One natural protective mechanism used by
the body to avoid poisoning is vomiting. Some hazardous medica-
tions are coated with an odorless, tasteless emetic that induces vomiting in the event of an overdose.

Obviously, alcohol users and producers are likely to resist this
type of solution. Physiological differences between individuals are
sufficiently large that it would be difficult to calibrate the quantity
of the emetic to ensure that it would (1) not inconvenience some
light drinkers, (2) fail to prevent drunkenness in some heavy drinkers, and (3) avoid hazardous side effects on some individuals who
may be particularly sensitive to the proposed protective additive.
Liability suits likely would prevent the widespread use of an additive
that produced even mild discomfort. It appears very unlikely that
technology will produce a product acceptable to the public which
will discourage excessive consumption of alcohol.

D. Provision of BAC Information

Avoiding DUI requires that the drinker be able to estimate his or
her BAC or impairment level. A number of methods exist for pro-

viding the alcohol consumer with either a direct measurement or a reasonable estimate of BAC. Unlike tests conducted in an enforcement or medical setting in which measurements can be performed by technicians under relatively controlled conditions, self-testing devices must be easy to understand and to use, and if possible highly reliable, because they will be used under adverse conditions (poor lighting, noise, distraction) by unskilled operators who may be impaired by alcohol. A variety of devices for estimating BAC have been offered to the public.

1. BAC CALCULATORS

Early in this century, Widmark (1914) produced a simple equation for predicting peak BAC from the amount of alcohol consumed and the weight of the drinker:

$$C = \frac{a}{p \cdot r}$$

where the peak BAC (C) is equal to the amount of alcohol consumed (a), divided by the weight of the drinker (p) times a ratio (r) of the water content of the body to the water content of blood, commonly called the Widmark factor. This formula has been used to produce "know your limits" (KYL) wallet cards, such as the one illustrated in figure 13.1, which can be used to estimate the BAC level if drinkers know their weight and count their drinks accurately.

All such cards considerably oversimplify BAC prediction. The proportion of water in the body (the Widmark factor) varies with age, sex, and amount of body fat. Because fat contains little water, it will absorb less alcohol, and the Widmark formula will underestimate the BAC of overweight persons. Because women's bodies contain a higher proportion of fat, Widmark developed separate values of his factor for men (0.68) and women (0.55). These complexities are rarely accommodated, however, in the KYL cards. Burns and Moskowitz (1980) note that such cards appear to be in error for significant segments of the population, particularly women and overweight males.

More significant factors affecting accurate BAC estimation are variations in the alcoholic content of drinks, the time over which alcohol is consumed, and the amount of food in the stomach. Variations in alcohol content between typical drinks served in bars thwarts any accurate estimation of BAC by simple counting of drinks and referring to a KYL card. In addition, because food in the stomach slows absorption and can reduce peak BAC as much as 50 percent,

DRINK CHART CARD

Your Weight	NUMBER OF DRINKS (Over A Two Hour Period) 1½ ozs. 80 Proof Liquor or 12 oz. Can of Beer											
100	1	2	3	4	5	6	7	8	9	10	11	12
120	1	2	3	4	5	6	7	8	9	10	11	12
140	1	2	3	4	5	6	7	8	9	10	11	12
160	1	2	3	4	5	6	7	8	9	10	11	12
180	1	2	3	4	5	6	7	8	9	10	11	12
200	1	2	3	4	5	6	7	8	9	10	11	12
220	1	2	3	4	5	6	7	8	9	10	11	12
240	1	2	3	4	5	6	7	8	9	10	11	12

DRIVE WITH CAUTION BAC TO .05%	DRIVING IMPAIRED .05% — .09%	DO NOT DRIVE .10% & UP

Fig. 13.1. "Know your limits!" card.

and because the liver metabolizes alcohol at about one drink an hour, these pocket charts will considerably overestimate peak BAC if not corrected for the time over which drinking has occurred and whether food was consumed.

Moreover, individual response to alcohol varies significantly. For example, O'Neill, Williams, and Dubowski (1983) found that the low dose of whiskey provided to drinkers in their experiment resulted in variation in BAC from a low of .035 percent to a high of .109 percent. This variation prompts questions not only of the utility but the safety of these KYL cards.

Various solutions have been developed or proposed to address the multiplicity of influences on BAC. For example, some cards attempt to present more than two scales within the table; others use a slide rule that accommodates several factors. The California motor vehicle department, when instructed by the state legislature to provide BAC information to motorists, developed a system whereby in only 5 percent of the cases would the BAC be underestimated (Arstein-Kerslake 1986). In addition, charts used separate body weight intervals so that the two-dimensional nomograph could be presented in terms of number of drinks and the time over which these drinks were consumed.

Because of the many factors that can influence BAC, and their natural concern over liability, KYL chart makers have tended to make the charts highly conservative. Snyder (1984a) evaluated three cards and found that one overestimated actual BAC for between 76 and 96 percent of his subjects, a second card overestimated BAC for one-third of the subjects, while the third was more accurate but could only be applied to a small number of subjects because of the limited data presented. Although this may be a responsible approach, it runs the risk of the charts being rejected by the drinking public when it finds that they seriously overestimate BAC.

Although the complexity of the factors that determine peak BAC may frustrate simple nomographs, it is easily handled by the small credit-card-sized pocket computers used by many individuals to record checks and balance their accounts. NHTSA has received a number of proposals for the development of a computer for the know-your-limit problem. Such hand computers will allow the user to enter, in advance, information on weight, sex, and favorite beverage. When drinking, the user would enter each drink as consumed using a preset value or entering the type of drink and whether it was a single or a double. In addition, the user will enter time (though this could be automated) and whether food was being consumed. Such devices will provide current BAC and possibly a projection of BAC for the next several hours, assuming no further consumption.

Whether a significant portion of the drinking public would purchase and carry such devices, and whether the BAC estimates produced would affect drinking-and-driving behavior, remain to be determined. Know-your-limits nomographs have been provided to patrons of restaurants and bars on placemats and drink coasters, but no evaluation of this method of providing BAC information has occurred.

An important use for this type of information, which has not been applied to date, is in regulating beverage service to patrons. Server training programs generally emphasize recognizing individuals who are already under the influence so that service can be denied. Many of the patrons who leave drinking establishments with BACs over the legal limit, however, have consumed all their alcohol at that one location. Thus, a simple count of the drinks, coupled with keeping track of the time, frequently would provide information about when to deny service. Cash registers in most bars and restaurants are reasonably sophisticated computing devices that record the number and type of drinks sold, the server, and the time of service. Adding the capability to keep track of the clients and calculate alcohol consumption over time would not be a major technical problem.

COIN-OPERATED MACHINES.

Some have argued that the establishment of BAC limits for driving places a responsibility on the state to provide a means for motorists to determine their BAC:

> The driver, even though prohibited from driving above a certain BAC, has no practical means of measuring his personal BAC prior to driving. To this extent, such a law is vicious because the information the driver needs to determine his BAC prior to driving is unavailable, but he commits a criminal offence if he drives with too great a BAC. An analogous situation might be one in which it was an offence to exceed a given speed limit but only the police had speedometers. (Picton 1977, 327)

This concern has prompted some legislatures to require the state department of motor vehicles to provide a method for drivers to estimate their BACs. One method frequently proposed, but not yet legislated in the United States, is mandating that drinking establishments provide coin-operated machines to measure BAC. Attempts to introduce such machines in the United States over the past two decades since the first model based on the Breathalyser was developed in 1970, have not been commercially successful. However, the Breath Alcohol Analyzer,[2] using a fuel cell sensor, has been a commercial success in New South Wales, Australia, where police enforce DUI laws by a very active program of random breath testing (Breakspear 1986).

Test results of these units illustrate both their potential value and their many significant problems. Picton (1981) conducted extensive tests with the Alcohol Guard,[3] a coin-operated tester using a Taguchi sensor. He found a high correlation between the Alcohol Guard results and standard, evidential-quality breath or blood tests *when users were assisted by an operater*. However, he found the machine was much less accurate when users were unassisted. When Picton attempted to simulate real-life operating conditions, he found that eleven of seventeen subjects were unable to operate the unit correctly without assistance. One-third of the subjects activated the unit without reading the instructions and eleven out of seventeen attempted to provide a breath sample without waiting the required five minutes after their last drink. Overall, of fifty-six tests on fourteen participants, 57 percent were within .02 percent of the correct BAC, while 36 percent were in error by .03 percent or more.

Many critics of coin-operated units also argue that they will be used as game machines and that tavern patrons will vie with each other to see who can obtain the highest BAC. In addition, studies have not examined whether users understand the meaning of the BAC obtained. Picton, however, did test recall of the last test result. He found that seven of eleven subjects recalled all three digits of the last test result while three more were able to recall only the first two digits and one could not recall the result at all.

3. *Self-Test Devices.* Self-test devices represent another method for providing BAC information to the public. Three types of units are commonly available: (a) length of stain tubes (balloon testers); (b) electronic self-testers; and (c) saliva tests. Crystal-filled tube testers have been used for many years primarily by the police as preliminary screening devices to determine whether a suspect should be arrested and taken to the station for an evidential breath test. These units consist of a glass tube filled with a yellow crystalline material (potassium dichromate) that changes to green when breath containing alcohol passes through the tube. A balloon attached to one end of the tube controls the amount of exhaled air passing through the unit.

Tests generally have indicated that these units are not very accurate. Anderson (1984), reporting on laboratory tests conducted on Lucky Laboratories' DM-2, found that this unit gave results that were too low. His subjects with a BAC of .10 percent or greater were provided with false negative readings (BACs below .10 percent) more than 60 percent of the time. Earlier tests by Prouty and O'Neill (1971), (O'Neill and Eiswirth (1972), Bjerver, Bonnichsen, and Andreasson (1966), and Day, Muir and Watling (1968) found that tube testers resulted in many false positives, that is, drivers with BACs below .10 percent were given positive results. It appears unlikely that this type of technology will provide the inexpensive but reasonably accurate measurement required in a self-testing device.

The development of electronic pre-arrest breath test devices has led to the marketing of small hand-held units, which generally employ a Taguchi or semiconductor sensor and sell for between $40 and $100. It is questionable whether the public will be willing to invest this much in a self-test unit, despite the fact that, if used frequently, the per-test cost will be less than that of the balloon test. Noteworthy in this connection is that radar detectors, which are considerably more expensive, have been a commercial success, even though the penalties for speeding are mild compared to DUI sanctions.

Table 13.1. Evaluation of Hand-held Electronic Self-testers with Numeric and Three-light Displays.

Percentage of Actual Values Falling in Each Displayed BAC Range for 3 Electronic Breath Testers with Numeric-Only Displays
(420 Spaced Trials, 72° F.)

| Displayed BAC | Actual BAC | | |
	.00–.04	.05–.09	.10–.15
.10–.15	0	3	48
.05–.09	0	24	51
.00–.04	100	73	2

Percentage of Actual Values Falling in Each Displayed BAC Range for 3 Electronic Breath Testers with Light-Only Displays
(280 Spaced Trials, 72°F.)

| Displayed BAC | Actual BAC | | |
	.00–.04	.05–.09	.10–.15
Red	0	33	100
Yellow	13	55	0
Green	88	13	0

Source: Snyder (1984a).

Snyder (1984b) reported on NHTSA tests on six of these electronic units. Table 13.1 shows the results for three devices that provide numerical readouts and for three that use a three-light readout (red, amber, green). In the NHTSA study, the devices using numerical readouts dangerously underestimated the true BAC, while those using lights generally erred by overestimating BAC.

The limited accuracy of these units makes public acceptance unlikely and subjects the manufacturers to liability suits. However, tin-oxide (semiconductor) technology is advancing rapidly and may provide a means of producing more reliable, less expensive units in the future (Crary 1986). Another limitation of these breath testers is that purchasers are not provided with a means to test their accuracy or to calibrate them, so it is likely that their sensitivity to alcohol will shift over time. Self-testers using fuel cell sensors have yet to be actively marketed in this country, and those used by the police (the Alcosensor or the SD-2 Alcohol Analyzer) are too expensive ($350 to $440) to be attractive for individual use. Less expensive ($150) fuel cell sensors such as the Lion Laboratories Intoxitest are under development. Such units, combined with a simple and inexpensive method for calibration, may have some potential for commercial success. However, until less expensive or more reliable electronic devices are available, or the public's fear of arrest for DUI increases, such units are likely to have limited commercial success in the United States.

A more promising technology for self-testing is the development of simple saliva tests for alcohol. The Addiction Research Foundation of Canada has been developing a "dip stick" saliva test for individual use and the Lifescan Company of Mountain View, California, currently markets a "litmus" test that uses a color change on a small strip of sensitive paper. This Alcoscan test involves applying saliva to a strip of sensitive paper treated with the enzyme alcohol-oxidase. The ethanol in the saliva sample is oxidized and produces, among other products, hydrogen peroxide, which reacts with chromogens (dyes) in the paper to produce a blue color. The BAC is estimated by comparing the color change against a color-comparator chart. Although the color change can be measured with some precision with a photometer, reading the test by eye provides only a rough indication of BAC (Frank and Flores 1986).

Although this test currently is sold primarily to police departments and probation agencies in multiple test packages, it can be sold in single units at a moderate price (approximately $1.00). Because the unit can be conveniently carried and stored, it has considerable potential for being widely used. Moreover, liquor stores and bars may distribute free tests as they have with know-your-limit cards.

The success of these methods for providing BAC information to the potential drinking driver is dependent on one critical issue: if drinkers are provided with reliable BAC information, will they alter their behavior so as to avoid driving while impaired? The evidence on this question is not reassuring. Oats (1976) reported on a program that offered breath tests to patrons of drinking establishments. Those participating were informed of the meaning of the resulting BAC with respect to driving impairment and the DUI laws. These volunteers were then observed as they left the bar. Unfortunately, the study found no difference in the frequency of driving by individuals who had been informed that they had BACs over the legal limit and those informed they were under the legal limit. This finding is particularly significant because the tests were accurate (they were performed by a trained technician) and the meaning of the test had been carefully explained. This ensured that neither self-testing errors nor misunderstanding of the results could account for the failure of the test to influence driver behavior.

Another significant problem for programs that attempt to intervene between drinking and the start of driving is that, by the time the issue arises, the drinker is already committed to driving home, having traveled to the bar or friend's home in his or her own vehicle. Even if provided with a free ride, the drinker is faced with the necessity of retrieving the car. The inconvenience of returning to the drinking site to pick up the vehicle, as well as the embarrassment of admitting he or she is incapable of driving, provides a powerful incentive to ignore the high BAC level. The easiest time to make driving decisions is before leaving for the bar or friend's house. At this point, it is possible to consider (while still sober) the advantages of taking along a "designated driver" or arranging to go by public transportation. Bar owners that provide free taxi rides home might consider providing free rides to their establishment. Once at the premises without a car, the drinker is forced to use public transportation. The failure to respond to information that they are at or above the legal BAC limit, suggests that many drinking drivers perceive the probability of a DUI arrest as low, and are not deterred from drinking and driving. To make this information more effective, a higher level of general deterrence is required.

III. Vehicle Control of Impaired Driving

If excessive drinking cannot be controlled by altering alcohol beverages, and if providing information on BAC to potentially impaired drivers does not influence their driving behavior, then the next line of defense is the automobile. For some time there has been interest in the possibility of equipping vehicles with devices that could prevent their operation by impaired drivers. The first device for this purpose, Quickey,[4] was developed in the late 1960s. In a paper presented in 1970 entitled "Cars that Drunks Can't Drive," this investigator (Voas 1970) attempted to provide an overview of the possibilities and problems in this technology:

> A car that could sense the capability of its driver and refuse to operate if that driver was not capable of safe performance, provides the most parsimonious approach to the problem of the impaired operator. If the vehicle could measure driver capability, even driver licensing tests might be unnecessary. Certainly a great reduction in those accidents which are due to the physiological or psychological impairment of the driver would be expected. This would include the fifty percent of fatal accidents in which alcohol plays a role. . . . Clearly, this utopian concept lies a number of years in the future. The closest we have come to this in the past has been to build in a man (called a chauffeur) who performed these functions.

While a car with a complete diagnostic capability has not been seriously proposed, a modification of this concept involving the detection of intoxicated drivers has been frequently suggested. The recent development of relatively reliable methods for determining blood alcohol levels has led to proposals for ignition interlock devices which would block the starting of a vehicle, based on a breath sample from the driver. Clearly, this is an attractive approach to the problem of drinking and driving. Society has no basic desire to keep the drinking driver from using the roads as long as he is sober. One of the major problems in achieving complete enforcement of drinking-driving laws is the unwillingness of juries to take away the license of offenders for fear of interfering with their ability to earn a livelihood. Any system which would limit the driving prohibition to those times when the individual was actually drinking rather than take it away completely, would find sympathy and support among law enforcement and court officials. Thus, the proposal for an Alcohol Safety Ignition Interlock System (ASIS) must be seriously considered. . . .

A. Performance Interlocks

In October 1970, NHTSA invited potential manufacturers to submit ideas for an Alcohol Safety Interlock System (ASIS). Twenty-five firms replied to this solicitation, and ten devices were screened by the Department of Transportation. None of the units were acceptable for application at that time, but several showed promise. Thus began a decade of development activity by NHTSA (Snyder 1984b).

Three significant decisions were made early in the course of this development. First, by 1976, experience with breath test technology suggested that it was too susceptible to circumvention to be practical in an interlock system. Moreover, these units were difficult to maintain and required frequent calibration. As a result emphasis was given to performance-measuring devices.

Second, it was obvious that preventing the starting of the vehicle was dangerous because it might preclude vehicle use in legitimate emergencies and might create emergencies if the engine stalled during normal operation. The expectant father who is so excited he cannot pass the test and start the car to take his wife to the hospital is one example of such an emergency. Another is the frustrated driver blocking traffic in the middle of a busy intersection because he or she cannot pass the interlock test. To avoid these problems, a decision was made to have the system signal other motorists (and the police) by causing the headlights to flash and the horn to sound. Thus, ASIS was changed to Drunk Driver Warning System (DDWS).

Third, there was little possibility that the general public would pay for and accept a DDWS as a standard feature on all new cars. Although some units performed reasonably well in passing zero-BAC drivers and stopping high-BAC drivers, all systems would produce some false positives. The annoyance and embarrassment produced by even a few failures would be likely to prevent the government from ordering, or the industry from implementing, such devices in all cars. The public outcry that resulted from the Department of Transportation's attempt to require safety belt interlocks illustrates this problem. More recently, General Motors of New Zealand mounted an intensive advertising campaign in that country to sell a breath test interlock system, but failed and the manufacturers went bankrupt (Yanek 1986).

Snyder (1984b) suggests that the potential applications for DDWS systems are those shown in table 13.2. He sees three classes of

Table 13.2. Analysis of the Most Likely Uses for Vehicle Interlock Systems

Control/locus Mode	Applications Categories with Some Examples Use Class		
	I	II	III
	Legally restricted drivers	Voluntary use by owners (or their desigees)	Users of vehicles available to the public
A. Outside-strict	Court DDWS[a]		
B. Outside-moderate		Insurance Parents/teenagers Fleetowners Drinkers in treatment	Rental cars Vehicles for sale
C. Driver information and option		Car owners	Rental cars Vehicles for sale

Source: Snyder (1984b).
[a]Drunken Driver Warning System.

users: I—legally restricted drivers; II—owners acting voluntarily; and III—drivers of rental cars. The application of the units would involve varying amounts of outside control: A—strict (probation requirements); B—moderate (insurance company inspection, employer supervision); and C—none (owner election of unit for personal information). To date, the principal interest in the DDWS has been in connection with controlling the driving of convicted DUIs.

NHTSA's research program has been limited principally to developing performance-measuring devices. Figure 13.2 illustrates the relationship of test scores to BAC for four units NHTSA tested in 1973. The four units compared are:

1. The Critical Tracking Task (CTT): a meter with a pointer that is driven off center by a noise generator. The operator is required to keep the needle centered.

2. Reaction Analyzer (RA): a device with two lights, one of which varies randomly in intensity. The subject has to control the other light to match it.

3. Complex Coordinator (CC): a device with two five-light columns and two levers. The subject has to manipulate the levers to keep the same number of lights lit in each column.

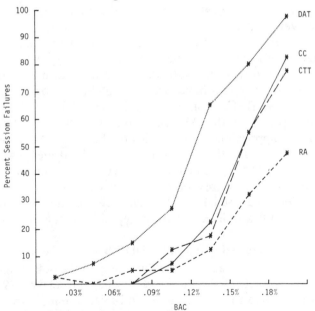

Fig. 13.2. Test failures and blood alcohol concentrations for four drunk driver warning systems (Snyder 1984).

4. Divided Attention Test (DAT): a tracking task (performed with the vehicle's steering wheel) combined with a task that required reacting to numbers and pushing buttons with right or left thumb or with right or left foot.

As figure 13.2 demonstrates, failure rates on all these devices increased with BAC. Some, however, such as the DAT, had relatively high failure rates at BACs below .05 percent. None of the units failed as many as 50 percent of the trials by individuals with BACs at or above the legal limit of .10 percent. Further improvement has occurred since that time, and Snyder, by applying new scoring procedures to recently collected data on the CTT and DAT tests, suggests that the accuracy level shown in figure 13.3 can be obtained.

To better understand the implications of these results, it is necessary to consider the consequences of these scores in relation to the frequency of driving at various BACs. Snyder suggests that if the test is failed, the driver should be made to wait ten minutes before being allowed to try again. Using the data from the studies of the DAT 2 devices, Snyder estimates how often a driver at three different BACs will be required to wait ten or more minutes. These data are shown in figure 13.4.

In evaluating these estimates, it is important to keep in mind that most drivers make far more zero-BAC than positive-BAC trips. A typical driver may make two trips a day five days a week to work, and ten more trips during the week for shopping, while using the car only once to come home from the bar on Saturday night. In this case, the driver would have twenty zero-BAC trips for every trip with a positive BAC. From the data in figure 13.4, we can see that the driver would fail the DAT test and be forced to wait ten minutes or more on approximately one-third of the zero-BAC trips. Therefore, for every time this device prevented the driver from starting the car because he or she had a BAC over .10, the same driver would have one-third of twenty or six delays when sober. This type of inconvenience can be legitimately enforced on the convicted drinking driver, but is unlikely to be acceptable to the general driving public.

The only major field study of a DDWS system conducted to date was performed by Allen, Stein, Summers, and Cook (1983) under a NHTSA contract. DDWS units were built into eleven 1979 Novas that were loaned to seventeen second-DUI offenders for a twenty-six-week test period. The CTT used in this experiment allowed four attempts to achieve a pass. Laboratory tests of the device indicated

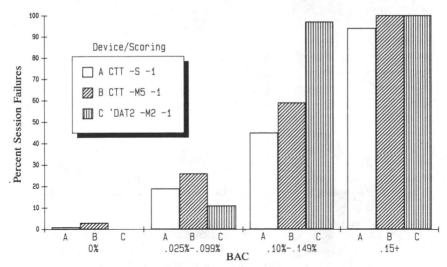

Fig. 13.3. Percent of vehicle starts delayed/deterred by blood alcohol content for three types of drunk driver warning systems (Snyder 1984b).

that, at a cost of failing 7.5 percent of the sober trials, it would fail 46.0 percent of attempts at .10 percent BAC and 95.0 percent of attempts at .15 percent BAC. A sensor in the driver's seat prevented a substitute from taking the test. In addition to the CTT itself, the experimental vehicles were equipped to record attempts to start the car, CTT scores, and driving over 10 MPH without passing the test (which would cause the lights to flash and horn to sound).

During the course of this study none of the subjects were involved in an accident or a DUI arrest. One was cited for driving a non-DDWS car (a violation of probation) and another cited for speeding while driving a non-DDWS car but not charged with a probation violation. The authors reported no attempts to tamper with the DDWS equipped cars, and the recorded data indicated that over more than two thousand person days of operation only ten trips involving fifty-three minutes of operation were made with the horn sounding and the lights blinking.

Snyder (1984b) concludes from this test that the DDWS is a feasible alternative to sentencing for DUIs. He notes that some hardware improvements to correct maintenance problems encountered in the test would be required, along with a redesign to reduce the price of the CTT units from around $10,000 to $1,000 or $500. Aside from these technological improvements, cooperation between local

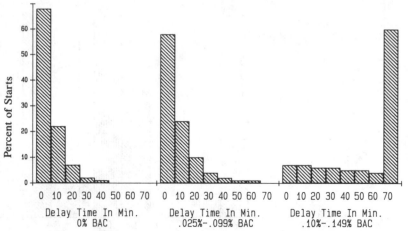

Fig. 13.4. Distribution of projected delay times by blood alcohol content for DAT 2 (80-U) drunk driver warning system (Snyder 1984b).

courts, police departments, and the state driver licensing agency would be required. Finally, the cost of the devices to the user would have to be sufficiently low to attract the clientele needed to make the unit a commercial success.

B. Breath Test Interlocks

Although NHTSA abandoned the breath alcohol measurement system for the DDWS in the mid-1970s, interest in this system continued. With the renewed attention to the drinking-driving problem in the first half of this decade, several manufacturers have developed breath test units. The continuing advances in semiconductor (tin-oxide) gas sensors have made breath test devices less expensive and more accurate, thus making this technology more practical than in the mid-1970s (Crary 1986). In September 1986, NHTSA sponsored a workshop on in-vehicle alcohol test devices, at which presentations were made on five units: Autosense, Guardian Interlock, Lincoln Co-driver, Lion Analytic VBM, and Safety Interlock (*Federal Register* vol. 51, no. 120, 23 June 1986).

The breath test units presented at the NHTSA conference employed various means to overcome some of the principal issues raised by critiques of these systems:

Bogus breath samples. To prevent the actuation of the units by air-filled balloons and other means, sysystems were included that required the sample to meet certain temperature requirements, or to provide a specified pressure level.

Mechanical tampering. Most manufacturers propose a system for recording operation of the car when the test has not been passed so that tampering, if not prevented, could at least be reported to the court.

Filtered air samples. In addition to using temperature and pressure to defeat filters, it was proposed that other breath elements could be sensed to ensure that the sample was not being filtered.

Substitute test takers. One device required a stop-and-go blowing procedure that the manufacturer claimed could not be learned in less than three trials and noted that after three trials the unit would turn off and another test could not be taken for an hour. Another approach provided by one manufacturer was to require repetition of the test after eight minutes.

Blood alcohol in absorption phase. The problem presented by a rising BAC was reduced by one manufacturer by requiring a retest within a few minutes if the first test indicated alcohol was present but below the BAC level which would have prevented engine ignition.

A number of the manufacturers provided special features such as a timer to prevent all use of the car during certain high-risk hours (6 PM to 6 AM) or to enable the breath test system only during such hours. The option of recording the breath test results is also a feature of some systems. Only one paper reported price information: the unit could be purchased for approximately $140 and installed for $12.

The federal government has also conducted some limited tests on two breath test units (the Soberlizer[5] and ABIC[6]) (Frank 1985). These two were selected for testing because they employed systems designed to frustrate efforts to provide a bogus breath sample; however, Frank reported that bogus samples could be introduced in both units. In addition, NHTSA determined that by blowing through appropriate filtering materials, enough alcohol could be filtered out of the breath sample to "fool" the protective systems on one of the units. The other required so much pressure that a filter could not be used but, on the other hand, some drivers would probably not be able to blow hard enough to operate the unit.

The availability of these units has attracted sufficient attention to cause the California legislature to authorize testing of alcohol ignition interlock units in four counties, and to permit their use in other areas of the state. The California Office of Traffic Safety is responsible for determining which counties will participate in the field test and for approving the units to be tested. The users will pay a fee or purchase the units, and manufacturers will be required to provide units for indigent offenders. The performance requirements for the units have not been finalized; however, initial requirements call for the interlock to engage at a BAC between .025 percent and .035 percent. If the field test, which is scheduled to run until January 1, 1990, is successful, several thousand DUIs may have these units installed in their cars for six months or more. This would provide a sufficiently large sample to determine the effectiveness of these devices in reducing accidents and recidivism.

IV. Detection and Apprehension of Drinking Drivers

If the vehicle itself does not prevent the impaired operator from driving, then the next line of defense must be the police. Unfortunately, the probability that a drinking driver will be apprehended in the United States is very low. The most careful measurements of the probability of arrest (Beitel, Glauz, and Sharp 1975; Hause, Voas, and Chavez 1982) indicate that the chances of being arrested in an area with a high level of DUI enforcement is approximately one in two hundred drunk (.10 percent BAC or higher) trips. Where no special DUI enforcement effort is made, the probability may be as low as one in two thousand (Borkenstein 1975). An effort has been made to develop technology to improve DUI enforcement procedures. This investigator (Voas 1982b) has suggested that the DUI apprehension process can be broken down into three phases: (1) detecting vehicles operated by impaired drivers, (2) detecting alcohol in the driver, and (3) measuring impairment through sobriety tests.

A. Detecting Vehicles Operated by Impaired Drivers

The proportion of vehicles being operated by impaired drivers (BAC at or above .10 percent) varies by time of day and location. Fox and Borkenstein (1966) found that, when vehicles were sampled at random locations seven days a week between the hours of 7 PM and 3 AM, approximately 1.6 percent of the drivers were at or above .10 percent BAC. Other studies that limited data collection to accident sites or to weekend evenings have obtained higher proportions of drivers over the .10 percent limit. National roadside surveys of weekend drivers between the hours of 10 PM and 3 AM conducted in 1973 and 1986 found 4.9 percent and 3.1 percent respectively above the .10 percent BAC limit (Wolfe 1974, 1986b).

A critical factor in DUI enforcement programs is the efficiency with which police officers can select these high-BAC drivers from the general traffic flow. Research has been directed at developing both improved observational systems for use by officers patrolling the highway and electronic devices that might identify impaired operators through their driving characteristics.

1. Visual Detection

Harris, Howlett, and Ridgeway (1979) conducted a study of the driver behaviors that police commonly use to identify vehicles being driven by drinking drivers. Observers accompanied police officers on patrol and recorded the vehicle maneuvers that brought 643 individuals to the attention of the police. The observer conducted a pre-arrest breath test on all drivers stopped (whether or not they were ultimately arrested). With these data, the researchers were able to correlate cues with BAC and develop probabilities that a driver would be found to be above the limit based on the type of abnormal driving observed by the police. Descriptions of each of the twenty-three cues developed through this process, with the probability that the driver who exhibits them is impaired, are listed in table 13.3.

To date, the use of this detection guide has not been proven to increase the numbers of DUI arrests. Harris, Dick, Casey, and Jarosz (1980) tested the guide at ten police departments in different locations across the country and found an overall increase of 12 percent in DUI arrests after its introduction. However, no control groups were employed, and the increase in numbers of arrests was possibly due to increased priority being given to DUI enforcement rather than to the use of this guide. Vingilis, Adlaf, and Bletgen (1983) evaluated the guide and found that it was no more effective in increasing arrest rates than an informal discussion of drinking and driving. They found that experienced officers used the same cues before and after the training, suggesting that the guide identified cues that the police traditionally use and that the guide's primary value is for training novices, rather than increasing overall apprehension rates.

2. Electronic Sensing

Several studies have measured the impairment of driving performance produced by alcohol in experiments involving drinking subjects operating instrumented cars on closed (protected) courses (Huntley 1973; Perrine 1976). A logical result of this research has

Table 13.3. DWI Detection Guide

---

1. The number to the right of each cue listed below is the percentage of nighttime drivers expected to have a BAC equal to or greater than ($\geq$) 0.10, if that cue is observed.

Stopping (without cause) in traffic lane	70
Following too closely	60
Turning with wide radius	60
Appearing to be drunk	60
Driving on other than designated roadway	55
Straddling center or lane marker	55
Almost striking object or vehicle	55
Slow response to traffic signals	50
Headlights off (at night)	50
Signaling inconsistent with driving actions	45
Weaving	45
Tires on center or lane marker	45
Drifting	45
Swerving	45
Accelerating or decelerating rapidly	45
Slow speed (more than 10 MPH below speed limit)	45
Fast speed (more than 10 MPH above speed limit)	35
Failing to respond to traffic signals or signs	35
Braking erratically	35
Stopping inappropriately (other than in lane)	35
Turning abruptly or illegally	30
Driving into opposing or crossing traffic	30
Driving with vehicle defect(s)	30

2. If one additional cue is observed, add 5 to the larger of the two percentage values to obtain the expected percentage of drivers with BAC $\geq$ 0.10. If two or more additional cues are observed, add 10 to the largest percentage to obtain the expected percentage of drivers with BAC $\geq$ 0.10.

3. To obtain the expected percentage of drivers with BAC $\geq$ 0.05, add 20 to the percentage obtained for drivers with BAC $\geq$ 0.10.

Source: Harris, Howlett, and Ridgeway (1979).

been to ask whether similar driving characteristics can be observed in drivers using public roads, and whether these behaviors can be recorded electronically to provide an effective enforcement tool. Perrine (1976) and Damkot et al. (1977) reported on an experiment conducted in Vermont in which radar was used to record the braking behavior of drivers coming to a stop at a roadside breath test survey. Once stopped, the drivers were requested to provide a breath sample that permitted the correlation of BAC with stopping behavior. Data from this study are shown in figure 13.5. Drivers at low BAC (0.01

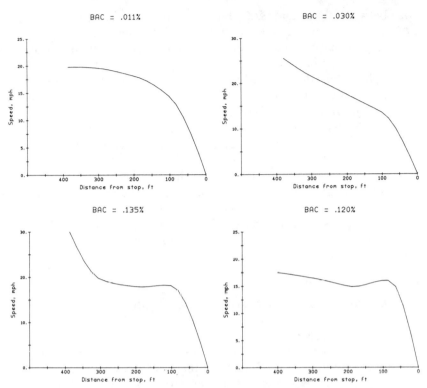

Fig. 13.5. Smoothed plots of speed as a function of distance from stopping point for four motorists at two roadside surveys (Perrine 1976, 36).

percent and 0.03 percent) stopped their vehicles with a relatively smooth deceleration, whereas drivers at illegal BACs maintained their speed until almost at the survey site and then applied the brake hard. This suggests that police with radar units could detect impaired drivers by timing their approach to a stop sign. Although officers frequently combine DUI enforcement with radar speed enforcement, to this investigator's knowledge, no attempt has been made to use these braking patterns in DUI enforcement.

Another approach to automatic detection of impaired drivers was investigated by Bragg, Dawson, Kirby, and Goodfellow (1981). Building on earlier work by Bragg and Wilson (1980), they used two pneumatic loops placed thirty meters apart on the roadway. With these loops placed in front of a roadside survey site, they measured speed and alignment of passing motorists and correlated these data with BAC measured at the survey site. They found no relationship between speed and BAC, but did find a significant correlation with lane position. They noted that, as a driver encountered the first set of pneumatic tubes, he or she would hear the rumble of the tires and change lane positions slightly: sober drivers would move to the right, while drinking drivers went to the left. This change in lane position was measured by the second set of tubes. Based on their results, Bragg and his coworkers estimated that, if drivers at checkpoints were stopped based on their performance on this test rather than at random, the proportion of drivers with BACs at or above .08 percent would rise from 6.9 percent to 10 percent. However, 79 percent of the drivers who failed this test would have BACs below .05 percent. Thus, using this measure, six sober drivers would still be stopped for each drunken driver apprehended. Therefore, this sensing system would have only limited value outside of checkpoints where large numbers of drivers are to be routinely interviewed.

3. RANDOM STOPPING

An alternative method advanced to identify impaired motorists is the "sobriety checkpoint" procedure in which all, or a random sample of all, drivers using a roadway are stopped and examined for alcohol impairment. This controversial enforcement system appears to be effective in producing an increase in perceived risk of DUI arrest. The key to the effectiveness of this system is the rapid but accurate processing of a large number of motorists through the checkpoint.

Because of the many limitations and specifications courts have placed on the operation of checkpoints (Ifft 1983), a checkpoint "technology" has developed that requires extensive preparations as well as considerable staff and equipment at the site. The requirements for this process have been described by Compton and Engle (1983) and will not be covered in detail here. Some courts have required that checkpoints be used only at times and places where alcohol-related accidents occur. They must provide for motorist safety, and involve sufficient show of force to make it clear to the public that all cars are being stopped and no individuals are singled out. The courts also require that vehicles be selected at random and that the intrusion on the public be minimized by keeping interviews short and avoiding long lines of waiting cars.

Complying with these requirements involves extensive advanced surveying of sites, training of officers, and development of informational materials. Checkpoint operations tend to be logistically complex and involve a number of officers with associated equipment, flares, barriers, signs, and breath testing apparatus as well as patrol cars. Because checkpoint operations involve significant amounts of time and personnel, there is considerable controversy within police departments as to whether they are cost-effective. In many checkpoint operations, few DUIs are arrested. Voas, Rhodenizer, and Lynn (1985) have demonstrated, however, that more arrests per officer hour can be made at a checkpoint than during regular patrols if efficient methods are used in checking drivers for alcohol. Furthermore, police contact with drivers at lower BACs at checkpoints may have an important influence on deterrence (Voas 1982a), particularly because the drivers contacted at checkpoints are more similar to accident-involved drivers than those arrested by traditional patrol methods (Voas et al. 1985).

B. Detecting Drinkers

Once the police have selected and stopped a vehicle, the next critical step in the enforcement process is to determine whether the individual is impaired by alcohol. This activity occurs in at least three contexts. First, the stop may be part of routine traffic enforcement operations. In such a situation, the officer may be primarily concerned with writing a traffic citation rather than attending to subtle cues that the individual has been drinking. Second, the stop may involve an officer on special DUI patrol who is specifically looking for drinking drivers. Finally, the stop may occur at a sobriety checkpoint where the officer is looking for drinking drivers, but has only thirty seconds or less to determine whether the individual has been drinking.

In Scandinavia, where police physicians previously were required to examine individuals accused of DUI to certify their impairment, several studies found that physicians identify as impaired only about half of the drivers who are at .10 percent BAC (NSC 1976, 11). The police officer must make a judgment under more adverse circumstances, and, therefore, it is not surprising that many high-BAC drivers are not identified at the roadside. In a study of DUI arrests by regular patrol officers, Taubenslag and Taubenslag (1975) found that officers arrested less than half of the drivers with BACs of .10 percent or greater with whom they came in contact. Studies of police detection of drinking drivers at checkpoints also demonstrate that many high-BAC drivers are missed. Vingilis et al. (1982) found that Canadian police who interviewed motorists briefly at checkpoints failed to detect 95 percent of drivers over .08 percent BAC. Jones and Lund (1985) found that officers at checkpoints in Charlottesville, Virginia, detected only 45 percent of drivers at or above .10 percent.

There is some evidence that officers on dedicated DUI patrols identify a greater proportion of the high-BAC drivers they stop (Lund and Jones 1986), perhaps because their knowledge of impaired driving cues results in their stopping only drivers with very high BACs in the first place. The average BAC for drivers arrested by officers on patrol tends to be higher than the BAC of drivers arrested at checkpoints (Voas et al. 1985).

1. Visual Cues to Drinking

Once the vehicle is stopped, the officer interviews the motorist to determine whether to ask the driver to exit the car for further testing. The officer makes this determination primarily from traditional indicators of impairment, such as bloodshot eyes, fumbling with keys or the driver's license, and slurred speech.

Compton (1985) has reported on an attempt to determine the validity of these cues in a simulated checkpoint situation. In this study, seventy-five male volunteers consumed sufficient quantities of alcohol to produce two BAC levels (.12 percent or .07 percent) or took a placebo to produce a zero-BAC control. These volunteers then drove a vehicle down a protected roadway to where they were stopped by participating police officers who, without knowledge of their BACs, interviewed them to determine whether they were above the legal limit (.10 percent BAC). The officers were provided with the checklist of the personal appearance signs shown in table 13.4, which are believed to indicate intoxication. For each item, the proportion of the drivers who were recorded as exhibiting that indictor was recorded by BAC category. As can be seen, all but two items did discriminate significantly between the BAC categories. These results suggest that these traditional signs of drinking can be useful in detecting drinkers.

Teplin and Lutz (1985) have taken this observational procedure a step further by developing an Alcohol Symptom Checklist (ASC) on 672 randomly selected emergency room patients. They began with a twenty-eight-item checklist, which, through an item analysis procedure, was reduced to eleven: smell of alcohol, impaired fine motor

Table 13.4. Percentage of Drivers at Each BAC Level Observed Exhibiting Various Personal Appearance Variables

	BAC		
Driver behavior	.00–.04	.05–.09	.10–.15
Odor of alcohol	7% (0–14%)*	39% (5–68%)	61% (8–100%)
Face flushed	7% (0–11%)	29% (5–45%)	53% (14–72%)
Speech slurred	3% (2–3%)	14% (7–25%)	20% (0–29%)
Eyes dilated	15% (7–22%)	41% (20–50%)	56% (7–25%)
Demeanor	4% (2–5%)	14% (1–15%)	20% (7–25%)
Hair disheveled	3% (2–5%)	5% (0–10%)	9% (7–14%)NS**
Poor dexterity	1% (0–2%)	2% (0–5%)	12% (0–17%)
Clothes disheveled	3% (0–7%)	2% (0–5%)	14% (0–22%)
Other observations	17% (5–25%)	26% (0–38%)	34% (0–100%)NS**

Source: Compton (1985).
*These figures are the minimum and maximum average percentage of drivers observed by the different police agencies.
**This difference was not statistically significant at the $p \leq .01$ level.

coordination, impaired gross motor coordination, slurred speech, change in speech volume, decreased alertness, sweating, slowed respiration, sleepiness, changes in pace of speech, and red eyes. They found that this scale had an interrater reliability of .89 and a correlation with the breath test criterion of .85. With an optimal cutoff point of 4 on this scale, they identified 72 percent of the patients with a .10 percent BAC, while keeping the false positive rate to 8 percent. Although this is a relatively impressive performance, it should be kept in mind that the observers in the emergency room probably had a somewhat longer and better opportunity to observe the patient than do most police officers in the field. Nevertheless, these results, together with those of Compton (1985), suggest that the development of a standardized rating scale for the natural signs of drinking could be a useful addition to current enforcement technology.

2. IN-VEHICLE NYSTAGMUS TEST

The lateral-gaze nystagmus test has been advanced as a method of identifying impaired drivers while they are still seated behind the wheel. This test was devloped as one part of the "sobriety test" battery to be used by officers after they had decided to ask the suspect to leave the vehicle (Burns and Moskowitz 1977; Tharp 1981). The test consists of having the subject follow with his eyes a pen light as the officer moves it from the center of the visual field toward the right and left. The officer watches for the onset of nystagmus (jerkiness) as the pupil moves toward the side. Each eye is scored on three items: smooth pursuit, point of onset of nystagmus, and presence of nystagmus at maximum deviation.

Although this test is best performed while the subject is standing facing forward, some highly trained police officers claim they are able to perform the test well enough with the driver seated in the car to determine whether the driver is impaired. In the study reported by Compton (1985), this test, when conducted and scored by the officers participating in the checkpoint simulation, correctly identified 74 percent of the drivers at or above .10 percent BAC. However, it also incorrectly identified fifteen of the zero-BAC drivers as being over the limit. Because eight out of ten drivers at a checkpoint will be at zero-BAC, even this low rate of false positives may be unacceptable.

3. PRE-ARREST BREATH TESTS

The fastest and most accurate method for determining whether a motorist has been drinking is the use of a small, hand-held pre-arrest breath test device.

Until the early 1970s, the only breath test devices available for police use at the roadside were the balloon-type testers that were found to be relatively inaccurate and difficult to read (Prouty and O'Neill 1971). The use of this type of tester in the enforcement of the highly successful Road Safety Act of 1967 in Britain, however, stimulated interest in roadside testing in the United States. As a result, the Department of Transportation encouraged the development of hand-held test units, and NHTSA established a test laboratory to evaluate these units and funded the development of a prototype.

By 1977, Harriot was able to report on the initial tests of seven such devices. These units used four different sensing systems: fuel cell, catalytic burner, infrared, and semiconductor. In the decade since these early instruments were developed, fuel cell devices have tended to dominate the field of enforcement because they are smaller and have greater accuracy and stability. As already noted, however, semiconductor units are being marketed as self-testers and the technology of tin-oxide gas sensors is progressing rapidly so it is possible that this type of unit may come back into vogue (Crary 1986).

At one time, NHTSA intended to develop a "Qualified Products List" for pre-arrest test devices, similar to the one established for evidential breath testers. Although this plan was never implemented, three of the pre-arrest units currently on the market have been found to qualify under the evidential standards. Several thousand of these units have been sold to police departments; however, their usefulness has been limited by the belief that the Fourth Amendment requires that the officer must have "reason-to-believe" that the suspect is impaired before requesting a test. Whether the Fourth Amendment does indeed have such a requirement has not been resolved by the federal courts. Nevertheless, this limitation prevents the use of these highly accurate devices in the initial interview with the motorist, and forces the officer to depend upon observation of the traditional signs of drinking described above or on the passive sensor described below.

4. Passive Sensing

The concept of passive sensing was first described by the present investigator in 1972 in a Department of Transportation memorandum that noted a need for a sensing unit which could be used by police without "probable-cause" or "reason-to-believe" that the suspect had been drinking. This led to the postulation of a sensor that would draw air from in front of the face and make a rough determination of the extent of drinking by measuring a combination of exhaled air and environmental atmosphere. To determine the potential for this system, NHTSA requested the industry to submit concepts for a passive sensor. No satisfactory responses were obtained from this solicitation when it was issued in 1972. However, several studies of the potential utility of such a device were sponsored by NHTSA during the 1970s (Voas 1983a).

The first mention in the literature of a passive sensing device was that reported by Harger in 1974. The device that he describes, however, was not marketed generally in the United States, and a passive sensor unit only became available in 1981 when the Japanese police began to use a unit developed under contract to Honda Motors by the Nippon-Seiki Company. With support from the Insurance Institute for Highway Safety, this researcher arranged for the import and testing of several of these units (Voas 1983a).

The laboratory and field tests indicated that the Honda unit, which was based on a semiconductor or Taguchi sensor, demonstrated a number of desirable features for enforcement, but also revealed a number of limitations. The police, for example, felt that the sensor needed to be integrated with a flashlight so that both could be operated with only one hand. Extensive use of the Taguchi sensor demonstrated that it tended to drift and to be poisoned by environmental contaminants so that the sensitivity declined over time. Despite these limitations, field use of the unit (Voas 1984a; Voas and Layfield 1983) indicated that it could be highly effective, particularly in sobriety checkpoint applications where it increased both speed and accuracy in identifying drinkers among the drivers interviewed. Compton (1985) obtained further evidence for the utility of passive sensing in his simulated checkpoint study. He found that police using the Honda unit identified 94 percent of the drivers above .10 percent BAC, while misidentifying only 10 percent of the .00-.04 percent BAC cases.

Because of the limitations of the Taguchi sensor, the Insurance Institute for Highway Safety contracted with Lion Laboratories of Cardiff, Wales, to produce a passive sensor unit using a fuel cell sensor. This sensor proved to be considerably more stable (see Jones 1986). Application of this sensor in a field operation (Jones and Lund 1985; Voas, Rhodenizer, and Lynn 1985) demonstrated that the unit could be highly effective at checkpoints in increasing detection of .10 percent BAC drivers and in minimizing the numbers of nondrinking drivers unnecessarily detained. Lund and Jones (1986) reported on the use of the sensor in a traditional dedicated DWI patrol situation. The purposes and advantages of using a passive sensor have been described by Dubowski (1986) and Voas (1982b, 1983b). Recently, mass production of an improved version of this sensor has begun in the United States. Thus, the passive sensing system is currently supported by laboratory research that demonstrates the basic validity of the system and by field research that shows police can use the system effectively not only to increase apprehension of drunken drivers, but also to minimize the delays to nondrinking drivers.

Three independent legal studies have been made of the Fourth Amendment issues raised by the use of a passive sensor. The earliest of these was Ruschmann, et al. (1980) that concluded the passive sensor would not constitute a search under the Fourth Amendment and, therefore, could be used by police in their investigation prior to establishing "probable cause." More recent reports by Manak (1984) and Fields and Hricko (1986) have reached similar conclusions. Thus, although no case law currently exists specifically involving the passive sensor, there is reason to believe that it can be used by police as a tool for screening DUI suspects.

C. Detecting Impairment

DUI laws traditionally required not only evidence that the accused had been drinking, but also that his or her behavior clearly indicated impairment. The rapid development and use of breath tests for alcohol resulted in increasing reliance by the courts on chemical tests, culminating in the adoption from Europe of the illegal per se concept, which defines a DUI offense with only two elements—operating or controlling a vehicle and having a BAC at or above the prescribed level—and theoretically requires no evidence that the behavior of the accused was impaired (Voas 1982b). Despite the fact that forty-four of the fifty states currently have such laws, successful prosecution in most courts still places the burden of demonstrating impairment on the police officer. As a result, once the officer has "reason-to-believe" that the driver is impaired by alcohol, the next step in the apprehension process is to conduct a set of "sobriety tests."

1. FIELD SOBRIETY TESTS

Prior to court acceptance of the blood and/or breath test for alcohol as presumptive evidence of impairment, conviction of a driver charged with DUI was almost entirely dependent upon the police officer's testimony regarding the behavior of the suspect. To strengthen their testimony, officers developed simple performance tests, such as walking a straight line, which could provide an opportunity to make observations useful in detecting impairment. These psychomotor tests, developed from the practical experience of police officers, varied among police departments, as well as among individual officers. Only in the last decade has there been a significant effort to improve the technology of performance assessment by systematizing and validating these tests. Snapper, Seaver, and Schwartz (1981) reviewed the literature on performance impairment by alcohol and drugs in an effort to identify tests applicable to enforcement programs. In 1976, NHTSA funded a research program by Burns and Moskowitz (1977) in which six tests were administered by ten police officers to 238 subjects with BACs ranging from 0.00 to 0.15 percent. A discriminant analysis indicated that three tests—the "one-leg stand," the "walk-and-turn," and the "lateral gaze nystagmus"— correctly identified 83 percent of the subjects as having BACs of 0.10 percent or higher.

NHTSA adopted these three tests as a standard part of the training program for officers specializing in DUI enforcement. This agency also has developed an instructor training program and certification system for such instructors. As previously described, the lateral gaze nystagmus test consists of three observations for each of the two eyes, yielding a score between zero and six. The subject is requested to fixate a small pen light and follow it with his or her eyes as the officer moves it slowly toward the left or right periphery of the visual field. One point is assigned if nystagmus (jerkiness) occurs in the pursuit movement of the eye. The second observation is obtained by forcing the pupil to the extreme corner of the eye and scoring a point if nystagmic movements occur with the eye in this position. A third observation is made at the location where the pupil deviates forty-five degrees from the centerline. According to Tharp (Tharp 1981; see also Goding and Dobie 1986), this is the point at which nystagmus first appears when BAC reaches 0.10 percent.

The walk-and-turn test and the one-leg stand are designed to test postural steadiness (Rhomberg) and the ability to divide attention, two skills known to be affected by BAC (Moskewitz 1974). The motorist is required to stand still with feet together while given the instructions for the test and then told to walk heel-to-toe exactly ten steps forward and back. Points are scored for (1) failure to remain balanced and still during the instructions, (2) stopping, (3) stepping out of line, (4) using the arms to maintain balance, and (5) taking too many or too few steps. The one-leg stand requires the motorist to stand on the preferred leg for thirty seconds. Points are scored for (1) failure to count to thirty, (2) losing balance, and (3) using the arms to maintain balance.

Tharp et al. (1981) studied the use of these tests in actual field operations. They found that after training police officers in these three tests, the arrest rates of drivers with BACs of 0.10 percent or higher rose from 62 to 69 percent. The relatively limited improvement resulted in part from the fact that the officers used these tests on only 50 percent of the drivers in the 0.10 to 0.149 percent BAC range both before and after training. Anderson, Schweitz, and Snyder (1983) also studied the validity of this three-test battery in the field with five different police departments. The proportion of suspects tested varied from 70 to 88 percent depending on the department. The highest usage rate occurred with the Maryland State Police, who also had the highest accuracy in identifying drivers at or above .10 percent BAC. They identified 92 to 96 percent of the impaired drivers depending on the test. Overall, the accuracy of the three-test battery as used by the five departments studied was 83 percent. Of the 17 percent misclassified, 16 percent were drivers at BACs lower than .10 percent who were identified as impaired, while 1 percent were false negatives, drivers above .10 percent assessed as not impaired.

NHTSA (1986e) has provided extensive training support for these tests, and they have become very popular with police departments. The Los Angeles Police Department has extended sobriety testing, including the use of the nystagmus test, to the identification of drug-impaired drivers. This program, which involves a large number of behavioral and physiological tests and is conducted by specially trained "drug recognition experts," has been evaluated by the NHTSA (Bigelow, Bickel, Roche, Liebson, and Nowowieski 1985; Compton 1986a) and found to be surprisingly effective not only in identifying impaired drivers but in specifying the dose of drug consumed.

2. ELECTRONYSTAGMOGRAPH

The sobriety tests used by the police involve behavior that, in some cases, can be measured with greater sensitivity using laboratory or electrophysiological recording equipment. For example, in the early 1940s, Goldberg (1943) constructed a platform for measuring Romberg motion in subjects dosed with alcohol. This apparatus was never used in enforcement operations and little effort has been made to develop other equipment for this purpose. Recently, however, Westerman and Gilbert (1981) have developed evidence that the electronystagmograph (ENG), which is commonly used to diagnose problems in the labyrinth system of the ear and in the postural control system of the brain stem, can detect the effects of drugs on these systems. Moreover, they claim that the electrical output of the ENG associated with the major drug categories is sufficiently specific so that the general class of drug consumed can be identified. Their findings have led to the development of a field analysis system using a portable computer (the Veritas[7], which analyzes the ENG output from three electrodes placed on the forehead and indicates the presence of alcohol and several other major drug groups (marijuana, cocaine, and narcotics). Field tests of this system are just beginning. Whether the unit has practical importance for use in DUI enforcement programs remains to be demonstrated.

The feature that makes the Veritas and similar performance-measuring equipment of special interest is that, at least in theory, they measure the extent of the impairment produced by the substance, not just the quantity of the drug found in the blood. Because the relationship of drug concentration in the blood to performance is very complex compared to the relatively simple monotonic relationship of BAC to impairment (Chester 1985), measuring performance may be the only method for apprehending drug-impaired drivers.

3. THE USE OF VCRs TO RECORD PERFORMANCE

In the absence of objective tests, the officer frequently has difficulty describing the behavior of the DUI suspect with sufficient clarity to convince the jury that the driver was impaired. The advent of low cost video recording equipment permitted the recording of the suspects performance on the sobriety tests and the presentation of that performance directly to the jury. In practice, these tapes usually persuade the accused to plead guilty when the on-camera behavior clearly demonstrates impairment. Initially, the availability of video recordings was welcomed, not only because they served to record impaired performance, but also because they protected the officers by demonstrating that they behaved properly toward the accused and proceeded in accordance with legal requirements. However, in some cases, the defendants, despite high BACs, show little apparent impairment. In these cases, the defendants' attorneys frequently subpoena the tapes for presentation in court in defense of their clients. On a number of occasions, the prosecution has lost cases that, considering the defendant's BAC, would normally have been won. Experience with police use of VCRs during the Alcohol Safety Action Project program sponsored by the Department of Transportation indicated that while fifteen of the thirty-five ASAP sites adopted this technique, thirteen discarded the procedure by the end of the three-year project period (NHTSA 1979). Although a number of police departments continue to videotape DUI offenders, careful use of standardized sobriety tests and proper attention to filling out arrest forms probably reduces the need for this type of technology.

D. Evidential Tests

Analytical techniques for measuring alcohol in beverages and in bodily fluids have existed for over one hundred fifty years. During the last half century, tests for alcohol have become the most frequently performed forensic chemical test and more than three hundred methods for conducting such tests have been described. This technology is the core of modern drunk-driving enforcement programs and lends to this area a scientific aura less prominent in other areas of the criminal justice system. Not only are chemical tests for alcohol conducted as a part of the prosecution of the DUI charge, but, beginning in 1936, Norway defined the DUI offense itself in terms of blood alcohol concentration. Nebraska adopted this type of per se legislation in 1963, and currently forty-four of the fifty states have such laws (Voas 1982a).

1. Methods

Until this past decade, blood tests were used almost exclusively in European DUI enforcement programs. In the United States, however, the breath test, first used for medical purposes by Bogen in 1927, has become the principal method for forensic analysis, primarily because of Borkenstein's development of a relatively simple photometric device that he named the "Breathalyzer." The current NHTSA (1986b) "Conforming Products List" includes fourteen manufacturers and thirty-nine models of breath-test devices. Some of these are no longer on the market. Dubowski (1986) lists ten evidential breath-test devices currently being marketed in the United States. The reader interested in the development and testing of breath-test devices and the state policies on their maintenance and operation should consult the manual prepared by the National Safety Council on "Alcohol and the Impaired Driver" (1976) and a recent review of this subject by Dubowski (1986).

2. Operational Issues

Because per se legislation makes the breath-test result the principal issue in a DUI trial, the test and testing procedures have come under considerable legal pressure in the last few years. The test is the only thing that the defense can attack, and because chemical tests tend to be esoteric to the laymen on a jury, there is often considerable latitude for the defense to raise doubts about the accuracy of the breath-test results. Some of the issues that have received the greatest attention in recent years include the following:

Blood versus Breath Tests. The earliest forensic tests were performed on blood samples and when breath tests began to be used, the results were expressed in terms of blood alcohol content, using a 2100 to 1 volume ratio. This procedure proved to be unfortunate because it permitted several challenges regarding the correlation between breath and blood alcohol concentration. In actuality, the measure of interest is the alcohol content of the brain, which cannot be measured directly, but must be inferred from the blood sample taken from a vein in the arm or from a deep-lung air sample. This problem has been partially resolved by rewriting DUI legislation to establish per se levels in terms of both measures: the Uniform Vehicle Code (Section 11-902.1[a]5), now states that "Alcohol concentration shall mean either grams of alcohol per 100 milliliters of blood or grams of alcohol per 210 liters of breath."

Contaminants. The possibility has frequently been raised that the test result might be influenced by substances in the breath other than alcohol. However, extensive testing in the laboratory and in the field has demonstrated that the breath of healthy persons contains no contaminants to which the devices currently in use respond to an extent that would produce a spuriously high result. Acetone, a product present in the breath of diabetics and allegedly in some individuals on special diets, has frequently been raised as a source of interference, particularly in infrared devices. A number of studies (summarized by Dubowski 1986) clearly demonstrate that acetone is rarely found in enforcement operations, and does not present a significant problem in evidential breath testing.

Radio Interference. Another challenge to the use of evidential breath-test devices was that their readout could be affected by radio-frequency interference from police communication equipment. This issue caused considerable consternation, and, at one point, prosecution of DUI cases was completely curtailed in some states. Improved shielding and grounding of test equipment as well as rules regarding the location of breath-test equipment relative to radio transmission equipment corrected the problem. Moreover, extensive tests have demonstrated that the units currently in use showed no measurable effects from radio-frequency interference over frequencies from 46 to 850 megahertz.

Operational Procedures. Dubowski (1986, 24) notes that "no (DUI) case has ever been overturned on the basis of recognizably faulty science, i.e., by rejection of the scientific principles employed in forensic alcohol analysis, although many reversals have resulted from the failure of law enforcement agencies to adhere to established technical or administrative procedures or to necessary scientific safeguards." To help ensure that proper procedures are followed and to minimize the possibility that the officer could produce a spurious result through error or intention, most states now require that testing equipment be automated so that the device operates on a prescribed testing procedure and requires the whole procedure to be repeated if any step is not performed correctly. Once the test procedure is completed, the device prints a tamper-proof report. As a result, the tests conducted as part of the DUI enforcement process tend to be highly reliable. The principal factor left to administrative supervision that could prejudice the result is ensuring that there has been a twenty-minute wait prior to testing to prevent the result from being affected by residual mouth alcohol.

Evidential breath-test devices have been developed to a high level of sophistication and accuracy. Small portable units that can operate on battery power or on a police car's electrical system already exist. There is a trend toward smaller equipment that is easier to use at the roadside. The extent to which this trend continues will depend upon the ability of police departments to adequately train operators and to supervise the use of such equipment in the field.

V. Technology in Court Operations

Once arrested and charged, the DUI suspect must be processed through the courts efficiently, and, if found guilty, given a sentence likely to prevent recidivism. Unfortunately, because DUI is the nation's most frequently committed crime and the courts are overloaded with cases, plea bargaining is frequently permitted in order to speed prosecution and avoid court backlogs (Ross 1983; Voas 1982a). The speed with which DUI cases must be handled (in some urban areas, a single judge may hear over a hundred cases a day) places a premium on the efficient collection of background data from court records, police files, and the state driver-record system. Background records are important in identifying offenders who are "problem drinkers" in need of treatment, in lieu of traditional sentences such as incarceration. Technology plays an important role in maintaining accurate records of offenders and in assessing their drinking problems.

Studies of drinking drivers in crashes (Filkins, Clark, Rosenblatt, Carlson, Kerlan, and Manson 1970; Perrine, Waller, and Harris 1971;

Waller 1967) have found evidence of prior alcohol-related problems and physical signs of symptomatic drinking, such as fatty liver changes (Waller 1967). These data suggest that a significant portion of these drivers may be classified as "problem" drinkers. This notion is supported by the very high (average 0.20 percent) BACs found among fatally injured drivers with alcohol. More extensive studies of drinking status have been conducted on drivers arrested for DUI than on fatally injured drivers. The Alcohol Safety Action Projects (ASAP) stimulated the use of alcohol education and treatment programs (Nichols, Weinstein, Ellingstad, Struck-Johnson, and Reis 1980) and the development of questionnaires for use by court personnel to identify problem drinkers (Filkins, Mortimer, Post, and Chapman 1973). During the ASAP period, these screening methods were used to classify into "problem drinker," "social drinker," and "unidentified" or "intermediate" drinker categories over 125,000 arrested drivers (Weinstein 1978). Validation of this classification scheme was limited by the lack of standard criteria for problem drinking. However, some validity was demonstrated by the finding that the recidivism rate for problem drinkers was twice that of social drinkers (Nichols et al. 1980).

Eagleston et al. (1975) and Ferguson and Kirk (1979) studied convicted drinking drivers entering treatment programs and found that they were consuming less alcohol, were less impaired, and more likely to be employed than patients entering treatment from other sources. Vingilis (1983) has published an extensive review addressing the question of whether alcoholics and drinking drivers are from the same population. She concludes that drinking drivers are not from the same population, but that 30 to 50 percent may fit the general nonspecific definition of alcoholism.

As a result of the general acceptance of the proposition that at least a portion of DUI offenders are problem drinkers, alcohol treatment programs have become a standard part of the sanctioning of these offenders. Studies of the effect of such programs on recidivism (Nichols et al. 1980; Reis 1982) indicated, as would be expected, that the length and content of the treatment program should be based on the extent to which the offender demonstrates a drinking problem. This requires that a procedure be established for identifying problem drinkers among convicted DUIs prior to sentencing. This presents a significant problem, because the courts lack health personnel trained in alcohol problems to make these assessments, and the heavy court caseload leaves little time for interviewing and testing offenders.

To provide measurement devices for court presentence investigators to identify problem drinkers in a short period of time, NHTSA funded the development of a psychometric questionnaire called the Mortimer-Filkins (M-F) Test (Mortimer, Filkins, Kerlan, and Lower 1973; NHTSA 1986c). The questionnaire was developed in the early 1970s for NHTSA and was used in most of the ASAPs as a court-ordered procedure to aid in identifying problem drinking drivers among the drivers convicted (but not yet sentenced) for DUI. Presentence investigators in the ASAPs attempted to classify drivers as either "problem drinkers" or "social drinkers" for sentencing and referral purposes. Mann, Leigh, Vingilis, and De Genova (1983) have published a critical review of the studies of the Mortimer-Filkins, and two validation studies (Ennis and Vingilis 1981; Wendling and Kolody 1982) of the Mortimer-Filkins Test have been conducted. Jacobson (1975) has provided an overall review and description of the available screening and diagnostic tests for identifying problem drinkers.

Overall, the M-F test and similar interview and questionnaire procedures have shown promise as tools for initial identification of problem drinking. However, scoring the self-report form and conducting the interview of the Mortimer-Filkins requires approximately forty minutes' time. Many court presentence investigators complain that they have as little as ten minutes per client because of the crowded court dockets. As a result, many presentence reports are based only on very brief questionnaires such as the Michigan Alcohol Safety Test (MAST, Selzer 1971) or simple record checks. If treatment for problem drinking is to be used effectively as a court sanction the available technology for quickly identifying the problem drinker will have to be improved, or a method found for diagnosing drinking status outside the court.

VI. Applying Technology to Penalties

Once a DUI has been convicted the court has the opportunity to apply a set of penalties best calculated to promote the rehabilitation of the offender as well as protect public safety by reducing the possibility that the individual will drink and drive in the future. The most effective penalties appear to be suspension of the driver's license and treatment for alcohol problems (Peck, Sadler, and Perrine 1985a; Sadler and Perrine 1984; Reis 1982; Mann et al. 1983). Other penalties commonly applied to DUIs have not been demonstrated to be effective in reducing recidivism (Voas 1986a and 1986b).

A. Using Jail Sentence for Diagnosis

Siegal (1985) (Siegal and Rudisill 1984) has developed an intensive diagnosis and referral program as an alternative to the mandatory short-term jail sentences that seventeen of the fifty states (NHTSA 1986b) provide for first-offense drunken drivers. This program offers an opportunity to compensate for the lack of court time for classifying the drinking status of DUI offenders by using the two or three days that would have been spent in jail to collect detailed information on the drinking behavior, to begin the process of breaking through the individual's denial mechanisms, and to develop an individualized treatment program. Further development of this assessment technique in a group setting appears to be desirable based on the preliminary results of an evaluation of this program (Siegal 1986).

B. Monitoring Drinking

Adequate coverage of the many treatment techniques applied to drinking drivers would go well beyond the space limits available for this chapter. The interested reader should consult the excellent review by Mann et al. (1983) of rehabilitation programs for drinking drivers. Aside from the therapeutic procedures themselves, technology has mainly been applied in the control of drinking by individuals in treatment.

1. ANTABUSE

A number of court programs (Marco and Marco 1980) have provided for supervised administration of Antabuse in an effort to ensure that DUI offenders do not drink during periods when they are on probation and receiving treatment. Reis (1982) found that the therapists in the programs which he evaluated felt that individuals on Antabuse were easier to work with and made more progress in therapy. However, he reported that half the offenders dropped out of the program even though this exposed them to additional sanctions. In the end he was not able to conclude that those on Antabuse had lower recidivism records. Temer, Peck, Perrine, and Borok (1986) found that supervised use of Antabuse was less effective in reducing recidivism among multiple-offender DUIs than attendance at Alcoholics Anonymous meetings.

2. BREATH TESTING

Prearrest breath-test devices such as the Alcosensor have been widely used to monitor drinking by individuals attending treatment sessions. Most therapists use these test devices only when they suspect drinking, so that some of their clients may continue to drink without the therapists' knowledge. More routine monitoring of drinking could be accomplished by using a passive sensor system placed at the entrance to the treatment agency. Even this procedure, however, monitors drinking only on the one or two days a week the offender attends treatment.

3. BLOOD TESTS

BAC is correlated with the immediate or acute effects of alcohol. There is evidence that some blood constituents, particularly liver enzymes, provide an indicator of heavy, chronic drinking. Tests for these substances have received some attention for monitoring the drinking of convicted offenders and evaluating their progress in treatment. One enzyme, gamma glutamyltranspeptidase (GGT) (Teschke, Brand, and Strohmeyer 1977), which is correlated with, but not specific for, alcohol-related liver injury, has been used by a California treatment agency to monitor the drinking of DUIs participating in treatment programs (Temer, personal communication). Their results leave some question as to the effectiveness of this test as a method of monitoring heavy drinking. Use of such physiological approaches to monitoring drinking may require a more complete battery of tests such as the one developed by Ryback, Eckardt, and Raulter (1979). Whether blood constituents can ultimately provide a method of tracking longer-term drinking practices remains to be determined.

C. In-Home Monitoring

Recently, an interesting alternative to incarceration that is applicable to DUIs has been used in some communities for monitoring offenders on parole or probation. Electronic monitoring systems, which employ a small transmitter attached to the arm or leg of the offender, are being used to verify that an offender is at home or at work as required by the terms of probation. A recent report by Ford and Schmidt (1985) for the National Institute of Justice lists six such units being tested in five states.

These devices provide an interesting alternative to the jailing of DUIs. Incarceration has been found to be ineffective in reducing recidivism and involves some risk of injury to the drunken driving offender who is sometimes victimized by the more hardened criminals with whom he or she may be imprisoned (Voas 1986a; NHTSA 1986b). Jail is not effective in reducing the risk of crash involvement because the period of incarceration is too short. Requiring the offender to remain at home at night, when most drinking and driving occurs, should serve to protect the public by reducing driving opportunities and may also support treatment objectives by reducing drinking opportunities. Because the individual lives at home and continues to work, the cost of this system of supervision is much less than jail and can be applied for a longer period of time. The evaluation of this penalty in conjunction with treatment for multiple DUI offenders should be undertaken as soon as possible.

D. Supervision of License Suspension

Even though most DUIs whose licenses are suspended continue to drive, research indicates that they have fewer total accidents and traffic citations than comparable groups of offenders who are not suspended (Peck, Sadler, and Perrine 1985a). In general, the reduction in accidents is greater for non–alcohol-involved accidents than for alcohol-related accidents. Considerable effort has been expended in studying ways in which license suspension might be supervised to prevent unlawful driving.

1. TRADITIONAL METHODS OF CHECKING DRIVERS' LICENSES

Driving with revoked or suspended licenses occurs because there is no way for police in an urban area to detect a suspended driver other than by stopping the individual for a traffic offense or at a checkpoint. Thus, the probability of detection is very low. Moreover, even when a driver is apprehended, conviction may be avoided because the state cannot prove that the offender received adequate notice since suspension notices are frequently sent through the mail rather than served by a sheriff's deputy. Because few are caught and convicted, deterrence is low and most offenders soon learn they can drive with relative impunity.

NHTSA (1970) funded a comprehensive study of the enforcement of driver's license suspensions and revocations that considered both traditional enforcement procedures and technological solutions to this problem. With respect to traditional enforcement, this report notes that at the time of the study somewhere between one in twenty and one in eighty police traffic contacts resulted in a license check. Thus, less than 10 percent of drivers have their licenses checked each year. Obviously, this rate of license checking could be greatly increased if police departments adopted the policy of checking the license of every driver who comes in contact with a police officer for whatever reason.

2. AUTOMATED LICENSE CHECKING SYSTEMS

NHTSA's report analyzed the motor-vehicle traffic enforcement system and concluded that the number of licenses checked, and therefore the proportion of unlicensed drivers detected, could be greatly increased by equipping police officers with improved communication equipment with which to interrogate license files. Even larger numbers of licenses could be checked using automated observation and checking systems. However, this would be expensive, and would encounter considerable legal and political opposition.

Some appreciation for the problem of enforcing license suspensions can be gained by considering the numbers involved. According to the Federal Highway Administration, in 1984 there were 172 million vehicles registered, and 155 million drivers licensed, in the United States. These records were spread through the files of the fifty states with some drivers holding licenses in more than one state. The proportion of the driving population that does not hold valid permits at any given time is not known but certainly is at least 1 to 3 percent of all motorists. Unlicensed drivers include those who have never applied for licenses, those who are late in renewing their licenses, and those suspended for failure to demonstrate financial responsibility, as well as those suspended for DUI or other serious law violations. A comprehensive system designed to detect individuals operating while suspended requires four elements: (1) a reference number (tag) for each driver and vehicle, (2) a system for sensing that reference number, (3) a system for transmitting the number and checking it against a reference file, and (4) the construction and maintenance of an appropriate reference file.

Tagging Vehicles and Drivers. Currently vehicles carry two identification numbers—the VIN or engine number applied at the manufacturer's plant and the state vehicle registration number. In addition, the driver has a state driver license number. Only the vehicle license plate is visible to the public. To identify a suspended driver using the vehicle license tag requires checking the number through the vehicle file, identifying the owner, and then checking the driver license file to see whether the owner is validly licensed. Alternatively, a special file of the tag numbers of vehicle owners with revoked licenses can be established. In either case, vehicle tag numbers must be observed and recorded at random at the roadside in an effort to detect the one to three in a hundred who may be suspended.

It has been frequently proposed that some special label should be placed on the cars owned by convicted drinking drivers. Although Minnesota and Ohio have experimented with issuing special license plates for violators, these provisions have not been widely used. To issue a special plate the court must impound the regular plates which usually requires a special hearing. Even when the court impounds the plate only about 5 percent of the offenders request such special tags. Many offenders may find other ways to get regular tags (for example, by reregistering the car in another family member's name).

Tagging the offender's vehicle with a label that clearly indicates that the owner has been suspended finds favor in some quarters as an appropriate punishment for drunken driving. In general, however, legislatures have been slow to adopt such procedures out of concern for the effect of this "scarlet letter" on innocent family members. Therefore, labeling schemes that do not call public attention to the driver, but make it easier for the police to identify vehicles belonging to suspended drivers, are more likely to be politically acceptable. Such systems might include a normal-appearing license plate with a code known only to the police, or a radio transmitter that responds to an electronic signal from the police vehicle. Such systems might not only indicate that the vehicle is owned by a suspended driver but also describe the prohibited driver (for example, male, age forty) so that the police could determine whether to stop the vehicle.

Sensing Vehicle or Driver License Numbers. The principal system for sensing a vehicle or driver identification number is the human eye. Because driver licenses are not available unless the driver is stopped, NHTSA proposed that consideration be given to placing the driver's license in a holder on the windshield when the individual was operating the vehicle. Funds were set aside for a field trial of this procedure but no state was willing to participate. The system was opposed beause it was viewed as an invasion of privacy, though the nuisance factor of having to take out and replace the license each time the vehicle was operated also played a role.

It is possible to develop electronic methods for sensing the vehicle registration numbers (NHTSA 1970). Some involve transponders on all cars (perhaps built into the license plate) that would respond to low-frequency induction signals from roadway transmitters. Others would involve no modification of the vehicles but would require automatic equipment at the roadside to record the vehicle tag number and the driver's face on film or videotape. Photography at nighttime (when most drinking and driving occurs) would be difficult unless special systems were used. All of these systems would involve considerable expense for equipment and field operations, and would certainly raise concern over personal privacy and other legal issues.

Transmitting Data and Interrogating Files. Several companies[8] already provide keyboard entry and digital communications devices for police vehicles that can be used to transmit license numbers to a control point for record checks (Nailen 1967). Once received, these messages must be directed to the correct location, the inquiry processed, and a response generated and relayed back to the police car. Traditionally, this process has been handled by voice messages from the officers in the field to a dispatcher at police headquarters who relays the information to the record center. This procedure may be adequate when the licenses of suspects already stopped and detained are to be checked. But it is far too slow to be used to identify vehicles in the traffic flow that are being driven by suspended drivers. By using the digital entry and transmission system and providing for the message to go directly to the central computer for processing, it is possible to receive a reply within a few seconds.

Using this system, police officers patrolling the highway can enter the vehicle tag number of cars at random and determine whether the vehicle belongs to a suspended operator in time to stop the car and interview the driver. The Insurance Institute for Highway Safety (Miller 1978) funded a test of this type of system called "TAGS" and found that it could be more successful in apprehending suspended drivers than traditional enforcement procedures. Using the TAGS system in Maryland, 9.6 offenders were identified per officer hour, compared to only .5 offenders per officer hour using traditional patrol methods. O'Neall and Crancer (1969) applied a random observation technique in Washington and found that 4 percent of their checks yielded either a stolen car or suspended driver. This could provide a very efficient apprehension technique if license checks can be made rapidly enough— for instance, one every thirty seconds. Much more rapid checking rates could be obtained by automatic equipment that could read license plates and transmit numbers to the central file, with information on suspects being transmitted to patrol cars.

Constructing Data Files. For any of these systems to function effectively, an up-to-date computerized file of vehicle and driver license information must be available. Developing such files presents major problems. Sheer size of the data base is a major factor in the larger states (California has over sixteen million records in its driver file). Out-of-state residents, which in some areas may run as high as 10 percent or more of the drivers on the road, present another significant problem. There is no *national* driver license registry, and passing information on offenses committed in one state by residents of another is, in many areas, unreliable, depending upon the effectiveness of local agreements ("compacts") between states and on the quality of the data system in those states.

Multiple licenses for a single driver also present a problem since operators suspended in one state can frequently obtain a license in a neighboring state. To prevent this, Congress established the National Driver Register (NDR). Participating states send identity information on suspended drivers to the NDR, which keeps them on file and provides the states with a source for checking new license applicants moving into the state to determine whether they have been suspended in another state. After considerable debate regarding the privacy issues presented by a centralized national file of suspended drivers, Congress approved an appropriation for automating the NDR so that states can transmit names of license applicants electronically and be referred to the appropriate state file when a motorist has been suspended in another state. The value of the NDR is limited by the failure of some states to participate by forwarding the names of drivers suspended or by failure to go to the expense of checking all their new license applicants.

The delays and inaccuracies that occur in court reports to the motor-vehicle departments, and the delays that may occur in processing records at the state level are another limitation in the data systems on which any automated checking system must be based. All in all, the problem of maintaining accurate and up-to-date files that can be rapidly interrogated by electronic means may be one of the more difficult problems to overcome in employing automated technology for checking licenses.

Recording Vehicle Operation. Because of the potential cost of these automated or semiautomated systems, considerable interest has been shown in devices that control the use of vehicles by convicted DUIs directly such as the Drunk-Driver Warning Systems discussed earlier. Another approach to direct control of driving by the DUI offenders is the Autotimer concept (Voas 1984c). This device is similar to the recorders used on commercial trucks and buses. It is a sealed, shoebox-sized unit with its own power source that does not interfere with the operation of the vehicle, but does make a record of when the car is used by combining a timer with a motion sensor. This device, which is locked on to the vehicle, is read once a month by a probation officer. With this unit, a court can supervise the driving by an offender who is given a limited license to drive to and from work but at no other time. The present investigator has received a grant from the National Institute for Alcohol Abuse and Alcoholism (NIAAA) to conduct a field study on the effectiveness of the Autotimer device in reducing the recidivism of one thousand drivers. Participating drivers will be given a limited license, to drive to and from work, in return for allowing this device to be placed on their cars. Their driving records will be compared with an equal number of drivers who receive full driving suspensions.

VII. Summary and Conclusions

From the material presented in this chapter, it should be clear that a large number of technological devices and procedures exist or are under development that can be applied to the drunken driving problem. This chapter has been devoted primarily to describing these techniques, rather than presenting an analysis of the social and political implications of their use. As in most areas of technological development, the speed with which the devices come into common use will depend upon the public demand for them.

Although there has been a significant increase in the consumption of "lite" or low-alcohol beverages, there has been no indication, so far, that the public will purchase personal breath testers, sober pills, or automobile interlocks. Most of the technology applied to the drinking-driving problem to date has been in enforcement or corrections, and, even here, the public has been ambivalent on the extent to which nonoffenders should be exposed to surveillance (as in sobriety checkpoints or radar speed traps) in an effort to reduce drunken driving. In addition to the problem of attracting sufficient public support to create a market for alcohol safety products, manufacturers face a significant problem in obtaining liability insurance.

A problem for those concerned with traffic safety is whether the adoption of these safety procedures or devices will result in the expected reduction in death and injury on the highway. Experience with other safety devices (use of safety belts, for example) indicates that they will be used by those who are least likely to be involved in accidents, so that while they provide a benefit to the user, the overall impact is less than would be expected if high-risk drivers used them with equal frequency. There is also a body of theory suggesting that individuals drive so as to maintain a constant perceived level of risk (risk homeostasis: Wilde 1976). If using a safety belt makes drivers feel safer, they may increase their level of risk-taking by driving at higher speeds or less carefully. Whether safety products such as low-alcohol beverages, sober pills, or BAC information might have such an effect is unknown. There is, for example, some basis for concern that knowledge of BAC might have an undesired effect on the moderate drinker. When driving after drinking, light drinkers may attempt to compensate by driving more carefully, because they assume that they are at or beyond the legal BAC limit. However, if given the opportunity to measure their BAC, they may come to realize that they are well below the limit, and they might drink more or compensate less.

The value of these technological innovations for traffic safety is generally unknown. Also unknown is their value in reducing alcohol problems outside the drinking-driving area. If low-alcohol beverages, sober pills, or BAC information reduce the incidence of alcoholism, or alcohol problems generally, then these technologies are likely to be implemented irrespective of their highway safety benefits. The risk, as always, is that these products will get widespread use prior to an adequate evaluation of their benefit (or threat) to public health and safety.

14 Law, Society, and the Drinking Driver: Some Concluding Reflections

Franklin E. Zimring

This volume attempts to summarize knowledge of social control of the drinking driver at an interesting historical moment in the United States and in many other Western nations. Nearly two decades have passed since policy toward driving under the influence of alcohol became an issue of governmental responsibility throughout the Western world. We thus have the opportunity to assess public policy toward drunk driving at mid-career.

Involvement of government agencies in the problems generated by drunk driving is as old as traffic law enforcement. But prior to the mid-1960s, with the exception of Scandinavia, it nowhere seemed necessary for governments to develop what could be called national-level drunk-driving policy, to debate policy alternatives, or to evaluate specific countermeasures or approaches. Driving while intoxicated was a crime. The law was enforced as an undifferentiated part of police traffic-enforcement strategy. The nature of legislation and the circumstances of its enforcement were rarely the concern of those in Western government who make and debate what are regarded as public policy decisions at the national level.

All that has changed. Traffic law policy is now both significant and controversial in many Western democracies and important in the United States for the federal government and the states.

Whatever the multiple reasons for this evolution, it cannot be attributed to a recent increase in the problem as objectively measured. The toll of alcohol-related accidents was astonishingly high in 1965, but probably no greater than for 1955 in the United States and many Western nations, and the death rate was lower in 1965 on a per-mile basis. But the costs of alcohol-related accidents, although always great, were not always known. One reason for the increased salience of the issue in recent decades has been the documentation of the extent of the problem that was accomplished by medical and social scientists from mid-century onward.

A second contribution to the growth of alcohol and traffic safety as a public policy problem was a growing belief that government policies could control traffic accidents generally and drunken driving behavior specifically. For four decades, the enormous toll of death and injury that occurred in the United States was regarded as accidental in almost a cosmic sense. The statistical toll of road accidents was collected and reported with an air of fatalism similar to attitudes toward earthquakes, tornadoes, or other natural disasters.

At the same time, the implicit causal model and the paradigm of responsibility began and ended with the personal fault of the parties to the accident. Unlike our attitude toward a hurricane, we traditionally searched for a human agent to blame for bad outcomes on the highway. But that human agent was "the nut behind the wheel" in the words of the National Safety Council. And if this individual nut-behind-the-wheel was the sole cause of our highway safety carnage, instrumentalities of government could not be held responsible for the occurrence of such harms.

The public perception now in the United States and throughout the Western world is that the manner in which roads are constructed, emergency medical services are provided, and laws are drafted and enforced can have important effects on highway deaths and injuries. Indeed, it is possible that public perception of the controllability of loss rates from traffic circa 1987 is often exaggerated. Part of this change of attitude can be related to the growth of consumer awareness in Western nations and the expanding role of government in pursuit of safety, but much of the change in public and governmental attitudes is also a response to scientific data on drinking and driving.

After twenty years, alcohol and traffic safety has its own history as a public policy issue. Initial policies have been evaluated and modified. Some of the bright new ideas of 1968 have become orthodoxies; others have been discarded.

This historical moment gives us an opportunity to look for some of the less obvious effects of early policy initiatives because twenty years is long enough to reveal latent as well as manifest functions of policy innovation. Moreover, the novelty of drunk driving as a public policy issue will have worn off to some extent after two decades. Citizens have long considered drunk driving to be a governmental concern; indeed, it is now a problem that must compete with many others for resources and priority.

Further, the perception of controllability by government that comes with the discovery of a new problem of importance has now had some time to wear thin. It is, after all, only after government efforts in particular problem areas are launched that we confront the limits of government effectiveness. Two decades might be enough time for the public to decide, in part because of government's limited ability to have a positive impact, that drunk driving is not such a high priority after all. Has this happened? Will it?

The discussion that follows is organized, somewhat eccentrically, as a progression from the general to the specific. I begin with a statement of common themes noted in the many different nations discussed in this text. I then discuss developments in the United States and its many political subdivisions. I defer this discussion because an assessment of important influences in the United States can derive a great deal from comparison with social and governmental phenomena in Western Europe and the Commonwealth countries.

My final two headings might be regarded as specific to the point of parochialism. I deal first with the jurisprudence of drunk driving in Anglo-American law. Finally, I examine our experiences with drunk driving for lessons for the study of the impact of law on society.

The conclusions in my discussion are personal, but they nonetheless depend on the enormous learning that has been marshaled by the contributions to this volume. The contributors to this collection are thus blameless for any infelicities that follow, but their efforts were indispensable to my enterprise.

Cross-National Perspectives

We did not set out to conduct a comprehensive survey of the industrialized nations of the Western world in this volume. As a result, we have reports on the national experience of only ten countries, and these countries are certainly not a representative sample, even of industrial Western nations, with respect to drunk-driving policy. Still, a volume that reports on recent developments in the four Scandinavian countries, in two on the European continent, in Great Britain, Canada, and Australia, as well as the United States, generates cross-national data of some value. Further, examining countries with substantial histories of concern with the issue is of value for studying the persistence of concern with drunk driving and the evolutionary development of policy.

Two common characteristics of recent national experience are worthy of special attention: the continuing salience of the issue in each of the countries reported on and the tendency toward convergence in approach of the various national-level policies. By salience, I mean the continued importance of drunk driving in the national policy agenda of these countries. By convergence, I mean the tendency of each of these countries to move toward features of drunk-driving countermeasure policy common to the other countries in the sample. Thus, countries with sharply contrasting drunk-driving priorities and points of emphasis at the beginning of the 1970s—for example, the Scandinavians and the Australians—come more to resemble each other in officially announced strategies in recent years. And reform proposals for the future promise even greater convergence.

Over recent decades, drunk driving does not appear to follow a cyclical pattern as a policy problem in Western democracies. In none of the ten countries discussed in these pages is the problem of the drinking driver a lower public priority in recent years than in the mid-1960s, nor did these countries experience any significant downcycle in governmental concern over the drinking driver. In Norway, the drinking driver was a high priority problem in the mid-1960s, and has remained so in the 1980s. In Finland, where there was a lower priority on alcohol and traffic safety as a governmental problem in the 1960s, the problem is regarded as more salient in recent years.

In those countries with traditionally low levels of concern over alcohol and traffic safety (Canada, Australia, and the United States are the examples in our sample), the drinking driver is regarded as a much more serious problem in 1986 than in 1966.

In those countries where the drinking driver has always been regarded as a serious problem, it remains so. In those nations with more tolerant social and political climates for drinking and driving, the problem has received more attention and policy has become more stringent. Why is this? What does it bode for the future?

To some extent, the mobilization of public opinion has been partially responsible for the increased prominence of drunk driving as a public policy issue. This is a frequently cited factor in the United States in the 1980s with the advent of mother and student organizations against drunk driving functioning as lobbies for further resources and more punitive legislation at the state and federal levels.

But the tendency for increased public concern about the drinking driver is nowhere near as uniform as the tendency for increased importance of the issue in government. Even in the United States, it is difficult to separate public opinion as a cause as opposed to an effect of the increased attention focused on alcohol and traffic safety. A long governmental information campaign preceded the birth of grass-roots lobbying organizations. Historians may just as well consider Mothers Against Drunk Driving as an effect rather than a cause of increased governmental concern about drunk driving in recent years.

On the European continent and in the Commonwealth countries, governmental elites rather than the ordinary citizens seem to be the key actors in maintaining or creating governmental measures aimed at drunk driving. In the United States, a scientifically-oriented administrative bureaucracy at the federal level founded in the late 1960s had as a primary mission the continued priority of this area. Although the tactics advocated to combat the drinking driver have varied with the contrasting styles of the Johnson, Nixon, Ford, Carter, and Reagan presidencies, priority accorded to the drinking driver has remained a common element. And I would argue that the public relations campaign in the U.S. by the federal government was a resounding success, even though we seldom associate the state-level political action of the 1980s with these earlier federal initiatives.

In those Scandinavian countries with traditionally high levels of concern about the drinking driver, governmental elites may also have played a role in the continued salience of the drinking driver. But in Scandinavia, two other factors deserve mention. First, as reported by Johannes Andenaes, public opinion is of some importance in those countries with national histories of the most stringent controls over drunk driving, notably in Norway. Second, as Andenaes is perhaps too modest to report, throughout the Scandinavian countries, the continued public importance of drunk driving owes much to a tradition of scholarly concern that has made this topic among the most important to scholars of the sociology of law as well as scholars of criminal law, such as Andenaes. The prominent Scandinavian scholars now in their fifties and older have been a significant force in the continued national priority of this issue and have also shaped the direction of policy reform.

In Great Britain, the Commonwealth countries, and the United States, this impressive scholarship is one explanation of the increased prominence of the drinking driver in the 1970s and 1980s. Sociologists and legal academics in the United States, Canada, and Australia have taken note of the pioneering work of American public health scholars on alcohol and traffic safety and the work on deterrence reported by Professor Andenaes and his colleagues. Issue-shopping politicians throughout the Western world have also noticed this work. In the United States, the salience of drunk driving received a major and permanent boost when one of the eminent public health practitioners, William Haddon, became an activist first in the federal bureaucracy and then in the automobile insurance lobby.

Civil servants and academic researchers in Australia and Canada in the late 1970s and early 1980s became responsible for replicating research on the connection between alcohol and traffic safety that had occurred much earlier in Scandinavia and somewhat earlier in the United States. To the extent that there is convergence in the priority of this aspect of highway safety or criminal justice programs, it is in part because policymakers have been reading the same data for a substantial period of time. The pen thus seems as mighty as the public opinion poll in the recent transnational career of this issue.

The convergence I speak of goes beyond discovery or maintenance of the drinking driver as a high priority in social control. There seems an emerging consensus, at least among governmental and scholarly elites, on an appropriate strategy toward drinking drivers, a consensus toward the moderately punitive.

The major elements of a moderately punitive approach include:
1. The use of the criminal law as the major governmental weapon against drunk driving;
2. The adoption of low per se limits for blood alcohol;
3. The use of heavy fines and short jail terms as sanctions of choice for drunk drivers;
4. A reliance on detection efforts and publicity to increase the credibility of threats rather than on escalation of sanctions to enhance deterrence.

Although there are still great differences among the countries studied, this broad outline shows the enforcement strategy toward which each of the countries seems to be moving. Furthermore, although countries still differ on the critical issue of the proper use of incarceration as a sanction, the degree of convergence that has taken place is impressive.

In traditional low-priority jurisdictions, such as the United States and the Commonwealth countries, the movement toward enthusiastically enforced per se laws was the major trend of the last fifteen years. In Scandinavia, with a history of regarding drunk driving as a serious crime, recent emphasis has been on enhanced enforcement with some discussion beginning of reducing the current extent of reliance on confinement as a sanction.

Most of the important political forces at work on the reformulation of drunk-driving policy operate at the national or subnational level in individual countries. There is, however, a policy community in each country that is alert to developments in other countries. Drunk driving is thus a domestic political concern that increasingly operates from a transnational data base.

In most countries, policy communities concerned with traffic safety seem confident that the cost of accidents can be curtailed by governmental intervention. Despite the frustrations of many policy interventions in the last fifteen years, there is nowhere in the scholarly or policy community concerned with the drinking driver the equivalent of the "nothing works" consensus generated by those who studied rehabilitative effects of prison programs in the United States and Great Britain.

Substantial variations in the death rate from accidents from country to country and the probable impact of seat belts, speed limits, and gas shortages on traffic death rates in recent years seem to have fostered confidence in the potential of legal controls for impact on drunk driving. There is widespread, though by no means universal, approval of deterrence-based programs. There is more skepticism about therapeutic interventions for identified drinking drivers, yet governmental support for such treatment programs continues.

No single treatment strategy has been lately identified as particularly promising. Similarly, despite years of discussion about high-tech sobriety checks, the shifting patterns of governmental response in the last two decades have occurred without any major technological change at the tactical level. Although some improvement in sobriety testing and drunk-driving detection can be anticipated, there is no reason to suppose that a major breakthrough in either detection or treatment of drinking drivers will occur soon as a function of improved technology.

The countries surveyed seem to display an evolutionary optimism about the efficacy of enforcement strategies that are based on traditional elements of social condemnation, law enforcement, and punishment. In each of these countries, it appears that alcohol and traffic safety policies of the proximate future will display large degrees of continuity with existing programs. And this is not viewed as an occasion for regret.

The American Experience

The American fashion concerning crime and criminal justice is to regard the national experience of the United States as unique beyond the values of comparative analysis. There are, of course, special features of American society, government, traffic, and criminal justice that should inspire caution in the most devout comparativist. Still, a review of recent American experience in light of the cross-national picture provides evidence of strong linkages between trends in the United States and those of its neighbors in the Western world. Indeed, the degree of continuity between American patterns and those noted elsewhere provides some counsel against attributing too much influence to some peculiar American developments of the recent past.

Recent history in the United States is consistent with both the increased salience of drunk driving to the general public and relevant levels of government as well as a tendency toward convergence in which American jurisdictions are moving from a historical position of lower-than-average penal priority for drunk driving toward the paradigm of moderate severity.

Although the broad sweep of American experience over the last two decades is consistent with the greater prominence of the drunk-driving problem, there have been shifts in both the focus of reform activity and the specific policies being emphasized that also deserve attention. Over the decade from 1965 to 1975, the federal government was the almost exclusive source of governmental initiative in the area of alcohol and traffic safety. Establishment of the National Highway Traffic Safety Administration, provision of funding for programs and research, and publication of the *Alcohol and Traffic Safety Report* in 1968 were followed by somewhat more federalistic rhetoric and the substantial action funding of the Nixon-era High Impact programs. It is difficult to assemble a consensus history of what happened next in the half-decade from 1975 to 1980. The federal bureaucracy continued its development, and both research and action funding by the government occurred, but there was a relative de-emphasis from the High Impact program days in the executive branch of national government. There also seemed substantial sentiment during the Carter years to regard the High Impact initiative as a failure.

Renewed interest in drunk driving in the 1980s has involved new governmental actors and in many cases different levels of government. The administrative bureaucracy was the major source of innovation at the federal level prior to 1975. Congress played a much more important role by the early 1980s, as shown by the mandated twenty-one-year-old drinking age. State and local governments have emerged as more important arenas for legislative change in the 1980s than before, and the switch in focus to state government has been caused or been accompanied by innovations in grass-roots citizen organizations such as Mothers Against Drunk Driving (MADD) and Students Against Drunk Driving (SADD).

The contrast in style and content between William Haddon and MADD is substantial. There is thus a temptation to see recent historical patterns as the product of a conglomeration of different initiatives at different historical times that were substantially unrelated to each other. This characterization is probably incorrect. The consciousness-raising grass-roots activities of the 1980s probably owe a substantial debt to the consciousness-raising efforts of scholarly and bureaucratic elites in the late 1960s and early 1970s.

The isolation of the drinking driver as a problem and the perception that the volume of crashes attributable to this problem could be responsive to variations in policy were almost certainly the product of the earlier initiatives.

The "get tough" rhetoric of grass-roots organizations and the punitive cast of much state-level legislation is not so much an argument against its earlier federal ancestry as it is an observation about inevitable changes in style that happen when criminal justice initiatives trickle down from federal to state legislatures and from elites to the generally conservative crime-control ideology of local America.

Despite this punitive cast, most policy initiatives in recent American experience have been basically convergent with the cross-national trends described above. The extension of per se legislation, judicial and legislative enabling of testing regimes, the legitimation of administrative controls, and the raising of the minimum age for alcoholic beverage consumption to twenty-one have been the major policy initiatives of the early 1980s for drunk driving in the United States. Without exception they are in the tradition of the moderate punitive approach noted in many other countries.

This continuity raises the question of both the extent and the direction of the impact of grass-roots lobbies, such as MADD, which are to date peculiar to the American experience. If many of the same results were obtained in other countries without such organizations, perhaps the role of these organizations in the United States has been overstated.

The question is one that deserves more sustained empirical study and analysis than I can provide. My impression is, however, that grass-roots lobbying has been an important part of the explanation for the pace of legislative change in many American states, and perhaps even in the United States Congress. The inertial forces in the American federal system are substantial. Grass-roots organizations have probably played an extensive role in overcoming these forces.

However, the importance of these organizations in determining the specific content of proposals may be easy to overstate. No particular movement can claim credit for the fact that the direction of state legislative intervention in this area is toward "getting tough." That is almost the inevitable direction of state-level innovation when public opinion regards prohibited conduct as a threat to public safety. My guess is that citizen action groups are a more important explanation of the passage of legislation in the 1980s than they are of the specific content of legislation.

The Sociological Jurisprudence of Drunk Driving

The most substantial change in the status of drunk driving in the United States and throughout the Western world is not a matter of either law or technology, but one of social psychology. Driving while intoxicated, always a crime in the statute books, has come to be regarded in society as more of a "real crime" worthy of condemnation by the general public and punishment by the criminal justice system. The criminalization of this offense is an occasion for study of the conditions under which law can serve as an instrument of social change.

To students of law and society, the complex interaction between social attitudes and governmental acts is acknowledged as important and incompletely understood. In recent years, much attention has been paid to the legal and social processes of what is called decriminalization, the strategic withdrawal, de facto or de jure, of the criminal law from the regulation of a number of behaviors.

The formal abolition of criminal sanctions against attempted suicide in Great Britain, against homosexual acts throughout the Western world, and against many forms of gambling, as well as the sharp reduction of penalties and occasional de facto recognition of certain kinds of narcotics use, are frequently cited examples of the tendency toward decriminalization in recent years. The major focus of decriminalization has been what are termed victimless crimes, those which lack both a complaining witness and what a majority in society would regard as a victim (other than the willing perpetrator) who suffers palpable harm.

Driving while intoxicated is one of a relatively small list of traditionally marginal crimes for which public pressure to condemn the behavior and support rigorous criminal sanctions has increased in recent years. A short list of other such behaviors might include minor forms of political corruption, willful damage to the environment through water and air pollution, spousal abuse, and other kinds of family violence.

A series of parallel questions can be asked about both the decriminalization and criminalization of behaviors in democratic societies. To what extent is change within the law or the machinery of enforcement a cause as opposed to merely a consequence of shifts in social attitudes? Are there events or characteristics that distinguish those behaviors that will generate pressure for increasing condemnation and those that will appear attractive candidates for decriminalization?

The particular history of drunk driving in the United States over the period since 1965 is an interesting proving ground for social theories about determinants of criminalization and decriminalization. The movement to condemn drunk driving more sharply seems the product of a governmental education and information campaign at the federal level. The key changes in social attitudes were public perceptions that driving after drinking was both harmful and culpable behavior.

The hardening of public attitudes about the dangers of driving after drinking is due in part to scientific demonstrations linking elevated blood alcohol with automobile crashes. The American public always believed that drinking, or at least elevated levels of intoxication, increased the risk of automobile crashes. But the public view that a substantial amount, even a majority, of all traffic fatalities were attributable to drinking and driving is a relatively new element in the American scene. Parallel to this general awareness about the high cost of drunk driving, much of the public believes that individual acts of driving while intoxicated generate an unacceptably high risk of crash involvement. Indeed, there is reason to suspect that the statistical risk of a fatal or injurious accident stemming from a single act of drunken driving is overestimated by a substantial fraction of the American public.

Perceptions of the risk of drunk driving play an important role not only in notions about the harmfulness of the behavior, but also in the consensus judgment that persons who drive after drinking are morally culpable and thus deserving of punishment. The apparent lack of blameworthiness of driving after drinking if it did not cause a crash was a major obstacle to having drunk driving considered a serious crime. The noncrash episode of drinking and driving is victimless in two senses: no one complains and no one is injured. The culpability of the drinking diver is mitigated by the fact that although the behavior may be intended, no injury or harm is intended by the act of drinking and driving.

The basis for blaming the drinking driver, in the formal law and in the public consciousness, is that knowingly taking a substantial and unjustifiable risk that harm will occur is blameworthy—indeed, for some, almost the equivalent of intending harm. This perception seems to have become a core North American attitude toward driving while intoxicated, at least for blood alcohol levels beyond .10.

The high aggregate social cost of crashes from drinking and driving has produced a perception of individual act risk that is high enough for many people to regard the offense as a serious crime. To what extent there exists a gap between this social perception and the reality of the risk generated by various types of driving after drinking is not currently known. The issue is an admirable candidate for cross-national research.

But the need to place blame on the intention to behave in ways that generate risks is a common characteristic of two of the more successful criminalization campaigns of recent years, pollution and drunk driving. In each case, the government played an important part in changing public attitudes with information and propaganda. In both cases, the shifts in criminal justice policy may properly be seen as the effect of changes in social attitudes, but social attitudes themselves were influenced by governmental campaigns, and more particularly by dissemination of scientific data about harms, risks, and causes. This is a somewhat novel and potentially important sequence of events in the criminal law of a postindustrial age.

Methods of Assessing Legal Impact

A concluding note on issues in the assessment of legal impact might seem like sociological special pleading in a volume of this nature. Why, after all, should most of us be concerned about methods of assessing the impact of legal change on social behavior? Yet limitations on our capacity to study legal impact over the long range have had a major influence on recent discussion of the impact of criminal sanctions on drinking and driving. And the methodological story teaches a humbling lesson about our capacity to measure important consequences of legal change.

The semiparadox that concerns me is that we are better equipped to study the impact of sudden and discrete change over the short run than we are to assess the impact of multiphase policy shifts introduced over a number of years which take effect gradually and in sequences that are not capable of precise advance specification. Yet the mechanical processes we can measure with precision are far less important than the gradual and multiphasic adjustments that are the essence of evolving criminal justice policies in the real world.

One case study that illustrates this contrast is the debate about the impact of the package of legislative changes that evolved into the distinctive penal policy of the Scandinavian countries to drunk driving. H. Laurence Ross has shown that no single policy initiative in prior years could be tied to discrete changes in crash fatalities that were substantial enough to rule out chance variation as an explanation. From this finding, and the all-too-evocative title of "the Scandinavian Myth," some observers were tempted to conclude that Scandinavia's lower-than-average rates of driving while intoxicated and somewhat lower than typical rates of alcohol involvement in crash fatalities could not be tied to differential legal threats. Other scholars, including John Snortum and Harold Votey, disagreed. (Most of the major contributors to this debate are authors in these pages.)

Neither that debate nor the cumulative impact of Scandinavian criminal justice innovations on accident and death rates can be definitively resolved in these pages. However, we can learn a great deal, methodologically, from that debate about the best way to assess legal impact in real-world settings.

There is a pressing need to develop methods of assessing the impact of legal change over the long term, and not simply with respect to alcohol and traffic safety. Most important changes to the criminal law take place episodically over a long period of time and operate on a social order cumulatively. Further, once legal change is set firmly in place, it is not clear that its most significant impacts will occur close to the time in which change is initiated. Many changes in the law, particularly those that must themselves generate or reinforce social-attitude change before becoming fully effective, may cumulate slowly and in unpredictable patterns.

The interrupted time-series analysis, so well suited to one-time trend-shifting events, is plainly inadequate to the task of assessing impact over the long term of cumulative changes. Yet episodic and cumulative shifts are the most important sources of change to be studied, as we have seen in relation to topics such as white-collar crime, gun control, imprisonment policy, indeed almost all of the critical topics in the recent reform of criminal law. What to do?

This volume contains several instructive examples of developing methods to assess long-term impacts of multiply-caused changes. Both Professors Ross and Snortum, disputants in the Scandinavian Myth debate, illustrate some creative steps that can be taken toward the assessment of legal impact over the relatively long term. Professor Ross combines the time-series perspective of his work in the 1970s with multi-site comparisons throughout the British Commonwealth countries in his chapter. This comparative work can be of particular importance when convergent trends are noted.

Professor Snortum's pioneering use of survey research results, both cross-nationally and in the United States, shows how relatively soft indicators can be cumulated to make a strong case for changed conditions. The common denominator of these methods is what I would choose to call a triangulation of proof, the use of multiple methods, each individually imperfect, to study the same question. If the various, individually imperfect, methods are flawed for different reasons, the cumulative portrait that we assemble from multiple measurement grows progressively more reliable.

This triangulation-of-proof tactic will lead to the use of not only different statistical techniques in trying to assess the long-term legal impact, but also different measures than we ordinarily employ for short-term assessment. Because the variety of measures used will be specific to the area under study, students of impact in the long run had better be well informed about the specific behaviors they seek to assess. The economist, psychologist, or lawyer is not well equipped to study the changes wrought by drunk-driving policies until he or she is an expert in the social corralates of drunk driving in a particular jurisdiction. Ross's and Snortum's contributions to this volume provide models in this regard that law-related scholars could emulate for a variety of topics. For law-related scholarship, the contributions collected here may be as important as a model of assessing legal impact as for any other reason.

And issues of special interest to scholars need not be arcane or unimportant. Indeed, one of the significant lessons from two decades of alcohol and traffic safety policy studies is that scholarship counts. The facts and figures of social scientists have been building blocks for changes in policy on a transnational basis throughout much of the Western world. A scholarly community long involved in this study of the relationship between alcohol and traffic safety has now generated a worldwide market for its wares. All the greater is the obligation of scholarship to remain both rigorous and relevant in the coming years.

Notes

Chapter One

1. Concentrations of alcohol in body fluids and breath can be expressed in various units of measurement. In this paper, two conventional BAC units have been used: (1) milligram percent (mg%), which specifies milligrams of alcohol per 100 milliliters of blood or other fluid; and (2) percent weight-volume (% w/v), which specifies milligrams of alcohol per 0.1 milliliter of body fluid. These units correspond as follows: 50 mg% = 0.05% (w/v), 100 mg% = 0.10% (w/v), 150 mg% = 0.15% (w/v), etc.

Chapter Two

1. A more detailed account of legislation and practice in the Scandinavian countries is to be found in *Drinking and Driving in Scandinavia,* Scandinavian Studies in Criminology, vol. 1 (Oslo: Universitetsforlaget, 1978).

2. H. L. Ross, "The Scandinavian Myth: The Effectiveness of Drinking-and-Driving Legislation in Sweden and Norway," *The Journal of Legal Studies,* 4, no. 2 (June 1975): 285.

3. H. L. Ross, "Scandinavia's Drinking-and-Driving Laws: Do They Work?" *Drinking and Driving in Scandinavia* (see n. 1, pp. 55–60).

4. Tidsskrift for den norske Lægeforennig (Journal of the Norwegian Medical Association) 1933: 81.

5. Act of June 16, 1936, amending the Motor Vehicle Act of 1926. Of course, under the per se law, a driver with a BAC under 0.5 per mille may still be convicted for driving under the influence if the prosecution can demonstrate impairment.

6. Srensk forfattoings samling (SFS) 1941: 397.

7. Danish act of June 10, 1976; Finnish act of December 10, 1976.

8. Norwegian act of June 19, 1959.

9. Ibid.

10. H. L. Ross, "Law, Science, and Accidents: The British Road Safety Act of 1967," *The Journal of Legal Studies* 2, no.7 (January 1973).

11. *Norsk Retstidende,* 1979: 11.

12. Danish act of May 27, 1981.

13. The reform and its effect on sentencing are described by Tapio Lappi-Seppälä in *Lakimies*, 1982: 598–633, and J. Andenaes in *Lov og Rett*, 1982: 382–86.

14. Norwegian act of April 12, 1985, no. 18.

15. For a more detailed discussion, see J. Andenaes, "The Effects of Scandinavia's Drinking-and-Driving Laws: Facts and Hypotheses," *Drinking and Driving in Scandinavia*, (see n. 1 above, pp. 35–53).

16. J. Andenaes, "The General-Preventive Effects of Punishment," *University of Pennsylvania Law Review* 114 (1966); reprinted in *Punishment and Deterrence* (University of Michigan Press, 1974).

17. P. Christensen, S. Fosser, and A. Glad, *Promillekjøring og trafikksikkerhet* (Drunken Driving and Traffic Safety) (Oslo: Transportøkonomisk institutt [Institute of Transport Economics], 1978 [see Table 8]). Comparative tables for Norway, Sweden, and the United States are presented by J. R. Snortum in "Alcohol-Impaired Driving in Norway and Sweden: Another Look at 'The Scandinavian Myth,'" *Law and Policy* 6 (1984), 21, 23.

18. See A. Glad, *Research on Drinking and Driving in Norway* (Oslo: Transportøkonomisk institutt [Institute of Transport Economics], December 1985) for a survey of recent research on drinking and driving and on drinking drivers.

19. J. R. Snortum, R. Hauge, and D. E. Berger, "Deterring Alcohol-Impaired Driving: A Comparative Analysis of Compliance in Norway and the United States," *Justice Quarterly* 3, 2 (1986): 139–65, esp. 150.

20. J. Andenaes and R. K. Sørensen, "Alkohol og dødsulykker i trafikken" (Alcohol and fatal accidents in traffic), *Lov og Rett* 18 (1979): 83–109.

21. See n. 18 above.

22. Norwegian Official Statistics, *Criminal Statistics*.

23. For a more detailed analysis, see R. Hauge, "Drinking and Driving: Biochemistry, Law, and Morality," *Drinking and Driving in Scandinavia* (see n. 1 above, pp. 61–68).

24. As reported in H. Koch, "Politipatruljering og sprotkorsel," *Tidsskrift for dansk politi*, 1979: 344.

25. On a more general level, the problem is discussed in J. Andenaes, "The Moral or Educative Influence of Criminal Law," *Punishment and Deterrence* (see n. 16 above, pp. 110–28). See also J. R. Snortum, "Controlling the Alcohol-Impaired Driver in Scandinavia and the United States: Simple Deterrence and Beyond," *Journal of Criminal Justice* 12 (1984): 131–48.

26. See n. 23 above.

27. See n. 19 above.

28. Liikennejuopumus Työryhmän mietintö, Helsinki, 1985, 27–29; Table 2, 119; Table 7, 124.

29. See n. 2 above.

30. H. Laurence Ross, *Deterring the Drinking Driver* (Lexington, MA: Lexington Books, 1982), 60–63.

31. See n. 28 above, 29–30, and Table 2, 119.
32. See n. 20 above.
33. For more details, see J. Snortum, "Alcohol-Impaired Driving."
34. Quoted in Nordisk Trafikksikkerhetsrad, Rapport nr. 36 (Report No. 36 from Nordic Council for Traffic Safety), 1984, 28.
35. See n. 9 above.
36. SOU 1986:14 Påföljd för brott, vol. 1, 118; vol. 2, 375–79.
37. NOU 1987:11 Promillekjøring.
38. Ross, *Deterring the Drinking Driver,* 109–15.

Chapter Five

1. The informal and interactive elements in the social organization of DUI have been analyzed and studied by myself and associates, and are described in my review of social and cultural contexts of drinking-driving (Gusfield 1985).

2. Bibliographies on American drinking and alcohol control movements can be found in Jessup (1979), and Gusfield (1963 and 1986, chap 8).

3. For one of the very few studies that attempted to count drunkenness events, see Polich and Orvis (1979).

4. But see the critique of methods used in these studies in Vingilis and De Genova (1984).

Chapter Six

1. See, e.g., T. Dalton, *The State Politics of Judicial and Congressional Reform* (Westport, CT: Greenwood Press, 1985), 71: "Like education, law enforcement and the administration of criminal justice is considered a matter of local control; leadership of most of the major elements of local criminal justice (e.g., police, prosecutors and courts) is selected through general elections."

2. See E. Fisher, *Vehicle Traffic Law* (Evanston, IL: Traffic Institute, Northwestern University, 1964), 62: "It is now recognized that the power to regulate and control the use of the public roads and highways is primarily the exclusive prerogative of the states." In 1924, President Coolidge, addressing the Conference on Statistics, Traffic Control, Construction and Engineering, City Planning and Zoning, Insurance, Education, Motor Vehicle and Public Relations, stated: "Highway control is primarily for the states, and it is best that this is so." Quoted in N. Damon, "The Action Program for Highway Safety," *Annals of American Academy of Political and Social Science* 320 (November 1985): 15–26.

3. 23 U.S.C. § 109 (1982); see also 23 C.F.R. § 625.1–625.7 (1986) (outlining review procedures and policy). Since the inception of federal aid for highway construction, some federal agency or officer has had the responsibility of reviewing state construction plans. See Federal-Aid Road Act of 1916, Pub. L. 64-156, § 6, 39 Stat. 355, 356 (1916) (conferring review au-

thority on secretary of agriculture); see also C. Dearing and W. Owen, *National Transportation Policy* (Washington, DC: Brookings Institute, 1949), 108: "In the cooperative work with the states, the federal role is one of financial and engineering management, involving approval of state [highway] plans and specifications, supervision of construction, and inspection of projects."

4. California Vehicle Code § 23212 (West 1985).

5. See, e.g., California Vehicle Code § 23206 (West Supp. 1986).

6. Act of June 5, 1794, ch. 48, 1 Stat. 376 (1794); see also Deficit Reduction Act of 1984, Pub. L. 98–369, tit. I, § 27(a)(1), 98 Stat. 494, 507 (1984) (raising tax rate of distilled spirits from $10.50 to $12.50 per proof gallon) (codified at 26 U.S.C. § 5001(a)(1) (Supp. III 1985)).

7. See D. Meister, "Don't Increase Liquor's Load," *New York Times,* 24 April 1984, A26, col. 1 (Letter to the Editor) (arguing against proposition that increased taxes will reduce drunken driving).

8. Henrick v. Maryland, 235 U.S. 610, 622 (1915).

9. NLRB v. Jones & Laughlin Steel Corp., 310 U.S. 1, 41 (1937) (federal government has power to regulate labor relations at a manufacturing plant because a work stoppage "would have a most serious effect upon interstate commerce"). See generally L. Tribe, *American Constitutional Law* (1978), §§ 5-4, 5-5, at pp. 232–37 (Mineola, NY: Foundation Press).

10. Pub. L. 64-156, 39 Stat. 355 (1916).

11. U.S. Department of Transportation, *1968 National Highway Needs Report* (Washington, D.C.: Government Printing Office, 1968), 4.

12. U.S. Bureau of the Census, *Statistical Abstract of the United States 1984,* Table 1055 (Washington, DC: Government Printing Office, 1984), 610.

13. Pub. L. 85-684, 72 Stat. 635 (1958). One such compact is the Drivers License Compact.

14. Highway Safety Act of 1966, 80 Stat. 731 § 402(a).

15. The Supreme Court has upheld the power of Congress to attach conditions to states' receipt of federal funding. Oklahoma v. United States Civil Service Commission, 330 U.S. 127 (1947) (highway funding can be cut off for failing to remove members of state highway commission who violated Hatch Act).

16. See W. Haddon and M. Blumenthal, "Foreword," in *Deterring the Drinking Driver,* rev. and updated ed., ed. H. L. Ross (Lexington, MA: D. C. Heath and Co., 1984), xv–xvi; see also House Committee on Public Works, *Highway Safety Program Standards, Report from the Secretary of Transportation,* Print no. 7 (Washington, DC: Government Printing Office, 1967).

17. Emergency Highway Energy Conservation Act, Pub. L. 93-239, 87 Stat. 1046 (1974), *extended by* Federal-Aid Highway Amendments of 1974, 23 U.S.C § 154.

18. W. Haddon and M. Blumenthal, "Foreword," xvi.

19. Pub. L. No. 97-364, § 101(a), 96 Stat. 1738.

20. Presidential Commission on Drunk Driving, *Final Report* (Washington, DC: Government Printing Office, 1983), 10. The report also recommended that federal legislation be enacted to force states to comply with the commission's recommendation.

21. L. Pearl, "The Party's Over: Controlling Drunk Drivers," *Urban Lawyer* 17 (1985): 813–26.

22. P. Cook and G. Tauchen, "The Effect of Minimum Drinking Age Legislation on Youthful Auto Fatalities, 1970–77," *Journal of Legal Studies* 13 (1984):169–87.

23. Eight states have refused to raise their drinking ages: Colorado, Idaho, Louisiana, Montana, Ohio, South Dakota, Tennessee, and Wyoming. *Los Angeles Times,* 2 December 1986, I4. The Supreme Court rejected the states challenge to the statute in South Dakota v. Dole, 107 S. Ct. 2793 (1987).

24. Foreword to *Uniform Vehicle Code* (1962), iv.

25. House Committee on Public Works. *Highway Safety Program Standards, Report from the Secretary of Transportation,* Print no. 7 (Washington, DC: Government Printing Office, 1967).

26. National Highway Traffic Safety Administration, *National Committee on Uniform Traffic Laws and Ordinances, Traffic Laws Annotated* (Washington, DC: Government Printing Office, 1979), 356 app.

27. The precise limits contained in the Indiana legislation came from the conclusions of the National Safety Council and the American Medical Association in 1938. In 1960, these organizations lowered the permissible limit to .10 percent.

28. The Uniform Vehicle Code reduced the maximum level from .15 percent to .10 percent in 1962. In 1972, the Uniform Vehicle Code was amended to make driving with a BAC of .10 percent a per se offense.

29. S. Thompson, "The Constitutionality of Chemical Test Presumptions of Intoxication in Motor Vehicle Statutes," *San Diego Law Review* 20 (1983):301–38, esp. 316.

30. New York Vehicle and Traffic Law § 1194 (1960–1961).

31. Uniform Vehicle Code § 11-902(c).

32. National Highway Traffic Safety Administration, *A Digest of State Alcohol–Highway Safety Related Legislation,* 4th ed. (Washington, DC: Government Printing Office, 1986).

33. Kolender v. Lawson, 461 U.S. 352, 357 (1983); see also Lanzetta v. New Jersey, 306 U.S. 451, 453 (1939): "No one may be required at peril of life, liberty or property to speculate as to the meaning of penal statutes. All are entitled to be informed as to what the State commands or forbids."

34. Courts are much more stringent in evaluating vagueness challenges to legislation that "inhibit[s] the exercise of constitutional rights." Village of Hoffman Estates v. Flipside, Hoffman Estates, 455 U.S. 489, 499 (1982). Thus, if a statute regulates activities not protected by the Constitution, courts are more willing to accept less precise definitions of prohibited conduct.

35. Determining the precise level of blood alcohol concentration proves to be a difficult task. Countless variables affect BAC levels in any particular driver. Several factors have been identified as affecting blood alcohol concentration: gender, health, weight, amount of alcohol consumed, time between when drinking began and when test taken, rate at which drinks consumed, water content of the body, liver size, amount of carbonation in the drink, food consumption, history of alcohol consumption of the individual, and relative fat content of the individual.

36. See, e.g., Burg v. Municipal Court, 35 Cal. 3d 257, 673 P.2d 732, 198 Cal. Rptr. 145 (1983), *cert. denied,* 104 S. Ct. 2337 (1984); Roberts v. State, 329 So. 2d 296 (Fla. 1976); State v. Keista, 455 N.E.2d 1370 (Ohio Mun. 1983); Commonwealth v. Mikulan, 504 Pa. 244, 470 A.2d 1339 (1983); Graves v. State, 528 P.2d 805 (Utah 1974); State v. Franco, 96 Wash. 2d 816, 635 P.2d 1320 (1982).

37. Presumably, states could prohibit driving after consuming any amount of alcohol. Such a prohibition would be upheld as long as it was rationally related to a legitimate government objective. See 14 C.F.R. § 91.11 (1986) (Federal Aviation Administration prohibits crew members from serving on commercial flights within eight hours after consuming alcohol).

38. Burg v. Municipal Court, 35 Cal. 3d 257, 673 P.2d 732, 741, 198 Cal. Rptr. 145, 154 (1983), *cert. denied,* 104 S. Ct. 2337 (1984); see also Fuenning v. Superior Court, 139 Ariz. 590, 680 P.2d 121 (1983): "Those who drink a substantial amount of alcohol within a relatively short period of time are given clear warning that to avoid possible criminal behavior they must refrain from driving."

39. 397 U.S. 358, 364 (1970).

40. See Ulster County Court v. Allen, 442 U.S. 140, 156 (1979).

41. *Id.* at 156, 157. The Supreme Court held that a permissive presumption that fulfills this test does not alter the burden of proof required of the prosecution. The permissive presumption does not shift the burden of proof to the defendant.

42, *Id.* at 166–67.

43. Heiner v. Donnan, 285 U.S. 312, 329 (1932).

44. Vlandis v. Kline, 412 U.S. 441, 451 (1973).

45. State v. Daranda, 388 So. 2d 759 (La. 1980).

46. See State v. Dacey, 138 Vt. 491, 418 A.2d 856 (1980); State v. Vick, 104 Wis. 2d 678, 312 N.W.2d 489 (1981).

47. See Coxe v. State, 281 A.2d 606 (Del. 1971); State v. Torrey, 32 Or. App. 439, 574 P.2d 1138 (Or. Ct. App. 1978); State v. Franco, 96 Wash. 2d 816, 639 P.2d 1320 (Wash. 1982).

48. See Commonwealth v. Neal, 392 Mass. 1, 464 N.E.2d 1356 (1984).

49. One commentator has explained the process of calculating blood concentrations from breath samples:

> Breath test machines actually measure the concentration of alcohol in the breath sample. Because it is assumed that the ratio of alcohol

in blood to breath is a constant, namely 2100:1, the amount of alcohol in the breath is simply multiplied by 2100 to arrive at the extrapolated amount estimated to be in the blood. Most breath test machines are designed to automatically make the extrapolation.

S. Thompson, "The Constitutionality of Chemical Test Presumptions of Intoxication in Motor Vehicle Statutes," *San Diego Law Review* 20 (1983):301–38, 323.

50. Armstrong v. Manzo, 380 U.S. 545, 552 (1965).

51. Mackey v. Montrym, 443 U.S. 1, 10 (1979).

52. See Mathews v. Eldridge, 424 U.S. 319, 335 (1976).

53. See, e.g., Ferguson v. Guthright, 485 F.2d 504 (7th Cir. 1973), *cert. denied*, 415 U.S. 933; *In re* Campbell, 250 N.W.2d (S.D. 1977) (absence of *Miranda* warnings during arrest irrelevant in license revocation proceeding).

54. See, e.g., Wells v. Malloy, 402 F. Supp. 856, 858 (D. Vt. 1975).

55. See Mackey v. Montrym, 443 U.S. 1, 10 (1979) (state must provide due process of law to driver's license suspensions because it involves "a protected property interest"); see also Dixon v. Love, 431 U.S. 105, 112 (1977); Bell v. Burson, 402 U.S. 535, 539 (1971): "Once licenses are issued, . . . their continued possession may become essential in the pursuit of a livelihood. . . . [Issued] licenses are not to be taken away without that procedural due process. . . ."

56. 443 U.S. 1 (1979). Some state courts have held that summary adjudication is sometimes permitted, but only when the penalty is license revocation, and not when a fine or imprisonment is involved. See, e.g., Heddan v. Durkswager, 336 N.W.2d 54 (Minn. 1983).

57. Heddan v. Dirkswager, 336 N.W.2d 54, 60 (Minn. 1983) (citing *Montrym*, 443 U.S. at 11–12).

58. 443 U.S. at 17 (quoting Dixon v. Love, 431 U.S. 105, 113 (1977)).

59. *Id.*

60. California v. Trombetta, 467 U.S. 479, 485 (1984) (quoting United States v. Valenzuela-Bernal, 458 U.S. 858, 867 (1982)); see also United States v. Agurs, 427 U.S. 97 (1976); Giglio v. United States, 405 U.S. 150 (1972); Brady V. Maryland, 373 U.S. 83 (1963).

61. See, e.g., Lauderdale v. State, 548 P.2d 376 (Alaska 1976); Scales v. City Court of City of Mesa, 122 Ariz. 231, 594 P.2d 97 (1979); People v. Hitch, 12 Cal. 3d 641, 117 Cal. Rptr. 9, 527 P.2d 361 (1974); State v. Humphrey, 104 Wis. 2d 97, 310 N.W.2d 641 (1981).

62. See, e.g., State v. Barker, 490 S.W.2d 263 (Mo. 1973); State v. Helmer. 278 N.W.2d 808 (S.D. 1979); Turpin v. State, 606 S.W.2d 907 (Tex. 1980).

63. 476 U.S. 479 (1984).

64. U.S. Const. amend IV. See generally W. LaFave and J. Israel, *Criminal Procedure,* § 3.2, student ed. (St. Paul, MN: West Publishing, 1985).

65. Almeida-Sanchez v. United States, 413 U.S. 266, 277 (1973) (Powell, J., concurring).

66. See Carroll v. United States, 267 U.S. 132, 153 (1925) (warrantless search permissible if "it is not practicable to secure a warrant because the vehicle can be quickly moved out of the locality or jurisdiction in which the warrant must be sought").

67. See, e.g., Almeida-Sanchez v. United States, 413 U.S. 266, 269-10 (1973) ("[T]he *Carroll* doctrine does not declare a field day for the police in searching automobiles. Automobile or no automobile, there must be probable cause for the search."); State v. Greely, 115 N.H. 461, 464, 465, 344 A.2d 12, 14, 15 (1975).

However, the requirements apply only if the person or object is actually seized or searched. Courts have held that mere questioning by a police officer is not a seizure "[u]nless the circumstances of the encounter are so intimidating as to demonstrate that a reasonable person would have believed he was not free to leave if he had not responded." INS v. Delgado, 104 S. Ct. 1758, 1763 (1984).

68. Carroll v. United States, 267 U.S. 132, 161 (1925) (quoting Stacey v. Emory, 97 U.S. 642, 645 (1878)).

69. Terry v. Ohio, 392 U.S. 1 (1968).

70. See, e.g., State v. Barber, 241 N.W.2nd 476 (Minn. 1976); State v. Rankin, 477 S.W.2d 72 (Mo. 1972); State v. Sharp, 702 P.2d 959 (Mont. 1985); People v. Ingle, 36 N.Y.2d 413, 369 N.Y.S.2d 67, 330 N.E.2d 39 (1975); see also United States v. Brignoni-Pounce, 422 U.S. 873, 881–82 (1975) (reasonable suspicion that car contains undocumented aliens permits stop and questioning to investigate).

71. See v. City of Seattle, 387 U.S. 541 (1967); Camara v. Municipal Court, 387 U.S. 523 (1967); see also Marshall's v. Barlow's, Inc., 436 U.S. 307 (1978) (warrant required for OSHA inspections).

72. Delaware v. Prouse, 440 U.S. 648 (1979).

73. See, e.g., United States v. Croft, 429 F.2d 884 (10th Cir. 1970); People v. Andrews, 173 Colo. 510, 484 P.2d 1207 (1971).

74. See, e.g., J. Jacobs and N. Strossen, "Mass Investigations Without Individualized Suspicion: A Constitutional and Policy Critique of Drunk Driving Roadblocks," *U.C. Davis Law Review* 18(1985):595–680.

75. See, e.g., People v. Scott, 63 N.Y.2d 518, 473 N.E.2d 1, 483 N.Y.S.2d 649 (1984); Little v. State, 300 Md. 485, 479 A.2d 903 (1984); State v. Superior Court, 143 Ariz. 45, 691 P.2d 1073 (1984); Stark v. Perpich, 590 F. Supp. 1057 (D. Minn. 1984).

76. See, e.g., Commonwealth v. Trumble, 483 N.E.2d 1102 (Mass. 1985); State v. Martin, 496 A.2d 442 (Vt. 1985).

77. See, e.g., State v. Koppel, 499 A.2d 977 (N.H. 1985).

78. E.g., Elam v. State, 690 S.W.2d 352 (Ark. 1985).

79. E.g., McNeil v. Wallace, 699 S.W.2d 534 (Mo. App. 1985).

80. Schmerber v. California, 384 U.S. 757, 765 n.9 (1966).

81. Holt v. United States, 218 U.S. 245, 252–53 (1910).

82. 384 U.S. at 765.

83. 459 U.S. 553, 561–62 (1983).

84. *Id*. at 563–64.

85. See, e.g., Campbell v. Superior Court, 106 Ariz. 542, 479 P.2d 685 (1971); State v. Vietor, 261 N.W.2d 828 (Iowa 1978); Sites v. State, 300 Md. 702, 481 A.2d 192 (1984); State v. Jones, 457 A.2d 1116 (Me. 1983); Spradling v. Deimeke, 528 S.W.2d 759 (Mo. 1975); State v. Petkus, 110 N.H. 394, 269 A.2d 123 (1970), *cert. denied*, 402 U.S. 932 (1971); Seders v. Powell, 298 N.C. 453, 259 S.E.2d 544 (1979); State v. Newton, 291 Or. 788, 636 P.2d 393 (1981); Law v. Danville, 212 Va. 702, 187 S.E. 197 (1972).

86. See, e.g., Sites v. State, 300 Md. 702, 481 A.2d 192 (1984); People v. Gursey, 22 N.Y.2d 224, 239 N.E.2d 351, 292 N.Y.S.2d 416 (1968); Troy v. Curry, 36 Ohio Misc. 144, 303 N.E.2d 925 (1973); State v. Newton, 291 Or. 788, 636 P.2d 393 (1981).

87. See, e.g., Gottschalk v. Sueppel, 258 Iowa 1173, 140 N.W.2d 866 (1966); State v. Jones, 457 A.2d 1116 (Me. 1983); State v. Braunesreither, 276 N.W.2d 139 (S.D. 1979).

88. 267 U.S. 132, 153 (1925).

Chapter Eight

1. Such programs may also have "rehabilitative" effects which are independent of the legal threat or supervisory monitoring. This topic is addressed in the chapter by Mann, Vingilis, and Stewart.

2. Hingson et al. (1986, 4) reported that, in 1985, the Maine Supreme Court declared the civil charge of "operating under the influence" to be unconstitutional "because it allowed police to handcuff and detain suspected offenders at police stations without due process."

3. Andenaes also speculates that the moral impact of the law may be greater within relatively homogeneous cultures and in countries with a traditional respect for formal law.

4. Fairfax County had no roadblocks and, therefore, served as a "control" for the roadblock testing program in neighboring Montgomery County, Maryland.

Chapter Nine

1. An increase in the number of secondary insureds on a policy will cause upward variance in an important insurance pricing variable—frequency rate (reflecting the probability of careless driving). Report of the FTC to the Department of Transportation, *Price Variability in the Automobile Insurance Market*, 1970, 38–39.

2. This is not meant to minimize the carnage and economic loss suffered on America's roadways. Motor vehicles are the most common cause of accidental death in the United States. Annually, approximately nineteen

million accidents occur, producing 46,200 deaths, and 1,700,000 disabling injuries (National Safety Council, *Accident Facts* 40 [1985]). Additionally, although most drivers are accident- and claim-free over the multiyear period pertinent to insurance rating, over a lifetime virtually every motorist will be involved in an accident (New York State Insurance Department, *In Whose Benefit?* 1 [1970]).

3. Insurance companies could, for example, require their insureds to provide a copy of driver licenses with the insurance application, or they could lobby for mandatory reporting of drunk driving convictions by courts or the department of motor vehicles to the defendant's insurance company.

4. See U.S. Bureau of the Census, *1980 Census of Population: Occupation by Industry* PC80-2-7c (Washington, DC, May 1984), 555–57. (Statistics demonstrating that the insurance companies employ a far greater number of people in the categories of financial managers, other financial officers, and managers of properties and real estate than in the categories of actuaries and statisticians.)

5. See generally All Industry Research Advisory Council, *State Motor Vehicle Records as a Source of Driver Performance Information* (1981) (unpublished manuscript). This important study found that (1) accident information is not available to automobile insurers in ten states, and in the remaining states only 36.9 percent of the serious accidents were reflected on motor vehicle records (MVRs), and (2) on a countrywide basis, only 22.3 percent of serious accidents resulted in a violation being recorded on MVRs. *Id.* at 1–3.

6. Most states regulate insurance surcharging. New York State, for instance, strictly limits points and surcharges to policies. Personal injury damage caused by an insured can only trigger a surcharge if the driver was at fault. NYCRR Section 169.1(c) (1985). Additionally, there is a threshold of $400 for surcharges predicated on property damage, unless the insured has had two or more prior accidents involving property damage. *Id.* § 169.1(a). Section 169.0(a)(2) allows insurance companies to add surcharges for drunk-driving convictions.

In New York State, the amount of the surcharge is governed by § 169.1(e). Under "additive" plans, surcharges can increase by up to three times the total limits premium per base class for liability coverage and three times the base for collision coverage. Under "multiplicative" plans insureds can be surcharged at twice the premium for both liability and collision coverage. *Id.*

7. It is difficult to identify a general trend favoring either drivers or insurance companies in New York State arbitration proceedings. See, e.g., NF-1178, 7 N.Y. No-Fault Arb. Rep. 7–8 (No. 12, 1983) (.20 BAC not enough to suspend policy); NF-1075, 7 N.Y. No-Fault Arb. Rep. 4–5 (No. 3, 1983) (BAC of .11 and arrest for drunk driving not conclusive); but see NF-1098, 7 N.Y. No-Fault Arb. Rep. 6 (No. 5, 1983) (.14 BAC is sufficient); NF-1102, 7 N.Y. No-Fault Arb. Rep. 7 (No. 5, 1983) (same).

8. The courts have frequently essayed to define the terms "intoxication" and "drunkenness," but, as has been said, the terms are scarcely susceptible of accurate definition for practical purposes, and are so familiar that they define themselves. "Intoxication" is a word synonymous with "inebriety," "inebriation," or "drunkenness," and is expressive of that state or condition which inevitably follows from taking excessive quantities of an intoxicant. To some men, it means being under the influence of an intoxicant to such an extent as to render one helpless, while others speak of a person as intoxicated when he is only slightly under such influence. . . . As far as the infliction of physical injuries upon a third party is concerned, it has been said that a person may be deemed intoxicated within the meaning of a civil damage act when his excessive use of intoxicants has produced such a material change in his normal mental state that his behavior becomes unpredictable and uncontrolled, and when, as a result, slight irritations, real or imaginary, cause outbursts of anger which find expression in acts of physical violence against another.
45 Am. Jur. 2d *Intoxicating Liquors* §21 (1964)

9. The traditional view is that intoxication does not obviate proof of negligence. See Dooley and Mosher, *Alcohol and Legal Negligence,*7 Contemp. Drug Probs. 145, 154–56 (1978); see also McKenna v. Volkswagenwerk A.G., 57 Hawaii 460, 558 P.2d 1018 (1977); Cain v. Houston Gen. Ins. Co., 327 So. 2d 526 (La. App.), *cert. refused,* 330 So. 2d 279 (La. 1976). Thus far, no jurisdiction has imposed strict liability for driving while intoxicated, although it was proposed by Professor Ehrenzweig in the 1950s. See Ehrenzweig (1955) ("tort fines" for drunk drivers). More recently, the New York State Insurance Commission proposed strict liability for drunk drivers. See New York State Insurance Department, *In Whose Benefit?* (1970).

Neither negligence per se nor traditional strict liability is synonymous with absolute liability. Negligence per se usually permits the defendant to raise excuses. See W. Prosser, *Law of Torts* 36, 4th ed. (1971), 197–98. Even under so-called strict liability, the defendant may plead the plaintiff's contributory negligence.

10. Commentators have frequently criticized punitive damages (see, e.g., 1 Long § 1.27:411; Walther and Plein 1965, 369). A major criticism is that punitive damages blur the distinction between criminal law, which seeks to achieve social control through punishment and deterrence, and tort law, whose primary goal, according to some theorists, is to determine who should bear the loss when some social activity results in an injury. Judge Richard Posner believes that the purpose of tort law should be to deter uneconomical accidents, or to put it differently, to produce the socially efficient number of accidents. Nevertheless, in his view, punitive damages should play a limited role because "If the defendant's liability exceeded accident cost, he might have an incentive

to incur prevention costs in excess of accident cost, and this would be un-economical." R. Posner, 2d ed. (1977), 143.

11. A typical jury instruction for calculating punitive damages is illustrative:

> In determining the amount of your award of punitive damages, should you decide in favor of such an award, you should consider any evidence that tends to throw light on defendant's wealth or poverty.
>
> The amount to be awarded as exemplary damage, if you award them, is for your good discretion. The law does not offer any precise formula for determining a ratio between compensatory and exemplary damages. They should not be totally disproportionate to the compensatory damages. You may not base your award upon influences such as passion, prejudice, or undue sympathy for either plaintiff or defendant.
>
> However, in deciding on an appropriate figure, you should give due consideration to the degree of outrageousness of the conduct involved.
>
> The court relies on your good judgment, if exemplary damages are to be awarded, in arriving at a sum which, considering all the circumstances, will serve not only to punish, but also to deter similar wrongdoing in the future.
>
> G. Douthwaite, Jury Instructions on Damages in Tort Action §§ 2-2, 2-6, at 80, 90n (1981)

12. States that permit punitive damages for drunk driving characterize it variously as either gross negligence, culpable disregard, or willful and wanton conduct. See, e.g., Ross v. Clark, 35 Ariz. 60, 274 P. 639 (1929); Homes v. Hollingsworth, 234 Ark. 347, 352 S.W.2d 96 (1961); Infield v. Sullivan, 151 Conn. 506, 199 A.2d 693 (1964); Taylor v. Superior Court, 24 Cal. 3d 890, 598 P.2d 854, 157 Cal. Rptr. 693 (1979); Busser v. Sabalasso, 143 So. 2d 532 (Fla. App. 1962); Madison v. Wigal, 18 Ill. App. 2d 564, 153 N.E.2d 90 (1958); Sebastion v. Wood, 246 Iowa 94, 66 N.W.2d 841 (1954); Southland Broadcasting Co. v. Tracy, 210 Miss. 836, 50 So. 2d 572 (1951); Svejcara v. Whitman, 82 N.M. 739, 487 P.2d 167 (N.M. App. 1971); Colligan v. Fera, 76 Misc. 2d 22, 349 N.Y.S. 2d 306 (1973); Harrell v. Ames, 265 Or. 183, 508 P.2d 211 (1973); Focht v. Rabada, 217 Pa. Super. 35, 268 A.2d 157 (1970); Pratt v. Duck, 28 Tenn. App. 502, 191 S.W. 562 (1945); Higginbotham v. O'Keefe, 340 S.W.2d 350 (Tex. Civ. App. 1960).

13. A typical dram shop law is Ill. Rev. Stat. ch. 43 § 135 (Supp. 1981):

> Every person who is injured in person or property by an intoxicated person has a right of action . . . against any person who by selling or giving alcoholic liquor, causes the intoxication of such person; Mich. Comp. Laws §436.22 (1978) provides: Every wife, husband, parent, child, guardian, or other person who shall be in-

jured. . . . by a visibly intoxicated person by reason of the unlawful
selling, giving, or furnishing to such persons of any intoxicating
liquor . . . shall have a right of action.

14. Twenty-three states have enacted some form of dram shop law. Of
those, eighteen states use dram shop laws only. There are eighteen states
that apply common law liability principles against the suppliers of alcoholic
beverages; of those, thirteen states use common law principles only. Five
states have both dram shop laws and common law liability. *Insurance Information Institute Fact Sheet* (Aug. 1984), 1–2. In stark contrast to this
trend, Tennessee recently amended its dram shop act to all but immunize
taverns and their owners. Humphrey, "Tenn. Sharply Cuts 'Dram Shop'
Liability," 19 *Nat'l L.J.* 3 (No. 8 1986).

15. Alcohol Beverage Control (ABC) laws in many states make it a
misdemeanor for a liquor licensee to sell alcohol to drunk customers. Some
states enforce ABC laws against both the establishment and the owner, as
well as against the bartender or waiter who served the drinks. Although a
few of these statutes impose strict liability, see, e.g., Wisc. Stat. Ann.
§ 125.07(3) (1982), making it irrelevant whether the bartender knew or should
have known that the patron was intoxicated, most require some type of
mens rea. See, e.g., N.Y. Alcohol Beverage Control Act § 165 (1982). Some
courts have grounded civil liability for liquor dispensers on the ABC laws,
e.g., Rappaport v. Nichols, 31 N.J. 188, 156 A.2d 1 (1959).

16. In March 1985, the South Dakota legislature abrogated the dram shop
liability created by *Walz*. See S.D. Comp. Laws Ann. § 35-4-78 (1985). The
Wisconsin Supreme Court established dram shop liability in Sorenson v.
Jarvis, Wis. 2d, 350 N.W.2d 108 (1984).

17. This is due, in great part, to the incredibly high turnover in bar
personnel. See American Bartenders' Association, 1984 Annual Report 3–
4 (turnover impossible to ascertain precisely, but is "undeniably large").

18. In civil cases, bartenders and waiters are not normally held to the
level of an expert in intoxicated behavior. *See* Coulter v. Superior Court,
21 Cal. 3d 144, 577 P.2d 675, 145 Cal. Rptr. 534 (1978); Kyle v. State, 366
P.2d 961 (Okla. Crim. App. 1961). The customer must be drunk enough to
raise the suspicion of a reasonable person of ordinary experience. State v.
Morello, 169 Ohio St. 213, 158 N.E.2d 525 (1959).

Negligence suits based on violation of an alcohol beverage act may involve heightened standards of care, such as the "reasonable bartender" or
even the "reasonable bartender of like experience." *See* W. Prosser, *Law
of Torts,* 4th ed. (1971), § 32, 161–66 (explaining higher standards of conduct).

19. Due mostly to liability insurance incentives, many taverns have implemented educational programs for bar personnel. These programs stress
the importance of not serving drunks, the identification of drunks, and
proper etiquette for "shutting off" a customer. C. Weiner, *The Politics of
Alcoholism* (1981), 242. There may also be insurance reductions available

to taverns that install breath testing equipment. *Id*. Leverage from insurance companies has also, in the estimation of many tavern owners, forced the bars to push more food and fewer drinks. *Beverage Bull.*, May 1, 1977, at 4.

20. The city of Boca Raton, Florida, for instance, has outlawed oversized drink glasses, such as those used in many establishments to serve margaritas. Boca Raton, Fla. Ord. 35-23.5 (1985). Many of these glasses exceed thirty-two ounce capacity and resemble fishbowls more than cocktail glasses.

21. A growing number of states have banned or strictly curtailed special liquor promotions, among them: Nebraska, New Jersey, Texas, Michigan, Ohio, Rhode Island, Arizona, and Oklahoma. 3 *Dram Shop and Alcohol Rep.* 1 (No. 2 1985).

22. Such a proposal is pending in the Vermont legislature:

> Under the proposed legislation, liquor sellers and providers would have to demonstrate proof of financial responsibility as follows:
> 1. A certificate that there is in effect for the period covered by the license an insurance policy or pool providing the following minimum coverages:
> (a) $100,000 because of bodily injury to any one person in any one occurrence, and subject to the limit for one person, in the amount of $200,000 because of bodily injury for two or more persons in any one occurrence, and in the amount of $10,000 for injury to or destruction of property of others in any one occurrence.
> (b) $100,000 for loss of means of support of any one person in any one occurrence, and, subject to the limit for one person, $200,000 for loss of means of support of two or more persons in any one occurrence; or
> (c) An annual aggregate policy limit for dram shop liability of not less than $300,000 per policy year may be included in the policy provisions; or
> (2) A bond of surety company with minimum coverages as provided in subsection (A); or
> (3) A certification of the state treasurer that the licensee has deposited with him $200,000 in cash or securities which may legally be purchased by savings banks or for trust funds having a market value of $200,000.
> 4 *Dram Shop and Alcohol Rep.* 1, 5 (No. 1, 1986)

23. In Coulter v. Superior Court, 21 Cal. 3d 144, 577 P.2d 675, 145 Cal. Rptr. 534 (1978), the California Supreme Court held that social hosts could be liable for the drunk-driving injuries of their guests. The California legislature soon reversed the court. Cal. Bus. & Prof. Code Ann. § 25602(b)(c) (West Supp. 1979) (eliminating all dram shop liability for commercial sellers and social hosts).

24. Four months after *Kelly*, the New Jersey legislature created a Commission on Alcoholic Beverage Liability. The commission has urged a more

limited approach to social host liability. It would require the plaintiff to show (1) that the host willfully and knowingly served alcohol to a guest who was either visibly intoxicated in the host's presence, or that he recklessly disregarded the effects of the guest's abusive drinking; (2) a reasonably foreseeable risk of harm; and (3) an injury caused by the intoxicated guest's negligent operation of a vehicle. 3 *Dram Shop and Alcohol Rep.* 1985 1, 5 (No. 11, 1985). The commission's proposal also includes a rebuttable presumption of sobriety for a BAC less than .15; "visibly intoxicated" would mean a state of intoxication accompanied by a perceptible act indicative of that intoxication.

25. Comprehensive personal injury policies would certainly cover suits based on social host liability, absent express contractual language to the contrary. Such policies cover the insured's legal obligation to honor personal injury judgments. See 7A W. Berdal, *Appelman on Insurance Law and Practice* § 4501.4 (Supp. 1983).

Coverage under homeowner policies may be more problematic. Service of alcohol is not what is traditionally thought of as a condition of the premises. However, nonpremises interests are occasionally protected under homeowner contracts. Thus far, homeowner policies do not expressly cover social host liability, but this is probably due to the current rarity of the theory.

Chapter Eleven

1. However, measures intended to control drinking and driving that fail might be justified on other grounds. For example, it may pay to attempt to control drinking because of the social harm that alcohol has for some individuals, but it might also be true that those who tend to drink and drive might be unaffected by such an effort. In this case, the temperance effort may be socially justifiable on other grounds but not on the basis of arguing that drinking driving benefits. The paradigm could be formulated to deal with the question of costs and benefits associated with reducing alcohol consumption and then such questions could be investigated in parallel with the drunken driving issue.

Chapter Thirteen

1. DUI (driving under the influence) is used throughout this chapter to refer to operating a vehicle at a BAC above the legally prescribed limit. In some jurisdictions, this is referred to as driving while impaired or intoxicated (DWI).

2. Breath Test Co., Analgas Australia Pty. Ltd., Cheltenham, Victoria.

3. Public Access Breath Testing Inc., Mississaga, Canada.

4. Robert D. Smith, 7860 Glade, Canoga Park, CA 91304.

Bibliography

Addiction Research Foundation. 1981. *Alcohol: Public Education and Social Policy*. Toronto: Addiction Research Foundation.

Ajzen, I., and Fishbein, M. 1980. *Understanding Attitudes and Predicting Social Behavior*. Englewood Cliffs, NJ: Prentice-Hall.

Albert, W. G., and Simpson, R. I. 1985. Evaluation of an Educational Program for the Prevention of Impaired Driving among Grade 11 Students. *Journal of Drug Education* 15:57–71.

Alberta Solicitor General. 1984. *Alberta Check-Stop Program. First Annual Report: November 1, 1973–October 31, 1974*. Edmonton: Office of the Solicitor General.

Alcohol Health and Research World. 1986. Server Training Programs: Profiles, 10:4, 22–23.

Allen, R. W.; Stein, A. C.; Summers, L. G., and Cook, M. L. 1983. *Drunk Driving Warning System (DDWS), Volume II, Field Test Evaluation*. Technical Report no. DOT-HS-806-460. Washington, DC: NHTSA.

Allsop, R. E. 1966. *Alcohol and Road Accidents*. Report no. 6. Crowthorne, Berkshire: Transport and Road Research Laboratory.

American Law Institute. 1979. *Restatement (Second) of Torts*. St. Paul, MN: American Law Institute.

Andenaes, J. 1984. Drinking-and-Driving Laws in Scandinavia. *Scandinavian Studies in Law* 1984:13–23.

———. 1978. The Effects of Scandinavia's Drinking and Driving Laws: Facts and Hypotheses. *Scandinavian Studies in Criminology* 6:35–53.

———. 1977. The Moral or Educative Influence of Criminal Law. In *Law, Justice, and the Individual in Society: Psychological and Legal Issues*, ed. J. L. Tapp and F. J. Levine, 50–59. New York: Holt, Rinehart and Winston.

———. 1975. General Prevention Revisited: Research and Policy Implications. *Journal of Criminal Law and Criminology* 66:338–365.

———. 1974. *Punishment and Deterrence*. Ann Arbor: University of Michigan Press.

———. 1952. General Prevention—Illusion or Reality? *Journal of Criminal Law, Criminology, and Police Science* 43:176–98.

Andenaes, J., and Sørensen, R. K. 1979. Alkohol og dødsulykker i trafikken. *Lov og Rett* 18:83–109.

Anderson, L. S.; Chiricos, T. G.; and Waldo, G. P. 1977. Formal and Informal Sanctions: A Comparison of Deterrent Effects. *Social Problems* 25:103–14.

Anderson, M., and Merrick, P. L. 1980. Dunedin Course for Impaired Drivers: A Model for New Zealand? *Australia and New Zealand Journal of Criminology* 13:133–41.

Anderson, T. E. 1984. *Performance Evaluation: Balloon-type Breath Alcohol Self-Tester for Personal Use*. Technical Report no. DOT HS-806-538. Washington, DC: NHTSA.

Anderson, T. E.; Schweitz, R. M.; and Snyder, M. B. 1983. *Field Evaluation of a Behavioral Test Battery for DWI*. Technical Note. Washington, DC: NHTSA.

Andreasson, R., and Bonnichsen, R. 1965. Alkoholpåverkade i vägtrafiken. In *Alkoholkonflikten 1963*. Stockholm.

Arbeitskreis, I. 1981. Die Nachschulung alkoholauffälliger Kraftfahrer und die gerichtliche Praxis. In *19. Deutscher Verkehrsgerichtstag* 7:38–80. Hamburg.

Argeriou, M.; McCarty, D.; and Blacker, E. 1985. Criminality among Individuals Arraigned for Drinking and Driving in Massachusetts, *Journal of Studies on Alcohol* 46:525–30.

Armitage, P. 1971. *Statistical Methods in Medical Research*. New York: Wiley and Sons.

Arstein-Kerslake, G. W. 1986. *Confidence Interval Approach to the Development of Blood Alcohol Concentration Charts*. Report no. AL-DMV-RSS-86-103. Sacramento, CA: California Department of Motor Vehicles.

Arthurson, R. M. 1985. *Evaluation of Random Breath Testing*. Sydney: Traffic Authority of New South Wales.

Assum, T. 1985. *Virkninger av fengselsstraff for kjøring med promille mellom 0,5 og 1,5. Sammenlikning av forhold i Norgeog Sverige*. Oslo: Det Kgl Samferdselsdepartment.

Attwood, D. A.; Williams, R. D.; Bowser, S. J.; McBurney, L. J.; and Frecker, R. C. 1981. *The Effect of Moderate Levels of Alcohol and Marijuana, Alone and in Combination, on Closed-Course Driving Performance*. Ottawa, Ontario: Transport Canada.

Babor, T. F.; Mendelson, J. H.; Greenberg, I.; and Kuehnle, J. 1978. Experimental Analysis of the "Happy Hour": Effects of Purchase Price on Alcohol Consumption. *Psychopharmacology* 58:35–41.

Babor, T. F.; Mendelson, J. H.; Uhly, B.; and Souza, E. 1980. Drinking Patterns in Experimental and Barroom Settings. *Journal of Studies on Alcohol* 41:634–51.

Bacon, S. D. 1984. Alcohol Issues and Social Science. *Journal of Drug Issues* 14 (Winter): 7–29.

————. 1973. Highway Crashes, Alcohol Problems, and Programs for Social Controls. In *Alcoholism: Progress in Research and Treatment*, ed. P. G. Bourne and R. Fox, 311–35. New York: Academic Press.

Baker, R. 1971. *The Highway Risk Problem.* New York: Wiley Inter-Science.

Baker, S.; O'Neil, B.; and Karpf, R. 1984. *The Injury Fact Book.* Lexington, MA: Lexington Press.

Barnes, R.; Landrum, J. W.; Cosby, P. J.; and Snow, R. W. 1986. An Analysis of Mississippi DUI Offenders: Heterogeneity Reaffirmed. Paper presented at the annual meeting of the American Society of Criminology, Atlanta.

Baum-Baicker, C. 1985a. The Health Benefits of Moderate Alcohol Consumption: A Review of the Literature. *Drug and Alcohol Dependence* 15:207–27.

————. 1985b. The Psychological Benefits of Moderate Alcohol Consumption: A Review of the Literature. *Drug and Alcohol Dependence* 15:303–22.

Beauchamp, D. E. 1980. *Beyond Alcoholism: Alcohol and Public Health Policy.* Philadelphia: Temple University Press.

Beaumont, K., and Newby, R. F. 1972. Traffic Law and Road Safety Research in the United Kingdom—British Countermeasures. Paper presented at the National Road Safety Symposium, Canberra, Australia.

Beck, K. H. In press. Adolescent Gender Differences in Alcohol Beliefs and Behaviors. *Journal of Alcohol and Drug Education.*

————. 1983. Psychosocial Patterns of Alcohol Abuse in a College Population. *Journal of Alcohol and Drug Education* 28(2):64–72.

————. 1981. Driving While under the Influence of Alcohol: Relationship to Attitudes and Beliefs in a College Population. *American Journal of Drug and Alcohol Abuse* 8:377–88.

Beirness, D. J., and Donelson, A. C. 1985. Noncompliance with Per Se Laws: Ignorance or Inability? In *Alcohol, Drugs, and Traffic Safety. Proceedings of the 9th International Conference on Alcohol, Drugs, and Traffic Safety,* ed. S. Kaye and G. W. Meier, 155–65. Washington, DC: NHTSA.

Beirness, D. J.; Haas, G. C.; Walsh, P. J.; and Donelson, A. C. 1985. *Alcohol and Fatal Road Accidents in Canada: A Statistical Look at Its Magnitude and Persistence.* Impaired Driving Report no. 3. Ottawa, Ontario: Department of Justice.

Beitel, G. A.; Glanz, W. D.; and Sharp, M. C. 1975. Probability of Arrest While Driving under the Influence of Alcohol. *Journal of Studies on Alcohol* 36:870–76.

Beneke, M. 1982. Gesetzliche Massnahmen und Alkoholverkehrsdelinquenz. Eine empirische Untersuchung zur Frage der Wirksamkeit des 0.80/oo-Gesetzes. *Blutalkohol* 19:137–70.

Berger, D. E., and Snortum, J. R. 1986. A Structural Model of Drinking and Driving: Alcohol Consumption, Social Norms, and Moral Commitments. *Criminology* 24:139–53.

————. 1985. Alcoholic Beverage Preferences of Drinking-Driving Violators. *Journal of Studies on Alcohol* 46(1):232–39.

Bierau, D. 1985. Erschreckende Zahlen—beredte Statistik. In *Alkohol und Strassenverkehr—Neue Fronten bei einem alten Problem: 4–5.* Düsseldorf: Bundesminister für Verkehr.

Bigelow, G. E.; Bickel, W. E.; Roche, J. D.; Liebson, I. A.; and Nowowieski, P. 1985. *Identifying Types of Drug Intoxication: Laboratory Evaluation of a Subject-Examination Procedure.* Report no. DOT HS-806-753. Washington, DC: NHTSA.

Bishop, R. W. 1973. Improving Teacher Competency Related to the Alcohol and Traffic Safety Topic. *Journal of Traffic Safety Education* 20:11–13.

Bjerver, K.; Bonnichsen, R.; and Andreasson, R. A. 1966. A Field Study on the Use of "Alcotest" in Sweden. In *Proceedings of the 4th International Conference on Alcohol and Traffic Safety, Bloomington, Indiana,* 190–94. Bloomington, IN: Indiana University Press.

Blount, W. R.; Reis, R.; and Chappell, J. 1983. The Effect of Drinking Driver Rehabilitation Efforts on Rearrest When Drinking Type Is Controlled. In *DWI Reeducation and Rehabilitation Programs—Successful Results and the Future,* 22–37. Falls Church, VA: AAA Foundation for Traffic Safety.

Blum, W., and Kalven, H. 1965. *Public Law Perspectives on a Private Law Problem—Auto Compensation Plans.* Boston: Little, Brown.

Blumenthal, M., and Ross, H. L. 1973. *Two Experiments in Traffic Law. Volume 1: The Effect of Legal Sanctions on DUI Offenders.* Washington, DC: U.S. Department of Transportation.

Blumstein, A.; Cohen, J.; and Nagin, D., eds. 1978. *Deterrence and Incapacitation: Estimating the Effects of Criminal Sanctions on Crime Rates.* Washington, D.C.: National Academy of Sciences.

Bonney, L. A. 1984. *Evaluation Report: Project SMASH.* Project Summary Paper commissioned by a California Office of Traffic Safety Grant, 16–20.

Borkenstein, R. F. 1985. Historical Perspective: North American Traditional and Experimental Response. *Journal of Studies on Alcohol,* Supplement no. 10:3–12.

————. 1975. Problems of Enforcement, Adjudication, and Sanctioning. In *Alcohol, Drugs, and Traffic Safety, Proceedings of the 6th International Conference on Alcohol, Drugs, and Traffic Safety, Toronto,* ed. S. Israelstam and S. Lambert. Ontario, Canada: Addiction Research Foundation of Ontario.

Borkenstein, R. F.; Crowther, R. F.; Shumate, R. P.; Ziel, W. B.; and Zylman, R. 1964. *The Role of the Drinking Driver in Traffic Accidents.* Bloomington, IN: Department of Police Administration, Indiana University.

Borkenstein, R. F.; Trubitt, H. J.; and Lease, R. J. 1963. Problems of Enforcement and Prosecution. In *Alcohol and Traffic Safety,* ed. B. H. Fox and J. H. Fox, 137–88. U.S. Public Health Service Publication no. 1043. Washington, DC: Government Printing Office.

Boston University School of Law–Medicine Institute. 1969. *Investigation of Thirty-one Fatal Automobile Accidents.* Washington, DC: U.S. Department of Transportation, Bureau of Highway Safety.

Bragg, B. W. E.; Dawson, N.; Kirby, D.; and Goodfellow, G. 1981. Detection of Impaired Drivers through Measurement of Speed and Alignment. In *Alcohol, Drugs and Traffic Safety,* Volume III, ed. L. Goldberg, 1341–52. Sweden: Almqvist and Wiksell.

Bragg, B. W. E., and Wilson, W. T. 1980. Evaluation of a Performance Test to Detect Impaired Drivers. *Accident Analysis and Prevention* 12:55–65.

Bratholm, A., and Hauge, R. 1974. Reaksjonene mot promillekjørere, *Lov og Rett* 1974:24–38.

Braucht, G. N., and Braucht, B. 1984. Prevention of Problem Drinking among Youth. Evaluation of Educational Strategies. In *Prevention of Alcohol Abuse,* ed. P. Miller and T. Nirenberg, 253–79. New York: Plenum Press.

Breakspear, R. 1986. Coin-Operated Self-Testers. Paper presented at the 9th International Conference on Alcohol, Drugs and Traffic Safety, Amsterdam.

Brenner, R. 1980. Economics—An Imperialist Science? *Journal of Legal Studies* 9:179–88.

Broughton, J., and Stark, D. C. 1986. *The Effect of the 1983 Changes in the Law Relating to Drink/Driving.* Crowthorne, Berkshire: Transport and Road Research Laboratory Report.

Bruun, K.; Edwards, G.; Lumio, M.; Mkel, K.; Pan, L.; Popham, R. E.; Room, R.; Schmidt, W.; Skog, O.-J.; Sulkunen, P.; and Østberg, E. 1975. *Alcohol Control Policies in Public Health Perspective.* Helsinki: Finnish Foundation for Alcohol Studies.

Buikhuisen, W. 1969. Criminological and Psychological Aspects of Drunken Drivers. Paper presented at symposium, The Human Factor in Road Traffic, Stockholm.

Buikhuisen, W., and von Wering, J. 1983. Vorspeelen van Recidivisme. *Nederlandse Tijdschrift voor criminologie* 5:223–40.

Bundesminister für Verkehr. 1984. *Verkehrssicherheitsprogramm 1984 der Bundesregierung.* Bonn: Bundesminister für Verkehr.

Burns, M., and Moskowitz, H. 1980. *Methods for Estimating Expected Blood Alcohol Concentration.* Technical Report no. DOT-HS-805–727. Washington, DC: NHTSA.

———. 1977. *Psychophysical Tests for DWI Arrest: Final Report.* Technical Report no. DOT-HS-5-01242. Washington, DC: NHTSA.

Burrell, R., and Young, M. 1978. Insurability of Punitive Damages. *Marquette Law Review* 62:1–33.

Bussman, E., and Gerhardt, B. P. 1984. Legalbewährung junger Alkoholverkehrsstraftäter. *Blutalkohol* 21:214–27.

Caghan, E. N. 1976. Attitude Change in Male DWI (Drinking While Intoxicated) Offender. Ph.D. thesis, Kent State University.

Calabresi, G. 1970. *The Costs of Accidents*. New Haven, CT: Yale University Press.

Calvert-Boyanowsky, J., and Boyanowsky, E. O. 1980. *Tavern Breath Testing as an Alcohol Countermeasure*. Technical Report. Ottawa, Ontario: Ministry of Transport.

Cameron, M.; Strang, P.; and Vulcan, A. 1980. Evaluation of Random Breath Testing in Victoria, Australia. Paper presented at the 8th International Conference on Alcohol, Drugs, and Traffic Safety, Stockholm.

Cameron, T. 1982. Drinking and Driving among American Youth: Beliefs and Behaviors. *Drug and Alcohol Dependence* 2:1–33.

―――――. 1977. Alcohol and Traffic. In *Alcohol, Casualties, and Crime,* ed. M. Arrens et al. Report C-18. Berkeley, CA: Social Research Group.

Carlson, W. L. 1973. Age, Exposure, and Alcohol Involvement in Night Crashes. *Journal of Safety Research* 5:247–59.

Carpenter, J. A. 1963. Effects of Alcohol on Psychological Processes. In *Alcohol and Traffic Safety,* ed. B. H. Fox and J. H. Fox, 45–90. U.S. Public Health Service Publication no. 1043. Washington, DC: Government Printing Office.

―――――. 1962. Effects of Alcohol on Some Psychological Processes: A Critical Review with Special Reference to Automobile Driving Skill. *Quarterly Journal of Studies on Alcohol* 23:274–314.

Carr, B.; Goldberg, H.; and Farbar, C. 1975. The Canadian Breathalizer Legislation: An Inferential Evaluation. In *Alcohol, Drugs, and Traffic Safety, Proceedings of the 6th International Conference on Alcohol, Drugs, and Traffic Safety,* ed. S. Israelstam and S. Lambert, 679–88. Toronto: Addiction Research Foundation of Ontario.

Carseldine, D. 1985. *Surveys of Knowledge, Attitudes, Beliefs, and Reported Behaviours of Drivers—on the Topic of Drink-Driving and Random Breath Testing*. Sydney: Traffic Authority of New South Wales.

Carstensen, G.; Takala, H.; Hauge, R.; and von Hofer, H. 1978. In *Drinking and Driving in Scandinavia. Scandinavian Studies in Criminology,* Volume 6. Oslo: Universitetsforlaget.

Cashmore, J. 1985. *The Impact of Random Breath Testing in New South Wales*. Sydney: New South Wales Bureau of Crime Statistics and Research.

Chafetz, M. 1984. Training in Intervention Procedures: A Prevention Program. *Abstracts and Reviews in Alcohol and Driving* 5(4):17–19.

―――――. 1983. *A Plan to Prevent Drunk Driving*. Washington, DC: Health Education Foundation.

Chambers, L.; Roberts, R.; and Voeller, C. 1976. The Epidemiology of Traffic Accidents and the Effect of the 1969 Breathaliser Amendment in Canada. *Accident Analysis and Prevention* 8:201–6.

Chapanis, A. 1967. The Relevance of Laboratory Studies to Practical Situations. *Ergonomics* 10:557–77.

Chester, G. B. 1985. Alcohol and Other Drugs in Road Crashes: What Does Pharmacokinetics Have to Do with It? *Alcohol, Drugs, and Driving Abstracts and Reviews* 1(3):1–20.

Christensen, P., and Fosser, S. 1980. *Analyse av 1053 promillekjøringssaker i Norge.* Oslo: Transportøkonomisk institutt.

Christensen, P.; Fosser, S.; and Glad, A. 1978. *Promillekjøring og trafikksikkerhat (Drunken Driving and Traffic Safety).* Oslo: Transportøkonomisk institutt (Institute of Transport Economics).

Christy, C. C. 1986. The Value of Server Intervention Training. Testimony before the California State Assembly: The Select Committee on Alcohol and Related Problems, 14 August 1986.

Cicourel, A. 1968. *Method and Measurement in Sociology.* New York: The Free Press.

Cisin, I. H. 1963. Social Psychological Factors in Drinking-Driving. In *Alcohol and Traffic Safety,* ed. B. H. Fox and J. H. Fox, 1–25. U.S. Public. Health Service Publication no. 1043. Washington, DC: Government Printing Office.

Clark, W. B. 1981. The Contemporary Tavern. In *Research Advances in Alcohol and Drug Problems,* Volume 6, ed. Y. Israel, F. B. Glaser, H. Klant, R. E. Popham, W. Schmidt, and R. G. Smart. Toronto: Addiction Research Foundation of Ontario.

Coase, R. H. 1978. Economics and Contiguous Disciplines. *Journal of Legal Studies* 7(2):201–12.

Collins, J. 1982. Alcohol Careers and Criminal Careers. In *Drinking and Crime,* ed. J. Collins, 152–60. London: Tavistock Publications.

Comment. 1982. Employer Liability for Drunken Employee's Actions Following an Office Party: A Cause of Action under Respondeat Superior. *California Western Law Review* 19:107–40.

Compton, R. P. 1986a. *Field Evaluation of Los Angeles Police Department Drug Detection Program.* Technical Report no. DOT-HS-807-012. Washington, DC: NHTSA.

———. 1986b. *A Preliminary Analysis of the Effect of Tennessee's Mandatory Jail Sanction on DWI Recidivism.* Washington, DC: Department of Transportation.

———. 1985. *Pilot Test of Selected DWI Detection Procedures for Use at Sobriety Checkpoints.* Technical Report no. DOT-HS-806-724. Washington, DC: NHTSA.

Compton, R. P., and Engle, R. E. 1983. *The Use of Safety Checkpoints for DWI Enforcement.* Technical Note. Washington, DC: NHTSA.

Comptroller General of the United States. 1979. *The Drinking-Driver Problem—What Can Be Done about It?* Washington, DC: General Accounting Office.

Cook, P. 1981. The Effect of Liquor Taxes on Drinking, Cirrhosis, and Auto Accidents. In *Alcohol and Public Policy: Beyond the Shadow of Prohi-*

bition, ed. M. Moore and D. Gerstein, 255–85. Washington, DC: National Academy Press.

Coppin, R., and van Oldenbeek, G. 1965. *Driving under Suspension and Revocation.* Sacramento, CA: Department of Motor Vehicles.

Cosper, R., and Mozersky, K. 1968. Social Correlates of Drinking and Driving. *Quarterly Journal of Studies on Alcohol,* Supplement no. 4:58–117.

Crary, S. B. 1986. Recent Advances and Future Prospects for Tin-Oxide Gas Sensors. Paper presented at the workshop on In-Vehicle Alcohol Test Devices. Washington, DC: NHTSA.

Cressey, D. 1975. Law, Order, and the Motorist. In *Crime, Criminality, and Public Policy,* ed. R. Hood. New York: The Free Press.

Curry, B. 1983. Drive for Safe Highways: Citizen Army Waging War against Drunks. *Los Angeles Times,* 26 September, I-1, 14.

Cutler, R. E., and Storm, T. 1975. Observational Study of Alcohol Consumption in Natural Settings. *Journal of Studies on Alcohol* 36:1173–83.

Damkot, D. K.; Toussie, S. R.; Akley, N. R.; Geller, H. A.; and Whitmore, D. G. 1977. *On-the-Road Driving Behavior and Breath Alcohol Concentration.* Technical Report no. DOT-HS-802-264. Washington, DC: NHTSA.

Day, M.; Muir, G. G.; and Watling, J. 1968. Evaluation of Alcotest R80 Reagent Tubes. *Nature* 219:1051–52.

Demick, J.; Inoue, W.; Wapner, S.; Ishii, S.; Minami, H.; Yamamoto, T.; and Nishiyama, S. 1986. Experience and Action of Automobile Seat Belt Usage: U.S. and Japan. Paper presented at the annual meeting of the American Psychological Association, Washington, DC.

Department of the Environment. 1976. *Drinking and Driving: Report of the Departmental Committee.* London: Her Majesty's Stationery Office.

Deutscher Verkehrssicherheitsrat. 1986. *Fahrerlaubnis auf Probe—Kurse für Fahranfänger.* Handbuch für Kursleiter. Ein Programm des DVR, des HUK-Verbandes und der Bundesvereinigung der Fahrlehrerverbände. Bonn: Deutscher Verkehrssicherheitsrat.

————. 1985. *Programm "Nüchtern fahren—Sicher ankommen."* Aktionsleitfaden mit programmunterstützenden Vorschlägen für Massnahmen "vor Ort." Bonn: Deutscher Verkehrssicherheitsrat.

Deutscher, I. 1973. *What We Say/What We Do: Sentiments and Acts.* Glenview, IL: Scott, Foresman.

————. 1966. Words and Deeds: Social Science and Social Policy. *Social Problems* 13:236–54.

Distilled Spirits Council. 1985. *Annual Statistical Review, 1984–1985.* Washington, DC: Distilled Spirits Institute.

Donelson, A. C. 1985a. *Alcohol and Road Accidents in Canada: Issues Related to Future Strategies and Priorities.* Impaired Driving Report no. 4. Ottawa, Ontario: Department of Justice.

————. 1985b. Between Molecule (Alcohol) and Mayhem (Road Crashes): The Case for Humane Intervention and the Role of Social and Behavioral

Sciences. In *Human Behavior and Traffic Safety,* ed. L. Evans and R. C. Schwing, 421–79. New York: Plenum Press.

Donelson, A. C. 1985c. Drinking and Driving in the Sociocultural Context: Research Needs and Opportunities. *Journal of Studies on Alcohol,* Supplement no. 10:78–89.

————. 1983. *Alcohol and Road Accidents: Future Strategies and Priorities.* Edmonton, Alberta: Alberta Alcohol and Drug Abuse Commission; Ottawa, Ontario: Traffic Injury Research Foundation of Canada.

Donelson, A. C., and Beirness, D. J. 1985. *Legislative Issues Related to Drinking and Driving.* Impaired Driving Report no. 2. Ottawa, Ontario: Department of Justice.

Donelson, A. C.; Beirness, D. J.; and Mayhew, D. R. 1984. *Characteristics of Drinking Drivers.* Ottawa: Traffic Injury Research Foundation of Canada.

Donelson, A. C.; McNair, J. W.; Ruschmann, P. A.; and Joscelyn, K. B. 1980. *The Incidence of Drugs among Fatally Injured Drivers: Feasibility Study.* NHTSA Contract no. DOT-HS-8-02024. Ann Arbor: University of Michigan, Highway Safety Research Institute (now Transport Research Institute).

Donelson, A. C., Marks, M. F.; Jones, R. E.; and Joscelyn, K. B. 1980. *Drug Research Methodology, Volume One. The Alcohol–Highway Safety Experience and Its Applicability to Other Drugs.* Report no. DOT-HS-805-354. Washington, DC: NHTSA.

Donelson, A. C.; Mayhew, D. R.; and Simpson, H. M. 1985. *Dealing with the Alcohol-Crash Problem: A Role for Health Promotion.* Ottawa, Ontario: Department of National Health and Welfare.

Donovan, D. M., and Marlatt, G. A. 1982. Personality Subtypes among Driving-While-Intoxicated Offenders: Relationship to Drinking Behavior and Driving Risk. *Journal of Consulting and Clinical Psychology* 50:241–49.

Donovan, D. M.; Marlatt, G. A.; and Salzberg, P. M. 1983. Drinking Behavior, Personality Factors, and High-Risk Driving: A Review and Theoretical Formulation. *Journal of Studies on Alcohol* 44:395–428.

Donovan, D. M.; Queisser, H. R.; Saltzberg, P. M.; and Umlauf, R. L. 1985. Intoxicated and Bad Drivers: Subgroups within the Same Population of High-Risk Men Drivers. *Journal of Studies on Alcohol* 46:375–82.

Douglass, R. L. 1982. Repeating Cycles of Concern and Complacency: The Public Interest and Political Response to Alcohol-Related Traffic Accidents. *Abstracts and Reviews in Alcohol and Driving* 3 (4):3–5.

————. 1980. The Legal Drinking Age and Traffic Casualties: A Special Case of Changing Alcohol Availability in a Public Health Context. In *Minimum-Drinking-Age Laws,* ed. H. Wechsler, 93–132. Lexington, MA: Lexington Books, D. C. Heath and Co.

Dubowski, K. M. 1986. Recent Development in Alcohol Analysis. *Alcohol, Drugs, and Driving: Abstracts and Reviews* 2 (2):13–46.

————. 1985. Absorption, Distribution, and Elimination of Alcohol: Highway Safety Aspects. *Journal of Studies on Alcohol,* Supplement no. 10:98–108.

Dubowski, K. M. 1984. Absorption, Distribution, and Elimination of Alcohol: Highway Safety Aspects. Paper presented at the meeting of the North American Conference on Alcohol and Highway Safety, Baltimore, MD.

————. 1963. Alcohol Determination—Some Physiological and Metabolic Considerations. In *Alcohol and Traffic Safety,* ed. B. H. Fox and J. H. Fox, 91–115. U.S. Public Health Service Publication no. 1043. Washington, DC: Government Printing Office.

Dunbar, J. A.; Pikkarainan, J.; and Penttila, A. In press. Detection of Problem Drinkers: A Comparison of Finland and Scotland. In *Proceedings of the 10th International Conference on Alcohol, Drugs, and Traffic Safety.*

Durell, J., and Bukoski, W. 1984. Preventing Substance Abuse: The State of the Art. *Public Health Reports* 99:23–31.

Eagleston, J., et al. 1975. *Continued Monitoring and Evaluation of NIAAA-Funded Problem Drinking Driver Programs.* Technical Report. Stanford, CA: Stanford Research Institute.

Ehrenzweig, A. 1955. "Full Aid" Coverage for the Traffic Victim. *California Law Review* 43:1–48.

Ennis, P., and Vingilis, E. 1981. The Validity of a Revised Version of the Mortimer-Filkins Tests with Impaired Drivers in Oshawa, Ontario. *Journal of Studies on Alcohol* 42:685–88.

Essex, D. W., and Weinerth, W. B. 1982. *Effects of Treatment on the DUI Offender in Ventura County.* Ventura, CA: Alcohol Services Program, Health Care Agency, County of Ventura.

Estep, R., and Wallack, L. 1985. *The Message and the Media: Drinking and Driving in Newspapers.* Washington, DC: U.S. Department of Transportation.

Evangelische Akademie Bad Boll (Hrsg.). 1982. Der alkoholauffällige Kraftfahrer. Ergänzende Massnahmen zum Sanktionssystem des geltenden Rechts aus verkehrspädagogischer Sicht. *Protokolldienst* 3/82.

Falkowski, C. L. 1986. The Impact of Two-Day Jail Sentences for Drunk Drivers in Hennepin County, Minnesota. *Journal of Safety Research* 17:33–42.

Farina, A. J. 1985. *Alcohol/Drink Equivalency and Evaluation of the Topic.* Technical Report. Washington, DC: NHTSA.

Farris, R.; Malone, T. B.; and Kirkpatrick, M. 1977. *A Comparison of Alcohol Involvement in Exposed and Injured Drivers.* Report no. DOT-HS-802-555. Washington, DC: NHTSA.

Farris, R.; Malone, T. B.; and Lilliefors, H. 1976. *A Comparison of Alcohol Involvement in Exposed and Injured Drivers: Phase I and II.* Technical Report no. DOT-HS-801-096. Washington, DC: NHTSA.

Federal Bureau of Statistics. 1973. Vorbericht 1973. *Fachserie H: Verkehr.* Reihe 6:8. Wiesbaden: Statistisches Bundesamt.

Feeley, M. 1979. *The Process Is the Punishment.* New York: Russell Sage Foundation.

Fell, J. C. 1985. *Alcohol Involvement in Fatal Accidents, 1980–1984*. Washington, DC: U.S. Department of Transportation.

————. 1984. *Alcohol in Fatal Accidents for Various Driver Age Groups*. Washington, DC: NHTSA.

————. 1982. Alcohol Involvement in Traffic Crashes. *Quarterly Journal of the American Association for Automotive Medicine* 4:31–38.

Fell, J. C., and Klein, T. 1986. *The Nature of the Reduction in Alcohol in U.S. Fatal Crashes*. Warrendale, PA: Society of Automotive Engineers, Inc.

Ferguson, L., and Kirk, J. 1979. *Statistical Report: NIAAA Funded Treatment Programs, Calendar Year 1978*. Rockville, MD: National Institute for Alcohol Abuse and Alcoholism.

Ferreira, J. 1970. *Quantitative Models for Automobile Accidents and Insurance*. Washington, DC: U.S. Department of Transportation.

Fields, N., and Hricko, A. R. 1986. Passive Alcohol Sensors—Constitutional Implications. Manuscript, available from Insurance Institute for Highway Safety, Washington, DC.

Fielding, J. E. 1977. Health Promotions: Some Notions in Search of a Constituency. *American Journal of Public Health* 67:1082–86.

Filkins, L. D.; Clark, C. D.; Rosenblatt, C. A.; Carlson, W. L.; Kerlan, M. V.; and Manson, H. 1970. *Alcohol Abuse and Traffic Safety: A Study of Fatalities, DWI Offenders, Alcoholics, and Court-Related Treatment Approaches*. Washington, DC: NHTSA.

Filkins, L. D.; Mortimer, R. G.; Post, D. V.; and Chapman, M. M. 1973. *Field Evaluation of Court Procedures for Identifying Problem Drinkers*. Technical Report no. DOT-HS-031-2-303. Washington, DC: NHTSA.

Fingl, E., and Woodbury, D. M. 1975. General Priciples. In *The Pharmacological Basis of Therapeutics*. 5th ed., ed. L. S. Goodman and A. Gilman, 1–46. New York: Macmillan.

Finkelstein, M. M. 1986. *Alcohol Statistics in Fatal Accidents: Update as of June 10, 1986*. Washington, DC: Department of Transportation.

Fishbein, M., and Ajzen, I. 1975. *Belief, Attitude, Intention, and Behavior: An Introduction to Theory and Research*. Reading, MA: Addison-Wesley.

Flay, B. R.; Di Tecco, D.; and Schlegel, R. P. 1980. Mass Media in Health Promotion: An Analysis Using an Extended Information-Processing Model. *Health Education Quarterly* 7:127–47.

Ford, D., and Schmidt, A. K. 1985. *Electronically Monitored Home Confinement*. Report no. SNI 194. Washington, DC: National Institute of Justice.

Forney, R. B., and Harger, R. N. 1971. The Alcohols. In *Drill's Pharmacology in Medicine*. 4th ed., ed. J. R. DiPalma, 275–302. New York: McGraw-Hill.

Fox, B. H., and Borkenstein, R. F. 1966. Patterns of Blood Alcohol Concentrations among Drivers. In *Alcohol, Drugs, and Traffic Safety*, ed. S.

Israelstam and S. Lambert, 51–67. Toronto, Ontario: Addiction Research Foundation of Ontario.

Foy, D. W., and Simon, S. J. 1978. Alcoholic Drinking Topography as a Function of Solitary versus Social Context. *Addictive Behaviors* 3:39–41.

Frank, J. F. 1985. *Laboratory Testing of Two Prototype In-Vehicle Breath Test Devices.* Technical Report no. DOT-HS-806-821. Washington, DC: NHTSA.

Frank, J. F., and Flores, A. L. 1986. *Laboratory Testing of Alcoscan Saliva-Alcohol Test Strips.* Technical Report no. DOT-HS-807-059. Washington, DC: NHTSA.

Freifeld, K., and Engelmayer, S. 1985. Booze Blockers. *Health* 17 (February), 44–47.

Gallup, G., Jr. 1985. Alcohol Use and Abuse in America. *The Gallup Report* (November), Report no. 242.

Gart, J. J. 1962. Approximate Confidence Limits for the Relative Risk. *Journal of the Royal Statistical Society* 24:454–63.

Garwood, F., and Johnson, H. D. 1969. Statistical Studies Leading to Breath Tests (Road Safety Act, 1967). Paper presented to the Manchester Statistical Society, England.

Gebauer, W. 1980. *Untersuchungen zu "Alkohol und Fahren."* Band 5: Teil 1—Literaturauswertung über Ursachen der Alkoholdelinquenz im Strassenverkehr sowie über Massnahmen und Erfahrungen bei ihrer Bekämpfung. PROGNOS. Teil 2—Zur Entwicklung des Alkoholkonsums in der Bundesrepublik Deutschland bis 1979. Forschungsberichte der Bundesanstalt für Strassenwesen, Bereich Unfallforschung. Heft 48. Köln:.Bundesanstalt für Strassenwesen.

Gebhardt, H.-J. 1981. Die Nachschulung alkoholauffälliger Kraftfahrer und die gerichtliche Praxis. In *19. Deutscher Verkehrsgerichtstag.* Hamburg.

Geller, E. S.; Altomari, M. G.; and Russ, N. W. 1984. Innovative Approaches to Drunk Driving Prevention. Special seminar on alcohol and driving. Warren, MI: Societal Analysis Department, General Motors Research Laboratories.

Geller, E. S.; Altomari, M. G.; Russ, N. W.; and Harwood, M. K. 1985. Exploring the Drinking/Driving Behaviors and Attitudes of College Students. *Resources in Education* Ms. no. ED252756.

Geller, E. S.; Kalsher, M.J.; and Lehman, G. R. 1987. Beer versus Mixed-Drink Consumption at University Parties: A Time and Place for LA Beer (under editorial review).

Geller, E. S., and Nimmer, J. G. In press. Social Marketing and Applied Behavior Analysis: An Integration for Quality of Life Intervention. In *Quality of Life/Marketing Interface,* ed. A. C. Samli. Westport, CT: Greenwood Press.

Geller, E. S., and Russ, N. W. 1986. Drunk Driving Prevention: Knowing When to Say When. In *Alcohol, Accidents, and Injuries.* Warrendale, PA: Society of Automotive Engineers, Inc.

Geller, E. S.; Russ, N. W.; and Altomari, M. G. 1986. Naturalistic Observations of Beer Drinking among College Students. *Journal of Applied Behavior Analysis* 19:391–96.

Ghiardi, J. 1972. The Case against Punitive Damages. *The Forum* 8:411–24.

Gibbs, J. P. 1975. *Crime, Punishment, and Deterrence.* New York: Elsevier.

Gjerde, H.; Sakshaug, J.; and Mørland, J. 1986. Heavy Drinking among Norwegian Male Drunken Drivers. *Alcoholism, Clinical Experimental Research* 2:209–12.

Glad, A. 1985. *Research on Drinking and Driving in Norway: A Survey of Recent Research on Drinking and Driving and on Drinking Drivers.* Oslo: Institute of Transport Economics.

Glatt, M. M. 1963. Recurrent Driving "Under the Influence." In *Alcohol and Road Traffic,* ed. J. D. J. Havard, 99–103. Proceedings of the 3rd International Conference on Alcohol and Road Traffic, 3–7 September 1962. London: British Medical Association.

Goding, S., and Dobie, R. A. 1986. Gaze Nystagmus and Blood Alcohol. *Laryngoscope* 96:713–17.

Goldberg, L. 1963. The Metabolism of Alcohol. In *Alcohol and Civilization,* ed. S. P. Lucia, 23–27. New York: McGraw-Hill.

————. 1943. Quantitative Studies on Alcohol Tolerance in Man. The Influence of Ethyl Alcohol on Sensory, Motor and Psychological Functions Referred to Blood Alcohol in Normal and Habituated Individuals. *Acta Physiol. Scand.* 5(Suppl. 16):1.

Goldstein, H., and Susmilch, C. 1982. *The Drinking-Driver in Madison; A Study of the Problem and the Community's Response.* Madison: University of Wisconsin School of Law.

Goodstadt, M. S. 1980. Drug Education—A Turn On or a Turn Off? *Journal of Drug Education* 10:89–99.

————. 1978. Alcohol and Drug Education: Models and Outcomes. *Health Educational Monographs* 6:263–79.

Graham, K. 1984. Determinants of Heavy Drinking and Drinking Problems: The Contribution of the Bar Environment. Paper presented at the symposium on Public Drinking and Public Policy, Banff, Alberta.

Graham, K. 1979. Liability of the Social Host for Injuries Caused by the Negligent Acts of Intoxicated Guests. *Willamette Law Journal* 16:561–89.

Grasmick, H. G., and Bryjak, G. J. 1980. The Deterrent Effect of Perceived Severity of Punishment. *Social Forces* 59:471–91.

Greenberg, D. F. 1979. *Mathematical Criminology.* New Brunswick, NJ: Rutgers University Press.

Greenberg, L. A. 1968. The Pharmacology of Alcohol and Its Relationship of Drinking and Driving. *Quarterly Journal of Studies on Alcohol,* Supplement no. 4:252–66.

Gusfield, J. 1986. *Epilogue to Symbolic Crusade.* 2d ed. Urbana: University of Illinois Press.

Gusfield, J. 1985. Social and Cultural Contexts of the Drinking-Driving Event. *Journal of Studies on Alcohol,* Supplement no. 10:70–77.

—————. 1982. Prevention: Rise, Decline, and Renaissance. In *Alcohol, Science, and Society Revisited,* ed. E. Gomberg, H. White, and J. Carpenter, 402–25. Ann Arbor: University of Michigan Press.

—————. 1981a. *The Culture of Public Problems. Drinking and Driving and the Symbolic Order.* Chicago: University of Chicago Press.

—————. 1981b. The Grass-Roots Movement against Drinking-Driving. *Abstracts and Reviews in Alcohol and Driving* 2 (12):8–9.

—————. 1972. A Study of Drinking Drivers in San Diego County. Unpublished.

—————. 1963. *Symbolic Crusade: Status Politics and the American Temperance Movement.* Urbana: University of Illinois Press.

Haddon, W. 1972. A Logical Framework for Categorizing Highway Safety Phenomena and Activity. *Journal of Trauma* 12:193–207.

Hagen, R. E. 1978. The Efficacy of Licensing Controls as a Countermeasure for Multiple DUI Offenders. *Journal of Safety Research* 10:115–22.

Hagen, R. E.; Williams, R. L.; and McConnell, E. J. 1979. The Traffic Safety Impact of Alcohol Abuse Treatment as an Alternative to Mandated Licensing Controls. *Accident Analysis and Prevention* 11:275–92.

Haight, F. 1985. Current Problems in Drinking-Driving: Research and Intervention. *Journal of Studies on Alcohol,* Supplement no. 10:13–18.

—————. 1983. *Road Safety: A Perspective and a New Strategy.* University Park: Pennsylvania Transportation Institute, Pennsylvania State University.

Hall, R. W. 1977. An Alternative to the Criminality of Driving While Intoxicated. *Journal of Police Science and Administration* 5:138–44.

Hames, L. N., and Petrucelli, E. 1980. A Plan for Influencing Teenage Drinking Drivers. In *Alcohol, Drugs, and Traffic Safety,* Vol. 3, ed. L. Goldberg, 1414–28. Stockholm: Almqvist and Wiksell.

Hamilton, C., and Collins, J., Jr. 1981. The Role of Alcohol in Wife Beating and Child Abuse. In *Drinking and Crime,* ed. J. Collins, 253–98. London: Tavistock Publications.

Hanson, D. J., and Engs, R. C. 1986. College Students' Drinking Problems. *Psychological Reports* 58:276–78.

—————. 1984. College Students' Drinking Attitudes. *Psychological Reports* 54:300–302.

Hanson, D. J.; Engs, R. C.; and Katter, H. 1985. College Students' Attitudes toward Drinking—1983: Exploring Socialization Theory. *College Student Journal* 10:425–29.

Harger, R. N., and Hulpieu, H. R. 1956. The Pharmacology of Alcohol. In *Alcoholism,* ed. G. N. Thompson. Springfield: Charles C. Thomas.

Harriott, W. F. 1973. *Status Report on Portable Breath Testers.* Cambridge, MA: Transportation Research Center.

Harris, D. H.; Dick, R. A.; Casey, S. M.; and Jarosz, C. J. 1980. *The Visual Detection of Driving While Intoxicated. Field Test of Visual Cues and*

Detection Methods. Final Report no. DOT-HS-805-051. Washington, DC: NHTSA.

Harris, D. H.; Howlett, J. B.; and Ridgeway, R. G. 1979. *Visual Detection of Driving While Intoxicated.* Technical Report no. DOT-HS-805-051. Washington, DC: NHTSA.

Hartunian, N. S; Smart, C. H.; and Thompson, M. A. 1981. *The Incidence and Economic Costs of Major Health Impairments: A Comparative Analysis of Cancer, Motor Vehicle Injuries, Coronary Heart Disease and Stroke.* Lexington, MA: D. C. Heath and Co.

Harwood, M. K. 1984. New Directions toward Increasing Awareness of Alcohol Impairment. Senior research paper. Virginia Polytechnic Institute.

Haskins, J. B., and Haskins, T. S. 1985. Major Social Action Groups against Drunken Drivers. *Journal of Studies on Alcohol,* Supplement no. 10:192–95.

Hauge, R. 1982. Alkoholbruk og promillekjøring. In *Lov og frihet. Festskrift til,* ed. J. Andenaes, A. Bratholm, N. Christie, and C. Smith, 151–64. Oslo: Universitetsforlaget.

————. 1978. Drinking-and-Driving: Biochemistry, Law, and Morality. *Scandinavian Studies in Criminology* 6:61–68.

Hauge, R., and Irgens-Jensen, O. 1986. The Relationship between Alcohol Consumption, Alcohol Intoxication, and Negative Consequences of Drinking in Four Scandinavian Countries. *British Journal of Addiction* 81:513–24.

————. 1980. *Road Traffic Accidents and Liquor Store Strikes.* Oslo: National Institute for Alcohol Research.

Hauge, R., and Nordlie, O. 1984. Beruselse og ordensforstyrrelse. In *Virkninger av lørdagsstengte vinmonopolutsalg,* 108–21. Oslo: National Institute for Alcohol Research.

Hause, J., and Chavez, E. 1979. *Implementation Manual for DUI Enforcement.* Report no. DOT-HS-5-01194. Washington, DC: NHTSA.

Hause, J.; Voas, R.; and Chavez, E. 1982. Conducting Voluntary Roadside Surveys: The Stockton Experience. In *Proceedings of the Satellite Conference to the 8th International Conference on Alcohol, Drug, and Traffic Safety,* ed. M. R. Valverius, 104–13. Stockholm: The Swedish Council for Information on Alcohol and Other Drugs.

Hawkins, G. 1971. Punishment and Deterrence: The Educative, Moralizing, and Habituative Effects. In *Theories of Punishment,* ed. S. E. Grupp, 163–80. Bloomington: Indiana University Press.

Hedlund, J.; Arnold, R.; Cerrelli, E.; Partyka, S.; Hoxie, P.; and Skinner, D. 1983. *An Assessment of the 1982 Traffic Fatality Decrease.* Washington, DC: NHTSA.

Hebenstreit, B. V.; Heinrich, H. Ch.; Klebe, W.; Kroj, G.; Spoerer, E.; Schneider, W.; Walther, R.; Winkler, W.; and Wuhrer, H. 1982. *Kurse für auffällige Kraftfahrer.* Projektgruppenberichte der Bundesanstalt für Strassenwesen, Bereich Unfallforschung. Heft 12. Köln: Bundesanstalt für Strassenwesen.

—————. 1981. *Kurse für auffällige Kraftfahrer—Zwischenbericht 1981.* Projektgruppenberichte der Bundesanstalt für Strassenwesen, Bereich Unfallforschung. Heft 11. Köln: Bundesanstalt für Strassenwesen.

—————. 1980. *Kurse für auffälige Kraftfahrer—Zwischenbericht 1980.* Projektgruppenberichte der Bundesanstalt für Strassenwesen, Bereich Unfallforschung. Heft 7. Köln: Bundesanstalt für Strassenwesen.

—————. 1979. *Kurse für auffälige Kraftfahrer—Zwischenbericht 1979: Erfahrungen und Perspektiven.* Projektgruppenberichte der Bundesanstalt für Strassenwesen, Bereich Unfallforschung. Heft 6. Köln: Bundesanstalt für Strassenwesen.

—————. 1978. *Kurse für auffällige Kraftfahrer—Modellversuche in der Bundesrepublik Deutschland.* Köln: Bundesanstalt für Strassenwesen.

Hedlund, J. H. 1985. Recent U.S. Traffic Fatality Trends. In *Human Behavior and Traffic Safety,* ed. L. Evans and R. C. Schwing, 7–19. New York: Plenum Press.

Heeren, T.; Smith, R. A.; Morelock, S.; and Hingson, R. W. 1985. Surrogate Measures of Alcohol Involvement in Fatal Crashes: Are Conventional Indicators Adequate? *Journal of Safety Research* 16:127–34.

Heinrich, H. Ch., and Hundhausen, G. 1982. Möglichkeiten zu einer Neugestaltung des Fahrerausbildungssystems. Forschungsberichte der Bundesanstalt für Strassenwesen, Berich Unfallforschung. Heft 73. Köln: Bundesanstalt für Strassenwesen.

Heise, H. A. 1955. Educational Procedures in the United States. In *Proceedings of the 2nd International Conference on Alcohol and Road Traffic,* 16–17. Toronto: Garden City Press.

Heise, H. E. 1934. Alcohol and Auto Accidents. *Journal of the American Medical Association* 103:739–41.

Henderson, R. 1977. No Fault Plans for Automobile Accidents. *Or. L. Rev.* 56:287–329.

Hilton, M. 1984. The Impact of Recent Changes in California Drinking-Driving Laws on Fatal Accident Levels during the First Post-Intervention Year. *Law and Society Review* 18:605–28.

Hingson, R.; Heeren, T.; Kovenock, D.; Mangione, T.; Meyers, A.; Morelock, S.; Smith, R.; Lederman, R.; and Scotch, N. A. 1986. *Effects of Maine's 1981 and Massachusetts' 1982 Driving-under-the-Influence Legislation.* Boston: Boston University of Medicine.

Hirsch, J. 1956. Public Health and Social Aspects of Alcoholism. In *Alcoholism,* ed. G. M. Thompson, 3–102. Springfield, IL: Charles C. Thomas.

Hirshi, T. 1969. *Causes of Delinquency.* Berkeley, CA: University of California Press.

Holcomb, R. L. 1938. Alcohol in Relation to Traffic Accidents. *Journal of the American Medical Association* 111:1076–85.

Holden, R. T. 1983. Rehabilitative Sanctions for Drunk Driving: An Experimental Evaluation. *Journal of Research in Crime and Delinquency* 20:55–72.

Homel, R. 1986. *Policing the Drinking Driver.* Canberra: Federal Office of Road Safety.

————. 1986. Australia's Experience with Random Breath Testing. Paper presented at the University of New Mexico, Albuquerque.

————. 1980. *Penalties and the Drink/Driver: A Study of One Thousand Offenders.* Sydney, Australia: Department of the Attorney General and Justice.

Horverak, O. 1983. The 1976 Strike at the Norwegian Wine and Spirits Monopoly. *British Journal of Addiction* 78.

Huntley, M. S. 1973. Alcohol Influences upon Closed-Course Driving Performance. *Journal of Safety Research* 5 (3):149–64.

Hurst, P. M. 1978. Blood Test Legislation in New Zealand. *Accident Analysis and Prevention* 10:287–96.

————. 1974. Epidemiological Aspects of Alcohol in Driver Crashes and Citations. In *Alcohol, Drugs, and Driving,* ed. M. W. Perrine, 131–57. Report no. DOT-IIS-801-096. Washington, DC: NHTSA.

————. 1970. Estimating the Effectiveness of Blood Alcohol Limits. *Behavioral Research in Highway Safety* 1:87–99.

Ifft, R. A. 1983. Curbing the Drunk Driver under the Fourth Amendment: The Constitutionality of Roadblock Seizures. *Georgetown Law Journal* 71:1457–86.

Infratest Gesundheitsforschung. 1979. *Alkoholaffinität/Biogrammdaten.* Tabellenband Alkoholaffinität. München: Infratest.

Insurance Institute for Highway Safety. 1986. Highway Death Rate Cut More Than Half Since Safety Acts. *Status Report* 21 (11):1–3, 5.

————. 1984. Teenagers Admit Illegal Driving and Other Traffic Violations. *Status Report* 19 (18):1–7.

Irgens-Jensen, O. 1984. Virkninger av lørdagsstengning ved vinmonopolets utsalg for omfanget av promillekjøring. In *Virkninger av lørdagsstengte vinmonopolutsalg,* 138–52. Oslo: National Institute for Alcohol Research.

Irwin, A. 1985. *Risk and Control of Technology: Public Policies for Road Traffic Safety in Britain and the United States.* Manchester, England: Manchester University Press.

Irwin, D. 1986. Many Drunk Drivers Not Prosecuted, Study Finds. *Los Angeles Times,* 1 December, 1–19.

Jacobson, G. R. 1975. *Diagnosis and Assessment of Alcohol Abuse and Alcoholism.* DHEW Pub. no. 76-228. Rockville, MD: National Institute for Alcohol Abuse and Alcoholism.

Janiszewski, H. 1981. Entziehung der Fahrerlaubnis und kein Ende. In *Bundesregierung der Bundesrepublik Deutschland: Gesetzentwurf zur Änderung des Strassenverkehrsrechts und des Strafgesetzbuches.*

Janiszewski, H. 1974. Neuerungen im Strabenverkehrsrecht. *Blutalkohol* 11:312–28.

Jellinek, E. M. 1960. *The Disease Concept of Alcoholism.* Highland Park, NJ: Hillhouse Press.

Jenkins, J. T. 1970. An Evaluation Investigation Concerned with Teaching Selected Concepts Related to Alcohol and Traffic Involvement. Master's thesis, Southern Illinois University.

Jessor, R., and Jessor, S. L. 1977. *Problem Behavior and Psychosocial Development: A Longitudinal Study of Youth.* New York: Academic Press.

————. 1975. Adolescent Development and the Onset of Drinking: A Longitudinal Study. *Journal of Studies on Alcohol* 36:27–51.

Jessup, J. 1979. The Liquor Issue in American History: A Bibliography. In *Alcohol Reform and Society: The Liquor Issue in Social Context,* ed. J. S. Blocker, Jr. Westport, CT: Greenwood Press.

Johnson, D. 1962. Drunken Driving—The Civil Responsibility of the Purveyor of Intoxicating Liquors. *Indiana Law Journal* 37:317–31.

Johnson, D. 1983. Drunkenness May Not Be Accurately Measured by Blood-Alcohol Levels: UCB Researchers Report. *Public Information Office News.* Boulder, CO: University of Colorado.

Johnson's Liquor Handbook. 1986.

Johnston, I. 1982. *Deterring the Drinking Driver—Australia's Experience.* Internal Report. Vermont South, Victoria: Australian Road Research Board.

Jones, I. S. 1986. *The Development and Evaluation of a Passive Alcohol Sensor.* Washington, DC: Insurance Institute for Highway Safety.

Jones, I. S., and Lund, A. K. 1985. Detection of Alcohol-Impaired Drivers Using a Passive Alcohol Sensor. *Journal of Police Science and Administration* 14 (2).

Jones, R., and Joscelyn, K. 1978. *Alcohol and Highway Safety, 1978: A Review of the State of Knowledge.* Technical Report no. DOT-HS-5-01207. Washington, DC: NHTSA.

Jones-Lee, M. W. 1976. *The Value of Life: An Economic Analysis.* Chicago: University of Chicago Press.

Judicial Council of California. 1985. *Annual Report of the Administrative Office of the California Courts.* Sacramento, CA: Judicial Council of California.

Justizminister Baden-Württemberg. 1981. *Symposium 1980: Nachschulung alkoholauffälliger Ersttäter.* Ein Schritt zur Verbesserung des Rechts der Entziehung der Fahrerlabunis. Stuttgart.

Kalsher, M. J., and Geller, E. S. 1987. Beer Consumption at University Parties: Stimulus Control of Brand Labels (under editorial review).

Karaharju, E. O., and Stjernval, L. 1974. The Alcohol Factor in Accidents. *Injury* 6:67–69.

Keenan, A. 1973. Liquor Law Liability in California. *Santa Clara Law Review* 14:46–96.

Keeton, R. 1971. *Insurance Law: Basic Text*. St. Paul, MN: West.

Keeton, R., and O'Connell, J. 1965. *Basic Protection for the Traffic Victim: A Blueprint for Reforming Automobile Insurance*. Boston: Little Brown.

Kerner, H.-J. 1985. *Untersuchungen zu "Alkohol und Fahren."* Band 11: Gesetzgebung, polizeiliche überwachung und Strafgerichtsbarkeit in der Bundesrepublik Deutschland. Forschungsberichte der Bundesanstalt für Strassenwesen, Bereich Unfallforschung. Heft 115. Bergisch Gladbach: Bundesanstalt für Strassenwesen.

Kitsuse, J., and Cicourel, A. 1963. A Note on the Use of Official Statistics. *Social Problems* 11:131–39.

Klein, D. 1985. *The Impact and Consequences of the 1982 Law on Drunk Driving Adjudication*. Oakland, CA: Office of Court Services, Alameda County, California.

Klein, D., and Waller, J. A. 1970. *Causation, Culpability, and Determination in Highway Crashes*. Report prepared for the U.S. Department of Transportation, Automobile Insurance and Compensation Study. Washington, DC: Government Printing Office.

Klette, H. 1978. On the Politics of Drunken Driving in Sweden. *Scandinavian Studies in Criminology* 6:113–20.

Klitzner, M.; Blasinsky, M.; Marshall, K.; and Paquet, U. 1985. *Determinants of Youth Attitudes and Skills towards Which Drinking/Driving Prevention Programs Should Be Directed. Volume 1: The State of the Art in Youth DWI Prevention Programs*. Washington, DC: U.S. Department of Transportation.

Kohn, P. M.; Goodstadt, M. S.; Cook, G. M.; Sheppard, M.; and Chan, G. 1982. Ineffectiveness of Threat Appeals about Drinking and Driving. *Accident Analysis and Prevention* 14:457–64.

Kolata, G. 1986. New Drug Counters Alcohol Intoxication. *Science* 234:1198–99.

Kornhauser, L. 1985. Review: Theory and Fact in the Law of Accidents. *California Law Review* 73:1024–42.

Kretschmer, E., and Riediger, G. 1979. Forschungskonzeption "Alkohol und Fahren." *Blutalkohol* 16:409–23.

Kretschmer-Bäumel, E., and Karstedt-Henke, S. 1986. *Untersuchungen zu "Alkohol und Fahren."* Band 13: Orientierungs und Verhaltensmuster der Kraftfahrer—Ergebnisse einer Befragung. Forschungsberichte der Bundesanstalt für Strassenwesen, Bereich Unfallforschung. Heft 128. Bergisch Gladbach: Bundesanstalt für Strassenwesen.

Kroj, G. 1982. Drinking and Driving: Data and Measures in the Federal Republic of Germany. In *Unfall—und Sicherheitsforschung Strassenverkehr*, Heft 39, 79–97. Köln: Bundesanstalt für Strassenwesen.

Landgericht Heilbronn. 1982. 3 OS 328/82. *Die Justiz* 9/82:338.

Landrum, J.; Miles, S.; Neff, R.; Pritchard, T.; Roebuck, J.; Wells-Parker, E.; and Windham, G. 1982. *Mississippi DUI Probation Follow-up Project*. Washington, DC: U.S. Department of Transportation.

Langenbucher, J. W., and Nathan, P. E. 1983. Psychology, Public Policy, and the Evidence for Alcohol Intoxication. *American Psychologist* 38: 1070–77.

Larson, J. H. 1985. *North Dakota's Response to Legal and Programming Intervention into Drinking and Driving: After Two Years*. Grand Forks: University of North Dakota.

Ledermann, S. 1964. *Alcool, alcoolisme, alcoolisation. Mortalité, morbidité, accidents de travail*. Paris: Presses Universitaires de France.

———. 1956. *Alcool, alcoolisme, alcoolisation. Donnees scientifiques de caractere physiologique, économique et social*. Paris: Presses Universitaires de France.

Legat, S. 1985. Die Nachschulung: Ein Kommunikationsproblem zwischen Richtern und Psychologen. *Blutalkohol* 22:130–39.

———. 1981. Rechtsprechung oder "operational research"? *Blutalkohol* 18:17–28.

Lelbach, W. K. 1974. Organic Pathology Related to Volume and Pattern of Alcohol Use. In *Research Advances in Alcohol and Drug Problems*, Vol. 1, ed. R. J. Gibbins et al., 93–198. New York: Wiley and Sons.

Lemberger, L., and Rubin, A. 1976. *Physiologic Disposition of Drugs of Abuse*. New York: Spectrum.

Levine, H. G. 1984. The Alcohol Problem in America: From Temperance to Alcoholism. *British Journal of Addiction* 79:109–19.

Levine, J. M.; Greenbaum, C. D.; and Notkin, E. R. 1973. *The Effect of Alcohol on Human Performance: A Classification and Integration of Research Findings*. Washington, DC: American Institute for Research.

Levine, J. M.; Kramer, G. G.; and Levine, E. N. 1975. Effects of Alcohol on Human Performance: An Integration of Research Findings Based on Abilities Classification. *Journal of Applied Psychology* 60:285–93.

Liban, C. B.; Vingilis, E.; and Blefgen, H. 1985. *Drinking-Driving Countermeasure Review: The Canadian Experience*. Toronto: Addiction Research Foundation.

Lightner, C. 1981. Chronicles of a Grass-Roots Organization: Mothers Against Drunk Drivers (MADD). *Abstracts and Review in Alcohol and Driving* 1:6–7.

Lin, Y.-J.; Weidler, D. J.; Garg, D. C.; and Wagner, J. G. 1976. Effects of Solid Food on Blood Alcohol Levels of Alcohol in Man. *Research Communications in Chemical Pathology* 13:713–22.

Lindén, P., and Similä, M. 1982. *Rättsmedvetandet i Sverige*. Stockholm: Brottsförebyggande rådet.

Linton, J. 1955. Recent Studies of Educational Procedures in Canada. In *Proceedings of the 2nd International Conference on Alcohol and Road Traffic*, 22–23. Toronto: Garden City Press.

Little, J. W. 1971. A Theory and Empirical Study of What Deters Drinking Drivers, If, When, and Why! *Administrative Law Review* 23:169–93.

Long, R. 1976. *The Law of Liability Insurance*. Albany, NY: Matthew Bender.

Los Angeles Times. 1987. Pushing to Put Lock on Drunk Drivers. 3 January 1987, II-1, 10.

Lubetkin, B. S.; Rivers, P. C.; and Rosenberg, C. M. 1971. Difficulties of Disulfiram Therapy with Alcoholics. *Quarterly Journal of the Studies of Alcohol* 32:168–71.

Lucas, G. W.; Kalow, W.; McColl, J. D.; Griffith, B. A.; and Smith, H. W. 1955. Quantitative Studies of the Relationship between Alcohol Levels and Motor Vehicle Accidents. In *Proceedings of the 2nd International Conference on Alcohol and Road Traffic*, 139–42. Toronto: Garden City Press.

Lund, A. K., and Jones, I. S. 1986. Detection of Impaired Drivers with a Passive Alcohol Sensor. Paper presented at 10th International Conference on Alcohol, Drugs, and Traffic Safety, Amsterdam.

Lund, A. K.; Williams, A. F.; and Zador, P. 1986. High School Driver Education: Further Evaluation of the DeKalb County Study. *Accident Analysis and Prevention* 18:349–57.

McGuire, F. L. 1978. The Effectiveness of a Treatment Program for the Alcohol-Involved Driver. *American Journal of Drug and Alcohol Abuse* 5:517–25.

McGuire, W. J. 1974. Communication-Persuasion Models for Drug Education. In *Research on Methods and Programs of Drug Education*, ed. M. Goodstadt, 1–26. Toronto: Addiction Research Foundation.

McKnight, A. J. 1986. Intervention in Teenage Drunk Driving. *Alcohol, Drugs, and Driving: Abstracts and Reviews* 2:17–28.

McKnight, A. J., and McPherson, K. 1986. Evaluation of Peer Intervention Training for High School Alcohol Safety Education. *Accident Analysis and Prevention* 18:339–47.

McKnight, A. J.; Preusser, D. F.; Psotka, J.; Katz, D. B.; and Edwards, J. M. 1979. *Youth Alcohol Safety Education Criteria Development*. Washington, DC: U.S. Department of Transportation.

McLean, A. J.; Clark, M. S.; Dorsch, M. M.; Holubowycz, O. T.; and McCaul, K. A. 1984. *Random Breath Testing in South Australia: Effects on Drink-Driving, Accidents, and Casualties*. Adelaide, Australia: National Health and Medical Research Council Road Accident Research Unit, University of Adelaide.

McLean, A. J., and Robinson, G. K. 1979. *Adelaide In-Depth Accident Study 1975–1979, Part One, An Overview*. Adelaide, Australia: National Health and Medical Research Council Road Accident Research Unit, University of Adelaide.

McNeely, M. 1941. Illegality as a Factor in Liability Insurance. *Columbia Law Review* 41:26–60.

MADD. 1982. *National Newsletter* (Spring).

Maisey, G. E., and Saunders, C. M. 1981. *An Evaluation of the 1980/81 Christmas/New Year Traffic Enforcement Blitz.* Perth: Road Traffic Authority of Western Australia Research and Statistics Report no. 16.

Mäkelä, K. 1978. Level of Consumption and Social Consequences of Drinking. In *Research Advances in Alcohol and Drug Problems,* ed. Y. Israel, R. B. Glaser, H. Kalant, R. E. Popham, W. Schmidt, and R. G. Smart. New York: Plenum Press.

————. 1974. *Types of Alcohol Restrictions, Types of Drinkers and Types of Alcohol Damages: The Case of the Personnel Strike in the Stores of the Finnish Alcohol Monopoly.* Helsinki: Social Research Institute of Alcohol Studies.

Mäkelä, K.; Room, R.; Single, E.; Sulkunen, P.; and Walsh, B. 1981. *Alcohol, Society, and the State: A Comprehensive Study of Alcohol Control,* Vol. 1. Toronto: Addiction Research Foundation of Ontario.

Malfetti, J. L.; Simon, K. J.; and Homer, M. M. 1977. *Development of a Junior High School Module in Alcohol Education and Traffic Safety.* New York: Teachers College, Columbia University.

Malfetti, J. L., and Winter, D. J. 1980. *Counseling Manual for Educational and Rehabilitative Programs for Persons Convicted of Driving While Intoxicated (DWI).* New York: Teachers College, Columbia University.

Manak, J. P. 1984. *The Legal Aspects of the Use of Passive Alcohol Screening Devices as Law Enforcement Tools for DWI Enforcement.* Draft report to the National Highway Traffic Safety Administration. Evanston, IL: Traffic Institute, Northwestern University.

Mangione, T. W. 1983. *Compliance with a Recent Law Change: The Massachusetts Experience with Raising the Minimum Drinking Age.* Boston: University of Massachusetts.

Mann, R. E.; Leigh, G.; Vingilis, E. R.; and De Genova, Y. K. 1983. A Critical Review on the Effectiveness of Drinking-Driving Rehabilitation Programmes. *Accident Analysis and Prevention* 15:441–61.

Mann, R. E., and Vingilis, E. R. 1985. Applying the Interactionist Model to Impaired Driving: Implications and New Directions. In *Proceedings of the Canadian Multidisciplinary Road Safety Conference IV,* 296–308. Montreal. École Polytechnique.

Mann, R. E.; Vingilis, E. R.; Adlaf, E.; Kijewski, K.; and De Genova, K. 1985. A Comparison of Young Drinking Offenders with Other Adolescents. *Drug and Alcohol Dependence* 15:181–91.

Mann, R. E.; Vingilis, E. R.; Anglin, L.; Suurvali, H.; Poudrier, L. M.; and Vaga, K. In press. Long-Term Follow-up of Convicted Drinking Drivers. In *Proceedings of the 10th International Conference on Alcohol, Drugs, and Traffic Safety.*

Mann, R. E.; Vingilis, E. R.; Leigh, G.; Anglin, L.; and Blefgen, H. 1986. School-Based Programmes for the Prevention of Drinking and Driving: Issues and Results. *Accident Analysis and Prevention* 18:325–38.

Marco, C. H., and Marco, J. M. 1980. Antabuse: Medication in Exchange for a Limited Freedom: Is It Legal? *American Journal of Law and Medicine* 5:295–330.

Mason, M. F., and Dubowski, K. M. 1976. Breath-Alcohol Analysis: Uses, Methods, and Some Forensic Problems—Reviews and Opinion. *Journal of Forensic Science* 21:9–41.

Masten, F. L. 1979. The Effect of a Three-Day Minicourse on Knowledge and Attitudes about Drinking and Driving of High School Driver Education Students. Ph.D. thesis, University of Missouri, Kansas City.

Maycock, G. 1986. Accident Modeling and Economic Evaluation. *Accident Modeling, Accident Analysis and Prevention* 18:169–174.

Mayhew, D. R.; Warren, R. A.; Simpson, H. M.; and Haas, G. C. 1981. *Young Driver Accidents: Magnitude and Characteristics of the Problem.* Ottawa: Traffic Injury Research Foundation of Canada.

Meier, R. B., and Johnson, W. T. 1977. Deterrence as Social Control: The Legal and Extralegal Production of Conformity. *American Sociological Review* 42:292–304.

Mercer, G. W. 1985a. *Convicted Drinking Drivers: Sex, Age, Other Traffic Convictions, and Traffic Accidents. British Columbia, June 1980–December 1984.* British Columbia: Ministry of Attorney General, CounterAttack Program.

————. 1985b. The Relationship among Driving While Impaired Charges, Police Drinking-Driving Roadcheck Activity, Media Coverage, and Alcohol-related Casualty Traffic Accidents. *Accident Analysis and Prevention* 17:467–74.

————. 1984a. *Drinking-Driving Police Blitz Activity, Media Coverage, and Alcohol-Related Traffic Accident Reduction.* Victoria, British Columbia: Ministry of Attorney General.

————. 1984b. *An Evaluation of the April-May 1984 Drinking-Driving Roadcheck, Enforcement, amd Media Blitz.* Victoria, British Columbia: Ministry of Attorney General.

Middendorf, W. 1985. The Effectiveness of Deterrence: Especially as far as Drunk Driving Is Concerned. Paper presented at the annual meeting of the American Society of Criminology, San Diego.

Milgram, G. G. 1975. A Descriptive Analysis of Alcohol Education Materials. *Journal of Studies on Alcohol* 36:416–21.

Miller, G. 1978. *Summary Report on Project TAGS—An Experiment in Mass Screening of License Plates to Identify Motor Vehicle Law Violators.* Washington, DC: Insurance Institute for Highway Safety.

Mitchell, M. C. 1985. Alcohol-Induced Impairment of Central Nervous System Function: Behavioral Skills Involved in Driving. *Journal of Studies in Alcohol,* Supplement no. 10:109–16.

Moore, M. H., and Gerstein, D. R., eds. 1981. *Alcohol and Public Policy: Beyond the Shadow of Prohibition.* Washington, DC: National Academy Press.

Mortimer, R. G.; Filkins, L. D.; Kerlan, M. W.; and Lower, J. S. 1973. Psychometric Identification of Problem Drinkers. *Quarterly Journal of Studies On Alcohol* 34:1332–35.

Mortimer, R. G.; Filkins, L. D.; and Lower, J. S. 1971. *Court Procedures for Identifying Problem Drinkers. Final Report. Report on Phase II.* Ann Arbor: Highway Safety Research Institute, University of Michigan.

Mosher, J. F. 1985. Alcohol Policy and the Presidential Commission on Drunk Driving. *Accident Analysis and Prevention* 17:239–50.

————. 1984. Alcohol Policy and the Presidential Commission: The Paths Not Taken. Presented at the 63rd Annual Meeting of the Transportation Research Board, National Academy of Sciences.

————. 1983. Server Intervention: A New Approach for Preventing Drinking Driving. *Accident Analysis and Prevention* 15:483–97.

————. 1979. Dram Shop Liability and the Prevention of Alcohol-Related Problems. *Journal of Studies on Alcohol* 40:773–98.

Moskewitz, H. 1974. Alcohol Influences upon Sensory Motor Function, Visual Perception, and Attention. In *Alcohol, Drugs, and Driving,* ed. M. W. Perrine. Technical Report no. DOT-HS-801-096. Washington, D.C.: NHTSA.

————. 1973. Laboratory Studies on the Effects of Alcohol on Some Variables Related to Drinking. *Journal of Safety Research* 5:185–99.

Mosley, G. W. 1955. The Distillers' Approach to Drinking and Driving. In *Proceedings of the 2nd International Conference on Alcohol and Road Traffic,* 24–30. Toronto: Garden City Press.

Muhlin, G. L. 1985. Ethnic Differences in Alcohol Misuse: A Striking Reaffirmation. *Journal of Studies on Alcohol* 46:172–73.

Mulder, J. A. G., and Vis, A. A. 1983. *Alcoholgebruik onder Automobilisten. Verslag van een onderzoek naar de rij—en drinkgewoonten van Nederlandse automobilisten, uitgewoerd in hetnajaar van 1981.* Leidschendam: SWOV.

Murphy, J., and Netherton, R. 1959. Public Responsibility and the Uninsured Motorist. *Georgetown Law Journal* 47:700–745.

Nader, R. 1964. *Unsafe at Any Speed.* NY: Grossman.

Nagy, T. 1982. *Norms and Attitudes Related to Alcohol Usage and Driving: A Review of the Literature. Volume II: A Metanalysis of Primary Prevention Studies.* Washington, DC: NHTSA.

Nailen, R. L. 1967. Teleprinter in Patrol Cars. *Law and Order* 15 (July): 1–3.

National Commission Against Drunk Driving. 1985. *A Progress Report on the Implementation of Recommendations by the Presidential Commission on Drunk Driving.* Washington, DC: Department of Transportation.

National Highway Traffic Safety Administration. 1986a. Amendment of Conforming Products List of Evidential Breath Test Devices. *Federal Register* 51 (68):12258 (19 April Notices).

_____. 1986b. *A Digest of State Alcohol–Highway Safety Related Legislation*. 4th ed. Technical Report no. DOT-HS-806-925. Washington, DC: NHTSA.

_____. 1986c. *The Drunk Driver and Jail*. Technical Report no. DOT-HS-806-761. 5 vols. Washington, DC: NHTSA.

_____. 1986d. *DWI Detection and Divided Attention Field Sobriety Testing*. Final Report under contract DTNH22-84-C-05092. Washington, DC: NHTSA.

_____. 1986e. *Procedures for Identifying Problem Drinkers: A Screening and Assessment Package for Courts and Treatment Agencies*. Washington, DC: NHTSA.

_____. 1986f. *Review of Information on Fatal Traffic Accidents in the United States in 1984*. Washington, DC: NHTSA.

_____. 1985a. *Alcohol and Highway Safety 1984: A Review of the State of Knowledge*. Washington, DC: NHTSA.

_____. 1985b. *Fatal Accident Reporting System. Annual Report*. Washington, DC: NHTSA.

_____. 1983. *Limited Electromagnetic Interference Testing of Evidential Breath Testers*. Technical Report no. DOT-HS-806-400. Washington, DC: NHTSA.

_____. 1980. *1980 Survey of Public Perceptions on Highway Safety*. Washington, DC: NHTSA.

_____. 1979a. *Alcohol Safety Projects: Evaluation Methodology and Overall Program Impact*. Washington, DC: NHTSA.

_____. 1979b. *A Message to My Patients*. Technical Report no. DOT-IIS-804-089. Washington, DC: NHTSA.

_____. 1979c. *Results of the National Alcohol Safety Action Projects*. Technical Report no. DOT-HS-804-033. Washington, DC: NHTSA.

_____. 1979d. *Summary of National Alcohol Safety Action Projects*. Washington, DC: NHTSA.

National Public Services Research Institute. 1984. *Alcohol Peer Intervention*. Alexandria, VA: National Public Services Research Institute.

National Safety Council. 1985. *Accident Facts*. Chicago: National Safety Council.

_____. 1978. *Recommendations of the Committee on Alcohol and Drugs 1936–1977*. Chicago: National Safety Council.

_____. 1976. *Alcohol and the Impaired Driver*. Chicago: National Safety Council.

New York State Insurance Department. 1970. *In Whose Benefit?*

Nichols, J. L.; Weinstein, E. B.; Ellingstad, V. S.; and Struckman-Johnson, D. L. 1978. The Specific Deterrent Effect of ASAP Education and Rehabilitation Programs. *Journal of Safety Research* 10:177–87.

Nichols, J. L.; Weinstein, E. B.; Ellingstad, V. S.; Struckman-Johnson, D. L.; and Reis, R. E. 1980. The Effectiveness of Education and Treatment Programs for Drinking Drivers: A Decade of Evaluation. In *Alcohol, Drugs, and Traffic Safety,* Vol. 3, ed. L. Goldberg, 1298–1395. Stockholm: Almqvist and Wiksell.

Noordzij, P. C. 1984. *Alcoholgebruik von Automobilisten 1983.* Dienst Sociaal Wetenschappellijk Onderzoek. Rijksuniversiteit Leiden.

————. 1983. Measuring the Extent of the Drinking and Driving Problem. *Accident Analysis and Prevention* 15:407–14.

————. 1977. The Introduction of a Statutory BAC Limit of 50 mg/100 ml and Its Effects on Drinking and Driving Habits and Traffic Accidents. In *Proceedings of the 7th International Conference on Alcohol, Drugs, and Traffic Safety,* ed. I. R. Johnston, 454–70. Canberra: Australian Government Publishing Service.

Nordisk Trafiksikkerheds Råd. 1984. Trafikonykterhet i Norden: Kartläggning och forslag till forskning. Stockholm: Nordisk Trafiksikkerheds Råd.

Nordlung, S. 1984. Lørdagslukningens innvirkning på alkoholomsetningen. In *Virkninger av lørdagsstengte vinmonopolutsalg,* 66–107. Oslo: National Institute for Alcohol Research.

Norström, T. 1983. Law Enforcement and Alcohol Consumption Policy as Countermeasures Against Drunk Driving: Possibilities and Limitations. *Accident Analysis and Prevention* 15:513–22.

————. 1981. *Studies in the Causation and Prevention of Traffic Crime.* Stockholm: Almqvist and Wiksell.

————. 1978. Drunken Driving: A Tentative Causal Model. *Scandinavian Studies in Criminology* 6:69–78.

Note. 1983. Social Host Liability for Injuries Caused by Acts of an Intoxicated Guest. *North Dakota Law Review* 59:445–77.

Note. 1980. Insurance Coverage of Punitive Damages. *Dickinson Law Review* 84:221–40.

Note. 1976. Insurance for Punitive Damages: A Reevaluation. *Hastings Law Journal* 28:431–75.

Oats, J. F. 1976. *Study of Self-Test Drivers.* Final Report no. DOT-HS-501241. Washington, DC: NHTSA.

O'Connell, J., and Henderson, R. 1976. *Tort Law, No-Fault and Beyond.* Abridged ed. NY: Matthew Bender.

O'Donnell, M. A. 1985. Research on Drinking Locations of Alcohol-Impaired Drivers: Implications for Present Policies. *Journal of Public Health Policy* 6:510–25.

Olsson, O., and Wikstrøm, P. O. 1984. Effekter av systembutikernas lørdagsstengning i Sverige. *Alkoholpolitik* 2:84–95.

O'Neall, P. A., and Crancer, A., Jr. 1969. *An Exploratory Study of the Yield from Observation of Large Numbers of Vehicles.* Report 027. Olympia, WA: Washington Department of Motor Vehicles.

O'Neill, B., and Eiswirth, R. 1972. Screening Drivers for Alcohol: An Application of Bayes' Formula. *American Journal of Public Health* 62:1468–72.

O'Neill, B.; Williams, A. F.; and Dubowski, K. M. 1983. Variability in Blood Alcohol Concentrations: Implications for Estimating Individual Results. *Journal of Studies on Alcohol* 44:222–30.

Organisation for Economic Cooperation and Development. 1978. *Road Research: New Research on the Role of Alcohol and Drugs in Road Accidents.* Paris: OECD Road Research Group.

————. 1975. *Young Driver Accidents.* Paris: OECD Road Research Group.

Pacific Institute for Research and Evaluation. 1985. *The California Driving under the Influence First Offender Program: Directory of Providers.* Walnut Creek, CA: Pacific Institute for Research and Evaluation.

Parkin, H. E.; Martin, G. E.; and Rockerbie, R. A. 1980. Blood Alcohol in Hospitalized Traffic Crash Victims. *British Columbia Medical Journal* 2 (22):58–60.

Partya, S. 1983. *Simple Models of Fatality Trends Using Employment and Population Data.* National Center for Statistics Analysis. Washington, DC: NHTSA.

Paternoster, R., and Iovanni, L. 1986. The Deterrent Effect of Perceived Severity: A Reexamination. *Social Forces* 64:751–77.

Paternoster, R.; Saltzman, L. E.; Chiricos, T. G.; and Waldo, G. P. 1982. Perceived Risk and Deterrence: Methodological Artifacts in Perceptual Deterrence Research. *Criminology* 73:1238–58.

Paternoster, R.; Saltzman, L. E.; Waldo, G. P.; and Chiricos, T. G. 1985. Assessments of Risk and Behavioral Experience: An Exploratory Study of Change. *Criminology* 23:417–36.

————. 1983. Perceived Risk and Social Control: Do Sanctions Really Deter? *Law and Society Review* 17:457–79.

Peck, R. C.; Sadler, D. D.; and Perrine, M. W. 1985a. The Comparative Effectiveness of Alcohol Rehabilitation and Licensing Control Actions for Drunk Driving Offenders: A Review of the Literature. *Alcohol, Drugs, and Driving: Abstracts and Reviews* 1 (4):15–40.

————. 1985b. The Role of Youth in Traffic Accidents: A Review of Past and Current California Data. *Alcohol, Drugs, and Driving: Abstracts and Reviews* 1 (2):45–68.

Pequignot, G.; Tuyns, A. J.; and Berta, J. L. 1978. Ascitic Cirrhosis in Relation to Alcohol Consumption. *International Journal of Epidemiology* 7:113–20.

Perrine, M. W. 1976. Alcohol and Highway Crashes: Closing the Gap between Epidemiology and Experimentation. *Modern Problems of Pharmacopsychiatry* 11:21–41.

————., ed. 1974. *Alcohol, Drugs, and Driving.* Report no. DOT-HS-801-096. Washington, DC: NHTSA.

————. 1973. Alcohol Influences on Driving-Related Behavior. A Critical Review of Laboratory Studies of Neurophysiological, Neuromuscular, and Sensory Activity. *Journal of Safety Research* 5:165–84.

Perrine, M. W.; Waller, J. A.; and Harris, L. S. 1971. *Alcohol and Highway Safety: Behavioral and Medical Aspects.* Technical Report no. DOT-HS-800-599. Washington, DC: NHTSA.

Persy, A.-M. 1985. *Untersuchungen zu "Alkohol und Fahren."* Band 12: Entwicklung des Alkoholkonsums in der Bundesrepublik Deutschland. Forschungsberichte der Bundesanstalt für Strassenwesen, Bereich Unfallforschung. Heft 119. Bergisch Gladbach: Bundesanstalt für Strassenwesen.

Peters, J. E. 1986. Beyond Server Training: An Examination of Future Issues. *Alcohol, Health, and Research World* 10 (4):24–27.

Phillips, L., and Ray, S. 1983. Deterrence: A Rational Expectation Formulation. In *Applied Time Series Analysis,* ed. O. D. Anderson. Amsterdam: North Holland Publishing Company.

————. 1982. Evidence on the Identification and Causibility Dispute about the Death Penalty. In *Applied Time Series Analysis,* ed. O. D. Anderson and M. R. Perryman. Amsterdam: North Holland Publishing Company.

Phillips, L.; Ray, S.; and Votey, H. L., Jr. 1984. Forecasting Highway Casualties: The British Road Safety Act and a Sense of Deja Vu. *Journal of Criminal Justice* 12:101–14.

Phillips, L., and Votey, H. L., Jr. 1987. The Self-Sorting Process of Choosing Involvement in Crime versus Legitimate Income Sources. *Contemporary Policy Issues* (forthcoming).

Picton, W. R. 1981. Breath Alcohol Self-Testing with an Alcohol Guard: A Laboratory Evaluation. In *Alcohol, Drugs, and Traffic Safety,* Vol. 3, ed. L. Goldberg, 1329–40. Stockholm: Almqvist and Wiksell.

————. 1979. An Evaluation of a Coin-Operated Breath Self-Tester. In *Proceedings of the 7th International Conference on Alcohol, Drugs, and Traffic Safety,* ed. I. R. Johnson, 327–31. Melbourne: Australian Government Publishing Service.

Pikkarainen, J., and Penttila, A. 1981. Screening of Arrested Drunken Drivers for Alcoholism. In *Alcohol, Drugs, and Traffic Safety,* ed. L. Goldberg, 288–99. Stockholm: Almqvist and Wiksell.

Polich, M. M., and Orvis, B. R. 1979. *Alcohol Problems: Patterns and Prevalence in the U.S. Air Force.* Report no. R-2308-AF. Santa Monica, CA: Rand Corporation.

Popham, R. E. 1970. Indirect Methods of Alcoholism Prevalence Estimation: A Critical Evaluation. In *Alcohol and Alcoholism,* ed. E. Popham. Toronto: University of Toronto Press.

————. 1956. Alcoholism and Traffic Accidents: A Preliminary Study. *Quarterly Journal of Studies on Alcohol* 17:225–32.

Popkin, C. L.; Li, L. K.; Lacey, J. H.; Stewart, J. R.; and Waller, P. F. 1983. *An Initial Evaluation of the North Carolina Alcohol and Drug Education Traffic Schools. Volume 1: Technical Report.* Chapel Hill, NC: University of North Carolina Highway Safety Research Center.

Posner, R. 1977. *Economic Analysis of Law.* 2d ed. Boston: Little Brown.

Presidential Commission on Drunk Driving. 1983. *Final Report.* Washington, DC: Government Printing Office.

Preusser, D. F.; Ulmer, R. G.; and Adams, J. R. 1976. Driver Record Evaluation of a Drinking Driver Rehabilitation Program. *Journal of Safety Research* 8:98–105.

Produktschap voor Gestilleerde Dranken. 1985. *Hoeveelalcoholhoudende dranken worden er in de wereld gedronken?* Schiedam: PGD.

Prosser, W. 1971. *Law of Torts.* 4th ed. St. Paul, MN: West.

Prosser, W., and Keeton, R. 1984. *On the Law of Torts.* 5th ed. St. Paul, MN: West.

Prouty, R. W., and O'Neill, B. 1971. *An Evaluation of Some Quantitative Breath Screening Tests for Alcohol.* Technical Report, Insurance Institute for Highway Safety. Washington, DC: Insurance Institute for Highway Safety.

Ranney, T. A., and Gawron, V. J. 1986. The Effects of Pavement Edgelines on Performance in a Driving Simulator under Sober and Alcohol-Dosed Conditions. Human Factors 28 (5):511–25.

Reed, D. S. 1981. Reducing the Costs of Drinking-Driving. In *Alcohol and Public Policy: Beyond the Shadow of Prohibition,* ed. M. H. Moore and D. R. Gerstein, 336–87. Washington, DC: National Academy Press.

Reed, J. D. 1985. Water, Water, Everywhere: At Work and at Parties, Americans Are Drinking Less and Enjoying It More. *Time,* 20 May, 68–73.

Reid, J. B. 1978. Study of Drinking in Natural Settings. In *Behavioral Approaches to Alcoholism,* ed. G. A. Marlatt and P. E. Nathan. New Brunswick, NJ: Rutgers University Center of Alcohol Studies.

Reinerman, C. 1985. *Social Movements and Social Problems: Mothers Against Drunk Drivers, Restrictive Alcohol Laws, and Social Control in the 1980s.* Paper presented to the Society for the Study of Social Problems, Washington, DC, 23–26 August.

Reis, R. E. 1983. The Traffic Safety Impact of DUI Education and Counseling Programs. In *DWI Reeducation and Rehabilitation Programs— Successful Results and the Future,* 38–61. Falls Church, VA: AAA Foundation for Traffic Safety.

————. 1982. *The Traffic Safety Effectiveness of Education Programs for Multiple Offense Drunk Drivers.* Technical Report, DOT Contract HS-6-10414. Washington, DC: NHTSA.

Ritchie, J. M. 1975. The Aliphatic Alcohols. In *The Pharmacological Basis of Therapeutics.* 5th ed., ed. L. S. Goodman and A. Gilman, 137–51. New York: Macmillan.

Roach, M. K. 1982. The Biochemical and Physiological Effects of Alcohol. In *Alcohol, Science, and Society Revisited,* ed. E. L. Gomberg, H. R. White, and J. A. Carpenter, 17–37. Ann Arbor: University of Michigan Press; New Brunswick, NJ: Rutgers University Center of Alcohol Studies.

Robertson, L. S. 1981. Alcohol, Behavior, and Public Health Strategies. *Abstracts and Reviews in Alcohol and Driving* 2 (2):1–4.

Robertson, L. S. 1980. Crash Involvement of Teenaged Drivers When Driver Education Is Eliminated from High School. *American Journal of Public Health* 70:599–605.

Robertson, L. S., and Zador, P. L. 1979. Driver Education and Fatal Crash Involvement of Teenaged Drivers. *American Journal of Public Health* 68:959–65.

Rockerbie, R. A. 1979. *Blood Alcohol in Hospitalized Traffic Crash Victims.* Vancouver, British Columbia: Ministry of the Attorney General, Drinking-Driving CounterAttack.

Rood, D. H., and Kraichy, P. P. 1985. *Evaluation of New York State's Mandatory Occupant Restraint Law: Attitudinal Surveys of Licensed Drivers in New York State.* Albany: Institute for Traffic Safety Management and Research.

Room, R. 1984. Alcohol Control and Public Health. *Annual Reviews of Public Health* 5:293–317.

————. 1982. Alcohol, Science, and Social Control. In *Alcohol, Science, and Society Revisited,* ed. E. L. Gomberg, H. R. White, and J. A. Carpenter, 17–37. Ann Arbor: University of Michigan Press; New Brunswick, NJ: Rutgers University Center of Alcohol Studies.

Rosenbluth, J.; Nathan, P. E.; and Lawson, D. M. 1978. Environmental Influences on Drinking by College Students in a College Pub: Behavioral Observation in the Natural Environment. *Addictive Behaviors* 3:117–21.

Ross, H. L. 1986. Britain's Christmas Crusade against Drinking and Driving. Paper presented at the 10th International Conference on Alcohol, Drugs, and Traffic Safety, Amsterdam.

————. 1985a. Deterring Drunken Driving: An Analysis of Current Efforts. *Journal of Studies on Alcohol,* Supplement no. 10:122–28.

————. 1985b. Summary of Topic C—Countermeasures. *Journal of Studies on Alcohol,* Supplement no. 10:207–209.

————. 1984a. *Deterring the Drinking Driver: Legal Policy and Social Control.* Rev. and updated ed. Lexington, MA: D. C. Heath and Co.

————. 1984b. Social Control through Deterrence: Drinking-and-Driving Laws. In *Annual Review of Sociology,* ed. R. Turner and J. Short. Palo Alto, CA: Annual Reviews, Inc.

————. 1983. Limitations on Deterring the Drinking Driver. *Abstracts and Reviews in Alcohol and Driving* 4 (4):3–7.

————. 1982. *Deterring the Drinking Driver: Legal Policy and Social Control.* Lexington, MA: Lexington Books.

————. 1977. Deterrence Regained: The Cheshire Constabulary's "Breathaliser Blitz." *Journal of Legal Studies* 6:241–49.

————. 1975. The Scandinavian Myth: The Effectiveness of Drinking-and-Driving Legislation in Sweden and Norway. *Journal of Legal Studies* 4:285–310.

————. 1973. Law, Science, and Accidents: The British Road Safety Act of 1967. *Journal of Legal Studies* 2:1–78.

Ross, H. L. 1960. Traffic Law Violations: A "Folk Crime." *Social Problems* 8:231–41.

————. n.d. Final Report of the Presidential Commission on Drunk Driving (Review). *Accident Analysis and Prevention,* 199–201.

Ross, H. L. and Hughes, G. 1986. Getting MADD in Vain—Drunk Driving: What Not to Do. *The Nation,* 13 December, 663–64.

Ross, H. L.; Klette, H.; and McCleary, R. 1984. Liberalization and Rationalization of Drunk-Driving Laws in Scandinavia. *Accident Analysis and Prevention* 16:471–87.

Ross, H. L.; McCleary, R.; and Epperlein, T. 1982. Deterrence of Drinking and Driving in France: An Evaluation of the Law of July 12, 1978. *Law and Society Review* 16:345–74.

Ruschmann, P. A.; Joscelyn, K. B.; Greyson, M.; and Carroll, H. O. 1980. *An Analysis of the Potential Legal Constraints on the Use of Advanced Alcohol-Testing Technology.* Report no. DOT-HS-805. Washington, DC: NHTSA.

Russ, N. W., and Geller, E. S. In press. Exploring Low Alcohol Beer Consumption among College Students: Implications for Drunken Driving. *Journal of Alcohol and Drug Education.*

————. 1987. Training Bar Personnel to Prevent Drunken Driving: A Field Evaluation. *American Journal of Public Health* 77: 952–54.

————. 1986. Using Sobriety Tests to Increase Awareness of Alcohol Impairment. *Health Education Research: Theory and Practice* 1: 255–61.

————. 1985. Changing the Behavior of the Drunk Driver: Current Status and Future Directions. *Psychological Documents* (December): 1–30.

Russ, N. W.; Harwood, M. K.; and Geller, E. S. 1986. Estimating Alcohol Impairment in the Field: Implications for Drunken Driving. *Journal of Studies on Alcohol* 47:237–40.

Ryan, G. A., and Slater, W. E. 1979. Drinking Habits, Social Characteristics and Blood Alcohol Concentrations of Road Crash Casualties. In *Proceedings of the 7th International Conference on Alcohol, Drugs, and Traffic Safety,* ed. I. R. Johnston, 120–26. Melbourne: Australian Government Publishing Service.

Ryback, R. S.; Eckardt, M. J.; and Raulter, C. P. 1979. Biochemical and Hematological Correlates of Alcoholism. Paper presented at the 6th National Drug Abuse Conference, New Orleans.

Sadler, D. D., and Perrine, M. W. 1984. *An Evaluation of the California Drunk Driving Countermeasure System: Volume 2. The Long-Term Traffic Safety Impact of a Pilot Alcohol Abuse Treatment as an Alternative to License Suspensions.* Report no. 90. Sacramento, CA: California Department of Motor Vehicles.

Saltz, R. F. In press. The Role of Bars and Restaurants in Preventing Alcohol-Impaired Driving: An Evaluation of Server Intervention. *Evaluation and the Health Professions.*

Saltz, R. F. 1986. Evaluation of a Server Intervention Program. Workshop presentation at Life Savers 5 Conference, San Diego, CA.

Salzberg, P. M., and Klingberg, C. L. 1982. The Effectiveness of Deterred Prosecution for Driving While Intoxicated Offenders. *American Association for Automotive Medicine Quarterly Journal* 4:35–41.

Salzberg, P. M., and Paulsrude, S. P. 1984. An Evaluation of Washington's Driving-While-Intoxicated Law: Effect on Drunk Driving Recidivism. *Journal of Safety Research* 15:117–24.

Schaefer, J. M. 1983. The Physical Setting: Behavior and Policy. Paper presented at Life Savers 3 Conference, Orlando, Florida.

Schaps, E.; DiBartolo, R.; Moskowitz, J.; Palley, C.; and Churgin, S. A. 1981. A Review of 127 Prevention Program Evaluations. *Journal of Drug Issues* 11:17–44.

Schlegel, R. P.; d'Avernas, J.; and Manske, S. R. 1984. Longitudinal Patterns of Alcohol Use: Psychosocial Predictors of Transition. Paper presented at the 13th International Congress of Psychology, Acapulco, Mexico.

Schumaier, S., and McKinsey, B. 1986. The Insurability of Punitive Damages. *American Bar Association Journal* 72 (March):68–72.

Schmidt, W., and Popham, R. E. 1978. The Single Distribution Theory of Alcohol Consumption: A Rejoinder to the Critique of Parker and Harman. *Journal of Studies on Alcohol* 39:400–19.

Schmidt, W., and Smart, R. G. 1963. Drinking-Driving Mortality and Morbidity Statistics. In *Alcohol and Traffic Safety,* ed. B. H. Fox and J. H. Fox, 27–43. U.S. Public Health Service Publication no. 1043. Washington, DC: Government Printing Office.

————. 1959a. Alcoholics, Drinking, and Traffic Accidents. *Quarterly Journal of Studies on Alcohol* 20:631–44.

————. 1959b. A Note on Alcoholics and Drunk Driving. *Criminal Law Quarterly* 1:419–22.

Schneider, J. 1978. Deviant Drinking as Disease: Alcoholism as a Social Accomplishment. *Social Problems* 25:361–72.

Schultz, D. 1982. Möglichkeiten und Grenzen des bisherigen verkehrsrechtlichen Sanktionssystems. *Blutalkohol* 19:315–34.

Schwerdtfeger, W., and Küffner, B. 1981. Analyse der Verkehrsteilnahme. *Schriftenreihe Unfall—und Sicherheitsforschung Strassenverhehr.* Heft 33. Köln: Bundesanstalt für Strassenwesen.

Sedman, A. J.; Wilkinson, P. K.; Sakmar, E.; Weidler, D. J.; and Wagner, J. G. 1976. Food Effects on Absorption and Metabolism of Alcohol. *Journal of Studies in Alcohol* 37:1197–1214.

Seeley, J. R. 1960. Death by Liver Cirrhosis and the Price of Beverage Alcohol. *Canadian Medical Association Journal* 2:367–72.

Selzer, M. L. 1971. The Michigan Alcoholism Screening Test: The Quest for a New Diagnostic Instrument. *American Journal of Psychiatry* 127:89–94.

Shaoul, J. 1975. *The Use of Accidents and Traffic Offenses as Criteria for Evaluating Courses in Driver Education*. Salford, England: University of Salford.

Shapiro, P., and Votey, H. L., Jr. 1987. Moral Compliance, Private Self-Interest, and Exposure to the Law: The Response of Swedish Drivers to Drunken Driving Controls. In *Econometric Analysis of Crime in Sweden*, ed. P. Shapiro and H. L. Votey. Stockholm: The National Council for Crime Prevention.

──────. 1984. Deterrence and Subjective Probability of Arrest: Modeling Individual Decisions to Drink and Drive in Sweden. *Law and Society Review* 18:583–604.

Sherman, L. W.; Gartin, P.; Doi, P.; and Miller, S. 1986. The Effects of Jail Time on Drunk Driving: An Indirect Experiment. Paper presented at the annual meeting of the American Society of Criminology, Atlanta.

Siegal, H. A. 1986. *Impact of a Driver Intervention Program on DWI Recidivism and Problem Drinking*. Washington, DC: Department of Transportation.

──────. 1985. The Intervention Approach to Drunk Driver Rehabilitation. Part II: Evaluation. *International Journal of Addictions* 20.675–89.

──────. 1982. *Weekend Intervention Program: A New Way of Confronting the Drunk Driver*. Dayton, OH: Wright State University, School of Medicine.

Siegal, H. A., and Rudisill, J. R 1984. The Weekend Intervention Program: Identifying and Confronting Problem Drinkers. *Family Practice Recertification* 6:25–38.

Simpson, H. M. 1986. Social Change: Prospects for the Future of Road Safety. Paper presented at the Highway Safety Outlooks Conference, Toronto, Ontario. Ottawa, Ontario: Traffic Injury Research Foundation of Canada.

──────. 1985. Polydrug Effects and Traffic Safety. *Alcohol, Drugs, and Driving: Abstracts and Reviews* 1:17–37.

──────. 1977. The Impaired-Driver Problem vs. the Impaired Problem-Driver. *Transactions of the Association of Life Insurance Medical Directors of America* 61:178–92.

Simpson, H. M.; Beirness, D. J.; Mayhew, D. R.; and Donelson, A. C. 1985. *Alcohol-specific Controlls: Implications for Road Safety*. Ottawa, Ontario: Traffic Injury Research Foundation of Canada.

Simpson, H. M.; Mayhew, D. R.; and Warren, R. A. 1982. Epidemiology of Road Accidents Involving Young Adults. *Drug and Alcohol Dependence* 10:35–63.

Simpson, H. M.; Page-Valin, L.; and Warren, R. A. 1979. A Data Base on Traffic Fatalities. *Canadian Society of Forensic Science Journal* 11:215–20.

Skog, O.-J. 1985. *Økt totalforbruk—flere trafikkulykker?* Oslo: National Institute for Alcohol Research.

Skog, O.-J. 1983. *The Distribution of Alcohol Comsumption. Part II. A Review of the First Wave of Empirical Studies.* Oslo: National Institute for Alcohol Research.

————. 1980. Liver Cirrhosis Epidemiology: Some Methodological Problems. *British Journal of Addiction* 75:227–43.

Smart, R. G. 1976. *The Effects of Two Liquor Store Strikes on Drunkenness, Impaired Driving, and Accidents.* Ontario: Addiction Research Foundation.

Smith, Y.; Lilly, A.; and Dowling, N. 1932. Compensation for Automobile Accidents: A Symposium. *Columbia Law Review* 32:785–824.

Snapper, K. J.; Seaver, D. A.; and Schwartz, J. P. 1981. *An Assessment of Behavioral Tests to Detect Impaired Drivers.* Report no. DOT-HS-806-211. Washington, DC: NHTSA.

Snortum, J. R. 1984a. Alcohol-Impaired Driving in Norway and Sweden: Another Look at "The Scandinavian Myth." *Law and Policy* 6:5–37.

————. 1984b. Controlling the Alcohol-Impaired Driver in Scandinavia and the United States: Simple Deterrence and Beyond. *Journal of Criminal Justice* 12:131–48.

————. 1984c. Rejoinder: On Myths and Morals. *Law and Policy* 6:42–44.

Snortum, J. R., and Berger, D. E. 1986. Drinking and Driving: Detecting the "Dark Figure" of Compliance. *Journal of Criminal Justice* 14:475–89.

Snortum, J. R.; Hauge, R.; and Berger, D. E. 1986. Deterring Alcohol-Impaired Driving: A Comparative Analysis of Compliance in Norway and the United States. *Justice Quarterly* 3:139–65.

Snortum, J. R.; Kremer, L. K.; and Berger, D. E. In press. Beverage Preference as a Public Statement: Self-Concept and Social Image of College Drinkers. *Journal of Studies on Alcohol.*

Snow, R. W.; Cunningham, O. R.; and Barnes, R. 1985. Age–Sex Structure and Drinking Locations of Mississippi Drunk Driving Offenders. *Sociology and Social Research* 70:89–92.

Snyder, M. B. 1985. Legal Countermeasures: Panel Discussion. *Journal of Studies on Alcohol,* Supplement no. 10:144–47.

————. 1984a. Accuracy of BAC Estimation in Driving-Related Situations. Paper presented at the 28th Annual Meeting of the American Association for Automotive Medicine, 8–10 October, Denver, Colorado.

————. 1984b. The Drunk Driver Warning System—Status Review. Paper presented at the 63rd Annual Meeting of the Transportation Review Board, 18 January, Washington, D.C.

Sobell, L. C.; Vanderspek, R.; and Saltman, P. 1980. Utility of Portable Breath Alcohol Testers for Drunken Driver Offenders. *Journal of Studies on Alcohol* 41:930–34.

Sommer, R. 1969. *Personal Space: The Behavioral Basis of Design.* Englewood Cliffs, NJ: Prentice-Hall.

Sommer, R. 1965. The Isolated Drinker in the Edmonton Beer Parlor. *Quarterly Journal of Studies on Alcohol* 26:95–110.

Spector, M., and Kitsuse, J. 1977. *Constructing Social Problems*. Menlo Park, CA: Cummings Publishing Co.

Speiglman, Richard. 1985. Issues in the Rise of Compulsion in California's Drinking Driver Treatment System. In *Punishment and/or Treatment for Driving under the Influence of Alcohol and Other Drugs*, ed. M. Valverius, 151–80. Stockholm: International Committee on Alcohol, Drugs, and Traffic Safety.

Spoerer, E. 1979. *Dokumentation verkehrserzieherischer und verkehrsuufklärerischer Massnahmen zur Bekämpfung des Alkohols am Steurer*. Forschungsprojekt 7612/3 der Bundesanstalt für Strassenwesen. Köln: Bundesanstalt für Strassenwesen.

Stephan, E. 1986. Die Legalbewährung von nachgedschulten Alkoholerstättern in den ersten zwei Jahren unter Berücksichtigungder BAK-Werte." In *Zeitschrift für Verkehrssicherheit*. 32. Jahrgang. Heft 1:2–9.

_____. 1985. *Wirksamkeit von Nachschulungskursen erstmals alkohoslauffälliger Kraftfahrer*. Forschungsprojekt 8035 im Auftrage der Bundesanstalt für Strassenwesen. Unpublished.

_____. 1984. Die Rückfallwahrscheinlichkeit bei alkoholauffälligen Kraftfahrern in der Bundesrepublik Deutschland. In *Zeitschrift für Verkehrssicherheit*. 30. Jahrgang. Heft 1:28–34.

Stichting Wetenschappelijk Onderzoek Verkeersveiligheid (SWOV). 1984. Alcohol in het Verkeer. Rijden onder invloed, politietoezicht en onderzoek. Nota bij het *DSWO-rapport "Alcoholgebruik von automobilisten 1983."* Leidschendam: SWOV.

_____. 1978. *Alcoholgebruik onder Automobilisten-Verslag en resultaten van het onderzoek Rij—en drinkgewoonten van Nederlandse automobilisten in weekeindnachten in het najaarvan de janre 1970, 1971, 1973, 1974, 1975, en 1977*. Voorburg: SWOV.

Stock, J. R.; Weaver, J. K.; Ray, H. W.; Brink, J. R.; and Sadoff, M. G. 1983. *Evaluation of Safe Performance Secondary School Driver Education Curriculum Demonstration Project, Final Report*. Washington, DC: Department of Transportation.

Stuart, R. 1974. Teaching Facts about Drugs: Pushing or Preventing? *Journal of Educational Psychology* 66:189–201.

Summers, L., and Harris, D. 1978. *The General Deterrence of Driving While Intoxicated*. Vol. 1. Technical Report no. DOT-HS-803-582. Washington, DC: NHTSA.

Sundby, P. 1967. *Alcoholism and Mortality*. Oslo: Universitetsforlaget.

Sutton, L. 1986. The Effectiveness of Random Breath Testing: A Comparison between the State of Tasmania, Australia, and Four States in the Eastern United States. Paper presented at the 10th International Conference on Alcohol, Drugs, and Traffic Safety, Amsterdam.

Suzdak, P. D.; Glowa, J. R.; Crawley, J. N.; Schwartz, R. D.; Skolnick, P.; and Paul, S. M. 1986. A Selected Imiidazo-benzodiazepine Antagonist of Ethanol in the Rat. *Science* 234:1243–47.

Swenson, P. R.; Struckman-Johnson, D. L.; Ellingstad, V. S.; Clay, T. R.; and Nichols, J. L. 1981. Results of a Longitudinal Evaluation of Court-Mandated DWI Treatment Programs in Phoenix, Arizona. *Journal of Studies on Alcohol* 42:642–53.

Sykes, G. 1984. Saturated Enforcement: The Efficacy of Deterrence and Drunk Driving. *Journal of Criminal Justice* 12:185–97.

Takala, H. 1973. Alkostrejkens inverkan på uppdagad brottslighet. *Alkoholpolitik* 1:14–16.

Task Force on Drinking and Driving. 1983. *Drinking and Driving: A Discussion of Countermeasures and Consequences.* Toronto: Ministry of the Attorney General.

Taubenslag, W. N., and Taubenslag, M. J. 1975. *Selective Traffic Enforcement Program (STEP): Fort Lauderdale, Pasco Services, Inc. Final Report.* Washington, DC: NHTSA.

Temer, R. G; Peck, R. C.; Perrine, M. W.; and Borok, R. D. 1986. Study of the Relative Effectiveness of Disulfuram vs. Alcoholics Anonymous Participants in the Treatment of Drinking Driver Offenders. Paper presented to the 10th International Conference on Alcohol, Drugs, and Driving, September, Amsterdam.

Teplin, L. A., and Lutz, G. W. 1985. Measuring Alcohol Intoxication: The Development, Reliability, and Validity of an Observational Instrument. *Journal of Studies on Alcohol* 46:459–66.

Terhune, K. W., and Fell, J. C. 1981. The Role of Alcohol, Marijuana, and Other Drugs in the Accidents of Injured Drivers. In *Proceedings of the 25th Conference of the American Association for Automotive Medicine,* 117–30. Arlington Heights, IL: AAMM.

Teschke, R.; Brand, A.; and Strohmeyer, G. 1977. Role of Increased Serum Gamma-Glutanyltransferase Activity in Early Detection of Alcoholism. Paper presented at the 23rd International Institute on the Prevention and Treatment of Alcoholism, Dresden.

Tharp, V. 1981. Gaze Nystagmus as a Roadside Sobriety Test. *Abstracts and Reviews in Alcohol and Driving* 1 (2):5–8.

Tharp, V.; Burns, M.; and Moskowitz, H. 1981. *Development and Field Test of Psychophysical Tests for DWI Arrest.* Technical Report no. DOT-HS-805-864. Washington, DC: NHTSA.

Thomas, C., and Hepburn, J. 1983. *Crime, Criminal Law, and Criminology.* Dubuque, IA: William C. Brown Co.

Thoresen, T., and Petersen, J. 1986. *Alkoholforbrug og trafikkulykker.* København: Alkohol—og narkotikarådet.

Tittle, C. R. 1980. *Sanctions and Social Deviance: The Question of Deterrence.* New York: Praeger.

Traffic Injury Research Foundation of Canada. 1983. *Development of Resources to Support Community-based Initiatives Related to Drinking and Driving.* Ottawa, Ontario: Department of National Health and Welfare.

Turnauer, M. S. 1973. A Comparison of High School Driver Education Students' Attitudes as Measured by the Mann Inventory and Vincent Attitude Scale after Receiving Two Types of Alcohol Instruction at Selected Illinois High Schools. Ph.D. thesis, Southern Illinois University.

Ungerleider, S., and Bloch, S. 1986. *Assessing the Various Components of a Drunk Driving Program from Prevention to Criminal Justice Intervention.* Unpublished manuscript.

U.S. Bureau of the Census. 1984. *1980 Census of Population: Occupation by Industry.* No. PC80-2-7c. Washington, DC: Bureau of the Census.

U.S. Congress, Committee on Public Works. 1968. *Alcohol and Traffic Safety.* Washington, DC: Government Printing Office.

U.S. Department of Health and Human Services. 1986. *United States Alcohol Epidemiological Data Reference Manual.* Vol. 1. Washington, DC: Government Printing Office.

U.S. Department of Transportation. 1970. *Price Variability in the Automobile Insurance Market.* Washington, DC: Government Printing Office.

U.S. Department of Transportation. 1968. *Alcohol and Highway Safety Report to the U.S. Congress.* Washington, DC: Government Printing Office.

Vasquez, H. 1986. Strategies for Separating Drinking from Driving: A Model Program for First Offender Drunk Drivers. Paper presented at the annual meeting of the American Society of Criminology, Atlanta.

Vayda, A., and Crespi, I. 1981. *Public Acceptability of Highway Safety Countermeasures.* Report no. DOT-HS-6-01466. Washington, DC: NHTSA.

Vegega, M. E. 1986. NIITSA Responsible Beverage Service Research and Evaluation Project. *Alcohol, Health and Research World* 10 (4):20–23.

———. 1984. Deterring Drinking-Driving among Youth. Some Research Needs. Paper presented at the annual convention of the American Psychological Association, Toronto.

Vingilis, E. 1984. Predispositional Factors toward Drinking and Driving. Paper presented at the National Institute on Alcohol Abuse and Alcoholism's Research Workshop on Alcohol and the Drinking Driver, May, Bethesda, Maryland.

———. 1983a. Drinking Drivers and Alcoholics. Are They from the Same Population? In *Research Advances in Alcohol and Drug Problems.* Vol. 7, ed. R. G. Smart, F. B. Glaser, Y. Israel, H. Kalant, R. E. Popham, and W. Schmidt, 299–342. New York: Plenum Publishing.

———. 1983b. *Drinking Driving Countermeasures: Theory, Practice, Results.* Technical Report. Toronto: Alcoholism and Drug Addiction Research Foundation.

———. 1981. A Literature Review of the Young Drinking Offender: Is He a Problem Drinker? *British Journal of Addiction* 76:27–46.

Vingilis, E. R.; Adlaf, E. M.; Blefgen, B. C. 1983. A Controlled Evaluation of the DWI Visual Detection Guide Training Programme for Police Officers. In *Proceedings of the 9th International Conference on Alcohol, Drugs, and Traffic Safety, San Juan, Puerto Rico,* ed. S. Kaye and G. Meier. Washington, DC: NHTSA.

Vingilis, E. R.; Adlaf, E. M.; and Chung, L. 1982. Comparison of Age and Sex Characteristics of Police-Suspected Impaired Drivers and Roadside-Surveyed Impaired Drivers. *Accident Analysis and Prevention* 14:425–30.

————. 1981. *The Oshawa Impaired Drivers Programme: An Evaluation of a Rehabilitation Program.* Toronto: Addiction Research Foundation.

Vingilis, E.; Blefgen, H.; Lei, H.; Sykora, K.; and Mann, R. 1985. *An Evaluation of the Deterrent Impact of Ontario's 12-Hour License Suspension Law.* Toronto: Addiction Research Foundation.

Vingilis, E. R.; Chung, L.; and Adlaf, E. M. 1981. *The Evaluation of a Toronto Drinking Driving Programme Called RIDE (Reduce Impaired Drivers Everywhere).* Substudy No. 1216. Toronto: Addiction Research Foundation.

Vingilis, E. R., and De Genova, K. 1984. Youth and the Forbidden Fruit: Experiences with Changes in Legal Drinking Age in North America. *Journal of Criminal Justice* 12:161–72.

Vingilis, E. R., and Mann, R. E. In press. Towards an Interactionist Approach to Drinking-Driving Behaviour: Implications for Prevention and Research. *Health Education Research.*

————. 1985. *The Interactionist Model: A New Approach to Conceptualizing Drinking-Driving Behaviour.* Toronto: Addiction Research Foundation.

Vingilis, E., and Salutin, L. 1980. A Prevention Programme for Drinking Driving. *Accident Analysis and Prevention* 12:267–74.

Voas, R. B. 1986a. Evaluation of Jail as a Penalty of Drunken Driving. *Alcohol, Drugs, and Driving: Abstracts and Reviews* 2 (2):47–70.

————. 1986b. Special Preventive Measures. Paper presented at the 10th International Conference on Alcohol, Drugs, and Traffic Safety, Amsterdam.

————. 1984a. Detection of Drinking: A Neglected Element in DWI Enforcement. *The Police Chief* 51 (3):69–75.

————. 1984b. Estimating Alcohol Involvement in Fatal Crashes: A Note on the Reporting of BAC in the FARS. *Abstracts and Reviews in Alcohol and Driving* 5 (1):20.

————. 1984c. *Use of the Autotimer to Monitor the Driving of Convicted DWIs.* Phase I Report on NIAAA Small Business Grant no. R44–AA–06532–02.

————. 1983a. Laboratory and Field Tests of a Passive Alcohol Sensing System. *Abstracts and Reviews in Alcohol and Driving* 4 (3):3–21.

————. 1983b. To Reduce Drunk Driving, a Bold, New Enforcement Initiative Is Required. *Journal of Traffic Safety Education* 30:7–8.

Voas, R. B. 1982a. *Drinking and Driving: Scandinavian Laws, Tough Penalties, and United States Alternatives.* Technical Report no. DTNH-22-82-P-05079. Washington, DC: NHTSA.

————. 1982b. Selective Enforcement during Prime-Time Drinking-Driving Hours: A Proposal for Increasing Deterrence without Increasing Enforcement Costs. *Abstracts and Reviews in Alcohol and Driving* 4 (3):3–21.

————. 1975. Roadside Surveys, Demographics, and BACs of Drivers. In *Alcohol, Drugs, and Traffic,* ed. S. Israelstam and S. Lambert, 13–20. Toronto: Alcohol Research Foundation.

————. 1970. Cars That Drunks Can't Drive. Paper presented at the annual meeting of the Human Factors Society, San Francisco.

Voas, R. B., and Fell, J. C. 1984. *Alcohol Fact Book 1984.* Washington, DC: NHTSA.

Voas, R. B., and Layfield, W. A. 1983. Creating General Deterrence: Can Passive Sensing Help? *The Police Chief* 50:56–61.

Voas, R. B.; Rhodenizer, A. E.; and Lynn, C. 1985. *Evaluation of Charlottesville Checkpoint Operations.* Technical Report, DOT Contract DTNH-22-83-C-05088. Washington, DC: NHTSA.

Voas, R. B., and Williams, A. F. In press. Differences in Age of Arrested and Crash-Involved Drinking Drivers. *Journal of Studies on Alcohol.*

Vogel-Sprott, M., and Barrett, P. 1984. Age, Drinking Habits, and the Effects of Alcohol. *Journal of Studies on Alcohol* 45:517–21.

Votey, H. L. 1984a. Recent Evidence from Scandinavia on Deterring Alcohol Impaired Driving. *Accident Analysis and Prevention* 16:123–38.

————. 1984b. The Deterioration of Effects of Driving Legislation: Have We Been Giving Wrong Signals to Policymakers? *Journal of Criminal Justice* 12:115–30.

————. 1983. Effectiveness of Alternative Sanctions for Control of Drunken Driving: The Swedish Case. Paper presented at the 9th International Conference on Alcohol, Drugs, and Traffic Safety, San Juan, Puerto Rico.

————. 1982. Scandinavian Drinking-Driving Control: Myth or Intuition? *Journal of Legal Studies* 11:93–116.

————. 1979. *The Control of Drunken Driving Accidents in Norway: An Uncertainty–Cross Section–Time Series Analysis.* Oslo: Institute of Transport Economics.

————. 1978. The Deterrence of Drunken Driving in Norway and Sweden: An Econometric Analysis of Existing Policies. *Scandinavian Studies in Criminology* 6:79–99.

Votey, H. L., and Shapiro, P. 1983. Highway Accidents in Sweden: Modeling the Process of Drunken Driving Behavior and Control. *Accident Analysis and Prevention* 15:523–33.

Wagenaar, A. C. 1981. Effects of the Raised Legal Drinking Age on Motor Vehicle Accidents in Michigan. *HSRI Research Review* 11:1–8.

Walker, N. 1975. Ethical and Policy Aspects of General Prevention. In *General Deterrence: A Conference on Current Research and Standpoints,* 271–82. Stockholm: National Swedish Council for Crime Prevention.

Waller, J. A. 1986. State Liquor Laws as Enablers for Impaired Driving and Other Impaired Behaviors. *American Journal of Public Health* 76:787–92.

————. 1985. Research Needs and Opportunities Concerning Human-Environmental Interactions in Crashes Involving Alcohol. *Journal of Studies on Alcohol,* Supplement no. 10:54–60.

————. 1971. Factors Associated with Police Evaluation of Drinking in Fatal Highway Crashes. *Journal of Safety Research* 3:35–41.

————. 1968. Suggestions for Educational Programs about Alcohol and Highway Safety. *Traffic Safety Research Review* 68:66–70.

————. 1967. Identification of Problem Drinking among Drunken Drivers. *Journal American Medical Association* 200:124–30.

Waller, J. A.; King, E. M.; Nielson, G.; and Turkel, H. W. 1970. Alcohol and Other Factors in California Highway Fatalities. In *Proceedings of the 11th Annual Meeting of the American Association for Automotive Medicine.* Springfield, IL: Charles C. Thomas.

Wallgren, H., and Barry, H. 1970. *Actions of Alcohol, Volume 1. Biochemical, Physiological, and Psychological Aspects.* New York: Elsevier.

Walls, H. J., and Brownlie, A. R. 1970. *Drink, Drugs, and Driving.* London: Sweet and Maxwell.

Walther, D., and Plein, T. 1965. Punitive Damages: A Critical Analysis. *Marquette Law Review* 49:369–86.

Warren, R. A. 1982. Rewards for Unsafe Driving? A Rejoiner [*sic*] to P. M. Hurst. *Accident Analysis and Prevention* 14 (3):169–72.

Warren, R. A., and Donelson, A. C. 1982. *Alcohol and Traffic Safety: Strategies and Priorities for the Future.* Ottawa, Ontario: Traffic Injury Research Foundation.

Warren, R. A., and Simpson, H. M. 1982. Exposure and Alcohol as Risk Factors in the Fatal Nighttime Collisions of Men and Women Drivers. *Journal of Safety Research* 12 (4):151–56.

Warren, R. A.; Simpson, H. M.; Buhlman, M. A.; Bourgeois, L. A.; and Chattaway, L. D. 1982. *Alcohol in Patients Reporting to Hospital for Treatment of Traffic-Related Injuries: The New Brunswick Study.* Ottawa, Ontario: Traffic Injury Research Foundation of Canada.

Wayne, E. J. 1963. Alcohol and Driving—The Pharmacological Background. In *Alcohol and Road Traffic,* ed. J. D. J. Havard, 113–18. London: British Medical Association.

Wechsler, H., ed. 1980. *Minimum Age Drinking Laws.* Lexington, MA: D. C. Heath.

Weed, F. 1985. Grassroots Activism and the Drunk-Driving Issue: A Survey of MADD Chapters. Paper presented at meeting of the Society for the Study of Social Problems, Washington, D.C.

Weick, K. E. 1984. Small Wins: Redefining the Scale of Social Problems. *American Psychologist* 39 (1):40–49.

Weiner, C. 1981. *The Politics of Alcoholism.* Ph.D. thesis, University of California, San Francisco.

Weinstein, E. B. 1978. *Alcohol Safety Action Projects: A Process Evaluation of the Rehabilitation Countermeasure System.* Washington, DC: NHTSA.

Weisz, J. R.; Rothbaum, F. M.; and Blackburn, T. C. 1984. Standing Out and Standing In: The Psychology of Control in America and Japan. *American Psychologist* 39:955–69.

Wendling, A., and Kolody, B. 1982. An Evaluation of the Mortimer-Filkins Test as a Predictor of Alcohol-Impaired Driving Recidivism. *Journal of Studies on Alcohol* 43:751–66.

Westerman, S. T., and Gilbert, L. M. 1981. A Non-Invasive Method of Qualitative and Quantitative Measurement of Drugs. *Laryngoscope* 91:1536–47.

White, H. R. 1982. Sociological Theories of the Etiology of Alcoholism. In *Alcohol, Science, and Society Revisited,* ed. E. L. Gomberg, H. R. White, and J. A. Carpenter, 205–32. Ann Arbor: University of Michigan Press; New Brunswick, NJ: Rutgers University Center of Alcohol Studies.

Wicker, A. W. 1971. An Examination of the "Other Variables" Explanation of Attitude-Behavior Inconsistency. *Journal of Personality and Social Psychology* 19:18–30.

————. 1969. Attitudes vs. Action: The Relationship of Verbal and Overt Responses to Attitude Objects. *Journal of Social Issues* 25:41–78.

Widmark, E. M. P. 1914. Alcoholic Excretion in Urine and a Simple Clinically Applicable Method for Diagnosing Alcoholic Intoxication in Drivers. *Upsala Lakaref. Forh.* 19:241.

————. 1976. The Risk Compensation Theory of Accident Causation and its Practical Consequences for Accident Prevention. Paper presented to Osterreichische Gesellschaft fur Untallchirurgle, Salzburg.

Wilde, G. J. S. 1975. Evaluation of Effectiveness of Public Education and Information Programmes. In *Alcohol, Drugs, and Traffic Safety,* ed. S. Israelstam and S. Lambert, 813–23. Toronto: Addiction Research Foundation.

Williams, A. F. 1986. Raising the Legal Purchasing Age in the United States: Its Effect on Fatal Motor Vehicle Crashes. *Alcohol, Drugs and Driving: Abstracts and Reviews* 2 (2):1–12.

————. 1985. Fatal Motor Vehicle Crashes Involving Teenagers. *Pediatrician* 12:37–40.

Williams, A. F., and Lund, A. K. 1984. Deterrent Effect of Roadblocks on Drinking and Driving. *Traffic Safety Evaluation Research Review* 3:7–18.

Williams, A. F.; Lund, A. K.; and Preusser, D. F. In press. Drinking and Driving among High School Students. *International Journal of the Addictions.*

Williams, R. L.; Hagen, R. E.; and McConnell, E. J. 1984. A Survey of Suspension and Revocation Effects on the Drinking-Driving Offender. *Accident Analysis and Prevention* 16:339–50.

Wilson, R. J., and Jonah, B. A. 1985. Identifying Impaired Drivers among the General Driving Population. *Journal of Studies on Alcohol* 46:531–37.

————. n.d. *Impaired Drivers Who Have Never Been Caught: Are They Different from Convicted Impaired Drivers?* Ottawa, Ontario: Transport Canada.

Winek, C. L. 1983. Blood Alcohol Levels: Factors Affecting Predictions. *Trial* 19 (1):38–46.

Winkler, W. 1985. Driver Improvement 1984—Anspruch und Wirklichkeit. In *Schriftenreihe Unfall—und Sicherheitsforschung Strassenverkehr.* Heft 50. Bergisch Gladbach: Bundesanstalt für Strassenwesen.

————. 1982. *Die Kontrolle der Wirksamkeit von Kursen für wiederholt alkoholauffällige Kraftfahrer nach dem Modell LEER mit Hilfe der sog. Legalbewährung.* Report 1/82. Hannover: Medizinisch-Psychologisches Institut, Technischer überwachungsverein.

Wolfe, A. C. 1986a. *Changes in the Incidence of Drunk Driving in the United States, 1973–1986.* Ann Arbor, MI: Mid-America Research Institute.

————. 1986b. *National Roadside Breathtesting Survey: Procedures and Results.* Washington, DC: Insurance Institute for Highway Safety.

————. 1974. *1973 U.S. National Roadside Breathtesting Survey: Procedures and Results.* Interim Technical Report no. DOT-HS-801-241. Washington, DC: NHTSA.

Wolfe, A. C., and O'Day, J. 1984. *Evaluation Report on the 1979–1983 Oakland County Alcohol Enforcement/Education Project.* Ann Arbor: University of Michigan Transportation Research Institute.

Yanek, A. J. 1986. The General Motors of New Zealand Co-Driver: A Breath Test/Ignition Interlock Device. Paper presented at the Workshop on In-Vehicle Alcohol Test Devices, NHTSA, Washington, D.C., 17 September.

Yoder, R. D., and Moore, R. A. 1973. Alcohol Consumption in Social Drinkers in an Experimental Situation. In *Proceedings of the 7th International Conference on Alcohol, Drugs, and Traffic Safety,* ed. I. R. Johnston, 277–83. Melbourne: Australian Government Publishing Service.

Zabel, G. E. 1985. Nachschulung für Alkoholtäter im Erst—und Wiederholungsfall. Versuch einer Standortbestimmung. *Blutalkohol* 22:115–29.

————. 1981. *Verkehrsforum "Nachschulung von Alkoholtätern."* St. Ingbert.

Zador, P. 1976. Statistical Evaluation of the Effectiveness of "Alcohol Safety Action Projects." *Accident Analysis and Prevention* 8:51–66.

Zaks-Walker, L., and Larkin, E. J. 1976. *Driving While Impaired Programs: The Relationship between Behaviour and Attitude Change.* Substudy no. 788. Toronto: Addiction Research Foundation.

Zelhart, P. F., and Schurr, B. C. 1977. People Who Drive While Impaired: A Review of Research on the Drinking-Driving Problem. In *Alcoholism, Physiology, and Psychological Bases,* ed. N. Estes and E. Heinemann. St. Louis: Mosby.

Zimring, F. E. 1971. *Perspectives on Deterrence*. Washington, DC: National Institutes of Health.

Zimring, F. E., and Hawkins, G. J. 1977. The Legal Threat as an Instrument of Social Change. In *Law, Justice, and the Individual in Society: Psychological and Legal Issues,* ed. J. E. Tapp and F. J. Levine, 60–68. New York: Holt, Rinehart and Winston.

_____. 1973. *Deterrence: The Legal Threat in Crime Control*. Chicago: University of Chicago Press.

Zylman, R. 1975. Mass Arrests for Impaired Driving May Not Prevent Traffic Deaths. In *Alcohol, Drugs, and Traffic Safety,* ed. S. Israelstam and S. Lambert, 225–37. Toronto: Addiction Research Foundation.

_____. 1974a. A Critical Evaluation of the Literature on "Alcohol Involvement" in Highway Deaths. *Accident Analysis and Prevention* 6 (2):163–204.

_____. 1974b. Semantic Gymnastics in Alcohol-Highway Crash Research. *Journal of Alcohol and Drug Education* 19 (2):7–23.

_____. 1973. Youth, Alcohol, and Collision Involvement. *Journal of Safety Research* 5:58–72.

_____. 1968a. Accidents, Alcohol, and Single-Cause Explanations. *Quarterly Journal of Studies on Alcohol,* Supplement no. 4:212–33.

_____. 1968b. Police Records and Accidents Involving Alcohol. *Quarterly Journal of Studies on Alcohol,* Supplement no. 4:178–211.

Index